THE GLOBAL ECONOMY
IN TRANSITION

THE GLOBAL ECONOMY IN TRANSITION

Edited by

P.W. DANIELS
and
W.F. LEVER

 LONGMAN

Addison Wesley Longman Limited
Edinburgh Gate, Harlow
Essex CM20 2JE, England
and Associated Companies throughout the world

First published 1996

British Library Cataloguing in Publication Data
A catalogue entry for this title is available from the British Library.

ISBN 0–582–25328–4

Library of Congress Cataloging-in-Publication data
A catalog entry for this title is available from the Library of Congress.

Typeset by 33 in 10/12pt Times

Printed in Great Britain by Henry Ling Ltd., at the Dorset Press, Dorchester, Dorset

CONTENTS

LIST OF FIGURES

LIST OF TABLES

LIST OF CONTRIBUTORS

Nigel Thrift (Chapter 2) is Professor of Geography at the University of Bristol. His main interests are in international finance, time, social theory, consumption and Vietnam. His most recent publications include *Money, Power and Space* (edited with S. Corbridge and R. Martin), *Money/Space* (with A. Leyshon), *Globalisation* (co-edited with A. Amin) and *Spatial Formations*.

Brian Holly (Chapter 3) is a member of the Geography Department faculty at Kent State University, Kent, Ohio. He earned his doctorate in geography at Michigan State University. Dr Holly has also held faculty teaching positions at Michigan Technological University, Michigan State University and Bowling Green State University. In 1985 he was a Visiting Research Fellow at the University of Liverpool, England, and, from 1991 to 1993, he served as Program Director for Geography and Regional Science at the US National Science Foundation in Washington, DC. At Kent State, Dr Holly teaches urban and economic geography, quantitative methods and spatial analysis courses. He also coordinates an interdisciplinary programme in Urban Studies and Planning in the College of Arts and Sciences.

His current research interests focus on industrial dynamics, advanced services and regional economic development. He is engaged at present in a project investigating the software engineering industry. His previous work has been supported by grants from the State of Ohio, the National Geographic Society and the US Department of Commerce. In addition to numerous chapters in collected volumes, his work has been published in *The Great Lakes Geography*, *The Professional Geographer*, *Environment and Planning*, *Urban Studies* and the *Journal of Wine Research*. He co-edited *Themes in Geographic Thought*, published by St Martin's Press in 1981, and is currently co-editing a special issue of *Papers in Regional Science* devoted to contemporary research on producer services. Dr Holly is a member of several professional organizations and he also serves on the editorial board of *The Professional Geographer*.

William J. Coffey (Chapter 4) is Professor in the Department of Geography at the University of Montreal. His research interests include metropolitan economic structure, the role of producer services in economic development and the international division of labour. Recent publications include: *The Evolution of Canada's Metropolitan Economies* (1994), *Les services supérieurs dans la région métropolitaine de Montréal, 1981–1989* (1993) and *Spatial Econometrics of Services* (1992).

Andrew Leyshon (Chapter 5) is a Lecturer in Geography at the University of Bristol, having previously taught economic geography at the School of Geography and Earth Resources, University of Hull. He is the co-author of *Money/Space* (Routledge, 1996) and *A Reversal of Fortune? Financial Services and the South East of England* (South East Economic Development Strategy, 1993) and has written numerous papers on the geography of money and finance.

David Charles (Chapter 6) is a Senior Research Associate at the Centre for Urban and Regional Development Studies, University of Newcastle upon Tyne. His main research interests are in regional aspects of technology policy, the geography of R&D and innovation, and the role of technology in corporate restructuring. He is the co-author of *Technology and Competition in the International Telecommunications Industry* and *Technology Transfer in Europe* and is currently editing books on European integration and on telematics and corporate geography.

Jeremy Clegg (Chapter 7) is Senior Lecturer in International Business at the School of Business and Economic Studies, University of Leeds. His research is in international business and the multinational enterprise. Recent publications include *Multinational Enterprise and World Competition* (1987) and (edited with Peter J. Buckley) *Multinational Enterprises in Less Developed Countries* (1991). He is co-editor, with Howard Cox and Grazia Ietto-Gillies, of *The Growth of Global Businesses* (1993).

Erik Swyngedouw (Chapter 8) is Lecturer in Geography at the University of Oxford and Fellow of St Peter's College. He holds a PhD in Geography and Environmental Engineering from the Johns Hopkins University. His research interests include economic restructuring, political economy, the relationship between society and nature and social theory. He co-authored *Towards Global Localisation* and co-edited *Regional Planning at the Crossroads* and *The Urbanisation of Injustice*.

Roger Hayter (Chapter 9) is Professor of Geography in the Department of Geography, Simon Fraser University. Within the field of industrial geography he has researched questions related to location, foreign investment, the employment impacts of recession and restructuring, technology policy and international trade. He is the author of two books, including *Technology Policy Perspectives in the Canadian Forest Product Industries*, Background Study 56, Science Council of Canada, Ottawa.

P. W. Daniels (Chapters 1, 10 and 18) is Professor of Geography and Director, Service Sector Research Unit, University of Birmingham. He has published articles and books on the location and development of office activities and on the emergence of service industries as key agents in metropolitan and regional restructuring as well as in the transition to an integrated, global economy. His books include *Office Location* (1975); *Service Industries: A Geographical Appraisal* (1985); *Services and Metropolitan Development* (1991) (ed.); and *Service Industries in the World Economy* (1993). Professor Daniels is currently President of the European Research Network on Services and Space (RESER).

David Drakakis-Smith (Chapter 11) is Professor of Economic Geography at the University of Liverpool. His main interests revolve around the social impact of rapid urban-based economic growth and he works extensively in south-east Asia and southern Africa. His most recent books are *Pacific Asia* (Routledge) and (with C. J. Dixon) *Economic and Social Development in Pacific Asia* (Routledge). He is currently writing a book with Ooi Giok Ling on Urbanisation and Basic Needs.

Robert Gwynne (Chapter 12) is Reader in Latin American Development at the School of Geography, University of Birmingham. His research has focused on the problems of economic development in developing countries, most notably those in Latin America. His early books examined the strategies for industrialization in Latin America and their spatial implications (*Industrialisation and Urbanisation in Latin America*, Routledge, 1985) and compared the experience of Latin America with that of East Asia (*New Horizons: Third World Industrialisation in an International Framework*, Longman, 1990). He is now working on a book critically examining the relationship between trade and economic development for Third World countries.

Michael Bradshaw (Chapter 13) is a Lecturer in Geography and an Associate Member of the Centre for Russian and East European Studies at the University of Birmingham. He is the author of *Regional Patterns of Foreign Investment in Russia* (Royal Institute of International Affairs, 1995) and editor of *Geography and Transition in the Post-Soviet Republics* (Wiley, 1996) and has written numerous papers on trade and regional development in the Soviet Union and Russia.

William Lever (Chapters 1, 14 and 18) is Professor of Urban Studies at the University of Glasgow, Scotland. His first degree and doctorate were in Geography at Oxford University from where he moved as a researcher on town planning and subsequently urban economics in the Department of Social and Economic Research at Glasgow. His interests include urban change in the new Europe and the evaluation of urban and regional economic policies. He has written and edited books on British town planning, industrial change, urban policy and economic and urban change in Europe. He has been a consultant to the British government, OECD and the European Union and he is currently editor of the journal *Urban Studies*.

Philip Cooke (Chapter 15) is Professor of Regional Development and Director of the Centre for Advanced Studies in the Social Sciences at the University of Wales, Cardiff. In 1992 he published *Towards Global Localisation* (UCL Press, 1992), reprinted in paperback in 1993. Other books include *Back to the Future* (Unwin Hyman, 1990), *Localities* (Unwin Hyman, 1989) and *Theories of Planning and Spatial Development* (Hutchinson, 1983). He is also editor of *European Planning Studies*, an interdisciplinary journal with an urban and regional policy focus.

Marie Howland (Chapter 16) is Director of and Professor in the Urban Studies and Planning Program at the University of Maryland, College Park. She is the author of *Plant Closing and Worker Displacement: The Regional Issues*, published by the Upjohn Institute, 1988, and *From Combines to Computers: Rural Services in the Information Age*, published in 1995 by SUNY Press, with Amy Glasmeier. She is also the author of articles on the relationship between national economic growth and the economies of cities and regions, urban national policy, rural economic development and worker displacement. Dr Howland has a PhD in Urban Studies and Planning from the Massachusetts Institute of Technology and a Masters of City Planning from the University of California at Berkeley.

Matthew P. Drennan (Chapter 17) an economist, is a Professor in the Department of City and Regional Planning, Cornell University. He has written extensively on the role of producer services in the transformation of US metropolitan areas, particularly in New York. His most recent articles have appeared in *Urban Studies, Environment and Planning A* and *Economic Development Quarterly*. He has developed a large-scale econometric model of the New York region described in his book, *Modelling Metropolitan Economies for Forecasting and Policy Analysis* (New York, NYU Press, 1985).

ACKNOWLEDGEMENTS

Although the scope of this volume is very different, its origins can be traced to *Industrial Change in the United Kingdom* (edited by W.F. Lever) which was originally published by Longman in 1987 and reprinted in 1991. The Industrial Activity and Area Development Study Group of the Institute of British Geographers played a large part in making that book possible and undoubtedly contributed to its success. The publishers believed that there was a case for a new edited volume along the same lines but economic processes in the 1990s take place on a much larger stage and play to a wider variety of tunes; thus the decision to go for a global rather than local approach to aspects of economic development and change.

Having persuaded our contributors that this was a worthwhile exercise, we would like to thank them all for their cooperation. As with all edited works, they have been required to work to tight deadlines, respond to comments and requests for changes from the editors and then patiently await the arrival of the finished product. In many ways our task has been smoother than we could possibly have expected because we believe that the contributors have worked closely to the brief provided at the beginning of the project. We are also indebted to an anonymous reviewer who made very constructive suggestions about ways to rework the original proposal upon which this book is based and who subsequently made helpful, supportive comments on the completed manuscript. While we have been glad to take many of the ideas and suggestions on board we do of course take full responsibility for the finished product.

Our particular thanks also go to Helen Dixon, Secretary in the School of Geography, University of Birmingham, who very ably and cheerfully provided the administrative support, including the production of a consolidated bibliography, necessary to ensure the delivery of a complete manuscript and supporting materials to the publisher. We are also grateful to Pauline Connelly, Secretary in the Department of Economic and Social Research, University of Glasgow, who also provided invaluable assistance. Last, but by no means least, we would like to thank Sally Wilkinson at Longman for her wholehearted commitment to this project from the very beginning. She has often listened patiently to excuses for missed deadlines and been very understanding. At the same time when we have needed some assistance or advice it has always been provided quickly and effectively. Dealing with harassed academics with so many conflicting demands on their time must be one of the less attractive aspects of being a commissioning editor!

Peter Daniels
William Lever
October 1995

We are grateful to the following for permission to reproduce copyright material: Fig. 3.1 from *Transactions* **18**(3) p. 313 (Fig. 1) Global interdependence and regional development ... Royal Geographical Society, Institute of British Geographers (G. Clark, 1993); Fig. 11.6 from *Debt and Development* (Fig. 2.3) Blackwell, Oxford (S. Corbridge, 1993).

Whilst every effort has been made to trace the owners of copyright material, in a few cases this has proved impossible and we take this opportunity to offer our apologies to any copyright holders whose rights we may have unwittingly infringed.

GLOSSARY OF APPROVED ABBREVIATIONS

AIDS	Acquired Immune Deficiency Syndrome
ASEAN	Association of South East Asian Nations
CACM	Central American Common Market
CAD	Computer Aided Design
CAM	Computer Aided Manufacture
CAP	Common Agricultural Policy
CBD	Central Business District
CEFTA	Central European Free Trade Area
CFP	Common Fisheries Policy
CIS	Commonwealth of Independent States
CMEA	Council for Mutual Economic Assistance
CPE	Centrally Planned Economy
CRAFT	Cooperative Research Action for Technology
DATAR	Délégation à l'Aménagement du Territoire et à l'Action Régionale
DG	Directorate General
EAGGF	European Agricultural Guidance and Guarantee Fund
EC	European Community (pre-1993)
ECE	European Commission for Europe
ECSC	European Coal and Steel Community
ECU	European Currency Unit
EEC	European Economic Community
EFTA	European Free Trade Association
EIB	European Investment Bank
EMS	European Monetary System
EMU	Economic and Monetary Union
ERDF	European Regional Development Fund
ERM	Exchange Rate Mechanism
ESCB	European System of Central Banks
ESF	European Social Fund
EU	European Union (post-1993)
FAO	Food and Agriculture Organization

FDI	Foreign Direct Investment
FEI	Foreign Investment Enterprise
GATT	General Agreement on Tariffs and Trade
GDP	Gross Domestic Product
GERD	Gross Domestic Expenditure on R&D
GNP	Gross National Product
ICR	Intelligent Character Recognition
IMF	International Monetary Fund
IMS	Intelligent Manufacturing Systems
IPR	Intellectual Property Rights
ISI	Import Substitution Industrialization
IT	Information Technology
LAFTA	Latin American Free Trade Area
LDCs	Less Developed Countries
MNE	Multinational Enterprise
NAFTA	North American Free Trade Agreement
NASDAQ	National Association of Securities Dealers Automated Quotations
NATO	North Atlantic Treaty Organization
NEWER-IDL	Newer International Division of Labour
NICs	Newly Industrializing Countries
NIDL	New International Division of Labour
OCR	Optical Character Recognition
ODA	Overseas Development Administration
OECD	Organization for Economic Cooperation and Development
OEEC	Organization for European Economic Cooperation
OPEC	Organization of Petroleum Exporting Countries
PCM	Product Cycle Models
PPS	Purchasing Parity Standard
R&D	Research & Development
RIEs	Rapidly Industrializing Economies
RISC	Reduced Instruction Set Computing
SAP	Structural Adaptation Programmes
SDL	Spatial Division of Labour
SEM	Single European Market
SMEs	Small and Medium-sized Enterprises
SPRINT	Strategic Programme for Innovation and Technology Transfer
UK	United Kingdom
US	United States
WTO	World Trade Organization

CHAPTER 1

INTRODUCTION
William Lever and Peter Daniels

A not uncommon exercise in primary or elementary school classes in the 1950s was for children to describe what they had had for breakfast that day and for the teacher to identify the origins of the foods and implements involved, often with the help of a large coloured map. The bread would, in the case of British schools, have come from wheat grown on the Canadian prairies, as would the breakfast cereal. The egg would be British, as would the bacon (unless it was exotically Danish). The tea would have come from India, Ceylon (as Sri Lanka was known) or East Africa. The marmalade would have been made from Spanish oranges with West Indian sugar. The cutlery would have come from Sheffield and the crockery from the potteries of the English Midlands. Thus the young English scholar would have grown up with a sense of world trade in which imperialism and the history of the Empire ran deep. In the United States, a much larger country without a formal empire, more of the breakfast goods would have come from home suppliers with perhaps Brazilian or Colombian coffee substituting for the tea.

By the 1970s, a similar classroom exercise might have focused upon British imports of foreign consumer goods, most obviously cars from Europe and subsequently Japan. In turn these would have been replaced or augmented by cars from Malaysia, South Korea and elsewhere in the Far East, whilst other cars increasingly were drawing their components from all around the developed world, attracting the sobriquet 'world car'. Britain's position in world trade had thus moved from a country drawing raw materials, foodstuffs and energy from colonial possessions (and the Middle East in the case of oil) and supplying them with finished capital goods (such as machinery and railway engines) and consumer goods. The United States, too, was experiencing the same transition, although relatively more self-sufficient in food, raw materials and energy. The increasing level of imports of finished products, most clearly typified by the arrival of Japanese 'compact' cars to replace larger American models, began to worry analysts of America's balance of payments.

By the 1980s three further trends could be identified. Firstly, the increasing flow of imports into the advanced economies of western Europe and North America were increasingly coming from a new wave of newly industrializing countries from India to Brazil. Secondly, whereas the first cohort of imported consumer goods were copies of goods (sometimes not very good copies) previously produced in the West, now the exporting companies were innovating, especially in areas such as electronics and electrical goods. Thirdly, it was becoming apparent that services as well as material goods were involved. Initially, this was a reference to tourism where the West Indies, Goa, Thailand and Gambia were added to the brochures which had formerly only featured Spain, Portugal or Greece, but subsequently other services were involved.

By the 1990s, the world's economy had been truly integrated or globalized. Whilst the world's economy was growing at about 3 per cent p.a. the flow of internationally traded goods was increasing by about 8 per cent p.a. There were several reasons for this but we can identify three salient ones. Firstly, the goods involved were lighter and had higher levels of value added. They were therefore better able to bear the costs of long-haul freight. Secondly, wage differentials between the advanced economies and many Third World countries increased such that they could overcome freight costs – how else, for example, could Colombian coal be imported into Britain at prices which could compete effectively with British coal? Lastly, whilst bodies such as the General Agreement on Tariffs and Trade, the Single European Market and the North American Free Trade Agreement were established to encourage freer (and more) trade between countries, the creation of multinational markets like the SEM forced exogenous companies to set up plants inside such markets to circumvent the tariff barriers with which they surrounded themselves, thus making companies more multinational.

Whilst levels of international trade in goods have risen steadily, the last decade has seen a much more rapid growth in services, especially in financial services. Changes in the patterns of the world's manufacturing inevitably brought about changes in global finance. Companies became more multinational so that foreign direct investment grew rapidly. In the 1960s governments such as that of the United Kingdom sought to restrict flows of capital overseas in the belief that if the capital could be kept 'at home' then more jobs would be created at home. With the global recessions of the 1970s, created in part by substantial rises in energy (oil) prices, companies had to be permitted to invest abroad, and it could be argued that it was only the repatriated profits of companies earned abroad which kept major companies in business. To stay financially viable, companies had to 'go global'. The increasing flows of foreign direct investment, the growth of multinational companies, and increasing relative shares of output being traded internationally put great strain on the world's financial system. Initially in the post-war period attempts had been made to provide stability in the world's finances through agreements such as that at Bretton Woods creating the International Monetary Fund and the World Bank, retaining fixed exchange rates and tying currencies such as the US dollar to a fixed value in gold. Under increasing strain fixed exchange rates were adjusted with increasing frequency and the gold standard was abandoned after 1971. With increasingly volatile exchange rates, multinational companies had to find ways of protecting themselves, whilst it became possible to speculate in the future values of currencies very profitably – hence the business of arbitrage was born, the buying of currency on the assumption that its value would rise relative to other currencies. Money therefore ceased to exist merely as a means of buying commodities, goods and services: it had an exchange value in its own right. Currency dealing for speculation grew, as did the number of ways of investing in the future value of other assets. The simplest were 'futures' in which investors sought to capitalize on shifts in the future prices of foodstuffs, energy, industrial raw materials and metals. In part this was a way by which manufacturers could insure themselves against sudden rises in the prices of their inputs, but in part it was speculation. Futures were followed by more complex financial instruments such as derivatives, in which the future values, not of raw materials and goods, but of stock exchange indices and less tangible assets were speculated upon. Lastly, in addition to currencies as stores of value, the 1980s saw the development of bonds, forms of credit, where money could be made by charging transaction costs on the transfer of such bonds. Some were backed by real assets, some (junk bonds) were not.

By the mid-1990s this trade in financial instruments globally had come to dominate trade in material goods. For every pound or dollar used to buy goods internationally it was estimated that seven or eight pounds or dollars were part of an international financial transfer in which goods were not involved. Whereas the movement of goods around the world economy requires transport, and distance and location are still therefore important in economic activity through the impact of freight charges, the movement of information, including financial information, is unaffected by distance where satellites or fixed line systems are utilized. This has led to the argument that 'geography is dead', a way of saying that distance and location are unimportant. However, we would argue that the globalization of the world economy and the growth in importance of financial services may mean that distance or space is unimportant but in consequence place or location is more important. To the multinational finance house the distance between London, New York and Tokyo may be unimportant, but what the places are like to live in, how appealing their business cultures are, and how accessible they are to information and people flows (through teleports, airports, etc.) is of quite crucial importance.

This volume is divided into four main parts which deal successively with theories of globalization, the processes involved, the way the world economy and economies have responded to globalization, and lastly the spatial outcomes of these processes. In describing the theories which account for globalization, Thrift examines the increasing internationalization of production and consumption both of material goods and in the increasingly important service sector. He notes how services have come to dominate transnational flows, the belief that services could only be local-serving having been exploded a long time ago. As we shift to the informational economy it is very easy to generate information in one place and instantaneously despatch it to locations which are far away. There remains a debate, however, on how much information, especially of a qualitative nature, is lost *en route*. Whilst routine and unambiguous information can be transmitted long distances without loss, the belief remains, most usually amongst senior businessmen but also amongst statesmen, that there can be no complete substitute for face-to-face contact. Holly examines theories of changes in the production system which are essential parts of globalization. As profits fell after the early 1960s, companies, which hitherto had adopted Fordist modes of production, with product rigidity, the use of large units of production, vertical integration, deskilling of the labour force and the emergence of truly global firms, were forced to adopt more flexible production systems. These post-Fordist systems were flexible in product type, in the volumes produced, in their use of labour and machinery, and in the use of networks rather than vertical integration. Enterprises moved from economies of scale (producing large quantities of a single good) to economies of scope (producing more types of goods). Post-Fordist systems led to the development of networks of smaller enterprises, often working collaboratively, where internal (scale) economies are of declining importance and external (agglomerative) economies are of increasing importance. Debate continues as to whether spatial concentrations, known as industrial districts, can consist solely of cooperating networks of small and medium-sized enterprises – as in middle or Third Italy's spatial concentration of clothing, furniture, footwear and jewellery firms – or whether such groupings are basically subcontracting concentrations which require one or more large plants to service, as in Baden-Württemberg in Germany, in southern California or in the Japanese *keiretsu* system.

These theoretical perspectives are extended by Coffey who depicts the global specialization of goods production in the 1970s, termed the new international division of labour, in which foreign direct investment in low wage Third World countries began to be replaced by the more modernized economies of the newly industrializing countries (NICs), which were capable of endogenous growth and new product development. In terms of the 'product life cycle' model these NICs were moving from the mass production stage to the new innovation stage. This pattern he contrasts with the newer industrial division of labour in which the global economy is comprised also of subcontracting of services by the NICs, outward investment by the NICs, the cross-investment between advanced economies as companies seek to avoid the tariff walls erected around the trading blocs such as the Single European Market, the North American Free Trade Agreement and Japan. Leyshon examines the role of space in financial flows. He points out that early financial systems were very localized as personal knowledge was often important in granting credit or determining values of assets. He contrasts the Great West of the American Plains, which was serviced by frontier banks which were small and vulnerable, and where rural merchants used personal knowledge to minimize risk, with the current global financial system of swaps and derivatives. Contemporary finance takes place in a world of homogenized space, now global in scale, which developed out of the national financial systems of the late eighteenth century. Finance is no longer embedded in a local system of trust and personal knowledge but now relies on global institutions, which with growing deregulation are less trustworthy than of old as recent transnational frauds indicate. He concludes, however, that perhaps as a response to the uncertainties of global and national financial systems, Local Exchange and Trading Systems (LETS) are now being developed using a highly localized and non-transferable form of currency. He argues that a new dualism in finance is now emerging.

As the book moves on to the processes of globalization, it becomes clear how important the flows of information and knowledge around the world are (knowledge can be defined as information which can be usefully applied). Charles describes the diversity of contemporary information technologies and their characteristics. The wealth of information now available has allowed industry to be 'informationalized', permitting new products to be developed, new markets to be identified and new production systems to be introduced. It is the use of computer assisted manufacture allied to robotics which has facilitated flexible production systems. No longer are thousands of identical models churned out by car manufacturers, but individually customized models in response to individual specifications are now available. Nor is this development restricted to consumer goods: one could for example argue that customized tourism is now rivalling package holidays because of the much higher levels of information available within that market. Information flows not randomly but between and within institutions, the most obvious of which are the multinational enterprises (MNEs). Clegg describes how MNEs have been instrumental in moving foreign direct investment and technology between countries. He charts how the process has flowed from the advanced economies to the developing ones and how service enterprises have come to join manufacturing ones in creating these transfers. Globally the patterns, too, are changing as flows into Asia and the Pacific have expanded but with relatively little movement into Latin America and Africa. Now flows are emanating from Asia and the Pacific, whilst the world order awaits the repositioning of China and of the former centrally planned economies of Europe and the former Soviet Union within the globalized economy.

Swyngedouw concentrates further upon the money flows in the world economy. The breakdown of financial regulation with the US dollar leaving the gold standard and the system set up to manage the world economy at Bretton Woods has brought problems. The use of the US dollar as the world currency, the development of the Eurodollar market and the use of petrodollars all reflect difficulties of managing a world economy when the dollar is weak. Schemes for avoiding the problems of currencies which are increasingly a vehicle for speculation rather than a means of purchasing goods and services include futures, derivatives and swaps. The geography of these financial flows is based on world centres such as London, New York and Tokyo, but business is moving to centres in Latin America, south-east Asia and eastern Europe and to tax havens and stateless deposits as the pursuit of lower taxes and more compliant regulatory systems continues. Lastly Hayter describes the role of research and development (R&D) in globalization. Enterprises engage in R&D to expand their knowledge base in ways which give them a comparative advantage, but it can be risky and expensive and not all R&D translates into commercial advantage. R&D has led industry out of the narrow specialism of Taylorist systems into more flexible systems; some is conducted in-house but much is available from external agencies such as universities. The relationship between R&D and globalization is usually articulated through multinational enterprises, which transmit waves of innovation from country to country. However, innovations are unlikely to percolate from bases in MNEs to the host economy and this in turn has left the newly industrializing economies to develop their own R&D base.

The corporate and national response to globalization can differ widely across space. Daniels points out that inherent indicators of globalization are foreign direct investment and multinational enterprises and that globalization has diluted the power of national governments. Four things drive the processes of globalization – markets, costs, competition and government regulation. Seven countries dominate foreign direct investment and five countries dominate the world trade in manufactured goods. Foreign direct investment is drawn to large local markets and good local labour. Large exporting countries tend to have high per capita incomes and thus tend to be attractive markets into which to export. Thus there tends to be a virtuous circle which increasingly separates the advanced economies from the less developed economies. This differential will be increased with the switch from manufacturing to services.

The position of the less developed countries is taken up by Bradshaw who examines the prospects of the post-Soviet economies and by Gwynne and Drakakis-Smith who examine the Third World countries. Bradshaw describes how *perestroika*, an attempt to reform the Soviet state socialist model, led to a much more thorough-going change to a marketized economy based on market prices and this in its turn led to political change. The integration of the Soviet and east European economy into the global system led to sharp price rises, the problem of monetary overhang (i.e. people using savings which they were previously unable to spend due to a lack of goods), and privatization using new (probably foreign) capital. He argues that the current position is one of transitional recession, and the management of the Russian economy will be key to the integration of the post-Soviet economies notwithstanding current levels of European assistance to the Vysegrad countries.

Gwynne argues that the developing countries have not always been helped by trade. Developing countries, defined as those where primary products are more than 70 per cent of all exports, have suffered continuous falls in the real prices of their exports. Price protection in the European market has restricted food exports from developing countries to Europe and non-food agricultural products have been especially hard-hit. In the mineral sector the volatility of prices has caused further difficulties. He thus repeats the point that developing countries have not done well out of globalization, except where countries like Taiwan have been able to break out of import dependence through moving to import substitution and then to exports via a sequence of economies which are successively factor-driven, investment-driven and then innovation-driven. Drakakis-Smith extends this argument by further defining 'dependency' in the less developed economies, especially for former colonies. Pre-1850 colonies supplied metals, spices and silks but after 1850 they supplied raw materials for the industrialization of western Europe. By the 1930s this pattern was beginning to break up under the impact of war and recession. Since independence there has been neocolonialism through the multinational enterprises, but, he argues, there is now multiple dependence as the core MNEs depend upon the LDCs' low-cost labour and raw materials. By 1990, however, the LDCs were finding life very difficult. Globalization was creating polarization, the crisis of debts taken out from bodies such as the International Monetary Fund and the World Bank was worsening, and structural adjustment programmes were increasing dependency. The answer in the mid- and late 1990s may be escalating emigration to Europe and North America, where frontiers such as the Mediterranean, the Rio Grande and the Caribbean are difficult to police. Ironically, as western Europe turns its attention increasingly to helping the countries of eastern Europe, supporting in part their new-found democracy, it may be doing so at the expense of areas such as Africa – Europe is now, as the saying goes, caught between the East and the South.

In the fourth and final part of the book, four chapters examine at a smaller scale some of the impacts of globalization. Drennan seeks to identify why three world cities – London, New York and Tokyo – have achieved and retained such pre-eminence in the world's capital markets. Capital, especially foreign direct investment, comes through multinational enterprises which are concentrated in these three large cities. The concentration of financial services in the three cities conflicts with neoclassical growth theory, which assumes constant returns to scale. There must be, he argues, scale and agglomerative economies, such as the removal of uncertainty created by imperfect information, which keep firms in world cities. This is true for services, if not for manufacturing where agglomeration diseconomies, such as traffic congestion and high space costs, get in the way of profit. These advantages for financial service firms in the world cities are continuous and cumulative enabling the big three cities to overcome major problems such as London's loss of empire.

Cooke argues that the emphasis of globalization should not blind us to the importance of the regional dimension. If, he argues, globalization has reduced the power of national governments, then this may enhance the power of regions. He uses a wide range of examples – Pennsylvania, the Basque region, Nord-Rhein Westfalia, and Wales – to show how regional economies can be developed and supported by policy through the use of networks and industrial districts. Cooperation and collaboration between enterprises and institutions may offer significant comparative advantages to these regions in the post-Fordist era.

Lever describes the tendency for nation states to form economic alliances to enhance their competitive power within globalization using the example of western Europe. In the aftermath of the Second World War and anxieties about east–west conflict in Europe, political concerns were transmuted into economic and social alliances as well as politico-military ones. The creation of a common market moved in the late 1980s into a recognition of the advantages for western Europe of a Single Market permitting the free movement of people, capital, goods and services. As the market has enlarged successive additions have brought new problems – Spain, Portugal and Greece brought an undeveloped south previously only represented by the Mezzogiorno; Austria, Sweden and Finland brought high incomes but exceptionally high expectations of welfare systems; Poland, Hungary and the Czech Republic will bring the problems of adjustment from non-market economies. Evidence suggests that the economies of the cities within Europe are becoming less alike, but this is in part because poorer cities are being fed in at the bottom of the ranking with market enlargement.

Lastly, Howland describes how 'going offshore' has become an increasingly popular option for businesses. The greater use of satellites and other telecommunications options has widened the locational choice for service companies, especially as labour has become more skilled without an equivalent rise in price. Computing services have moved to Taiwan and the Caribbean, for example, taking jobs from rural and small-town America. Tax haven status has moved banking to the Cayman Islands and Ireland where regulation is also less. The Newer International Division of Labour now reflects the quality and price of labour, as before, but also the telecommunications revolution of the past decade.

This volume offers a number of insights into the globalization of the world's economy, the winners and the losers, the long-run trends and the one-off incidents, but we hope you will be able to make the interconnections. By using cross-references and advice on further reading it should be possible to use this volume as the start of a more extensive study of globalization. Alternatively it may be used alone as a comprehensive and contemporary text on a truly worldwide phenomenon.

PART 1

GLOBALIZATION OF PRODUCTION SYSTEMS: THEORY

CHAPTER 2

SHUT UP AND DANCE,
Or, is the world economy knowable?
Nigel Thrift

> Order and disorder, the one and the multiple, systems and distributions, islands and sea, noises and harmony, are subjective as well as objective. Now I am a multiplicity of thoughts, the world is now as orderly as a diamond. What fluctuates are the order and disorder themselves, what fluctuates is their proximity, what fluctuates are their relationship to and penetration of one another.
>
> SERRES (1995), p. 131

INTRODUCTION

That there have been marked changes in the world economy can hardly be doubted. If we had been able to look down on the Earth over the period since the Second World War, the marks of change would be seen everywhere, year after year after year. For example, over east and south-east Asia we would have seen the expanding frontier of electric light at night, the pall of smoke from burning rain forests, the spreading highway networks, the multiplying wakes of container ships and the blinking beacons of more and more jumbo jets making their way across the sky. Or, over Britain, we might have had to try to read rather more ambiguous signs: the snuffing out of the glare from foundry furnaces, the spread of derelict industrial land, and the withering away of once great ports, mixed in with the spread of the motorway network, and retail warehouse parks, and shopping malls.

Yet, although we could see all these signs of activity, there is little or no agreement about *why* this activity has taken place. Despite the trite formulae for national economic success peddled by the management gurus like Michael Porter (1990), there is little or no agreement about why economic development has taken root in many of the countries of east and south-east Asia. For example, nearly all commentators seem to agree that high levels of education and low levels of inflation have something to do with the economic success of these countries, but they do not agree about how these factors are related to economic success or what the other elements of success might be. Again, most commentators seemed willing

11

to agree, until recently, that long-term relations between banks (the lenders) and corporations (the borrowers) are important, but now even this conventional wisdom has been challenged (e.g. Corbett, 1987).

Then again, despite the many analyses of Britain's economic decline, there is little or no agreement about why it has taken place. One popular explanation is that this decline is the result of an anti-industrial 'gentlemanly' culture which has poisoned the wells of enterprise (e.g. Wiener, 1981; Cain and Hopkins, 1993a, b; Rubinstein, 1991). But many commentators think that this kind of explanation is glib and argue that the answer lies elsewhere:

> in the past dependence induced by mercantilism, and the consequent inability to switch to vertically integrated, multidivisional forms of enterprise early enough to compete with upcoming American and, later, Japanese forms (Ingham, 1995)

I want to argue that these kinds of disagreement – though constitutive – are not so awful as might once have been thought. They are now thought of as the normal condition with which we have to live. The problem has been that until recently we were in love with expectations about what we could know and how we can know it which have only now, and rather painfully, been dismantled, and I want to show that that process of dismantling has been taking place in both the international intellectual *and* the international business communities with quite concrete (and not always equable or equitable) effects.

Therefore, in this chapter, I want to write about how we can know the world economy as much as about what we know, the two of course being interrelated. In the first part of the chapter, I want to suggest in a dry but still necessary section that we must move away from the assumption of 'transcendental rationality' which still hinders many debates on the world economy and which has allowed all kinds of monstrous myths to grow and proliferate. In the second part of the chapter, I want to chart some of these myths which have turned into monsters and to suggest why they have become increasingly unstable, not just because they are intellectually problematic (if that were the case, we would all have been overwhelmed many years back) but because, as I want to make clear in the third part of the chapter, they are being exposed by the changing vagaries of the world economy, symbolized by major events like the decline of the Bretton Woods system of international economic management and the fall of the Berlin Wall. I want to suggest that, just as academics and other commentators have been concerned with these problems, so have more practically inclined business communities and that, increasingly, we can see the results in the ways that economies are being practised by managers. Thus, in a sense, a new vision of how we know *is* becoming what we know, a result which, as I show in the conclusion, is not without its own ambiguities concerning the distribution of power and influence.

THE PERILS OF TRANSCENDENTAL RATIONALITY

Discourses are metalanguages that instruct people how to live as people. They are best represented as great rivers of communication, performances propelled into movement by talk and text, enframed by technologies like books, visual images, and other 'media', guided by procedures like rules and styles, and crowned by significant effects like particular subject positions or emotional states which establish the cultural importance of a discourse at gut level (Gumbrecht and Pfeiffer, 1994). One of the prevalent discourses in Western intellectual cultures of the last two thousand years, a discourse which has waxed and waned and which has adjusted to historical custom but which still holds true to a series of central tenets, has been what Jowitt (1992) calls the 'Joshua discourse'. This is a discourse that is founded on the idea of transcendental rationality, on the notion of a single, correct, God's-eye view of reason which transcends (goes beyond) the way human beings (or indeed any other kinds of things) think, and which imparts the idea of a world that is 'centrally organised, rigidly bounded, and hysterically concerned with impenetrable boundaries' (Jowitt, 1992, p. 306). This discourse usually involves a series of linked and self-supporting tenets (Lakoff, 1987), tenets such as that:

- the mind is independent of the body; reason is a disembodied phenomenon;
- emotion has no conceptual content but is a pure force;
- meaning is based on truth and reference; it concerns the relationship between symbols which represent things in the real world and is independent of the speeches of mind and body. Symbols are meaningless in themselves and only get their meaning by virtue of their correspondence to things in the world; and
- the categories we use are independent of the world, defined only by the internal characteristics of their members and not by the nature of the people doing the categorizing.

But, beginning in the 1940s and 1950s with the work of philosophers like Austin, Merleau-Ponty and Wittgenstein, the Joshua discourse began to retreat. Further, more recent batterings by other intellectual communities like cognitive scientists, feminists and social theorists have produced something close to a rout. So a new discourse has begun to take hold, a discourse which challenges the idea that a God's-eye view of reason is possible. There are, instead, many rationalities and these rationalities are all:

- embodied, relying on our bodily natures;
- going to engage the emotions, since feeling is conceptualized and conceptualization always involves feeling;
- based on a notion of meaning as concerning symbols which are constitutive of the world and not just mirrors of it. These 'symbols' are, in fact, imaginative processes which rely on our capacity to produce images, to store

knowledge of particular levels of complexity, and to communicate (Putnam, 1981); and

- reliant on categories that are not independent of the world but are defined by upgraded processes (like metaphor, metonymy and mental imaging) which mean that there can be no objectively correct description of reality (this does not, of course, mean that there is no objective world, only that we have no privileged access to it from some external viewpoint).

These tenets (Lakoff, 1987) lead to a view of the world that is very different from the Joshua discourse, which we might call, after Jowitt (1992) and Serres (1995), the 'Genesis discourse'. It is a view of the world in which 'borders are no longer of fundamental importance; territorial, ideological and issue boundaries are attenuated, unclear, and confusing' (Jowitt, 1992, p. 307). It is a view of the world in which knowledge has become an archipelago of islands of epistemic stability in a sea of disorder, flunctuations, noise, randomness and chaos. Whereas in the Joshua discourse order is the rule and disorder is the exception, in the Genesis discourse disorder is the rule and order the exception and, as a result, 'what becomes more interesting are the transitions and bifurcations, the long fringes, edges, verges, rims, brims, auras, crenellates, confines ... all the shores that leads from one to another, from the sea of disorder to the coral reefs of order' (Latour, 1987, pp. 94–95; Serres, 1982).

Obviously, such a view has a number of consequences, of which two are particularly significant. First, the favoured epistemological stance is, to use Wittgenstein's (1978) feline phrase, 'not empiricism yet realism'. That may sound like a contradiction in terms but it is, in fact, an argument for a limited but not total form of relativism which argues that individuals understand the same domain of experience in different and inconsistent ways and that this is a necessary condition of knowledge (Diamond, 1991). Since even the most disinterested of analysts is engaged in social projects any *a priori* claim to epistemological privilege is impossible. Second, knowledge is no longer seen as a form of empire building; 'a powerful critique being one that ties, like a bicycle wheel, every point of a periphery to one of the centre through the intermediary of a proxy. At the end holding the centre is tantamout to holding the world' (Latour, 1987, p. 90). At best, knowledge is, in Lakoff's (1987) phrase, 'radial'. That is:

> central truths are true by virtue of the directness of fit between the preconceptual structure of experience and the conceptual structure in terms of which the sentence is understood. But most of the sentences we speak and hear and read and write are not capable of expressing central truths; they are sentences that contain concepts that are very general or very specific or abstract or metaphorical or metonymic or display other kinds of 'indirectness' relative to the direct structuring of experience. Not that they need to be any less true, but they aren't central examples (Lakoff, 1987, p. 297)

MYTHS AND FABLES

Discourses produce power relations. Within them, stories are spun which legitimate certain kinds of constructs, subject positions, and affective states over others. The myths and fables of the Joshua discourse were particularly powerful. Specifically, four of these myths and fables did serious work in producing a particular kind of world which is now so often called 'modern' that we no longer realize the cultural specificity of the description or the strength of the investments we have placed in it. The first of these myths was an old Enlightenment 'chestnut' – the myth of total knowledge. Somehow – though we don't have this facility yet – we could get to know everything that is going on. Every movement of an ant and every rustling of a leaf could be tracked and explained. Every human culture could be laid open to inspection and documentation. Every practical skill could be analysed down to its last detail and then transcended. This myth was supported by a second, that the world was set up in such a way as to allow this: the world was an ordered, homogeneous, quantitatively different multiplicity. The world was defined by oneness, consistency and integrity which, in turn, acted as an ideal terrain on which purified theoretical orders could operate and permeate. The third myth was of a material world which could be separated out from the world of the imagination, from the world of symbols and semiotics. There was no sense, therefore, of a world in which materials are interactively constituted, in which 'objects, entities, actors, processes – all are semiotic effects' (Law and Mol, 1995, p. 277). The fourth myth was one of individuality. This was the idea that knowledge comes from the operation of a god-like gaze which emanates from an individual focal point. Human capacities, therefore, could be framed as being the result of an innate endowment that every individual received at the point of conception. There was, in other words, no grasp of the individual as being a modulated effect (Thrift, 1991), of human capacities as arising out of:

> emergent properties of the total developmental system constituted by virtue of an individual's situation, from the start, within a wider field of relations – including most importantly, relations with other persons. In short, social relations, far from being the mere resultant of the association of discrete individuals, each independently 'wired up' for cooperative or enthusiastic behaviour, constitute the very ground from which human existence unfolds (Ingold, 1995, p. 17)

All these myths were often put together in one final myth of how we are now: the myth of the 'modern'. Somehow, human life (in the West at least) had transited into a distinctive historical space where everything was different and, well, modern. Most of all, 'modernity' was characterized by a condition of speed-up and transience which, in its main characteristics, happened to coincide with the four myths outlined above. First, supralunar organizations were involved in a whirl of constant information-gathering which fed into systems of control which produced an 'iron cage' of surveillance and discipline. Second, these organizations were supported by myths of instrumental rationality which allowed the world to be trussed-up like a Christmas turkey, with nothing out of place. Third, and here was the lament, these organizations were able to drain sociality out of the world, leaving behind nothing but a systematized shell. Then, fourth, this world was populated by anomic and hard-bitten individuals who had to develop all kinds of asocial survival skills. And there was, of course, a price to pay for this hubris. Not so slowly, but certainly surely, modernity builds towards a climax, usually involving a runaway apocalypse based upon technology, or the arms race, or mass communications (Norris, 1995) in which, in one way or another, human subjectivity is annihilated.

We can track the reactions to these myths and fables in contemporary accounts of the world economy after the demise of the Bretton Woods system of international economic management and then the fall of the Berlin Wall. Currently, three of these accounts vie for attention, each of which has broken to a lesser or greater degree from the influence of the Joshua discourse.

The first account of the world economy that is on offer is an apocalyptic one. A common reaction to change through history (Bull, 1995), this account reads events like the demise of Bretton Woods and the fall of the Berlin Wall as evidence of a millenarian condition. Laced with phrases like the 'end of history' (Fukuyama, 1992), and 'fin-de-siècle', such an account provides a cosy rest home for old intellectual habits like teleology and eschatology, as well as satisfying an alluring sense of the dramatic. A second account of the world economy interprets events like the demise of Bretton Woods and the fall of the Berlin Wall as symbols of a new kind of modernity. Whether posing as 'hypermodernity', 'late modernity', 'postmodernity', 'supermodernity' or what have you, such an account usually retains some of the old features of modernity, most notably a sense of transience, fragmentation and anomie, but then either exaggerates these elements still further (as in Harvey, 1989) or adds new defining elements (Beck, 1992; Giddens, 1991). This kind of work provides a final resting place for social theorists who want to retain grand accounts of the world, but is also home to many social theorists who want to provide more nuanced accounts of the contemporary world (Alexander, 1995). However, even the most nuanced of these accounts rarely provide much of an anthropological sense, any sense of the world as a continually practised place in which the human is constantly redefined, and they thereby run the very real risk of exaggerating the differences between this era and previous ones.

That leaves a third, constructivist account of the world economy, one which acknowledges the importance of events like the demise of Bretton Woods and the fall of the Berlin Wall but sees them as both the distillation and illustration of three of its crucial tenets. First, there is the difficulty of achieving sustained control of human systems, which bubble with a stubborn and constant creativity, and which therefore have a tendency to sidestep established orders like the nation state. Second, there is the complexity of what we name in order to escape complexity. Thus systems like 'capitalism' and 'the market' which have apparently triumphed after the two B's are now revealed, in the apparent absence of opposition, as made up of institutions which are manifold, multiform and multiple. There is no one capitalism or market but only a series of different capitalisms and markets which do not converge on a mean. Third, there is the need to understand history as an undetermined unfolding, a fullness of events, a 'maximum of matter in a minimum of space' (Perniola, 1995, p. 8). We cannot know history as a clash of giant and opposing, almost natural, forces, as tidal waves of economic and social change which sweep across the human shore. We can only know history as a more modest and complexly determined set of 'actor-networks' (Latour, 1993; Callon, 1987; Law, 1994), practical orders which allow people and things to be translated into more or less durable entities which can exert force.

But although this latter account is clearly the most credible, in part because of the looseness of its story-telling structure which gives more points of entry to those who lack communicative resources, it is not without its own ability to generate relationships of power, and it is important to realize this. Nowhere is this point made clearer than in the intensely practical realm of international business where physical and nervous energies have to be constantly expended on the concerns of the moment. In this realm, just as in the intellectual realm, the Genesis discourse has gradually displaced the Joshua discourse and, just as in that realm, in doing so it has empowered some groups (such as managers with higher educational qualifications, which increasingly include middle-class women) at the expense of others (Van der Pijl, 1994). There is, in other words, as Foucault pointed out so often, no knowledge that is neutral, that is not a part of the power–knowledge couplet. A *cui bono* question always lies waiting to be answered.

SHUT UP AND DANCE: COPING WITH COMPLEXITY

In this penultimate section, I want to show that the kinds of cogitations which have been the subject of the previous sections have gained a purchase outside intellectual communities, especially in communities concerned with the management of increasingly global business organizations. I want to show that much of the managerial literature since the demise of Bretton Woods and the fall of the Berlin Wall is influenced by two principles: one, that the world is a messy place which we can never know entirely and, two, that business organizations need both to acknowledge this fact and to gear themselves up to take what advantage from it they can. In other words, understanding of the world economy has shifted profoundly, and in a way which is increasingly constitutive, that is this new managerial discourse is changing the shape of the world economy as much as the changing shape of the world economy is changing it (Daly, 1993).

The period after the Second World War and before the demise of the Bretton Woods system and the fall of the Berlin Wall was a period in which striated spaces abounded: the buttoned-down personality of the company man (Whyte, 1957; Sampson, 1995) for one; the enclosed, hierachical world of the multi-divisional corporation (Chandler, 1962, 1977), with its monolithic goals of achieving ever-greater size and scale by means of a single corporate strategy realized through a relatively static and formal bureaucratic inner core which passed information upwards from an 'external' environment and controlled slowly downwards from a closed-off headquarters, for another. Then there were the rigidities that resulted from rules of nation states, like fixed exchange rates, high tariff barriers, and so on. And finally, orchestrating the whole, was the idea of a management 'science' which would be able to produce the cognitive wherewithal to predict and thereby control the world. At least in the rhetoric of the time, then, the world was an organized place, made up of carefully closed-off spaces which could be rationally appropriated and controlled. We might, of course, argue about the accuracy of that rhetoric since any glance at the history of the time hardly suggests the stable, golden age of capitalism that is so often written about. Indeed, as early as 1965 management theorists like Emery and Trist were already writing about organizations that could deal with permanently turbulent environments.

But from the 1960s on, as the Bretton Woods system declined and then, later, the Soviet Union and eastern Europe split asunder, so the state of permanent turbulence that Emery and Trist wrote about began to look more like a successful prophecy and less like a struggling prescription, and for a series of reasons, including the following. First, there was the floating of exchange rates, the growth of various offshore capital markets, and finally the growth of markets in financial derivatives, which has produced the merry-go-round of monetary transmission, offshore borrowing and lending, and various hedging strategies, flavoured with a dollop of pure speculation, that we take for granted today. Second, there has been the exponential growth of information 'economies' generated by the intersection of the financial media, information technologies and the growth of economic research. Third, there has been the growth of numerous new players in the international business world, which have upset the old competitive equilibrium: the Japanese certainly, but also now overseas Chinese firms, Third World multinationals, firms from eastern Europe, and so on. Fourth, there has been the growth of a more differentiated production–consumption nexus in which a more differentiated set of demands on mass producers produces more differentiated consumers, and so on, increasing both the range and fickleness of many markets. Fifth, there has been a general speed-up in transportation and communications. This speed-up has had numerous differentiated, multiple, and sometimes contradictory effects, which mean that it cannot be bracketed within a general description like 'time–space compression' (Thrift, 1995), but that there have been effects which have been sufficiently extensive to allow commentators to write of a world of flows (e.g. Lash and Urry, 1994) seems less open to debate.

Given the scale of these changes, it is no surprise that new discourses have been produced which both frame them and force them. These discourses depend, first of all, on new metaphors which attempt to capture a more turbulent world. At first, the metaphors tended to be ones of excess, overload and saturation. But many of these early metaphors can now be seen as:

the product of the first hysterical reactions to information technologies. 'Overload' in reference to what? Saturated in reference to whom? The relative, historically contingent nature of these terms is seldom if ever entertained within the discourse, which prefers to present them as timeless . . . (Collins, 1995, p. 12)

But, very gradually, new metaphors began to emerge which began to refigure the business organization's relationship with the world, and the role of the manager within that organization. These metaphors were based on the notion of constant adaptive movement – 'dancing', 'surfing', and the like – and of organizational structures that could facilitate this constant adaptation, both by becoming more open to the changing world and by engaging the hearts and minds of the workforce in such a way that the organizations could exist as more open entities:

> We talked of structures and their systems, of inputs and outputs, of control devices and of managing them, as if the whole was one huge factory. Today the language is not that of engineering but of politics with talk of cultures and networks of teams and coalitions, of influences and power rather than of control, of leadership not management. It is as if we had suddenly woken up to the fact that organisations were made up of people after all, not just 'heads' or 'role occupations' (Handy, 1989, p. 71)

What each of these new metaphors has in common, then, is a concern with looser organizational forms more able to 'go with the flow' (Peters and Austin, 1985; Peters, 1989; Handy, 1991; Kanter, 1991). In particular, these new metaphors have become embedded through a new, international discourse of managerialism which has become near to hegemonic. This discourse came from a smorgasbord of sources. There were, for example, early ideas about the importance of participative management (McGregor, 1960). There were new ideas about the ways in which the 'environments' of organizations could be described (for a review, see Taylor and Thrift, 1983). There were new ideas about how power could be exercised in and through corporations (e.g. Pfeffer and Salancik, 1978). And so on.

   Less important, in some ways, than the origins of the new managerialism were the agents which were responsible for its spread. These were of three kinds. The first of these was the demonstrable importance of an alternative model of management to the old multidivisional corporation: the Japanese firm, founded on consensus management, large networks of allied firms, and the like. The second was the growth through the 1960s and 1970s and into the 1980s of formal business education, and especially of the MBA course. Finally, there was the growing importance of 'management gurus' like Charles Handy, Theodore Levitt, Charles Naisbitt, Tom Peters, Rosabeth Moss Kanter, Kenichi Ohmae, and the like, as embodiments of new managerialist arguments. These gurus were responsible for the diffusion of a whole host of the 'business fads' taught on management courses which, jointly and singly, promoted a new managerial world-view, including quality circles, the paperless office, the factory of the future, entrepreneurship, brands, strategic alliances, globalization and, latterly, business process reengineering (Lorenz, 1989).

The new managerialism depends on the notion that the world is uncertain, complex, paradoxical, even chaotic (*Journal of Management Inquiry*, 1994). The manager must somehow find the means to steer a course in this fundamentally uncertain world, which she or he does by five main means (for a comprehensive review, see Ghoschal and Bartlett, 1995). First of all, there is an emphasis on the competitive advantage, in a business world that is increasingly constituted by information, that is incurred by knowledge. Whereas managers:

> used to think that the most precious resource was capital, and that the prime task of management was to allocate it in the most productive way, now they have become convinced that their most precious resource is knowledge and that the prime task of management is to ensure that their knowledge is generated as widely and used as efficiently as possible (Woodridge, 1995, p. 4)

Second, the task of the manager is increasingly seen as the harnessing of knowledge for the good of the organization, most especially by tapping the existing tacit skills and talents of the workforce, and then enhancing these competencies; informally by providing greater communication between workers within the organization so that beneficial practices spread, and formally by instituting means of gaining further qualifications (Allen and de Gay, 1993). Third, the manager no longer aims to produce an overall corporate strategy which is then mechanistically instituted in and through a corporate bureacracy. Rather, the aim is to produce an emergent 'evolutionary' or 'learning' strategy which is 'necessarily incremental and adaptive, but that does not in any way imply that its evolution cannot be, or should not be analysed, managed, and controlled' (Kay, 1993, p. 359). Such a strategy will be based on what are seen as the particular capabilities of a business organization, which are then amplified via informal methods of control which rely on a much greater grasp of the issues involved, and which also mean that whole layers of bureaucracy, most of whose time was taken up with oversight, can be shrunk or, in the jargon, 'delayered'. Fourth, in order to achieve evolutionary strategies, and informal control, the manager has to become a kind of charismatic itinerant, constantly imbuing the business organization's values and goals, constantly on a mission to explain and motivate an increasingly multinational workforce in an increasingly global firm. Not surprisingly, such a task is not easy. For example, Bruns (1995) finds that top managers in multinational corporations now spend most of their time talking to people, via either electronic means or direct face-to-face communication. And much of the rest of the time they spend travelling, spending as much as three out of every four weeks on business trips as they personally try to weave the culture of their organization together. In other words, the example of these managers shows the chief business of business organizations is talk, talk and then more talk (Boden, 1994). Fifth, the manager must not only weave the organization together but must also ensure that, through dedicated networking, he can produce and sustain external relationships of trust with other firms, which become vital conduits of information and future business. Thus the manager not only builds an internal but also an external relational 'architecture' (Kay, 1993).

Thus the rational company man of the 1950s and 1960s, skilled in the highways and byways of bureaucracy, has become the corporate social persona of the 1990s, skilled in the arts of social presentation and 'change management'. And the giant multidivisional corporation of the 1950s and 1960s has become a leaner 'networked organization', a looser form of business which can act like a net floating on an ocean, able to ride the swell and still go forward.

Now this new managerial discourse is undoubtedly an exaggeration that, in turn, exaggerates its own importance. For a start, it reflects 'cultural variations' which are not just variations but root and branch differences. The Japanese firm, with its cultural emphasis on informal reciprocity, is quite clearly a different animal from the US firm, with its emphasis on formal contract (Kay, 1995). And both types of firm are different from overseas Chinese or European firms (Thrift and Olds, 1996). Then again, it overstates the degree to which it has been adopted: many business organizations remain bureaucratic and monolithic. But, what seems clear is that this 'new managerialism' is now the hegemonic account of both what the post-Bretton Woods business world is like, and how best to exercise corporate power within it:

> It has contributed to some changes in management practice (however unevenly) and forms of organisational transformation. It has also provided a new and distinctive language of management which has played a significant role in legitimating claims to both organisational and social leadership (Clarke and Newman, 1993, p. 438)

CONCLUSIONS

The hegemony of this new managerialist ideology has three main consequences, each of them uncomfortable. The first is that it has what used to be called 'material consequences', effects that can be measured out in terms of pain, heartbreak, and shattered lives. Each of the business organizations that has taken the managerial ideology on board has become involved in programmes of direct 'downsizing', cutting back on the workforce with all the human misery this brings, made more of a shock, perhaps, because so many 'redundant' middle management 'layers' have been stripped out, as well as the jobs at the bottom of the occupational hierarchy which are always targeted and forfeited. Business organizations have also been involved in considerable indirect 'downsizing; for example through programmes that lay off significant numbers of subcontractors so as to produce a core network of closely allied firms. Then, not to be taken lightly, organizational change has brought with it other forms of stress and strain, from the 50-year-old executive who is being shunted into a part-time consultancy to the new graduates who must downsize their expectations of a corporate career. In other words, this new form of the exercise of corporate power is not necessarily any 'nicer' than what has gone before; for all the caring rhetoric, lean can just as easily be mean and learning can mean stomach-churning. The sword of management is, as always, two-edged: economic success is, now as then, bought at the cost of the workforce, as much as to its benefit.

Then there is a second consequence of this new managerialist ideology. It makes it even clearer (if this never needed saying) that there is no intellectual community which can be separated off from other communities, in which the intellectual community has the power to decode the world, whilst all the other communities just slope ignorantly about. As Bauman (1987) has pointed out, the intellectual community has moved from a position as legislator of the world to simply one of a number of interpretive communities. In the case of the relationship between the international intellectual and international business community this tendency has been strengthened by increased traffic between the two communities (for example, as a result of the growth of management education, and the increasing use of intellectual ideas in management), by the growth of an independent intelligence and analytical capacity within international business, and by the growth of the media as a powerful disseminator of and trader in ideas between the two communities.

There is one more consequence of the new managerialist ideology. It exposes the problem that there is no theory that is not, or cannot be made, complicit. Just as Marx's and Heidegger's theories could become some of the ingredients of a totalitarian discourse, so notions of radical indeterminacy can be turned to all manner of ends, not all of which are pure or pleasant. But this is the chief point about discourses: they may contain elements of theory but they are not theoretical. They are practically oriented orders bent to the task of constructing more or less durable social networks and they are constantly redefined in order to cope with the vagaries of that task.

What is certain, what is indeed the only certainty, is that the new view of what we know, whether it is found in the intellectual or business communities, demands a change of style which is also – inevitably – a change of content. We need to move away from the comforting nostrum that we can contain the world in theories, and realize that these theories are not just about seeking out new knowledge but also about telling stories about an uncertain world which can, however briefly, stabilize that uncertainty, and make it appear certain and centred. How else, for example, can we explain the currency of stories like 'postmodernism' which often seem to be simply a means of rolling over old antinomies, thereby providing an unfamiliar landscape with some familiar landmarks? Old habits die hard and the habit of searching for centred stories that tell all dies hardest of all, living proof, if proof were needed, of the human need to fend off uncertainty:

> The anxiety would be lessened, tensions allayed, the total situation made more comfortable were the stunning profusion of possibilities somewhat reduced, were the world a bit more singular, its occurrences more repetitive, its parts better marked and separated: in other words – were the events of the world more predictable, and the utility or uselessness of things more immediately evident. One may say that because of their 'fundamental constitution' human beings have inborn (hereditary) vested interests in an orderly structured world free of mysteries and surprises. They also have similar vested interests in being more clearly defined

themselves, and having their inner possibilities pre-selected for them, turned into the source of orientation rather than being a cause of confusion and distress (Bauman, 1995, p. 141)

Now both the international intellectual and international business communities understand the ramifications of this insight. We must learn to live with some of the consequences while striving to prevent them from being turned into a new orthodoxy.

FURTHER READING

Amin, A. (ed.) 1994 *The post-Fordism reader.* Blackwell, Oxford.

Amin, A., Thrift, N.J. (eds) 1994 *Globalization, institutions, and regional development in Europe.* Oxford University Press, Oxford.

Corbridge, S., Thrift, N.J., Martin, R. (eds) 1994 *Money, power and space.* Blackwell, Oxford.

Johnson, R.J., Taylor, P.J., Watts, M. (eds) 1995 *Geographies of global change.* Blackwell, Oxford.

CHAPTER 3

RESTRUCTURING THE PRODUCTION SYSTEM
Brian P. Holly

INDUSTRIAL RESTRUCTURING IN THE LATE TWENTIETH CENTURY

In a recent book, the American political economist, Bennett Harrison, observes that since the mid-1960s the portion of gross domestic product of OECD countries accounted for by corporate profits fell by anywhere from 12 to 37 per cent. These profit rates, defined for the seven richest industrialized nations as net operating surplus divided by net capital stock at current prices, diminished from 25 per cent in 1965 to 12 per cent in 1980. Taken across all sectors, the average profit rate declined from 17 to 11 per cent (Harrison, 1994b, pp. 125–126). There are almost as many explanations for this so-called 'profit squeeze' as there are commentators on contemporary industrial processes, but its net effect has been to induce major changes in international economic competition. The crisis has brought on two decades of deindustrialization which have wrought significant changes in the manner in which industrial production is organized and carried out. Two direct consequences of this industrial restructuring are an increased emphasis on flexibility in the management of production and distribution, and a greater degree of integration by firms, both large and small, in their mutual economic transactions.

It is the purpose of this chapter to examine both the causes and consequences of the reconfiguration of industrial production in an ever increasing global economic system, and to lay out in particular the variety of geographical outcomes that have evolved out of the transition of the industrial system of the past two decades. The chapter begins with a brief discussion of contemporary patterns of industrial organization, focusing on the transition from a Fordist to a post-Fordist mode of production. It then explores the transactions approach to industrial organization, wherein market transactions produce an endless variety of ways in which firms organize their production base. The final section of the chapter attempts to describe the major spatial configurations that result from differences in how production is organized in a post-Fordist economic system.

FORDISM AND INDUSTRIAL RESTRUCTURING

Any discussion of the dramatic restructuring of production on a global basis over the past twenty years must begin with a treatment of the dominant form of industrial organization which preceded the contemporary crisis. Rightly or wrongly, the middle two-thirds of the twentieth century have been labelled the period of Fordism by many observers (Storper and Scott, 1992). During this period, the manufacturing systems of advanced capitalist nations were dominated by a mode of production named after the industrialist Henry Ford and the practices he brought to the manufacture and assembly of automobiles. These included the mobilization of masses of labour in huge factories to produce large batches of standardized goods for mass consumption. Production was organized within vertically integrated firms which operated increasingly across the globe (Dicken, 1992a). The Fordist organization of production was complemented by Taylorist principles of scientific management, including a finely developed technical division of labour within the plant (Scott, 1988b).

According to Sayer and Walker (1992) Fordism embodied rigidity, mass production, dedicated machinery, standardized products, large inventories (just-in-case), labour deskilling, vertical integration, and global firms. By comparison, the post-Fordist regime incorporates flexibility, small batch production, flexible machinery, differentiated products, minimal inventories (just-in-time), skill upgrading, vertical disintegration, and industrial districts. While this dualistic framework tends to oversimplify the differences, it serves as a convenient foundation on which to commence an analysis of contemporary industrial organizational forms which emerged out of the profit crisis described by Harrison. In particular, it is noteworthy that new forms of production have concentrated in areas outside the traditional centres of Fordist activity.

Although the breakdown of Fordist-style production systems can be traced to the profit crisis described by Harrison, a number of other developments contributed to the apparent shift away from Fordism and towards a different, or neo-Fordist, manufacturing regime. Three areas of change stand out in particular: technology, markets, and labour practices. First, in the realm of technology, new methods of production have emerged which are classified under the rubric of Flexible Manufacturing Systems (Knudsen, 1994). These technological innovations normally include reprogrammable machine tools and handling devices as well as supervisory computers and computer numerical control systems. These technologies have been blended with computerized systems for product design, inventories, production scheduling, and financial management, among other aspects, to allow flexibility in both product specification and mix (Coombs and Jones, 1989).

Second, traditional mass markets for standardized products have become increasingly segmented as a result of higher rates of innovation and shorter product life cycles. As markets have become more global, and as transnational corporations compete in more national and regional markets, producers have become increasingly flexible in their product lines and manufacturing techniques. Finally, within the workplace, labour organization has taken on new forms such as functional integration of tasks, team-based work effort, and the integration of both mental and physical skills of workers (Kenney and Florida, 1993). This model sees the worker as more than just another 'input' into the production process, but rather as an active participant in product development, refinement, and manufacture.

In their extensive critique of the conventional characterization of Fordism, Sayer and Walker (1992) observe that Fordism, being far from obsolete, has taken on new forms in Japan through such innovations as just-in-time inventory practices, and that even in its heyday, Fordist production accounted for a minority of outputs, labour, and firms. As Jessop claims,

> Fordism à la Henry Ford was actually quite limited in diffusion and was never fully realized even in Ford's own plants in North America – let alone those in Europe . . . only a small part of manufacturing output is produced in Fordist conditions and only a small proportion of the labour force is employed in Fordist manufacturing. Both charges hold even for the supposed golden years of Fordism (Jessop, 1992, p. 53)

By one estimate, only 700000 British workers toil directly on assembly lines, out of a total workforce of 20.4 million (Littler, 1985). Nevertheless, Fordism reflected an important form of work organization, and it influenced the thinking of generations of management theorists, social scientists, and business writers.

INDUSTRIAL ORGANIZATION: FLEXIBILITY

The Fordist mode of organizing production has been replaced by one that is far more complex and less easily captured in a single term. Piore and Sabel (1984) were the first to bring forward the term flexible specialization to characterize the way in which small firms in the north of Italy were able to capitalize on their advantages of small size and proximity to adjust rapidly to new consumer tastes, technological innovation, changing markets, and labour organization. Soon, flexibility came to be associated with industrial districts across the globe, from Los Angeles to Tokyo, and from Seoul to São Paulo. Flexibility can be many things according to Sayer and Walker (1992). They have identified several types of flexibility, none of which may be necessarily mutually exclusive:

- flexibility in the volume of output as demand changes
- flexibility in product configuration in response to changing markets
- flexibility in labour practices
- flexibility in the use of machinery such as programmable automation
- flexibility in restructuring production
- flexibility in forms of organization as in the case of networks of specialized producers

A common explanation for the rise of flexible specialization in manufacturing is that mass markets have been breaking up into specialized niches. Hansen

(1995) attributes this trend to increasing flexibility in production processes coupled with falling costs in product design, thus creating new opportunities for manufacturers to customize output in small batches. Sayer and Walker argue from another perspective:

> ... part of the answer is that it is simply the general, structural tendency of capitalism to multiply the number of different kinds of commodities over time (and with it, increase the division of labour). The increased range and diversity of demand from all kinds of consumers is hardly new, for the changes wrought by capitalism, in production and ways of life, continually create new needs (Sayer and Walker, 1992, p. 203)

In addition, the internationalization of manufacturing and the rise of newly industrializing economies in Asia and Latin America has resulted in foreign penetration of national markets, thus increasing the total number of goods sold in any market. The intensification of competition within and between markets has promoted greater flexibility in the use of both technology and labour by large and small firms, but especially by small and medium-sized enterprises (SMEs). The emergence of flexible technologies, such as computerized numerically controlled machines, computer aided design and manufacturing, and computerized scheduling of information and materials, has benefited SMEs in terms of the quality and productivity of their output (Hansen, 1995). It is also true that many large firms, with their greater access to capital reserves, are adopting programmable factory automation at an accelerated pace, especially where there are resultant economies of scale (Harrison, 1994b).

By placing large and small firms in opposition to each other in a rigid dualistic framework, one misses many of the fundamental processes operating to produce the wide variety of production forms and the networks of relations which bind them together into production systems. It is necessary, therefore, to delve more deeply into how individual firms and establishments combine inputs of labour, capital, technology, information, and materials in the process of manufacturing products for both mass and specialized markets.

INDUSTRIAL ORGANIZATION: SCALE AND SCOPE

This section begins with the proposition that the industrial organization of manufacturing firms or production units conforms to a continuum with small, more flexibly specialized producers at one end and large, mass production entities at the other end (Scott, 1983, 1988b, 1993; Gertler, 1988; Schoenberger, 1989). This continuum has been given various labels but it relates mainly to the degree of integration of production processes embedded within the production unit or workplace. Different production systems exhibit varying degrees of organizational integration and disintegration (Harrison 1994b; Scott, 1993; Walker, 1988). Indeed, Storper and Walker refer to the '... rich tapestry of organizational forms that link up and overlap in complex and flexible ways'

(1989, pp. 26). This diversity in organizational forms of production raises the question of which processes invariably lead to particular types of organizational structure. A related question involves empirical attempts at verifying the relationship between specific industrialization processes and their derivative organizational structures. A third question addresses the particular geographical arrangements which various forms of production can adopt.

Any discussion of how production is organized requires that terms, which are often used interchangeably, be defined more precisely so as to facilitate analysis. Both Walker (1988) and Storper and Harrison (1991) argue for the need to build a vocabulary of terms to reduce confusion in the discussion of economic development. The following terms are given definition for that purpose.

- Firm – a legal entity, the central administrative structure designed to organize production under capitalism.
- Production unit – the physical entity, usually at a single location, where manufacturing takes place. Otherwise referred to as the factory, establishment, or workplace.
- Division of labour – the division of a production system into different sectors, with a concomitant specialization in specific tasks by each sector. This Scott (1993) terms a social division of labour.
- Input–output system – intersectoral flows of commodities and services, usually across many production units.

SCALE AND SCOPE ECONOMIES

Production units, regardless of size, attempt to achieve operating economies in two ways: internally and externally. Internal economies are achieved by reducing costs within the plant or workplace, while external economies result from reducing the cost of relations outside the establishment. Scott (1993) has related these cost reducing relationships to the effects of scale and scope. Scale economies are sought internally by increasing output in the workplace; external scale economies result when the number of production units increases quantitatively. Internal economies of scope accrue when a firm can produce two or more different, but related, products more efficiently or more cheaply in tandem than separately (Malecki, 1991). An increase in the variety or range of different producers within an industrial complex or agglomeration is an indicator of external scope economies. That is, the scope of the entire production system widens as the scope of individual firms or units narrows through specialization. Diseconomies of scale and scope result from the inefficiencies inherent in expanding production to a point of increasing average costs, thus encouraging the proliferation of separate production units which are smaller and more functionally specialized (Storper and Harrison, 1991; Scott, 1993).

Firms or production units seek to maximize both internal and external economies. Scott and Storper (1992) show how scale and scope in production networks can be subdivided into internal and external economies, which in turn leads to a taxonomy of production systems ranging from small isolated workshops to large-scale assembly systems. They develop a fourfold schema of production systems based on combinations of internal and external economies of scale and scope:

- Isolated specialized workshops – low internal and external economies of scale and scope.
- Process industries – high internal economies, but low external economies of scale and scope.
- Disintegrated network production – low internal economies, but high external ones.
- Large-scale network production – both high internal and external economies of scale and scope.

Thus, where internal economies are low and external economies are high, disintegrated network production should be the norm. Here one finds a system of small producers who practice extensive subcontracting (Scott and Storper, 1992). This type of production system comes closest to representing the classic vertically disintegrated, flexibly specialized complex of firms. Firms or production units which engage in more flexibly specialized production based on small batches, quick turnaround, and sophisticated products are more likely to engage in external market transactions than are units based on large batches of relatively uniform output. Thus, the flexibly specialized firm is more likely to participate in subcontracting arrangements within a network of tightly meshed firms ranging from small to large. The fourth category, that of large-scale assembly industries, encompasses classical Fordist mass-production sectors such as automobiles as well as those which produce small numbers of large and complex products such as satellites, rockets or aircraft. Scott (1993) refers to the latter as 'systems houses'.

The first category in the above schema consists exclusively of small production units with few connections, as in many craft industries. The second category reflects the typical Fordist, vertically integrated system with large factories which internalize most production tasks. Examples would include a modern petrochemical complex or a vertically integrated automobile factory such as the Ford-owned Rouge plant in Michigan (Walker, 1988). The remaining two means of organizing production can be classified as being vertically disintegrated because they consist of large numbers of firms and establishments, which exhibit an advanced social division of labour, with many transactions occurring between units. Two general forms are given by Scott and Bergman (1993). The first form consists of many small to medium-sized units linked together through a web of transactions consisting of subcontracting, strategic alliances, services contracts, distribution agreements, and more. This type of complex exhibits both vertical and horizontal disintegration, whereby many firms are spread across all levels of production. The electronics, machine tool, jewellery and clothing industries are characteristic of this form of network. The second form describes a complex of large core assembly plants, positioned at the downstream end of a many-tiered supply system. Horizontally integrated complexes such as these might include contemporary automobile assembly operations using just-in-time inventory practices, or large-scale systems houses producing aircraft or communications satellites in small batches (Scott and Bergman, 1993).

Storper and Harrison (1991) further refine this schema by dichotomizing production networks, containing both large and small firms, into dispersed and agglomerated forms. Dispersed production networks of mostly small firms, while not common, can be organized around such activities as consulting engineering or specialized apparel (Clark, 1993a). Dispersed network production based on some large units is typified by the personal computer industry with its far-flung networks of subcontractors shipping components to assembly plants as in the case of IBM. Agglomerated networks can be of two types: those consisting of primarily small and medium-sized units such as the textile districts of Capri or Prato in the 'Third Italy' (Piore and Sabel, 1984), and large firm-led districts typified by aerospace in southern California, semiconductors in 'Silicon Valley', aircraft in Toulouse, and automobiles in Toyota City (Storper and Harrison, 1991).

PRODUCTION SYSTEMS

Modern industrial organization centres on the production system, which is more than an input–output system consisting of intra- and inter-firm transactions. 'Production-systems have a certain technological integrity revolving around a common set of outputs or around a common set of inputs, which rests on a shared technology (such as microelectronics)' (Walker, 1988, p. 380). The French have termed this a 'filière'. Production systems take many forms, but their logic does not rely solely on the purpose inherent in their fundamental input–output relations. They must be integrated so that flows of material, labour, and information are regulated, so that labour processes are coordinated, and so that systems are physically linked (Walker, 1988). Thus, a governance structure has emerged which ensures that integration, coordination, and linkage are regulated and directed. Governance, according to Storper and Harrison (1991), requires both a hierarchy and leadership to effectively coordinate the input–output system. This leads to sets of asymmetrical and symmetrical power relationships which may be organized by and around large firms in the first instance, or contain no lead or coordinating large firm in the second.

Putting aside the classically vertically integrated, Fordist firm for the moment, most production systems function as production networks. Indeed, it is '... the creation by managers of boundary-spanning networks of firms, linking together big and small companies ...' that, according to Harrison, '... is the signal economic experience of our era' (Harrison, 1994b, p. 127). As noted above, production networks can be either small-firm-led or large-firm-led, and each can display either dispersed or agglomerated forms. Transaction costs, particularly over space, play an important role in determining the degree to which such networks will agglomerate or not. Scott has argued that, where inter-firm transactions are small in scale, variable and unpredictable in character, and require significant face-to-face contact, producers will locate in close proximity to each other. A locationally dispersed complex, on the other hand, will likely result from the opposite conditions (Scott and Bergman, 1993).

Through an illuminating case study of one specialized apparel firm located in the Pacific, Clark (1993a) shows how dispersed production networks can exist and be maintained by relatively small companies which are not part of territorial agglomerations. Corporation X, as Clark identified it, is a small, privately owned company which employs about 100 people directly. It markets both winter and summer sportswear for sale in Asia, Australia, Europe, and the US, but all of its products are manufactured by a series of small subcontractors located in south-east Asia and China. As it does not own retail outlets, Corporation X sells its products through large retailers and speciality stores. These backward and forward linkages account for a substantial portion of the retail price of its products. This firm typifies a particular kind of small to medium-sized company which has entered the global economy in increasing numbers. It operates locally, regionally, and globally, depending upon the kind of function or linkage involved (see Figure 3.1).

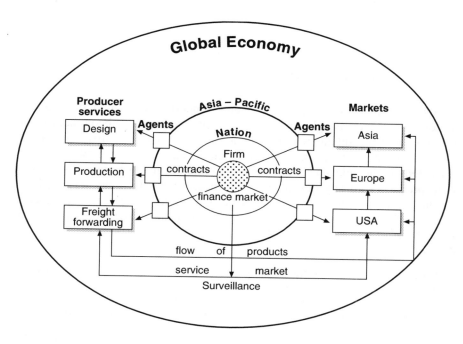

Figure 3.1   Chain-of-links through the global economy (from Clark, 1993a, Figure 1)

At the other extreme is the large-firm-led production network exemplified by the clothing manufacturer Benetton. Headquartered in Treviso near Venice in north-east Italy, the company operates eight factories and warehouses, and uses some 500 independent subcontractors, 90 per cent of which are located within the Veneto region. Benetton also uses numerous other small contract shops and home workers located throughout southern Italy and other countries. The firm distributes its output through a global network of franchised outlets which is connected to various regional offices and warehouses via computer networks. High skill tasks such as design, cutting, and dyeing operations, using computer technology, take place in the Veneto region, while most labour-intensive assembly, pressing, and embroidery are contracted out to small, specialized, non-union shops located farther afield, and who work exclusively for the parent firm. This system of 'putting out' has proved to be very profitable for Benetton, positioning it as a truly global company in retail clothing manufacture (Harrison, 1994b).

Corporation X and Benetton are but two examples of the many ways in which small-firm-led or large-firm-led production networks can be organized within a system of inter-firm transactions that can be either dispersed or agglomerated. In both cases, the lead firms succeed through the formation and maintenance of supplier and distribution networks based on subcontracting, franchising, distributional arrangements, strategic alliances, and more. On the production, or input, side of the equation, it is the variety and spatial extent of subcontracting which give definition to the networks. It is to that topic which this chapter now turns.

SUBCONTRACTING SYSTEMS

As the case studies of Corporation X and Benetton reveal, modern production systems rely increasingly on linkages with suppliers, subcontractors, distributors, and consultants who may be located next door or halfway around the globe. The complexity of subcontracting requires that relations between firms be regulated, predictable, and enforceable if production and distribution of products is to proceed with any degree of confidence, especially if the relationship is conducted over a long distance. Known as outsourcing in modern parlance, the practice of putting out work to subsidiary establishments or independent firms dates back to the early years of industrialization in Europe (Walker, 1988). According to Scott,

> Subcontracting involves the farming out of packets of work to independent producers who undertake to perform – according to given instructions – a specialized set of tasks. The work is then usually returned in semifinished form to its point of origin for further fabrication and finishing (Scott, 1988b, p. 55)

Under its modern guise subcontracting can be practised in a number of different forms, but two primary articulations are those of speciality and capacity subcontracting (Holmes, 1986; Scott, 1988b). Speciality subcontracting refers to the putting out of work which complements the primary functions of the firm. Here the subcontractor plays an important role in the design of fabricated parts. Thus, this form of subcontracting involves somewhat more sophisticated labour processes than does that of capacity subcontracting. This second form consists of excess work, technically able to be done in-house, but which results from a temporary level of demand in excess of capacity. Speciality subcontracting, according to Scott (1988b), reflects vertical disintegration in production, whereas capacity subcontracting is a form of horizontal disintegration. For a sample of technologically advanced firms in a part of the American manufacturing belt, Clarke (1994) found that over 90 per cent of firms putting out work did so for capacity reasons, while only 60 per cent of those firms taking in work did so for this reason. Also, capacity subcontracting dominated in the chemicals and machinery sectors, whereas specialization work was more common among electronics and instruments firms. These differences reflect the standardized production regimes and products associated with scale economies in chemicals and machinery as opposed to the more specialized output of electronics and instruments industries.

The primary interest in subcontracting among geographers has been, not surprisingly, in whether this aspect of production exhibits predictable spatial patterns, and whether the geography of subcontracting can be linked to fundamental changes in the organization of industrial production. Differences in production subcontracting behaviour vary by industry, type of product, degree of vertical disintegration, transaction costs, and distance, among other reasons. Donaghu and Barff (1990), for example, studied the athletic footwear industry through a case study of Nike Incorporated. They observe that Nike subcontracts 100 per cent of its footwear production to firms located mainly in south-east Asia through a combination of capacity and specialization outsourcing. The global athletic footwear market is constantly changing and intensely competitive, prompting Nike to seek production partners who could produce mass quantities of standardized goods quickly and flexibly in response to market changes, while at the same time keeping costs low. Nike found this combination of needs best met by agglomerations of firms in the low-wage countries of south-east Asia.

The personal computer manufacturing industry exemplifies a different type of production subcontracting system. The ability to manufacture personal computers is now a global phenomenon not confined to advanced industrial nations. The intensification of price competition and the narrowing of profit margins have reduced the once dominant position of US-based producers. As a result, final assembly of personal computers occurs in each of the three major market areas of North America, Asia, and Europe, but the majority of components and subassemblies are sourced from countries in south-east Asia and Mexico. High-technology components such as disk drives and microprocessors tend to be manufactured within final demand countries, whereas more standardized, mass produced components tend to be subcontracted to low-wage areas of the world (Angel and Engstrom, 1995).

What the above case studies demonstrate is that subcontracting has spatial manifestations as well as specific content characteristics. It can be found in highly localized industrial districts comprised of many small to medium-sized firms engaged in intensive sets of transactions such as in the Third Italy or Silicon Valley. But the subcontracting of production can also be organized globally by individual firms as in the cases of Benetton and Nike, and by entire industries as in the example of personal computers.

FROM FIRMS TO NETWORKS: JAPANESE KEIRETSU

Harrison's hypothesis that the networked production system typifies modern industrial organization finds support in both Europe and Japan, albeit in different forms. Indeed, the Japanese system of production organization combines a Fordist-style, standardized, mass production approach with a decentralized, flexibly specialized hierarchy of suppliers and subcontractors, known as 'societies of business' or '*keiretsu*' (Harrison, 1994b). A substantial social science and business literature has developed around Japan's industrial organization, and the following discussion is drawn from two reviews of that literature by Harrison (1994b) and Sayer and Walker (1992). Two basic forms of keiretsu exist: Gurupu, or financial keiretsu; and Keiretsu, or supply keiretsu. The former, descending from the pre-Second World War, family-owned zaibatsu, contain groups of firms, usually organized around a lead bank from which the group derives its name (e.g. Sumitomo, Mitsui, Mitsubishi). Each conglomerate operates one company in each of the major industries (e.g. steel, automobiles, chemicals, shipbuilding, trading, engineering) with financing provided through low interest loans from the gurupu bank. Firms are bound to each other through a complex pattern of overlapping ownership, preferential treatment in inter-firm transactions, protection of member firms from takeover, and a focus on long-term growth and stability. Not every major firm belongs to a financial keiretsu, especially in the newer information technology industries, but most large firms affiliate with one of them through technology agreements or various strategic alliances.

The second form of keiretsu is organized around supply relations, with major companies organizing their supplier and subcontractor firms into multiple tiers. Supply keiretsu are most common in industries where final products contain many components and subassemblies such as in automobiles (Toyota), consumer electronics (Sony), and machinery (NEC). Lead firms serve mainly as final assemblers sitting at the downstream end of a pyramidal supplier system comprised of layers of subcontractors ranging from large first tier companies to small lower tier ones. Firms higher in the pyramid generally enjoy longer-term transactional relations with the lead firm, and in turn dominate many lower tier suppliers. This system is known as 'relational contracting', where the parent firm directly manages relations with top tier firms, who in turn are charged with the responsibility of managing companies at lower levels in the hierarchy. Figure 3.2

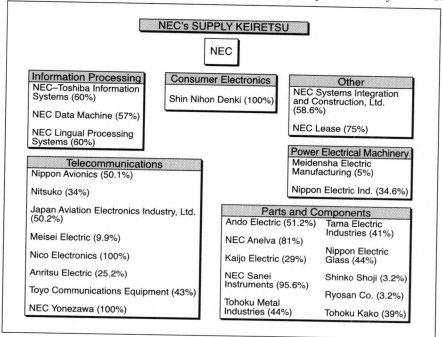

Figure 3.2 NEC's supply keiretsu (adapted from Harrison, 1994b)

portrays the upper tiers of NEC's supply keiretsu, together with the equity share NEC holds in each firm. NEC, in turn, is itself a member of the Sumitomo financial keiretsu or conglomerate. Matsushita's keiretsu is comprised of over 600 firms, and in 1980 Toyota's consisted of 168 first tier, 4700 second tier, and 31600 third tier subcontractors.

Often groups of subcontractors become organized into cooperation groups, or 'kyoryokukai', by first or second tier supply firms to which they sell. The parent or core firm in this part of the keiretsu may provide financial and technical assistance to members, instruct them in quality control, and promote communication among and between member firms. The kanban, or just-in-time, inventory system relies heavily upon reliable and quick flows of information among suppliers between tiers. Relational contracting's success depends on a certain degree of mutual obligation among firms between tiers. Suppliers are expected to invest in new equipment, innovate, incur debt, and continuously update the skills of managers and workers. In response, suppliers expect parent firms to commit to long-term procurement contracts and equity investments, provide technical assistance, and even exchange personnel with them. The benefits from such a system include limiting and channelling direct price competition, discouraging takeovers, spreading downsizing during periods of decline, and regulating entry into the industry. Far from constituting a cosy, comfortable system, suppliers are under constant pressure to improve their performance, continually innovate, and reduce costs and therefore delivery prices to the buyer firm.

Whereas the flexible specialization literature argues that vertically disinte-grated production systems are organized around non-routine kinds of production, the Japanese mass production industry keiretsu, while vertically disintegrated, emphasize large numbers of small firm subcontractors engaged in the kind of repetitive work characteristic of more integrated Western companies. Thus, while the system can be thought of as being flexible, individual supplier firms are not. The more specialized suppliers, with their greater assets of informa-tional, human, and physical capital, are likely to enjoy a high degree of independence from their parent firms. In the Japanese colour television sector, specialized independent suppliers sell not only to NEC, Matsushita, and Sony, but also to other customers, both domestically and internationally.

The combination of increased competition from newly developing nations and pressure from the West to open up its domestic economy to imported industrial products has spurred many Japanese companies to globalize their operations through a combination of strategic alliances, building plants on foreign soil, purchasing existing plant capacity in other nations, and encouraging their own suppliers to branch out around the globe. In a recent book on Japanese transplants in the US, regional planners Martin Kenney and Richard Florida have documented the transplantation of Japanese industrial capacity into the industrial heartland of America (Kenney and Florida, 1993). Since about 1980, almost 1300 manufacturing operations of Japanese firms or Japanese–American joint ventures have opened in the traditional Rust Belt of North America, including 11 auto assembly plants, 320 automotive suppliers, 72 steel mills, and 21 rubber and tyre plants. The investment behaviour of Japanese firms has not been confined to heavy industry. Japanese multinationals are also establishing product development centres and research and development laboratories at the same time as they build their own computer and electronics manufacturing facilities and place capital in US microelectronics, software, biotechnology, and semi-conductor firms in such localities as Silicon Valley (Kenney and Florida, 1993).

A key element in the globalization of Japanese industry is the accompaniment of investment by the Japanese system of production organization. Kenney and Florida characterize this system as a model of 'lean production', which includes efficient resource use, low inventories, and the practice of just-in-time production and delivery. It also involves harnessing the intellectual as well as physical labour of workers, resulting in a synthesis of innovation and production which they refer to as 'innovation-mediated production'. At the same time, variations of the keiretsu are being transplanted as the core firms encourage their suppliers to globalize by building branch operations abroad. The automotive sector has been especially aggressive in this regard. Indeed, Kenney and Florida argue that Japan '. . . is at the center of an epoch-making new model of technology, work, and production organization that is now being transferred to the United States and elsewhere around the globe' (Kenney and Florida, 1993, p. 4). They further believe that the Japanese innovation-mediated production model is directly transferable to other societies because it consists of a basic set of organizational practices.

THE NEW GEOGRAPHY OF PRODUCTION

A critical question in all of the discussion about industrial restructuring, production systems, and networks of flexibly specialized producers concerns how it all plays out on the geographical landscape. One inescapable fact is that production has been decentralizing or dispersing as companies search for cheaper labour and resources, try to escape congestion and labour unions, or to satisfy governments' demands that production must locate where consumption takes place (Harrison, 1994b). But dispersal has also been accompanied by concentration as inter-firm production networks encourage clustering of subcontractors around lead firms in an attempt to reduce transaction costs. One hypothesis put forward to explain the new geography of production is the emergence of industrial districts containing spatially concentrated networks of mainly small and medium-sized firms that are embedded in highly localized networks of linkages, and often using flexible production techniques such as computer numerical control systems. Such proximity encourages the sharing of information, exchange of assets and personnel, and the continual formation and dissolution of production networks in response to external market signals. The quintessential industrial districts are located in north and north-east Italy, sometimes referred to as the Third Italy (Piore and Sabel, 1984). Other industrial districts based on similar structures have been identified in the Los Angeles area, Silicon Valley, Britain's M4 corridor, Taiwan, and other locations. Whether this form of industrial district will form the centrepiece of the new industrial geography is open to question, and is increasingly seen as merely one outcome of the globalization of production.

It is clear that the city-based region remains the locus of production in modern economies. Whereas in the past territorially based production complexes were organized around lead industries and served mainly regional and national markets, contemporary complexes are bound up with the global economy through complex relations with firms and networks of firms around the globe. The regional planners Manuel Castells and Peter Hall suggest that cities and regions as production complexes are being influenced by three interlinked historical processes:

- a revolution based on information technologies
- the formation of a global economy
- the emergence of knowledge as the basis of productivity and competitiveness.

Networks, according to Castells and Hall, have become the web binding both large corporations and small firms together in the flexible process of production.

The resulting industrial space is given form by the location of new industrial sectors and by the adoption of new technologies by all sectors of production (Castells and Hall, 1994).

Thus, as the influence of the nation-state declines in the transition to a global economy, cities and regions benefit from their capacity to shape economic development and to adapt to changes in markets, technology, and culture. Some older major city-based regions such as Paris, London, and Tokyo have maintained themselves as national and global centres of innovation and production while others such as New York and Berlin have lost their formerly dominant position to southern California and Munich, respectively. But new production complexes, based on dynamic technologies such as microelectronics, computers, bioengineering, lasers, and robotics, have sprouted in Silicon Valley and Orange County in California, around Austin in Texas, Portland in Oregon, the Midi in France, 'Silicon Glen' in Scotland, and Seville in Spain. In addition, newly industrializing countries in Asia, including South Korea, Taiwan, Hong Kong, Singapore, and Malaysia, have developed highly competitive economies based on electronics sectors (Castells and Hall, 1994).

Both neo-Fordist and post-Fordist production regimes organized around large-firm-led production networks, as in the case of the Japanese supply keiretsu, continue to thrive in more traditional industrial regions of Japan, North America and Europe. As the reach of these production networks becomes more global, newer areas are opened up to production in parts of the developing world. The maquiladora branch plants of northern Mexico and the electronics and textile factories of south-east Asia constitute the upstream component of extended, global production networks which rely upon cheap, low-skilled labour, using modern production technology to manufacture standardized products in huge quantities. The extensive use of outsourcing in the production of both intermediate and final products has stimulated the dispersal of manufacturing to peripheral regions, while at the same time reinforcing the dominance of long-established core districts in the developed nations. At the same time, firms outside the traditional orbit have seized upon new manufacturing techniques and forms of organization to free themselves of the limitations of place. Nike and Benetton are but two of the more notable examples of firms that continually scan the globe in search of partners with whom to link up.

Whatever spatial configuration may evolve out of the restructuring of the global production system, it is clear that a very different system exists today from the one which emerged from the ashes of the Second World War. The dominance of the United States as the leading producer nation of the world is no longer assured. Both Japan and Germany pose challenges to US hegemony in manufacturing for the world's economy, and newly industrializing nations of Asia and Latin America are vying for position and influence in the global economy. All of these changes are the result of a fundamental restructuring of production and markets, and they have generated a wide variety of organizational forms and production technologies which are transforming the industrial map of the world.

FURTHER READING

Castells, M., Hall, P. 1994 *Technologies of the world: the making of 21st century industrial complexes*. Routledge, London.

Harrison, B. 1994 *Lean and mean: the changing landscape of corporate power in the age of flexibility*. Basic Books, New York.

Piore, M., Sabel, C. 1984 *The second industrial divide*. Basic Books, New York.

Sayer, A., Walker, R. 1992 *The new social economy: reworking the division of labor*. Blackwell, Oxford.

Scott, A.J. 1993 *Technopolis: high-technology industry and regional development in southern California*. University of California, Berkeley, CA.

Storper, M.J., Harrison, B. 1991 Flexibility, hierarchy and regional development: the changing structure of industrial production systems and their forms of governance in the 1990s. *Research Policy* **20**: 407–22.

Storper, M., Walker, R. 1989 *The capitalist imperative: territory, technology and industrial growth*. Blackwell, New York.

Walker, R. 1988 The geographical organization of production systems. *Society and Space* **6**: 377–408.

CHAPTER 4

THE 'NEWER' INTERNATIONAL DIVISION OF LABOUR
William J. Coffey

THE DIVISION OF LABOUR

The division of labour is one of the basic principles of the organization of human society. Very early on in their social evolution human beings rapidly became aware that, rather than each individual family or household attempting to provide for the entire range of its material and non-material (e.g. intellectual, psychological, spiritual) requirements, it was much more efficient for each to *specialize* in a very small number of products or processes. A certain proportion of the fruits of such specialized activities could then be exchanged, directly by barter or through the medium of money, for the output of other specialists, thus satisfying the basic needs of the social unit. This common-sense form of organization became the *raison d'être* underlying exchange economies.

The concept of the division of labour was formalized by Adam Smith (1776), who demonstrated that this practice was a major source of economies in the production process. Smith clearly documented the advantages of the division of labour within an individual production unit, using the example of a pin-making factory. Rather than having each individual worker perform all of the steps required for the fabrication of a pin, considerable advantages in efficiency (increase in speed and skill of operation, elimination of time lost in switching from one task to another, utilization of specialized machinery) and productivity (output per worker per hour) were to be obtained by having specific workers specialize in one of the discrete stages of the production process: wire drawing, straightening, cutting, sharpening, and so forth. In this manner, workers were led to apply their labour power more effectively. The division of labour reached its culmination in twentieth century assembly lines where an individual worker's function often consisted entirely of repeatedly tightening a specific bolt on each product passing before him on a conveyor belt.

The example of Smith's pin-making factory illustrates only one of the three major forms of the division of labour:

- The *technical division of labour* refers to the disaggregation of a given production process into discrete stages, and the consequent specialization of

40

workers in each of these stages, as exemplified by Smith's pin-making factory. The technical division of labour generally occurs within a given plant or firm and in the past has been closely associated with the concepts of 'Taylorism' (scientific management based on the use of flowcharts and stopwatches) and 'Fordism' (mass production based upon assembly line techniques).

■ The *social division of labour* is a more general concept. On the one hand, it refers to the specialization of functions performed by individuals in society; some persons are factory workers, while others are teachers, members of the clergy, poets, farmers or football players. On the other hand, the social division of labour also denotes the specialization of organizations, of firms or of a firm's establishments. Corporations such as Ford, General Motors or Toyota, for example, are not 100 per cent vertically integrated; that is to say, they do not perform internally all of the functions associated with the design, fabrication and sales of their automobiles. Rather, while performing certain functions and producing certain components, they rely heavily on inputs (e.g. tyres, design and advertising services, radios) obtained from independent specialist firms. As Scott (1988a) has noted, in modern production systems the notion of 'the firm as organization' is being rapidly replaced by that of 'the organization of firms'.

■ The *spatial division of labour* implies the specialization of production by geographic zones, and manifests itself at various spatial scales. (As we shall discover below, such geographic specialization often reflects the spatial division of labour within a firm; different activities within a firm may have different locational requirements.) For example, metropolitan space is generally divided into office, manufacturing and retail districts, and so forth. At a regional level, we often speak of the zones such as the Rust Belt (the north-eastern US, dominated by declining 'heavy' industries), the Gun Belt (the south-western US, where economic development has largely been stimulated by defence contracts), and France's Bordeaux and Bourgogne wine producing regions. At the national scale, too, certain degrees of specialization may be identified, giving rise to international trade flows. For example, Japan specializes in the production of automobiles and consumer electronic equipment, Germany in automobiles and precision instruments and equipment, Saudi Arabia in crude oil and refined petroleum. It is this *international division of labour* that is the focus of the present chapter.

The specialization inherent in the social and spatial divisions of labour enhances efficiency and productivity in the same manner as the technical division of labour in Smith's pin factory. Out of such specialization, it is argued, will accrue greater benefit to all. At a national scale, the division of labour allows a country to increase its productivity by eliminating the need for it to internally produce all of the goods and services that it consumes. A nation can thereby specialize in those activities in which its firms are relatively more productive and import those products and services for which its firms are relatively less productive.

THE CHANGING INTERNATIONAL DIVISION OF LABOUR: AN OVERVIEW

Walton (1985) identifies three phases of the international division of labour. In its first phase, corresponding to the early period of European colonization, the division of labour was characterized by the extraction of agricultural products and minerals from the periphery (i.e. the less developed countries of the New World), often by means of the forcible application of labour (e.g. slavery). At the same time, the core units themselves (i.e. the more advanced European economies) engaged in agricultural, mineral and rudimentary commodity production, and traded mainly with other core units. The second phase, which characterized most of the nineteenth century and the first half of the twentieth century, saw the expansion of industrial production in the core (a concept which expanded as more countries attained higher levels of development), and of asymmetric flows of industrial and resource commodities between core and periphery (a concept which also evolved over time), with the latter continuing to specialize in agricultural products and minerals. According to international trade theory, this particular form of the international division of labour, and its related trade flows, was the result of the respective *comparative advantages* of the nations involved (Appendix 1). From a political–economic perspective, however, it is clear that the observed international division of labour and the consequent pattern of exchanges between core and periphery largely involved western European and, later, North American colonialist states and their colonies or former colonies.

At the beginning of the 1960s, after well over 100 years of a 'traditional' international division of labour, a third or 'new' phase began. One of the first uses of the term 'new international division of labour' (NIDL) was by Ladreit de Lacharrière (1969), although the concept was popularized by Palloix (1977, first published in French in 1975) and, especially, by Fröbel *et al.* (1980, first published in German in 1977). As evident in the early literature, the novel aspect of the NIDL involved a major level of foreign direct manufacturing investment in the periphery by firms from core economies. (Note that the definitions of core and periphery continued to evolve over time, with the former concept now including Japan, for example.) Expressed more simply, firms from the industrialized countries began to establish branch plants in the less developed countries (LDCs). In addition, this 'outward' foreign direct investment (FDI) on the part of firms from developed nations was often part of a broader process involving the simultaneous closure of domestic manufacturing facilities, thus raising concerns about the 'deindustrialization' of core economies (Bluestone and Harrison, 1982). Note also that, as we shall see below, manufacturing FDI in LDCs has helped to create a new class of economies: the newly industrializing countries (NICs), often considered as the 'semi-periphery' of the world economy.

If, as indicated in the literature, the principal characteristic of the NIDL is foreign direct manufacturing investment in LDCs by firms from core countries, it becomes appropriate to identify a fourth phase in the trajectory of the international division of labour. In this 'new NIDL' or 'NEWER-IDL', four more recent processes have begun to take on increasing significance, overlaying (but not necessarily displacing) the original dimensions of the NIDL. (In a sense, these more recent developments may be viewed as extensions of the third phase, in that they were in existence during that period. We believe that a distinction is warranted, however, in that the processes in question were much more generalized after the early or mid-1980s, depending upon the specific countries involved.) First, firms from developed countries have increasingly begun to exploit the comparative advantages of LDCs without needing to resort to FDI. By entering into relatively stable supply relationships with independent local subcontractors in LDCs, 'manufacturing' firms in advanced economies perform less and less of their own physical production. This type of arrangement is an excellent example of 'the organization of firms' (the social division of labour) on a global scale.

Second, although the 'traditional' NIDL literature deals almost exclusively with manufacturing, it is obvious that an increasing share of the activities relocated from the core to peripheral or semi-peripheral economies involves the provision of services rather than the fabrication of goods. This development, primarily affecting standardized 'back office' functions, is not at all surprising given the rising importance of services in the world economy over the past two decades. (See Chapter 16 for more detail on services in offshore production.) Third, some of the LDCs that were among the original destinations for FDI by core nations have developed to the point that their own firms have begun to engage in outward FDI channelled towards countries that are even less advanced. The 'Asian tigers' – South Korea, Taiwan, Hong Kong and Singapore – are perhaps the most striking examples of this phenomenon. Fourth, an increasing level of outward FDI by firms in advanced nations is destined for other core economies. Conceptually, this represents a new dimension to the emphasis in the NIDL literature upon FDI in the periphery and the semi-periphery, although it must be noted that cross-investment between core economies has long existed.

This overview has provided a brief and schematic portrait of the changing international division of labour. The remaining sections of this chapter provide more detail concerning the nature and underlying causes of the phenomena presented here. Before embarking upon these amplifications, however, it is necessary to make a fundamental distinction between two uses of the term 'NIDL'. On the one hand, in its more general sense, NIDL is often employed to signify 'recent developments' in the international division of labour. On the other hand, in its narrower sense, NIDL also reflects a specific theoretical framework or *problématique* coming from radical political economy, one that is often identified with dependency theory and neo-Marxist approaches. In this sense, NIDL is used to describe relations of dominance and dependency between nations and, specifically, the shift of standardized forms of industrial production from core to periphery in order to increase profits. In this latter sense, the concern is not simply with describing which countries perform which functions, but rather with a whole range of social and political relations involving both the core and the periphery (for examples of this second approach see Fröbel *et al.*, 1980, and Henderson, 1989). Thus the thrust of the former interpretation of NIDL could be stated in terms of 'who does what in the world', while that of the latter might be better described as 'who does what to whom'. In reality, it is perhaps not feasible (nor desirable) to separate the two approaches entirely. In the remainder of this chapter, while our focus is primarily upon recent developments in the IDL, we cannot ignore the socio-political aspects of these changes.

DIMENSIONS OF THE INTERNATIONAL DIVISION OF LABOUR

The global distribution of economic activity has changed considerably since the end of the Second World War. In the early 1950s, the world's production of manufactured goods was still confined to two dozen industrialized countries. Most of the rest of the world (excluding the so-called Second World, consisting of the Soviet bloc and China, which was for all intents and purposes outside the global economic system and thus exerted virtually no influence on the international division of labour) was lumped together under the term 'the Third World', and was generally regarded as a supplier of natural resources. Currently, however, the international division of labour has taken on much more complex dimensions (Appendix 2).

In general, there are three major types of indicators that one may employ to examine the division of labour among the world's nations. A first indicator involves patterns of international trade: the principal imports and exports of each nation, as well as its main import origins and export destinations. This indicator is fairly complex to construct and to interpret, given the multiplicity of trade flows that must be taken into consideration. Further, many trade flows are more apparent than real, in the sense that they represent internal transfers within multinational corporations rather than 'arm's-length' commercial exchanges between sovereign states. In addition, the relationship between production and trade is not an exact one; some countries that are significant producers are less important in terms of exports (e.g. US, India, Brazil). A second indicator is the distribution of a nation's labour force among the major sectors of its economy; the proportion of workers engaged in various activities provides a reasonable first approximation of the relative specialization of individual countries. A third indicator is the proportion of a nation's gross domestic product (GDP) that is derived from the various economic sectors. This measure represents an improvement over labour force distribution in that it takes into account sectoral differences in worker productivity due to the use of capital and technology.

Figure 4.1 presents one perspective on the international division of labour by indicating the contribution of three major sectors to the GDP of ten selected nations in 1991. While the four 'developed' countries (US, UK, Japan and the former West Germany) are characterized by low shares of primary production and correspondingly high shares of service production, manufacturing produc-

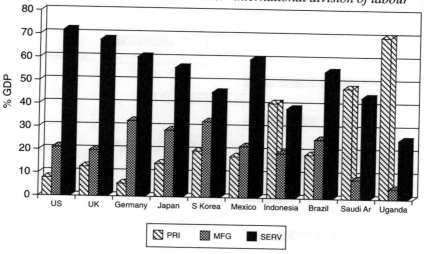

Note: PRI includes agricultural and extractive industries, plus construction; MFG indicates manufacturing; SERV denotes service industries. Germany indicates Federal Republic of Germany before unification.

Source: World Bank, *World Development Report 1992; The Economist World in Figures 1994.*

Figure 4.1 Sectoral contribution to GDP, selected nations, 1991

tion in the latter two countries is substantially more important than in the former two. The three NICs (South Korea, Mexico and Brazil) and the 'aspiring' NIC (Indonesia) all have proportions of manufacturing production that are at least the equivalent of those in the US and the UK; that of South Korea is significantly higher. Finally, in Saudi Arabia and Uganda, manufacturing plays a very minor role in national economic structure; on the other hand, the role of primary activities is highly significant. Figure 4.2 indicates the evolution of sectoral contributions to GDP in these same national economies over the past quarter-century. Note the shift towards services and out of primary and manufacturing activity on the part of the four developed nations. (This trend has led some cynics to refer to these nations, and others like them, as the NDCs – the newly *deindustrializing* countries.) On the other hand, South Korea, Mexico and Indonesia are characterized by increasing shares of manufacturing production, as implied by the term NIC (see also Chapter 12). The proportion of manufacturing production in Brazil, however, has remained stable over the past quarter-century; although it is relatively industrialized (with 26 per cent of GDP coming from manufacturing), its stability calls into question the current usage of the term 'newly' industrializing. Uganda is alone among our selected countries to have experienced a positive shift in primary activities, mainly due to its coffee production.

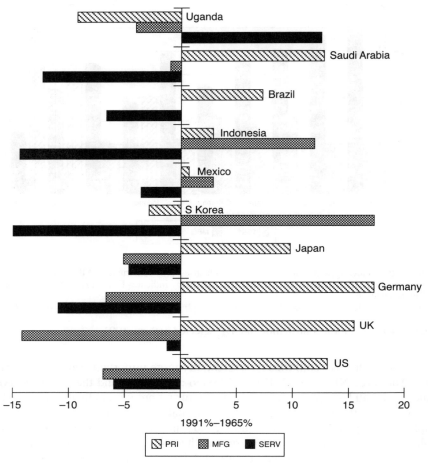

Note and source: see Figure 4.1.

Figure 4.2   Changes in sectoral contribution to GDP, 1965–91

FACTORS SHAPING THE INTERNATIONAL DIVISION OF LABOUR

What, then, are the principal factors underlying the trends identified in the previous sections? In order to answer this question, we first look at a number of processes influencing the international division of labour, in its widest and most general sense, and then turn to those affecting the NIDL and NEWER-IDL, as more specifically defined (see also Chapter 11).

International division of labour

The dimensions of the international division of labour, broadly defined, are the result of a number of major global economic processes. Principal among these are the evolution of production systems in developed economies, and changes in less developed countries involving national economic policies and rising levels of development.

Changes in the nature of production systems in developed economies

The recent evolution of production systems in developed countries has involved modifications in the sectoral, occupational and functional composition of the economy, and the increasing complementarity between manufacturing and service activities. In terms of *sectoral composition*, one of the major phenomena that has marked the economies of developed countries in the latter half of the twentieth century has been the growth of service industries. The provision of services has replaced the production of goods as the principal form of economic activity in these countries, where services currently account for between 60 and 75 per cent of total employment and generally more than 60 per cent of total economic production (gross domestic product). In addition, the growth of services, whether measured in employment or in output, has been impressive over the last two decades, accounting for approximately three-quarters of all new jobs created. These facts are indicative of a long-term structural evolution which is fundamentally modifying the production systems of advanced economies, and has led some observers to speak of a Second (Non-) Industrial Revolution. The process that is occurring in manufacturing is comparable to the historical evolution of agricultural production in developed countries: we are producing an increasing volume with a decreasing proportion of the labour force.

In addition, new types of *occupations and functions* are replacing those linked to the traditional industrial classification. On the one hand, there is an increasing shift from blue collar occupations towards those of a white collar nature; in Canada, for example, the share of 'white collar' occupations (management, medical, educational and technical categories) in the economy rose from 19 to 28 per cent between 1971 and 1991, while that of 'blue collar' occupations (resource extraction, transformation, manufacture, assembly and repair categories) declined from 41 to 28 per cent; 'grey collar' occupations (clerical, sales and service categories) remained relatively stable, shifting from 40 to 44 per cent. On the other hand, even occupation is not entirely satisfactory as an indicator of the nature of economic activity. In many ways, a person's position in the world economy increasingly depends more upon the nature of the function performed than upon the occupation, sector or industry in question. Reich (1991) identifies three major groups of functions that characterize the modern economy: routine production functions, in-person service functions, and symbolic–analytical functions.

Routine production functions are performed by many blue collar workers and 'pink collar' (i.e. female grey collar) workers performing clerical and information processing tasks. These functions currently account for approximately 25 per cent of jobs in developed economies and are declining at a brisk pace, largely because of a shift from high-volume standardized production, where profit margins are decreasing due to the lack of barriers to entry, to high-value-added production, where inputs involve a high proportion of specialized information and technology. Routine production can be done anywhere, often, as we will see below, where wages are lower. One indicator of the declining importance of this function is the decrease in union membership in the US: 35 per cent of non-agricultural workers belonged to a union in 1960, but the figure was only 17 per cent in 1989. *In-person service* functions involve simple and routine tasks in the retail, consumer services and health sectors; they currently represent about 30 per cent of employment and are declining, although more slowly and unevenly than routine production functions. These functions are often associated with lower wages and benefits and with part-time work, in large measure due to competition from labour-saving machinery such as automatic tellers and self-service gas pumps. *Symbolic–analytical* functions currently involve approximately 20 per cent of the labour force and are rapidly expanding. These functions – generally performed by scientists, engineers, consultants, and other professionals – involve identifying and solving problems and strategic brokerage, and have the capacity to be traded across the globe. (Of the remainder of the labour force, approximately 5 per cent is in the primary sector, while 20 per cent is involved in public and parapublic activities.)

Finally, modern economies are characterized by a growing *complementarity between services and manufacturing*. The relation between computer hardware and software is often cited as an example of this complementarity; neither is able to function without its counterpart. The relationship between goods production and services is an intimate one; service inputs are an integral part not only of the physical production process itself, but also of activities that are both upstream (e.g. design, R&D) and downstream (e.g. marketing, advertising) of the latter. Rather than neatly partitioning an economy into goods production and services production activities, it is more desirable to conceptualize it in terms of an *integrated production system*, the specific elements of which represent individual points on the goods–services continuum. In this integrated production system, however, information is rapidly replacing physical material as the principal 'natural resource', leading Porat (1977) to coin the term 'the information economy', and Reich (1991), as we have seen, to identify 'symbolic–analytical' activities (i.e. involving the manipulation and exchange of symbols) as the backbone of modern economies.

The interdependence between goods production and the provision of services manifests itself in important transformations in *what* types of goods are produced, and in *how* these goods are produced. In terms of *what* is produced, there has been a marked trend towards greater product differentiation as consumers are attracted to specially tailored, non-standardized products and as producers target special groups of consumers. In addition, as the length of the life cycle of most consumer products becomes increasingly abbreviated, the design, marketing and distribution aspects of goods production have become increasingly important. At the same time, many services closely related to consumption have come to the fore: maintenance, finance, and instruction. General Motors Acceptance Corporation, for example, a division of one of the United States's largest manufacturers, was originally established to assist consumers in the purchase of their motor vehicles by providing credit; GMAC has now emerged as one of that country's largest and most diversified financial establishments.

In terms of *how* goods are produced, there has been a marked tendency to substitute specialized knowledge and high-technology-embodied capital for labour in goods-producing processes. This has allowed management's attention to be shifted away from physical production, where processes are increasingly routinized, towards other areas which previously had been regarded as deserving of only secondary priority. The primary function of most high-value enterprises, even those in the manufacturing sector, is now to provide specialized research, design, engineering, sales, marketing, consulting, strategic, financial and management services (see also Chapter 9). For example, of IBM's 400000 employees, only 20000 are actually involved in physical production; only 10 per cent of the purchase price of a typical personal computer goes to the actual manufacture of the machine (Reich, 1991). In addition, increases in the size and complexity of manufacturing firms and the proliferation of government regulation in many countries have necessitated the incorporation of more diversified and more advanced levels of management expertise. Nowhere is the interdependence between goods production and services more evident than in the case of the set of activities commonly referred to as *producer services*.

Changes in less developed economies

Broad changes in the international division of labour may also be attributed to certain processes and policies within the less developed countries themselves. Two major factors stand out: the modernization of a significant number of LDCs, and the role played by selected national economic policies. In terms of *modernization*, evidence suggests that, due to a whole set of economic, social, demographic, political and institutional factors – factors that are both endogenous and exogenous (e.g. improved education, health, and housing; access to information and technology; reshaping of societal values; rural–urban migration; economic and political relations with other nations) – many of the LDCs have been undergoing a process of development analogous to that experienced more than 100 years ago by what we presently designate as the advanced economies. (In some cases, such as Japan, modernization occurred much more recently.) Often referred to as an urban–industrial transition (Preston, 1988), this process fundamentally alters the nature of the economies of developing countries, as a significant shift occurs out of 'traditional' sectors (primary activities, in particular) towards more 'modern' sectors such as manufacturing and services.

In addition, this process generally involves a growing integration between these modern sectors and the rest of the economy. Thus, manufacturing may no longer be viewed exclusively as a core region activity, as it had been for over 200 years. Developed countries like the US no longer possess the unique position in skilled labour and intermediate technology that they once did, and a wider range of nations now have the basic infrastructure required for most manufacturing industries. In addition, more and more of these developing countries have begun to establish an active service sector, at least in their major cities.

In specific cases, *national economic development policies* have also played a role in shaping the nature of economic activity in the LDCs. As we will see in the following section, during the 1960s or 1970s, primarily because of the availability of low-cost labour, many LDCs became the destination for inward FDI (mainly through the establishment of branch plants) by firms from the more advanced economies. In certain instances, this elicited no response from the national government of the destination economy. In other case, the FDI elicited what might be called a *passive* response; believing that such inward investment would ultimately lead to the development of an autonomous industrial structure through the provision of employment and through the transfer of technology, certain national governments took measures to provide a more hospitable environment for the inward investment. Thus, infrastructure was provided, export processing zones (also referred to as free production zones) were established, restrictions on international transfers of goods and materials were lifted, tax credits and tax holidays were instituted, and laws were established (or existing laws were relaxed) in order to make the labour force more accessible and compliant for foreign firms. While generally not having lasting effects upon the level of national economic development, in the sense that little technology or knowledge transfer occurred and few linkages to the local economy were formed, such policies did succeed in shifting a significant portion of the labour force from the primary sector to the manufacturing sector.

In still other instances, national governments reacted in a more *active* manner, not being satisfied with merely serving as a platform for foreign-owned plants. Rather, the inward foreign investment was treated as an opportunity to create the conditions for endogenous economic development. Several of the Asian NICs adopted this aggressive response, with South Korea and Taiwan perhaps representing the best examples. Henderson (1989) provides evidence concerning the role of the state in the development of the South Korean electronics and semiconductor industry. The national government first fostered the growth of a domestic consumer electronics industry by means of protectionist tariff barriers, and then by means of an import ban on foreign-made electronics. The only way for foreign firms to penetrate the local market was to produce goods inside Korea by means of wholly owned subsidiaries, joint ventures or licensing agreements. The state also provided substantial amounts of low-interest capital in targeted sectors, thus ensuring that industrial development was jointly planned by the state and private capital, with the state emerging as the dominant partner. In addition, the government has continued to invest heavily in electronics R&D and conducts basic semiconductor design work, which is then passed on to individual firms who adapt the design for their own particular purposes. The result is that one out of every twenty personal computers now manufactured in the world comes from South Korea. This strategy has not been limited to electronic products; similar successes have been registered in the steel, shipbuilding, apparel, footwear, and automobile sectors, among others. In Taiwan and Singapore economic development has been similarly financed and guided by highly interventionist and relatively authoritarian governments.

The new international division of labour

A series of more specific factors and processes also come into play in shaping the division of labour between nations. These forces manifest themselves at the level of the firm – more precisely at the level of the multinational enterprise (MNE). Indeed, it is impossible to understand the NIDL without examining the behaviour and strategies of the MNC. (See Chapter 7 for more detail on the MNE.)

Redeployment of the factors of production

The NIDL conceptual framework (which, in its 'classical' formulation, deals uniquely with manufacturing activity) explicitly concerns falling levels of domestic investment and employment in the major industrialized countries, and a corresponding shift of investment and employment towards developing countries. This phenomenon, in turn, is the direct result of firm-level strategic, administrative and operational decision making. While firms operating within the context of a single nation are relatively restricted in terms of available strategies, such is not the case with the MNE. The latter competes by means of strategies involving global markets, global component and material sourcing, and the international dispersion of production activities in order to take advantage of low factor costs. Above all, the MNE has the ability to decouple itself from the factor endowments (see Appendix 1) of a single nation and to locate the elements of the manufacturing process internationally according to the most advantageous combination of factors of production. Where and how effectively the various elements of the production process are deployed often proves to be the key to success.

What are the reasons underlying the decision by MNEs to undertake a redeployment of factors of production? During the 1970s (although Fröbel *et al.* (1980) argue that the process actually began in the early 1960s), many firms in advanced economies were faced by declining profits due to rising factor costs, rising levels of competition from less developed countries, and the entry of many mass-produced consumer products into a declining phase of their product life cycle (Figure 4.3). In an effort to boost sagging profits, firms embarked upon a dual strategy of attempting to enlarge their markets and lower their production costs; this strategy was generally based upon export expansion, foreign subcontracting

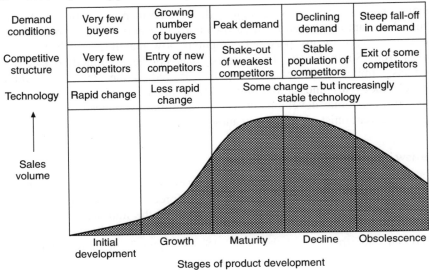

Demand conditions	Very few buyers	Growing number of buyers	Peak demand	Declining demand	Steep fall-off in demand
Competitive structure	Very few competitors	Entry of new competitors	Shake-out of weakest competitors	Stable population of competitors	Exit of some competitors
Technology	Rapid change	Less rapid change	Some change – but increasingly stable technology		

Sales volume

Initial development | Growth | Maturity | Decline | Obsolescence

Stages of product development

Figure 4.3   The product life cycle

and foreign direct investment. Note that, in certain cases, the imperatives were sufficiently strong so as to induce 'national' firms to become MNEs.

The nature of the process used to fabricate a specific product varies systematically according to the stage of that product in its life cycle. Associated with each stage is a different mix of factors of production (Figure 4.4). The different mixes of factors of production, in turn, are closely linked to different 'optimal' geographic locations where the most important factor inputs are relatively available and/or inexpensive. For example, products in the mature phase of their life cycle require a large proportion of semi-skilled and unskilled labour, which tends to be significantly more inexpensive in the less developed countries. Thus the shift of certain types of manufacturing activity (or certain parts of the production process of a specific good) towards less developed countries – the hallmark of the NIDL – may be seen primarily as the result of the 'push' of lower profits and higher factor costs (in particular, high wages due to increasing labour militancy) in developed countries, and the corresponding pull of lower factor costs – for labour, in particular – in developing countries. This shift is most likely to occur where the product or process in question is characterized by a high degree of labour intensity and by a high degree of standardization, as is usually the case in the mature stage of the product life cycle. Production systems thus become spatially (internationally) and functionally differentiated on the basis of location-specific factor cost advantages.

In order for this international economic redeployment to occur, however, three preconditions were necessary (Fröbel *et al.*, 1980). The first requirement

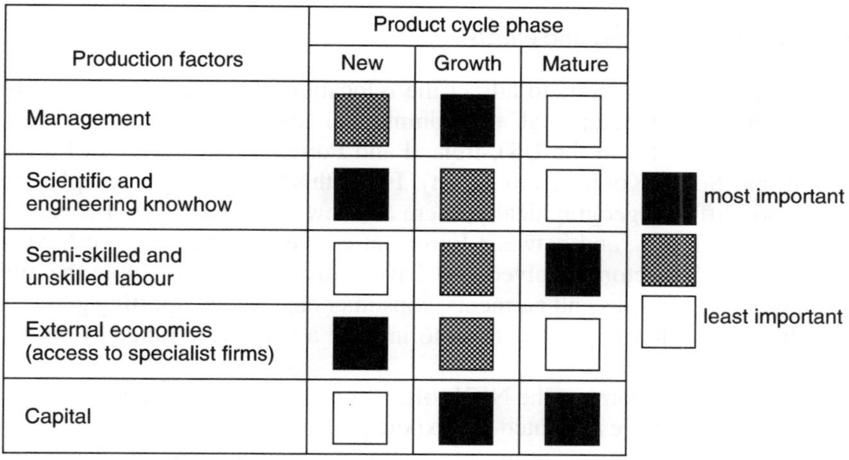

Production factors	Product cycle phase		
	New	Growth	Mature
Management	▨	■	☐
Scientific and engineering knowhow	■	▨	☐
Semi-skilled and unskilled labour	☐	▨	■
External economies (access to specialist firms)	■	▨	☐
Capital	☐	■	■

■ most important

▨

☐ least important

Figure 4.4   The relative importance of production factors at various stages in the product life cycle (from Hirsch, 1972)

was a deepening of the technical division of labour (see 'The division of labour' above), permitting increased organizational and spatial separation of the production process within a firm. New process technologies permitted the division, subdivision and standardization of specific tasks which could be easily learned and carried out by unskilled or semi-skilled labour, and subsequently assigned to whatever part of the world could provide the most profitable combination of factors of production. In this way, the more de-skilled and labour-intensive processes have been relocated to the periphery in order to take advantage of cheap labour, while the more skilled and technologically advanced processes have remained in the core economies (see Appendix 3). A second requirement was advances in transport and communications technologies, permitting a firm to coordinate widely dispersed elements of the production process. In the area of transportation technology, the appearance of containerization and air freight capabilities were of particular significance, while satellite links, fibre optics and computers led the way in communications. Thus the time and relative cost of transferring materials, products, services, people, information and money have fallen significantly. The third prerequisite was the emergence of a large and practically inexhaustible reservoir of disposable labour in developing countries. This labour force was distinguished not just by its willingness to accept low wages (by the standards of developed countries), but also by its lack of militancy and by the large number of hours that it worked per year (due to fewer holidays and longer daily shifts). The emergence of 'this global industrial reserve army' is primarily the result of rural–urban migration in developing countries and of the undermining of traditional social and economic structures.

Redeployment: examples and effects

The first peripheral nations to attract the relocation of economic activity were those with close geographical and commercial links to the core economies: Mexico and Haiti (from the US), Ireland and Portugal (from western Europe), Taiwan and South Korea (from Japan). From this initial stage, redeployment grew more diffused geographically; there are now significant links between the US and Asian LDCs, and between European core economies and north Africa, for example. The sectors involved, too, have evolved over time. From the initial redeployment in textiles and garments, consumer electronics, sporting goods and toys, the process has expanded so as to include a very wide range of products and sectors.

In peripheral economies, the NIDL often implies production in the context of 'world market factories' located in 'export processing zones' (free production zones). As implied by these terms, production is almost exclusively destined for export, rather than domestic consumption, and is confined to a small number of industrial enclaves having virtually no forward or backward linkages to the local economy except for the utilization of cheap labour and, occasionally, some local material inputs. In addition, the production process itself tends to be partial in nature, consisting of either the fabrication of intermediate components or the assembly of the final product from components produced elsewhere. Thus, typically, inputs are imported from outside the country, are processed by the local labour force (e.g. sewing, soldering, assembling) and are then exported. For example, pre-cut material for trousers is sent from Germany to Tunisia for sewing and then returned to Germany in its finished form. For many years, until the recent period of political instability, the raw materials involved in manufacturing baseballs were sent from the US to Haiti, where they were assembled and shipped back to the US. US watchmakers send components (some of which are manufactured in Switzerland) to American Samoa for assembly and re-export. US and Japanese consumer electronics producers send many of their components to Thailand for assembly and re-export. In these processing stages there is virtually no transfer of technology from the core countries to the LDCs. In any event, due to the imperatives of the technical division of labour, the technologies involved tend to be quite simple.

The typical employee of a world market factory is a woman between the ages of 16 and 26 years. In general, MNEs prefer women as they are more compliant than men in accepting working conditions that are significantly inferior in terms of security of employment, safety, shift work, wages and fringe benefits. In general, these women work between 20 per cent and 30 per cent more hours per year than their counterparts in the labour force of developed countries – as much as 50 per cent in some cases. On the other hand, wages tend to be only between 10 per cent and 20 per cent of those paid in core economies. For example, experienced female labour can be paid as little as $US0.15 per hour in Indonesia; this figure rises to $US0.36 in Thailand, $US0.57 in El Salvador, and $US0.89 in Mexico. In some instances, these wages barely provide for the basic necessities of life. Under these conditions, the labour force is quickly worn out and, in a given production unit, a complete labour force turnover every 1–2 years is not uncommon. In spite of these working conditions, however, the productivity per worker tends to be only slightly below that of developed countries.

A small number of NICs notwithstanding, it is clear that the NIDL has done little to improve the level of national economic development of the LDCs or the level of well-being of individual workers. World market factories entail few linkages to the local economy and virtually no multiplier effects; the flow of corporate profits is towards the advanced economies and no local control is exercised over what is produced or how it is produced; little transfer of technology occurs, working conditions are poor, and no industrial base providing for the needs of the local population is developed. As many observers (e.g. Fröbel *et al.*, 1980; Walton, 1985; Henderson, 1989) have argued, the NIDL perpetuates the dependency of peripheral economies and does not represent a major improvement over traditional plantation agriculture.

The 'newer' international division of labour

As noted in the 'overview' section, the four trends associated with the 'newer' international division of labour (NEWER-IDL) by no means represent a clean break with the NIDL; the processes and phenomena involved were in existence during the NIDL period (from the late 1960s up to the early 1980s) but were much less generalized. In this section we look at both the dimensions of the four major trends and their underlying factors.

Subcontracting In an attempt to create organizations that are 'leaner' and more flexible (see Chapter 3), an increasing number of 'manufacturing' firms in developed economies have eliminated or vastly reduced their capacity for physical production. The creation of stable supply relationships with subcontractors – many of which are in LDCs – allows firms to reduce expenditures on overhead, physical capital, wages and benefits. The well-known American athletic footwear 'producer', Nike, provides an excellent example of this process. Owning only a very minor proportion of its physical production facilities, Nike defines itself as a firm of 'marketers and designers'; virtually all of its 8000 employees work in management, sales promotion and advertising. Nearly 100 per cent of Nike's shoe production takes place in factories in China, Indonesia and Thailand, many of which are owned by local firms or by South Korean corporations (Barnet and Cavanagh, 1994). Benetton, the northern Italian clothing company, and several American computer manufacturers are similarly organized. Such firms are not so much MNEs – in the traditional sense of sprawling corporations with branch plants located across the globe – as fluid networks that add value by coordinating activities across geographic and corporate boundaries.

Services A similar trend is underway in service activities. An increasing number of firms in advanced countries are directing their service operations towards LDCs, through either outsourcing or FDI. Once again, flexibility of production (Coffey and Bailly, 1992) and access to an inexpensive pool of labour are the principal motivating factors. For example, the US data processing firm Saztec International, which provides specialized computer services to US corporations, actually employs workers in Manila; the annual salary of $US2650 paid by Saztec is significantly higher than the average annual Philippine income of $US1700. Similarly, the data and word processing functions of a large number of other firms in core economies are now performed in peripheral or semi-peripheral zones: Manhattan law offices fax drafts of letters and documents to Barbados for typing; American Airlines processes used airline tickets in Barbados and the Dominican Republic; claims made to the New York Life Insurance Co. are processed in Ireland, as is McGraw-Hill magazine subscription and marketing information; Texas Instruments performs a significant proportion of its computer programming and software development in India, where Swissair has now moved its accounting services.

Outward investment by NICs   The semi-peripheral economies (or NICs), particularly those in Asia, have recently begun to emulate the advanced nations by decentralizing elements of their own production processes to even less advanced economies. Increasing levels of economic development and sophistication, including a general up-skilling of the labour force, have created a situation in which these NICs have become increasingly expensive places to do business, particularly in comparison with their less developed neighbours. Thus many firms from the semi-periphery have begun to successively shift their own standardized, de-skilled tasks to peripheral economies characterized by lower wages and a more compliant work force. While an experienced worker in South Korea typically costs $US3.60 *per hour*, the cost is only $US2.90 *per day* in Thailand. A growing number of 'world market' assembly plants located in export processing zones in countries such as Thailand and Indonesia, for example, are owned by firms from South Korea and Taiwan; as before, the principal sectors involved include consumer electronics, luggage, toys, textiles and clothing. This phenomenon reinforces the point that the international division of labour is dynamic: yesterday's low-wage LDC is today's source of outward FDI. Japan is the most striking example of such transformation. In the 1950s, the current high-technology economic giant was principally known for its cheap toys and low-order consumer products; the label 'made in Japan' was virtually synonymous with 'junk'. The fact that NICs are becoming increasingly expensive environments also means that they are starting to be avoided by firms from advanced economies. In the early 1980s, for example, AT&T shifted its telephone assembly operations from Shreveport, Louisiana, to Singapore, where the same tasks were performed at a far lower cost. In 1989, however, AT&T switched its operations to Thailand, where the cost of the same operation was only a small fraction of that in Singapore.

Cross-investment by core economies The interpenetration of advanced economies has long been a fact of life. In recent years, however, this phenomenon has begun to assume staggering proportions. By 1991, for example, foreign firms (British, Dutch and Japanese, in particular) owned more than 13 per cent of US manufacturing assets and employed more than 8 per cent of US manufacturing workers, controlling major shares of domestic US production in certain industries: 50 per cent of consumer electronics, 33 per cent of chemical production, 20 per cent of the automobile industry, 70 per cent of the tyre industry, and 50 per cent of the film and recording industry (Barnet and Cavanagh, 1994). Similar trends are found in many other advanced economies. To a considerable extent, however, Japan has resisted inward FDI, much to the frustration of the US government, which wishes its domestically owned firms to have direct access to the booming Japanese market. Note that the production processes involved in this cross-investment are generally not as standardized and fragmented as those traditionally decentralized towards the LDCs.

In the NEWER-IDL, certain less urbanized areas of developed countries have begun to play the role of LDCs in the strategies of foreign MNCs. US inward FDI is an instructive example. During the NIDL period (mid-1960s to early 1980s) the relocation of US firms abroad created chronically high domestic unemployment and stagnating or falling real incomes for workers. Certain areas of the US therefore became favourable locations for technologically advanced production by west European and, later, Japanese firms. In comparison with countries like the former West Germany, specific places in non-metropolitan America are characterized by lower levels of unionization and by lower wages and social benefits; on the other hand, the number of hours worked annually is high. In addition, a long list of investment incentives has been made available by job-hungry economic development promotion agencies: financing, tax concessions, provision of site and infrastructure, and worker training. Much of this inward FDI has occurred in small southern cities such as Dothan, Alabama (population 50000), which is home to Sony and Michelin plants. The highest concentration of foreign investment is, however, in South Carolina, which is now host to almost 200 non-US firms. BMW pays its workers an average salary of $US12 per hour in South Carolina, rather than $US28 in Germany.

While cost factors play a major role in this type of inward FDI, the importance of market-oriented strategies must not be overlooked. Indeed, as Schoenberger (1988), among others, has argued, although virtually ignored in the traditional NIDL literature, a significant proportion of FDI is motivated by attempts at market expansion; by circumventing tariff and other trade barriers, thus improving market access, revenue can be maximized. Market access may be equally as important as labour cost minimization in both the new and newer forms of the international division of labour. Both factors have certainly contributed to the increasing cross-investment by MNEs from core economies.

CONCLUSION

The result of the processes outlined here has been the shift of major portions of the production systems of advanced economies towards the developing world – in particular, technically standardized and fragmented processes, on the one hand, and products in the mature phase of their product life cycle, on the other. Conversely, in developed economies the emphasis has shifted to specially tailored, non-standardized, and high-value products (and, more recently, services) generally involving a high level of technological expertise, information, and knowhow. These high-value products and services cannot be easily duplicated by less skilled competitors around the world since the principal barrier to entry is skill in finding the right mix between particular technologies and particular markets, rather than factor costs.

The international division of labour has been largely regulated by the MNE through its decisions to invest or not invest in particular countries, and through the resulting international flows of raw materials and finished goods. Indeed, world trade is increasingly involving flows of commodities between the establishments of the same firm spread throughout the world; a meaningful fraction of the imports of advanced nations is accounted for by transfers within a nation's own MNEs (Porter, 1990). These transactions are not subject to external market prices but, rather, to internal transfer pricing. While MNEs are key actors in the NIDL and NEWER-IDL, the extent to which they can pursue their strategies is limited by the attitudes and behaviours of national governments, whether acting singly or within supranational blocs. The international division of labour is thus the outcome of complex interactions between the competitive strategies of MNEs and the economic and trade policies of national governments.

FURTHER READING

Barnet, R.J., Cavanagh, J. 1994 *Global dreams: imperial corporations and the new world order*. Simon & Schuster, New York.
Daniels, P.W. 1993 *Service industries in the world economy*. Blackwell, Oxford.
Dicken, P. 1992 *Global shift: the internationalization of economic activity*, 2nd edition. Guildford Press, New York.
Fröbel, F., Heinrichs, J., Kreye, O. 1980 *The new international division of labour*. Cambridge University Press, Cambridge.
Henderson, J. 1989 *The globalisation of high technology production*. Routledge, London.
Porter, M.E. 1990 *The competitive advantage of nations*. The Free Press, New York.
Reich, R. 1991 *The work of nations*. Random House, New York.

APPENDIX 4.1   THE CONCEPT OF COMPARATIVE ADVANTAGE

In seeking to explain the role of international trade in creating 'the wealth of nations', Adam Smith (1776) introduced the concept of *absolute* advantage: a nation will produce and export those items for which it is the world's low-cost producer. Ricardo (1817) refined this notion to one of *comparative* advantage, recognizing that market forces will allocate a nation's resources to those economic activities in which it is *relatively* most productive. Thus, a nation might still import a good where it could be the low-cost producer if it were even more productive in other industries.

The dominant version of comparative advantage theory, due initially to Heckscher (1919) and Ohlin (1933), is based on the idea that nations differ in their endowments of the factors of production: land, natural resources, labour and capital. Nations gain factor-based comparative advantage in industries that make intensive use of factors that they possess in abundance; they export goods derived from these industries and import goods produced by industries in which they have a comparative factor disadvantage. Nations with abundant, low-cost labour such as Indonesia or Thailand, for example, will export labour-intensive goods such as apparel. Nations with rich endowments of raw materials or arable land will export products that depend on these factors. Sweden's strong historical position in the steel industry, for example, developed because Swedish iron ore deposits have a very low content of impurities, resulting in higher quality steel.

While national differences in factor costs and factor endowments have certainly played a role in determining the international division of labour and the resulting patterns of international trade, the concept of comparative advantage does not suffice as an explanation. Indeed, most world trade takes place between countries with similar factor endowments. Porter (1990) argues that the notion of *competitive advantage* – a broader concept based upon differences in national economic structures, values, cultures, institutions, and histories – is more useful in explaining the role of individual nations in the world economy.

APPENDIX 4.2   DIVISION OF LABOUR AMONG SEVEN GROUPS OF NATIONS

1. Twenty-four highly developed countries, including the US, Canada, Japan, Australia, New Zealand, South Africa, and the nations of western Europe, account for about 80 per cent of the world's economic activity. Most world trade and investment, research and development, and high-order services are found within this group.
2. Seven nations, although poor by many measures, have entered the industrial age to become large-scale manufacturers of a broad range of products: Brazil, Mexico, Argentina, India, and the so-called 'Asian tigers' – South Korea, Taiwan, and Hong Kong. With the exception of India (which has long

been in the process of industrialization), these economies are often referred to as the 'newly industrializing countries' (NICs).

3. About two dozen aspiring NICs (e.g. China, Thailand, Indonesia and Malaysia), although still predominantly dependent on natural resources, have achieved some limited industrialization. Unlike the NICs, however, the role of these countries has been almost exclusively to welcome foreign-owned, labour-intensive assembly operations into their territory. Within each country, industrialization tends to be concentrated in a small number of enclaves.

4. The former communist nations of eastern Europe are finding the path to capitalism painful and difficult. Hungary is the strongest of the group, largely due to its success in attracting plants of global corporations; it attracted about half of all foreign investment in eastern Europe in the first two years after the fall of Communism. Due to political instability, the former Soviet republics are not yet faring well.

5. The dozen Organization of Petroleum Exporting Countries (OPEC) occupy a special niche in the international division of labour. In spite of the oil-generated wealth that gives them the ability to import entire factories, these nations have no more than a veneer of industrialization.

6. Approximately forty poor countries, the majority in Africa and Latin America, continue to play the same role in the current world economy that they played in the colonial era: specialized suppliers of natural resources for export. Copper accounts for 98 per cent of Zambia's export earnings, for example.

7. Approximately fifty 'least developed countries', almost all of which are in Africa, maintain very few economic connections with the rest of the world, except for exporting small quantities of natural resources. For all intents and purposes, they are external to the world economic system.

Source: After Barnet and Cavanagh (1994)

APPENDIX 4.3   THE INTERNATIONAL DIVISION OF SEMICONDUCTOR PRODUCTION

Henderson (1989) provides an example of the manner in which specific elements of the production of semiconductors by US firms were associated with specific locational factors during the 1980s. The production of semiconductors involves five disarticulated processes: R&D, mask making, wafer fabrication, assembly and testing. Each of these has widely varying needs in terms of capital investment, labour skills, specialized inputs, and so forth. In the early period of development and of specialized and limited markets, these processes were confined to the US (in places like Silicon Valley). With the rise of more standardized products, broader markets, and Japanese competition, the conditions necessary for internationalization began to emerge. R&D requires access to highly trained scientists and engineers. This type of personnel is more abundant in the urbanized areas of developed countries, where universities and research institutes are relatively numerous. Thus, this function slowly began to diffuse from the US to places like Britain, France and Switzerland. Many of the same conditions apply to the location of mask-making and wafer-fabrication facilities. Local conditions, plus the need to penetrate the markets of other advanced economies and to avoid tariff barriers, stimulated US firms to transfer portions of these activities (wafer fabrication, in particular) to other developed countries (e.g. Japan and the nations of western Europe). Assembly and testing are typically unskilled operations with fewer locational constraints. These activities were increasingly relocated to the international periphery, in particular to east Asia. While investment in east Asia was initially motivated by supplies of cheap labour, a regional core (or semi-periphery) characterized by good quality engineering and technical labour began to develop (e.g. South Korea, Taiwan, Singapore). On the basis of this specialized labour, in combination with local entrepreneurial talent and government intervention, these Asian NICs subsequently began to establish their own autonomous semiconductor industries.

CHAPTER 5

DISSOLVING DIFFERENCE?
Money, disembedding and the creation of 'global financial space'
Andrew Leyshon

INTRODUCTION

> 'Money talks' because money is a metaphor, a transfer, and a bridge. Like words and language, money is a storehouse of communally achieved work, skill and experience. Money, however, is also a specialist technology like writing; and as writing intensifies the visual aspect of speech and order, and as the clock visually separates time from space, so money separates work from the other social functions. Even today money is a language for translating the work of the farmer into the work of the barber, doctor, engineer, or plumber. As a vast social metaphor, bridge, or translator, money – like writing – speeds up exchange and tightens the bonds of interdependence in any community. It gives great spatial extension and control to political organizations, just as writing does, or the calendar. It is action at a distance, both in space and in time (McLuhan, 1964, p. 136)

This chapter analyses the ways in which money acts as a form of communication which overcomes the friction of distance and brings about an 'annihilation of space' through time. The spread of money over space has important geographical implications because, to a certain extent at least, the diffusion of money over space causes processes of economic exchange to fall in line with the abstract and rational imperatives of financial capital. In very general terms, therefore, it is possible to argue that the spread of money over space tends towards a homogenization of economic space. These more or less homogenized economic spaces may be described as financial spaces, for it is the geographical extension of money and finance which defines such spaces, as economic activities proceed within financial systems that have clearly defined spatial boundaries (see Chapter 8).

Before we go any further, it is important to note that this is not to argue that 'everywhere is becoming the same' or that the financial system is bringing about the 'end of geography', as some commentators have asserted (for example, see O'Brien, 1991). There are at least two reasons why this particular view is mistaken. First, even within homogenized financial spaces, there is considerable variation in the levels of economic development, as a very large body of urban and regional research has demonstrated over many years. Second, the world remains made up of a patchwork of different financial spaces or systems, and although there has been considerable integration of financial practices and processes across such systems in recent years, we are still a long way from the seamless global financial space described by some commentators. Even if such a space were to materialize, it too would be characterized by uneven development, in the same way that national financial spaces are. Nevertheless, the traditional borders of financial space are undeniably in flux, having the effect of increasing the similarity between financial practices in different financial spaces, which suggests that a homogenization of financial space on a global scale is underway.

The chapter is organized as follows. The next section introduces the concept of disembedding and examines the interconnections between the disembedding, money and the process of financial homogenization. The following two sections each present examples of the process of financial homogenization, drawing upon historical and contemporary examples in turn. The penultimate section considers the role of space and place in the historical geography of the financial system and argues that we are witnessing the emergence of 'post-national' financial space. The final section concludes the chapter.

MONEY, MODERNITY AND THE 'DISEMBEDDING' OF ECONOMIC LIFE

Over a long period of time, social theorists have argued that the development of money-based societies introduces a degree of homogeneity and standardization into inter-subjective social relations. According to Zelizer, social theorists 'from Karl Marx to Jürgen Habermas, from Georg Simmel to Robert Bellah' (Zelizer, 1994, p. 2) have been 'impressed by the fungible, impersonal characteristics of money ... [and so have] emphasised its instrumental rationality and apparently unlimited capacity to transform products, relationships, and sometimes even emotions into an abstract and objective numerical equivalent' (Zelizer, 1989, p. 347). Traditional social theory has argued that the spread of money is associated with a fundamental shift in the nature of social relations, 'necessarily replacing personal bonds with materialist concerns' bringing about 'the inexorable homogenisation and flattening of social ties' (Zelizer, 1994, p. 2).

Zelizer draws attention to this characteristic of social theory to argue that such treatments of money overplay its homogenizing and rationalizing tendencies, and that there is more room for agency than such traditional accounts suggest. According to Zelizer, people 'mark' or inscribe money with a wide variety of different values and meanings, effectively creating their own currencies, or 'special monies', which are subject to social and cultural influence (Zelizer, 1989, 1994). While Zelizer's critique of traditional social theory's treatment of money is clearly an important redress to any tendency to overemphasize the power of money and its ability to dissolve all difference, it would be mistaken to dismiss entirely the social theory consensus on the homogenizing influence of money. Any objective historical survey of the geography of money would reveal that a process of financial homogenization has been underway over a long period of time. In what follows we shall draw from a relatively recent theoretical strain within the social theory canon to argue how the spread of money may well indeed serve to 'flatten' economic and financial space. To do this, specific reference will be made to the role of money in the work of Anthony Giddens.

In some of his more recent work, Giddens (1990, 1991) has sought to trace the implications of 'modernization' for the conduct of social life through space and over time. Money is seen by Giddens to be a particularly important agent of the process of modernization, in as much as the rise of money and the emergence of modern financial systems facilitates the process of time–space distanciation, which Giddens identifies as being critical to the rise of modern societies (Giddens, 1981, 1984). The concept of time–space distanciation is used by Giddens to refer to the way in which social relations between human subjects have tended to be 'stretched' over space. In pre-modern societies social and economic life was dominated by the here and now, as social relations were entered into with social actors present in time and space (Giddens, 1991, p. 16). With the rise of modern societies, social relations have become increasingly 'distanciated', as social relations are entered into with social actors absent from the here and now. The friction of distance, which acts as a barrier to social interaction, is overcome through advances in transportation and communications technology, thereby extending the space over which social relations may be conducted in modern societies.

Money is an important form of modern communication in this regard because it acts as a 'bridge' which can link places distant in space and time (Giddens, 1990; McLuhan, 1964). The ability of money to link places distant in time and space (time–space) is due to the peculiar qualities of money, which are expressions of the roles it plays in the process of economic exchange. As almost every economic textbook on the subject will relate, money performs several roles in an economic system. In fact, it is possible to identify at least five specific functions of money:

1. as a unit of account: that is, a medium which serves as the base of all economic accounting systems;
2. as a common measure of value: as well as being 'counted' in numbers of monetary units, commodities are valued or measured against or in money;
3. as a medium of exchange: by performing the role of a unit of account and a measure of value it becomes possible for money to become a medium of exchange; that is, the process of commodity exchange between two or more economic actors is done through the medium of money;
4. as a means of payment: the ability of money to intervene in processes of exchange means that it becomes a 'universal equivalent', exchangeable for all other commodities, and so becomes a desirable commodity in its own right, making it an ideal commodity to be used as a means of payment; and
5. as a store of value: because of all these roles, money becomes a store of value in an exchange system.

The universality of money, and its role as a store of value in particular, helps to explain why money is able to link places distant in space and time (see also Chapter 8). The development of money means that economic exchange no longer needs to revolve around a system of barter, a system of exchange which only works where there is a mutuality of want. Money-based exchange has several advantages over barter systems. In particular, money is more portable and durable than most commodities, and its insertion into the exchange process as a universal equivalent removes the need for a mutuality of want, thereby overcoming the inherent 'cumbersome awkwardness' of barter (Davies, 1994a, p. 9), speeding up economic exchange and hastening its extension over space in the process.

The spread of money-based economic exchange also tends to bring about a homogenization of economic space. Giddens refers to this process as one of *disembedding*, where the spread of institutions and practices associated with modern life displaces longer-standing social practices in local places, so that the spread of money helps to move social life away from the fixities of tradition:

> ... 'money proper' is ... an inherent part of modern social life ... It is fundamental to the disembedding of modern economic activity generally. One of the most characteristic forms of disembedding in the modern period ... is the expansion of capitalistic markets (including money markets), which are from relatively early on international in scope. 'Money proper' is integral to the distanciated transactions which these involve (Giddens, 1990, p. 26)

As a universal equivalent, money becomes a form of communication about economic value, which can link social actors separated by vast tracts of space and time. This form of communication acts to impose a uniformity of economic action across geographical space, as economic 'logic' becomes informed by the abstract rationality of monetary exchange and the desire to maintain the value of money.

Let us now consider in turn two particularly illustrative examples of the homogenization of financial space.

THE HOMOGENIZATION OF FINANCIAL SPACE I: THE 'GREAT WEST' IN THE NINETEENTH CENTURY

It follows from the preceding argument that money's colonization of space should serve first to disembed economic practices and then replace them by practices which conform more to the abstract conventions and rationalities of the community of money and capital. A historical example of these processes in action may be discerned in William Cronon's reading of the relationship between Chicago and the 'Great West' of the United States (Cronon, 1991).

In the early nineteenth century, before the advance of the railroads, the Great West was very much part of the frontier of the United States. It was even distant in time and space from the thriving metropolitan centre of Chicago, a city which was fast becoming the site of a wide range of modern social and economic practices. The agricultural communities of 'EuroAmericans' in the Great West were so remote from the rest of the US economy and society in dimensions of time–space that they tended to be chronically short of conventional money, such as gold and silver coins or the bank notes issued by large reputable banks from the financial centres of Chicago or New York (Cronon, 1991). These forms of conventional money were widely sought after because they were readily accepted as unambiguous expressions of value in abstract form which could serve as media of exchange across vast expanses of space. These conventional money forms could act as universal equivalents for one of two reasons: either they possessed an 'inherent value', as in the case of coins made from precious metal, such as silver or gold (commodity money), or because the value of money was guaranteed by the reputation and standing of the issuing financial institution, as in the case of bank notes. In other words, these forms of money were widely accepted as unambiguous expressions of economic value and as universal equivalents because they expressed a durable monetary value that would survive across vast expanses of space and time.

The absence of commodity money or 'reputable' bank notes meant that the money that circulated most freely in such places tended to be the bank notes issued by small 'frontier' banks. However, these banks tended to be extremely financially fragile so that their notes could not be relied upon to maintain their usefulness as universal equivalents over time (and through space). The fragility of the issuing institutions meant that the value of these notes tended to be extremely volatile, varying in direct relation to the perceived level of financial soundness and general trustworthiness of frontier banks (Cerny, 1993).

The absence of an unambiguous, abstract symbol of monetary value created potentially insurmountable barriers to economic exchange in such areas. In some places the shortage of money caused farmers to resort to exchange by barter (Cronon, 1991, p. 105). But in other areas, the barrier to exchange created by the shortage of conventional money was successfully circumvented through the creation of what were, in effect, localized financial systems. These local financial systems did not depend upon the issue of abstract tokens of value, as embodied in proper money forms such as coins or bank notes; rather, they were local credit systems, which pivoted around agricultural merchants who acted as 'translators between the world of rural barter and the world of urban money' (Cronon, 1991, p. 105). Merchants in remote rural areas bridged these two worlds by first establishing a link to the world of conventional money through an alliance with a merchant located in an established urban centre who had access to the financial system through a bank account. The alliance effectively guaranteed the 'worth' of the rural merchant, and provided a necessary link back to the world of abstract value embodied by conventional money. This link having been established, the rural merchant was then free to engage in exchange purely on account; that is, by effectively creating a 'virtual' financial system whereby exchange was entered into on a credit and debit basis through the transfer of personal notes of credit between the merchant and farmer.

The network of credit links which revolved around rural merchants allowed frontier economies to function despite a shortage of 'real' money. The circulation of 'credit money' in such economies was necessarily heavily dependent upon substantive social relationships and the cultivation of relations of trust between merchants and other economic actors. The 'currency' upon which exchange was based was the trusting social relationships between buyer and seller, which depended upon the relationship between the merchant and farmer. Merchants had created their own 'embedded' local financial systems.[1] The geography of such systems was quite restricted, because the calculation of value was based upon a highly localized and idiosyncratic accounting system, within which the willingness of rural merchants to extend credit to farmers depended upon trust and deep local knowledge.

The development of these moneyless financial systems enabled economic actors to continue trading until some time in the future when they took possession of 'conventional' money in the form of coins or extra-local bank notes, in which accounts were settled and credits and debits reconciled. In the Great West, acts of financial settlement and reconciliation occurred on a seasonal basis, because during the winter it was virtually impossible to reach the world beyond the frontier as the river system, which was the main artery of transport and communications, froze over. It was only with the arrival of spring that the communities of the frontier could once more make contact with the markets of the east and expect to receive in return payment in the form of the conventional money which circulated easily beyond the frontier region. The local credit systems, therefore, enabled rural communities to survive during the part of the year when winter 'locked up capital' (Cronon, 1991, p. 321).

The advance of the railroads throughout the nineteenth century served to push the frontier westwards. As they did so, the credit money systems of the frontier were destroyed. The railroads meant that formerly remote rural localities were brought closer to large metropolitan centres in dimensions of time–space, as locomotives effectively 'shrunk' the distance between the Great West and commercial centres such as Chicago (Cronon, 1991). The extension of the railroad network, therefore, made it far easier for more conventional monies to

---

[1] Embeddedness is a sociological concept which attempts to chart an analytical course between the traditional interpretations of 'the economic' developed by neo-classical economists on the one hand, and Marxism on the other. The concept was first proposed by Karl Polanyi (1944) in his criticism of both liberalism and Marxism for their transhistorical economism, and for what he took to be their fatal conceit in assuming that the importance afforded to 'the economic' within social life during the nineteenth century was a characteristic that had endured throughout human history. Polanyi argued that market-based societies were historically contingent, and represented a fairly recent development within social history:

> For Polanyi, nineteenth-century society was unique in the way that economic imperatives had become dominant in shaping human life. In earlier societies, the economy – the arrangement for ensuring humanity's livelihood – was *embedded* in social relations, subordinated to religions, politics, and other social arrangements. In opposition to Adam Smith, Polanyi stressed that the orientation toward individual economic gains played only a minor role in these earlier societies. Only in the nineteenth century did economic self-interest become the dominant principle of social life (Block and Somers, 1984, p. 63, *emphasis added*)

dominate processes of exchange, thereby removing the need for local credit systems based solely upon inter-subjective relations of trust and local knowledge. With the collapse of these local credit networks, the rural economies of the Great West became increasingly integrated with more distant centres of financial calculation, as coins and bank notes minted or issued elsewhere circulated more freely.

This development had important implications for the trajectory of the rural economies and for local economic actors in the Great West. The arrival of the railroads transformed the nature of the risk faced by farmers. The level of short-term risk tended to decrease, as farmers were able to maintain more frequent contact with the market, which in turn ensured a more regular supply of income. The difficulties of reaching the market in the days before the arrival of the railroad had forced farmers to despatch large, irregular consignments of produce to urban markets which, in the absence of a system of insurance, meant that an accident on the way to market would often bring with it financial ruin. The arrival of the railroads virtually eliminated this kind of short-term risk. But risk was not eliminated altogether. Short-term risk was merely replaced by a longer-run type of risk.

The westward advance of the railroads made metropolitan markets accessible for more frontier farms. In turn this led to an increase in the volume of agricultural produce sold in such markets, thereby intensifying competition in the sphere of agricultural production and forcing down prices. As the Great West was opened up to the east by the railroads, and economic exchange with metropolitan centres like Chicago and cities even further east was eased, so the volume of conventional money circulating within the rural economies increased. The rise of conventional money led to a process of disembedding, where processes of economic exchange and, in particular, financial exchange, became less dependent upon long-standing inter-subjective personal relations.

Just as economic risk was not so much reduced but transformed from short- to long-term, the penetration of money into the frontier communities was similarly double-edged. On the one hand, the circulation of 'proper' money was advantageous in a number of important respects. It probably loosened the ties of dependence which made farmers reliant upon individual merchants and, in particular, upon the merchant's assessment of the value of agricultural produce and their willingness to extend credit to individual farmers. The possession of conventional money meant that farmers were able to enter into economic exchange with a wider range of economic actors, far beyond the tightly knit, merchant-dependent credit money systems of the pre-railroad days, and which even held out the possibility of obtaining lower prices for commodities necessary for continued agricultural production.

Therefore, the growing circulation of conventional money in the rural communities of the frontier was to some extent empowering for local economic actors. However, in as much as the rise of 'proper' money served to integrate these communities with the abstract world of money represented by financial centres such as Chicago and New York, these developments were disempowering of local economic actors. To be sure, farmers were no longer so dependent upon the willingness of rural merchants to extend credit, for farmers could now appeal directly to the financial institutions based in centres such as Chicago. But while this opened up the possibility of gaining access to larger lines of credit than hitherto, it also meant that the granting of credit to farmers in the Great West became dependent upon extra-local assessments of credit risk. Farmers wishing to bridge the time–space gap between the production and sale of their output increasingly had to demonstrate their creditworthiness to bankers and financiers located in financial centres such as Chicago.[2]

These developments meant that the conduct of social and economic life in the formerly remote rural communities of the Great West fell into line behind an extra-local economic logic, so that agricultural production was increasingly run in accordance with a capitalist rationality. Similar processes were taking place in other relatively remote places that had been 'opened up' by the disembedding caused by the advance of capitalist modernity. It is in this sense that the advance of modern money can be said to bring about a 'flattening' of economic space.

THE HOMOGENIZATION OF FINANCIAL SPACE II: FINANCIAL SWAPS

The process by which financial space is 'flattened' was not just a product of the 'dromocratic revolution' of the nineteenth century (Virilio, 1986), when a cluster of transportation and communication technologies not only brought about a remarkable change in the perception of space and time and a shrinking of the world in dimensions of time–space (Kern, 1983; Leyshon, 1995) but also brought more economies and societies under the influence of the institutions and practices of modern capitalism. The homogenization of financial space is an ongoing process, although in many ways the flattening of financial space today owes as much to revolutions within the realm of financial ideas and concepts as it does to the production of material technologies that facilitate the rapid movement of people, commodities or information over space.

In the past, the process of financial homogenization was due in large part to the ability of concrete transport and communication technologies to permit social relations to be extended over larger expanses of space, one of the effects of which was to bring economic and social practices more into line with the dictates and imperatives of financial capital. This is still an important process of course. Indeed, one of the most notable features of the international financial system of the last 10 to 15 years or so has been the way in which revolutions in information and communication technologies penetrated the financial labour process, thereby

---

[2] The process by which financial space was flattened accelerated considerably during the 1860s when, in response to the financial crisis brought on by the Civil War, the Federal government of the United States enacted regulations to bring about a more ordered and structured 'national' financial system (see the Discussion later in this chapter).

facilitating the 'globalization' of financial markets (O'Brien, 1991; Solomon, 1991, Chapter 8). These technologies mean that although the buyers and sellers of financial products may be very distant from one another in geographical space, the time–space distance between them may be negligible, if not quite non-existent. But within the context of this technological background, global financial space is being flattened in a way that owes as much to a manipulation of financial symbols and concepts as it does to a process of innovation within the sphere of information and communication technologies (Bonetti and Cobham, 1992; Davis, 1991; MacDonald, 1992; Bank for International Settlements, 1992; Remolona, 1993; Robinson, 1992; Stafford, 1992).

The example of financial homogenization that we examined earlier involved the flattening of financial space in the US Great West made possible by a material technological innovation – the railroad – which brought about an 'annihilation of space through time' (Thrift, 1990). The second example of financial homogenization in this chapter is brought about by more 'immaterial' means.

The financial swap is an example of a financial product that exists only in conceptual terms. It is a highly idiosyncratic arrangement where a financial institution organizes an exchange of debt repayments between economic agents in order to effect a beneficial financial outcome. This form of 'financial engineering' is undertaken by a community of financiers that fall into the category of workers that Robert Reich has described as 'symbolic analysts':

> Symbolic analysts solve, identify, and broker problems by manipulating symbols. They simplify reality into abstract images that can be rearranged, juggled, experimented with, communicated to other specialists, and then, eventually, transformed back into reality (*sic*). The manipulations are done with analytic tools, sharpened by experience. The tool may be mathematical algorithms, legal arguments, financial gimmicks, scientific principles, psychological insights about how to persuade or to amuse, systems of induction or deduction, or any set of techniques for doing conceptual puzzles (Reich, 1991, p. 178)

Whether a 'financial gimmick' or not, the financial swap has become an increasingly important feature of the contemporary global financial system (Figure 5.1). It is a 'derivative' financial instrument, one of many such products that have been developed since the mid-1970s. Other derivative financial instruments, such as futures and options, were developed for purposes of risk management and hedging in increasingly fast-moving and turbulent financial markets. However, the swap was initially developed to eradicate what were seen to be anomalies and irregularities in the price of money and credit over space. The financial swap makes it possible to effect 'arbitrage' opportunities in financial markets, thereby overcoming geographical differences in the risk assessment of economic agents to the financial advantage of all involved. Such differences reflect important disjunctures in global financial space. The contemporary global financial system, as Susan Strange has observed, is something of a hybrid, being 'partly a truly global system, and partly still a series of national financial and monetary systems, even though all of these are increasingly

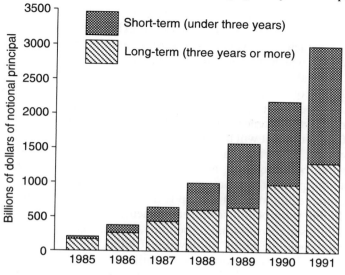

Note: Values for 1985 and 1986 are estimates based on reports by fifteen dealers.

Figure 5.1   Interest rate swaps by maturity (from Remolona, 1993, p. 29)

susceptible to influence and pressure from the world outside the frontiers of the state' (Strange, 1988, p. 88). According to Strange, the financial system

> ... is global in that all the major capital markets of the world are so closely linked together that in many respects they function as if they were one system. They react promptly and visibly to developments elsewhere in the system. The bankers and dealers in securities operate as though time zones were more significant than political frontiers ... The big operators have branches or offices in all the major financial centres; and their customers who deposit money are seldom content to put it in one national basket.
>
> But at the same time the continued co-existence of national currencies shows that frontiers still count. Within those frontiers, it is the government of the state that is held responsible politically ... for the weakness or strength of the national currency. It is the state that acknowledges this responsibility and does what it can to manage the value of money denominated in the national currency – in dollars or yen, marks or francs – so that it serves what it perceives as the national interest. Governments do not always succeed in achieving the goals they set themselves. But they have not yet abdicated their role as monetary managers ... In a nutshell, one may say that the markets are predominantly global, while the authorities are predominantly national (Strange, 1988, p. 88–89)

This is an important observation, in as much as it debunks the notion of a smooth, seamless global financial landscape; in reality, the global financial system consists still of a patchwork of financial spaces or 'regulatory surfaces', between which financial capital moves. The continued existence of national currencies, the values of which serve as expressions of the rate of return on capital within the economy to which they are attached, helps explain why interest rates vary from one national economy to another (Leyshon, 1993; Martin, 1994). Indeed, one should not overestimate the degree to which even capital markets have become integrated over space in the way that Susan Strange suggests; there remain important differences in the calculation of risk within different capital markets, for reasons that will be made clear a little later.

However, the differences that exist between national financial spaces *are* in the process of being reduced, and an important device in this respect is the interest rate swap. Figure 5.2 presents a highly simplified example of an interest swap. The first requirement for a swap is for there to be at least two companies with similar but reciprocal funding requirements. In our hypothetical example, USCO, a US-based transnational corporation, is planning to borrow £65 million to fund operations in Britain. Meanwhile, UKCO, a UK-based transnational corporation, is planning to borrow $100 million to fund its operations in the United States. At a nominal US dollar–sterling exchange rate of $1.53/£1 the funding requirements are identical in value, but denominated in different currencies and borrowed in different national financial markets; that is, USCO is planning to borrow sterling in Britain, while UKCO is borrowing dollars in the US. Therefore, our example is an interest swap involving US dollars and sterling, but it is important to note that similar arrangements are possible for counterparties from other countries using other currencies, such as Japanese and German firms swapping in yen and deutschmarks, or French and Australian companies swapping French francs and Australian dollars.

The parallel nature of financing needs means that it is possible that an interest rate swap between the companies might serve to lower the financing costs of both. But for a swap to be worthwhile one of the companies must enjoy a comparative advantage over the other in one of two credit markets. In our example, it is USCO that enjoys such an advantage. In the UK credit market, both companies are able to obtain funds at 8.25 per cent. But in the US credit market, USCO is able to obtain funds at preferable rates of interest. USCO can borrow at 5.0 per cent while the best rates for UKCO are 5.5 per cent (Figure 5.2, point 2).

There may be a number of reasons for this. A particularly important reason would be the role played by credit rating agencies. Since in our hypothetical example both USCO and UKCO are borrowing money via the issue of short-term money-market notes (commercial paper), credit rating agencies would play a critical role in determining the cost of each company's borrowings. Credit rating agencies provide assessments on a wide variety of debt instruments in financial markets. The ratings they provide 'are meant to indicate the likelihood of default or delayed payment' of the securitized borrowings of companies (Cantor and Packer, 1994, p. 3). The amount of attention paid to such ratings by the financial services industry has increased markedly within recent years, for

1. USCO wishes to borrow £65m to fund expansion in UK.
   UKCO wishes to borrow $US100m to fund expansion in US.

   Both wish to do so via issue of short-term money market notes of same time duration.

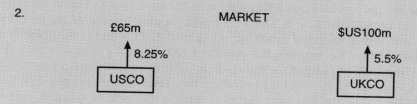

3. But: USCO can borrow $US at 5.0%   while: UKCO can borrow £ at 8.25%

   = comparative advantage of 0.5 percentage points

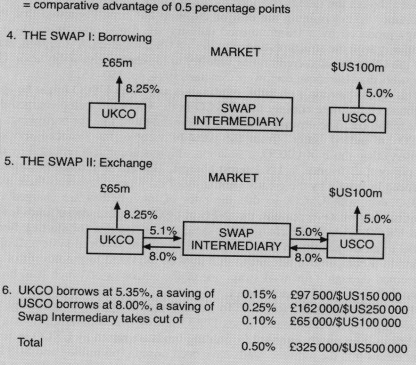

6. UKCO borrows at 5.35%, a saving of   0.15%   £97 500/$US150 000
   USCO borrows at 8.00%, a saving of   0.25%   £162 000/$US250 000
   Swap Intermediary takes cut of   0.10%   £65 000/$US100 000

   Total   0.50%   £325 000/$US500 000

Figure 5.2   Interest rate swaps and the homogenization of financial space

two main reasons. First, since the 1980s the global financial system has become increasingly disintermediated, so that securitized debt instruments and not banks are the predominant sources of credit. Second, since the early 1990s the financial services industry has become increasingly risk-averse, due to a growing awareness of the high systemic risk that accompanies a securitized financial system (Bank for International Settlements, 1992; Leyshon and Thrift, 1993).

The ratings provided by credit rating agencies have an effect upon the price of credit because the way in which the credit granting fraction of the industry deals with risk is to 'price' credit according to risk. This means that there is a positive relationship between the perceived riskiness of a borrower and the 'price' they will be charged for that credit in the level of additional interest they will be expected to pay over the prevailing base level of interest rates. In other words, the riskier the borrower, the more interest they will be charged, unless they are deemed so likely to default that they are excluded from the financial system altogether.

But although the ratings provided by credit rating agencies are of increasing importance in determining the cost of credit, it has been suggested that the ratings produced by a US-dominated industry are American-centric. Greater familiarity with the structures and practices of US companies, it is argued, may lead the US-dominated credit rating industry to look more favourably upon US borrowers than European borrowers (Sinclair, 1994, pp. 150–151).

This would provide a plausible explanation as to why USCO might be able to obtain credit more cheaply than UKCO in the US, while being charged the same in the UK. The obverse of this, of course, might be that the borrowings of USCO are indeed 'safer' (from the point of view of the financial services industry) than those of UKCO, a situation which is accurately reflected by the 0.5 per cent difference in US interest charges. But this difference is counterbalanced in Britain by the greater familiarity of the financial markets there with UKCO than with USCO, so that the rates of interest they are charged are identical. For whatever reasons, the ability of USCO to obtain dollar funds lower than UKCO while being charged the same rate of interest for sterling funds points to an irregularity in the operation of the global financial system. It also points to a comparative advantage that may be exploited to the benefit of all concerned through a financial swap, one of the outcomes of which is to bring about a 'flattening' of financial space.

The swap works as follows. To exploit the comparative advantage in borrowing dollar-denominated funds USCO borrows in dollars rather than in sterling as it originally intended to. Sterling funds are raised by UKCO instead. This means that the required funds have been raised (£65 million and $US100 million), but at a net saving of 0.5 per cent (£325 000 or $US500 000) (Figure 5.2, point 4). The companies can then swap the money raised with one another so they have the credit in the currency they require. The real 'financial engineering' of the swap, however, comes in the way that the comparative advantage of the swap – the 0.5 per cent interest saved – is realized through the reallocation of interest repayments. For if the companies only swapped the funds raised with one another then only USCO would win out, for UKCO would be left paying sterling interest rates of 8.25 per cent for dollar funds that it could have raised in the market for 5.5 per cent.

Point 5 of Figure 5.2 shows how the 0.5 per cent saved is divided up between the counterparties as they 'swap' repayments. UKCO's payments of 8.25 per cent are offset by 8.0 per cent repayments flowing from USCO. In turn, UKCO sends repayments of 5.1 per cent, via the financial institution that helped organize the swap, to USCO. When these payments are set out we find that both UKCO and USCO are able to borrow money at below market rates (Table 5.1).

Three important features need to be noted. First, all the parties in the transaction appear to 'win'. UKCO ends up obtaining dollars for 5.35 per cent, a saving of 0.15 per cent on the rate that it would have got if it had gone straight to the market. USCO, meanwhile, ends up by saving 0.25 per cent on the cost of borrowing. The financial institution that helps set up such deals is also better off. In our example, the swap intermediary receives payment to the value of 0.1 per cent of interest, which amounts to £65000 or $US100000. Second, note that not all the parties benefit to the same degree; USCO receives the lion's share of the discount in borrowing costs, because it was USCO that held the comparative advantage in dollar funding which made the swap possible. Third, and finally, note how the existence of swaps serves to flatten differences in financial space, reducing the differences in the interest rate surface of the global financial system.

Interest rate swaps are only possible because there exist geographical differences in the perceptions of the creditworthiness of individual borrowers between different financial markets. The swap could not have proceeded if UKCO and USCO had been seen as equivalent credit risks in both markets, nor if they had both enjoyed an advantage over each other in their respective home credit markets. The anomaly that allowed our hypothetical interest rate swap to work was that in the dollar-denominated credit market alone, USCO could obtain access to lower-cost funds than could UKCO. It is in this sense that the swap may be seen to be an instrument which has the effect of homogenizing

Table 5.1 Borrowing costs of UKCO and USCO after interest rate swap (per cent)

	Outgoings	Receipts	Balance
UKCO	8.25	8.00	0.25
	5.10		5.10
Total	13.35	8.00	5.35
USCO	5.00	5.00	0.00
	8.00		8.00
Total	13.00	5.00	8.00
Earnings of swap intermediary			
Total	0	0.10	0.10

financial space, for it overcomes the effect of 'embeddedness' in the process of credit assessment, allowing companies to obtain funds at costs that are less than the market-level rates of interest.

The number of interest rate swaps undertaken in the financial system has increased markedly over the last decade or so, in part because the market has become more organized. This has involved financial services firms moving away from swaps brokerage, intermediating between two swap counterparties, and towards market making, where the financial services firm acts directly as a counterparty in swaps with clients (Remolona, 1993). This speeds up the process, as financial institutions can organize swaps without having first secured a counterparty to match deals.

DISCUSSION: THE RISE AND FALL OF NATIONAL FINANCIAL SPACE

The examples of financial homogenization that we have examined in this chapter are just two fragments taken from a rich and varied historical geography of money. The way in which the financial system crosses space and subjugates local social and economic relations is a critically important process in the historical geography of capitalism, because financial capital's colonization of space has been instrumental in making and breaking the economic spaces upon which economic life is played out.

The creation of what can be described as 'national financial space' was part and parcel of the evolution of the state system between the sixteenth and eighteenth centuries, upon which the capitalist system was grounded. Along with the development of a centralized legal order and taxation system, the emergence of national monetary systems organized and policed by state authorities was central to the emergence of what later became the nation-state (Giddens, 1985; see also Chapter 17). National financial spaces were predicated upon the circulation of 'state' or 'fiduciary' money; that is, money that has no inherent value of itself, such as commodity money, but is guaranteed through the state's supervision and surveillance of the national financial system (Giddens, 1985, p. 155). In seeking to maintain the worth of fiduciary money, the state is forced to sanction those economic institutions that, through 'improper' financial practice, are seen to be undermining faith in fiduciary money as the medium of exchange and the measure of value in exchange. Through the social practice of regulation (Marden, 1992), the state seeks to control the institutions within a financial system, ushering in 'safe and sound' financial practice, while at the same time crowding out alternatives to fiduciary money within the national financial space.

This process may take many years. For example, consider the case of British 'financial space'. Although the Bank of England was created in 1694, it was not until the eighteenth century that it began to behave as a central bank, and not until the nineteenth century that it began to open a branch network throughout the country (Black, 1989). This development served two main purposes. First, to promote the replacement of locally issued bank notes by Bank of England notes. Second, to enable the Bank to 'supervise and survey the provincial economies' more closely (Black, 1989, p. 381), with the aim of preventing the periodic outbreak of financial crises in the regions which, thanks to the progressive improvement of intra-national communications (Thrift, 1990), rocked the British financial system as a whole as 'crises erupting in Liverpool or the West Riding rippled through the London money market and washed back out to correspondent banks in the provinces' (Black, 1989, p. 379).

Similar processes took place within other states. In the United States, a national financial space began to form after 1863 when the Congress established the legal basis for a system of financial regulation by allowing banks to incorporate under a federal banking charter as an alternative to state banking charters (Cerny, 1993; Zelizer, 1994). Those banks which submitted to the supervision of federal banking regulation were allowed to issue the national currency, the value of which was 'secured by the resources and financial prestige of the federal government itself' (Conzen, 1975, p. 324). In this way state-sanctioned money and financial institutions began to penetrate economic spaces formerly dominated by more idiosyncratic institutions and money forms, hastening a process of financial homogenization that was already being encouraged by a deepening web of contacts between widely dispersed banks which had the effect of increasing the power and influence of the New York banking community (Conzen, 1977). In this way the state began to standardize and normalize certain types of financial practices and institutions, which had the effect of flattening difference within national financial space.

In the late twentieth century, the national financial space, the territory which has so long been unproblematically accepted as the ground upon or between which economic processes are played out, is being undermined or 'decentred' (Corbridge, 1994) because of a process of 'deterritorialization'. This development has important geographical consequences, for national financial spaces have served to channel economic processes in distinctive ways, so that the patchwork that is the nation-state system also, to a certain extent at least, represents a geography of capitalisms (Agnew, 1994; Albert, 1993; Christopherson, 1993; Cox, 1986; Lash and Urry, 1994; Martin, 1994). However, processes of financial homogenization at play within the late twentieth century are conspiring to make national financial spaces increasingly similar and less different, as may be seen in the equalization of short-term interest rates and the convergence of national systems of financial regulation (Moran, 1991). In short, the distinctiveness of national financial space is being eroded, reflecting the empowering of financial capital over space and the disempowering of other economic actors, particularly those rooted in space, such as regulators and planners. As Robins (1991, p. 13) has argued,

With the triumph of flow, it becomes increasingly difficult for urban governments and planners to afford cohesion ... New kinds of network – physical and virtual – subvert 'traditional' territorial formations, deconstructing and recomposing them in more complex ways. In the process, established forms of urban community, culture and sensibility are disrupted. The key issue, then, is whether it is possible to manage these new dynamics of deterritorialisation.

The taken-for-granted world of financial space is being undermined in other ways too, as for example in the growth of electronic or plastic money, which is not tied to the nation-state in the same way that fiduciary money is. Indeed, it can be argued that the international credit cards issued by companies such as Visa, Mastercard and American Express represent a new form of post-national money which grants the holders of such money ease of movement across different financial spaces, transcending the need to translate different forms of fiduciary money from one national form into another.

The growing power of those financial institutions that operate beyond and across national financial spaces has important implications for the coherence of national financial space. As we saw earlier the process of disembedding was an important moment in the homogenization of financial space as local financial practices were overwhelmed by practices associated with more powerful financial institutions and financial centres. In Britain, for example, the process of disembedding led to the decline in importance of locally and regionally oriented financial institutions as the financial system became increasingly subject to processes of capital centralization and capital concentration (Duncan, 1993; Pratt, 1995), bringing about a high level of financial homogenization within the borders of the nation-state.

However, as financial institutions and financial capital have increasingly strayed beyond the borders of national financial space so a new 'post-national' financial geography has begun to emerge. At the heart of this geography sits a handful of increasingly powerful and influential financial centres that are made up of a dense network of financial institutions and markets, which increasingly radiate power on a global scale (Thrift, 1994; Thrift and Leyshon, 1994; Chapter 17). But this geography is detached from a necessary congruence with a set of tightly drawn national borders, as characterizes the traditional state form. The post-national state of the financial system transgresses national borders. Its own borders are constantly in motion, sometimes expanding, sometimes contracting. At present, the borders of the post-national financial system are contracting rapidly, withdrawing from spaces that were once subject to processes of financial disembedding and incorporated into national financial space (Leyshon and Thrift, 1994, 1995).

This process of abandonment has important implications for the geography of money and finance. On the one hand, within the borders of the post-national, transnational financial system, the process of financial homogenization is continuing to reduce difference. But outside these borders, there is likely to be a reversal of the process of homogenization in the wake of the retreat of the financial system. Abandonment can lead to a re-embedding of financial activity, as more locally oriented financial institutions and financial practices emerge to take the place of nationally and internationally oriented institutions that have retreated from predominantly poor and disadvantaged areas. To be sure, these institutions may be predatory and have a corrosive social and economic impact (Haas, 1992), and financial abandonment is fraught with all sorts of dangers as far as economic development is concerned, as evidence from the United States clearly testifies (Dymski and Veitch, 1992). However, some institutional responses to financial abandonment are more positive and may lead to a beneficial re-embedding of financial activity. One such example is the growth of Local Exchange and Trading Systems or LETS, which revolve around the creation of a highly localized and non-transferable form of currency (for example, see Williams, 1994).

What is clear is that such developments point to a new dualism emerging in the geography of money and finance, one which divides between processes of disembedding and homogenization on the one hand, and re-embedding and difference on the other.

CONCLUSIONS

The alphabet is a one-way process of reduction of nonliterate cultures into the specialist visual fragments of our Western world. Money is an adjunct of that specialist alphabet technology, raising even the Gutenburg form of mechanical repeatability to new intensity. As the alphabet neutralized the divergencies of primitive cultures by translation of their complexities into simple visual terms, so representative money reduced moral values in the nineteenth century. As paper expedited the power of the alphabet to reduce the oral barbarians to Roman uniformity of civilization, so paper money enabled Western industry to blanket the globe (McLuhan, 1964, p. 141)

In summary, then, the geographical spread of money tends to bring about a homogenization of economic space as economic practices tend to fall into line with the rationalities of financial capital. Such a process, allied with the regulatory intervention of governments within the financial sphere, has been responsible for the creation of more or less coherent financial spaces within the borders of the nation-state. In the late twentieth century we would appear to be entering a new phase of financial geography, in which the coherence of national financial spaces is dissolving. Some places that once were 'inside' national financial spaces are now finding themselves 'outside', while at the same time, in part because of innovative financial instruments such as swaps, many of the differences between financial systems are being eroded.

ACKNOWLEDGEMENTS

I would like to extend my thanks to Peter Daniels for his helpful comments on an earlier version of this chapter. The usual disclaimers apply.

FURTHER READING

Agnew, J., Corbridge, S. 1995 *Mastering space*. Routledge, London.

Corbridge, S., Martin, R., Thrift, N. (eds) 1994 *Money, power and space*. Blackwell, Oxford.

Daniels, P. W. 1993 *Service industries in the world economy*. Blackwell, Oxford.

Leyshon, A., Thrift, N. 1996 *Money/space*. Routledge, London.

PART 2

GLOBALIZATION OF PRODUCTION SYSTEMS: PROCESSES

GLOBALIZATION OF
PRODUCTION SYSTEMS:
PROCESSES

CHAPTER 6

INFORMATION TECHNOLOGY AND PRODUCTION SYSTEMS

David R. Charles

INTRODUCTION

The dramatic growth of information technology (IT) within the workplace during the 1980s has engendered a degree of familiarity and acceptance such that it is difficult to remember work before the micro. IT is everywhere these days, it seems: personal computer (PC) networks in the office, computerized tills with EFTPOS[1] and automatic stock reordering in retail, Computer Aided Design (CAD) systems in the drawing office, computerized instruments in the lab, Computer Integrated Manufacturing (CIM) and Flexible Manufacturing Systems (FMS) on the factory floor (along with PCs etc.) and PCs, stock control systems and automatic guided vehicles in the (increasingly automated) warehouses. Linking all of these systems together are various networks from small office networks to corporate data networks, to the new public information superhighways now being developed in the US, Europe and Japan. But if this explosion of IT systems and applications has occurred mainly during the last couple of decades, how has the geography of business been affected? If the pervasive nature of IT and the power given by the information carried has transformed society, as some would have it, then the geography of production systems must surely have been affected also.

In this chapter we will discuss the role of information and communication technologies in the globalization and restructuring of production systems. It is important to stress communications here, because it is only with the networking of IT systems that the full globalizing potential can be realized. Stand-alone IT systems can process information faster, but it still has to be printed or saved on magnetic media for transfer to another location by traditional methods. High-speed data communications networks permit a qualitative leap as a result of the speed of information flow, with users able to retrieve data and gain access to remote IT systems with the same ease as using the PC on their own desk, without needing to know where that resource is physically based. It is the qualities of

---

[1] Electronic Funds Transfer at the Point of Sale.

time–space compression and the blurring of traditional geographies arising from communication that are so important in understanding the dynamics of industrial systems against a background of increasing IT investment. Henceforth in this chapter we will use the term Information and Communication Technologies (ICT) as recognition of the consequences of communication between discrete IT applications.

In writing about ICT, it is difficult to avoid being either very future oriented, or very pessimistic, due to the highly uneven use of ICT. The optimists can take their message from study of the leading adopters of the new ICTs, but there remain enormous numbers of small firms that make little or no use of ICT beyond the telephone, typewriter, or possibly a PC to replace the typewriter. It is therefore important to remember in what follows that there are two main dynamics: one is the deepening dependence of the major multinationals on corporate ICT systems, and its considerable effects on their internal structure; the second is the gradual adoption of IT by the smaller firms in search of competitiveness or needing to become more integrated with their larger trading partners. The first is a process of intensification whilst the latter is more one of primary adoption. This chapter will focus more on the intensification of ICTs within the large and globally oriented firms rather than on the wider issues of diffusion to small firms, but the reader should bear this in mind and not make the presumption that the account that follows is always generalizable.

IT AND CORPORATE RESTRUCTURING

Developments in information handling and processing 'technologies' have always been at the heart of organizational evolution. The concept of the social division of labour, whether in the form of market relations or hierarchies, depends on the exchange of information, for example on production flows, prices and demand. Early telecommunications technologies in the form of the telegraph and then the telephone permitted new forms of spatial division of labour as outlined by Beniger (1986) in his concept of the 'control revolution'. Chandler (1990) also has explained the rise of the multi-regional firm in their exploitation of firm-specific advantages through the ability to control and coordinate these activities over distance, essentially using early forms of telecommunications.

Further developments in information processing since the 1960s have made considerable changes in corporate form. The advent of mainframe computers within business, initially for large-scale administrative tasks such as payroll and financial accounting, led to the formation of data centres, large back offices to manage the flows of data into and out of the machine and to tend carefully to the needs of these sensitive beasts. Such large-scale facilities, underpinned by 'clerical factories', fitted well into the spirit of scientific management, increased the span of control of management as a whole, and reinforced the development of large-scale Fordism.

In parallel the emergence of Computer Aided Design (CAD) was instrumental in the emergence of new, highly complex products, notably in industries such as electronics and aerospace, contributing to the pace of technological advance by permitting the development of products of such complexity that the design process could not be managed by humans alone. As such, computerization led to new demands for economies of scale in design and development that pushed certain industries further along the path to globalization. More recently, as we will discover, these design technologies have also been implicated in a set of new relations between suppliers and assemblers.

However, a key point to be made is that data networks have allowed the closer integration of geographically dispersed production, thereby affecting the potential structures and routines of the multinational firm, and the process referred to as globalization. Data networks are increasingly supplemented by video technology, more sophisticated information handling and sharing, interactive multimedia, etc. All these different forms of applications are essentially seeking to ease the flow of information and interpersonal communication across space, although despite the claims of some space has not been conquered, but rather new ways of exploiting spatial differentiation have been permitted.

Although IT networks are such an intrinsic part of economic life, and as we will see are having a substantial impact on the geography of organizations, the literature within geography is rather underdeveloped. Much of recent writing on industrial restructuring has glossed over the infrastructures that enable new forms of organization, whilst such work as exists on IT and restructuring takes an aspatial perspective. Even among communications geographers the emphasis has often been on global financial information flows rather than manufacturing and related services.

DIVERSITY OF IT INVESTMENT

Before looking further at the applications of IT and their effects on production systems and various aspects of corporate organization, let us examine the forms of IT in current use. There are a number of specific elements or types:

- *IT hardware* Typically in the form of the computer, this includes all sizes from the humble PC to departmental minis and mainframes. Considerable dynamic changes are occurring within the sector as changes in processing power bring the power of mainframes to the desktop, etc. In addition to computers themselves are all the machines that are controlled by their own computer such as machine tools, although single-chip computers seem to be invading all aspects of electrical and mechanical equipment.
- *Communications terminals* These include a wide range of equipment that can be connected to either physical or radio communications networks, telephones and small private switch systems, fax and other non-voice terminals, and more importantly perhaps the various interface equipment that permits computers to communicate over telecoms networks.

- *Network technologies* The heart of the communications networks are the switching and transmission equipment responsible for routing and manipulating voice and data between users. From the traditional electromechanical networks of the past, the telecoms networks now are becoming something like large computer systems themselves, as the technology embodied in the software permits flexible and 'intelligent' functions like automatic call distribution, and allows the handling of immense amounts of data including real-time video.

- *Software for networks and applications* Underpinning all of the above is the software that controls the equipment, interfaces with the users, and provides the applications. Most people are familiar with the software running on their PC, and perhaps recognize the enormous growth in size and complexity of newer Windows-type software that provides user-friendly interfaces, but aside from the system software on the computers themselves, there is software embedded in terminals as prosaic as the phone, and huge volumes of system software controlling the communications networks.

In all of the above the key issue is the systemic nature of the technology. Many aspects are systems by definition, but even in the case of discrete products such as a PC, the rise of networking massively increases the services and power available. Certainly, however, when it comes to the application of ICTs across multi-site organizations, it is the development of integrated systems, whether in office systems, manufacturing or technical support systems, that permits organizational transformation.

IT, FLEXIBILITY AND CORPORATE GEOGRAPHY

Concern over the benefits of investment in information and communication technologies has moved on from an initial focus on stand-alone systems and applications, albeit including mainframe computers, to the analysis of the integration of applications across networks (see Hepworth, 1989). It is a feature of the contagious spread into all aspects of business of PCs and workstations, with their ability to operate non-standard software and to manipulate new information, that a need for integration and networking has risen in priority. The large multi-site company has been in the vanguard of these developments with burgeoning investments in desktop computing and in networking technologies. Given the potential transformative power of these technologies, this then raises the question of how networking technologies, which link together geographically separated activities, affect the spatial structure of these large firms.

We may examine the geographical form of the organization as being the result of a historic pattern of investment, acquisition and restructuring. Firms originate in particular places at particular points in time and grow by means of expansion and acquisition. At each juncture, decisions are taken that influence the spatial distribution of investment and the form that it takes. New investments and more specifically rounds of restructuring and rationalization reshape the functional distribution of activities within the set of places that make up the firm and its industry (Massey and Meegan, 1979; Massey, 1984; Peck and Townsend, 1984). The spatial form therefore is rooted into specific places by local environmental conditions which influence the decisions to invest, and the forms that the investments may take. Similarly, the decisions taken by firms on the closure or rationalization of plants in specific localities are the outcome of organizational pressures and priorities as well as any locality-based influences (Fothergill and Guy, 1990). The spatial–functional form of the firm therefore is partly shaped by the response of the firm to local operating environments, but in turn the firm influences places through its investments in specific labour markets and external service and supplier networks. The functions of the firm in particular localities give those localities a position or role in a broader urban and regional functional system or division of labour.

Our concern here is therefore with how ICTs may be used in the restructuring and reshaping of the firm in this context of the external environment. In particular, in considering the spatial pattern of different functions such as R&D and production and the interfaces between them, we need to see the extent to which ICTs are enabling decentralization or centralization, both in terms of the overall pattern of investment and in terms of relativities between functions. Organizational developments may lead to activities in close proximity being separated in organizational terms without any relocation of people. Alternatively people may be shifted as different functions are merged onto one site.

At present there are a number of issues that exert pressure on the organization of the firm, leading to structural change:

- changes in the external operating environment, including issues of power relations between companies, the shifting balance of power between suppliers and assemblers, externalization of development, changing response times and product cycles;
- internal changes of strategy and organization, arising from internal power struggles and problems, especially the need to integrate new acquisitions, developing IT strategies, etc.;
- production factor issues such as labour requirements, technical change and costs.

In the past, rounds of restructuring have led to distinctive spatial forms of organization, whether by the concentration of business units on single sites, or through hierarchical divisions of labour and function within some form of core–periphery model. Hierarchical models of the organization have attracted particular interest, relating to levels of managerial control (Thorngren, 1970) and to differences in tasks and horizons (Chandler and Redlich, 1961). Multi-site and multi-divisional firms provide an opportunity for the spatial separation of these levels of activity within a division of labour. Such separation may relate either to whole functional activities such as R&D or marketing that tend towards a particular type of information linkage orientation, or to parts of functions (such as strategic R&D vs product development). Furthermore, there is an international dimension in the extent to which certain production processes may be separated between different regions of the world economy, and tied into this is the move towards a global form of organization.

This may be counterpointed by the need to pull together different functional groups into closer coordination, particularly between marketing and R&D and between R&D and production. The needs of new forms of lean production and of the faster response to product and market change are inducing a restructuring of organizations to smooth the flow of information between what have previously been discrete activities (Womack *et al.*, 1990).

Thus ICTs are assisting firms in the realization of what has been termed 'dynamic flexibility', in which short-term flexibility to cope with fluctuating demand patterns is combined with wider productivity gains from innovation in products and processes (technical and organizational). This can be viewed through three main processes, as identified by Bar *et al.* (1989):

1. Telecommunications as a productive force, in the application of ICTs to improving the efficiency of production processes, through administrative savings, higher quality and lower costs.
2. Telecommunications as an interface with the market, in which tele-communications assist in the capturing of market information, adjusting production to meet demand and exploiting scope economies through the target selling of complementary products or services.
3. Telecommunications as an integrating force, where the coordinating role of ICTs is used to better interlink different functions and production processes in a managed supply chain.

Throughout, the key is to better use and coordinate the information that is generated and accumulated as a by-product of normal business relations, to reapply that to deliver existing goods and services more effectively, and to innovate in using the information both to stimulate new demands and as a potential product in its own right.

These strategic effects of the use of ICT also impact on the spatial form of the organization in two ways. First, existing limits of control and coordination have been overcome allowing a greater variety of organizational forms to be implemented. Secondly, the new modes of production organization and patterns of inter-firm linkage lead themselves to new spatial requirements in the combination of factors of production, transport requirements and more importantly telecommunications infrastructure that they need.

Capello (1994) suggests the following six main characteristics of ICTs that affect processes of industrial restructuring.

1. *Flexible technologies* ICTs are flexible in that they are not necessarily dedicated to a specific task or product model, and can be reprogrammed to handle new forms of information or products. Thus as distinct from Fordist automation, which was largely dedicated to a specific task, modern ICT

investments can yield economies of scope as the same capital can be spread across different products or services. Capello points out, however, that economies of scale are not made completely irrelevant, but that a new balance emerges between economies of scale and scope. Indeed other aspects of ICTs assist the firm in new kinds of scale economies due to the ability to coordinate activities across greater distances within a reduced timescale. ICTs may also assist the firm to achieve economies of scope in the application of information through the obtaining of additional value from information by sharing it over a network – for example within an R&D unit or between a number of sites. This may apply to various forms of network application from databases, CAD and software tools to communications such as e-mail. The essence is to address the rising cost of R&D and other information processes by either reducing duplication or drawing upon a wider range of scarce expertise within a company.

2. *Speed of access to and processing of information* The network characteristics of ICTs and the ability to 'capture, manipulate and process information in ways and time spans that were hitherto impossible' (Capello, 1994, p. 193) has important implications for the way in which the firm responds to the market and restructures internal processes to 'compete in time' (Keen, 1988). A key development along these lines is the emergence of just-in-time (JIT) systems, where ICT networks are used to speed up the flows of goods within the production process, thereby cutting inventories and the costs of work-in-progress, and also sharpening the firm's ability to respond to short-term fluctuations in market demand.

3. *Ability to increase the control over decentralized systems* Control aspects of ICTs are commonly raised in studies of their impact on organizations (e.g. Zuboff, 1988; Knights and Sturdy, 1990), whether in terms of the control over the detailed working practices of individual employees or of the wider structural effects on the nature of middle management tasks. Changes in the patterns of control take two distinct dimensions. Typically ICT applications centralize power and control, but devolve responsibility. Responsibility is devolved in the sense that individuals may be given much greater access to information in the course of their jobs, so Zuboff's office workers are able to access corporate databases and change these data, making decisions about credit control, for example, which were previously passed to managers, and the applications assist this process through decision support tools and procedures. However, at the same time the ICTs allow managers to more tightly constrain the activities and organizational routines through the software, as well as monitor huge quantities of data on the performance of individuals without the filter of middle managers. This combination of a centralization of power with diffused responsibility allows the firm to expand spatially without the construction of additional tiers of bureaucracy.

4. *Creation of a common informational axis* Fundamental to processes just described is the sharing of information, both across a single function over territory, and between corporate functions. Such functional integration is a common theme in recent organizational studies, although in many cases it does not need to involve ICTs, such as for example where product development teams combine R&D, manufacturing and marketing staff. However, ICTs are increasingly underpinning these developments in leading-edge firms. In the aerospace industry, for example, shared engineering databases encompass design and manufacturing data, and can be remotely accessed by all staff involved in that project regardless of functional specialization. Whilst as Capello argues the ICT infrastructure is not sufficient to ensure success, it is increasingly becoming a necessary requirement in industries with complex products, or where timeliness is critical.

5. *Handling information with greater sensitivity* The increased ability to handle large amounts of data resulting from the use of ICTs implies also an ability to disaggregate data relating to specific customers or groups in order to customize products or deliveries more sharply to meet needs more precisely. In terms of the customization of production, we can see the benefits to Benetton of being able to use the sales data from stores to predict the level of demand for different colour variations in garments, to manufacture or at least dye the required quantities, and then allocate those garments to specific stores. In the car industry also, computer networks linking dealers and manufacturers allow high levels of customization in orders, with flexible production lines turning out hundreds of cars a day with no two being identical. Some of these cars are for specific customers, but others are made for stock, based on predictions of what the market wants, underpinned by analysis of sales databases. Some commentators argue that these trends lead to a demise of mass production in favour of customization, although what seems to be emerging is a more flexible form of mass production, in which overall commodity volumes may be rising but the degree of variety also increases.

6. *Linking spatially separate activities* The key spatial issue in much of the debate over corporate ICT networks has been the tension between the centrifugal and centripetal: between the decentralization of production and access to information and the centralization of control and power (Gillespie, 1993). In the latter respect particularly, new governance structures are emerging on an extra-corporate value chain basis, as key firms use information systems to exert control over trading partners beyond the ownership boundary of the firm. Such a reach is increasingly global as firms spread their production units more widely, interconnect multinational operations via product business units rather than geographically defined divisions, and implement global partnership (i.e., by control) sourcing.

We may observe examples of such global coordination of dispersed production in industries as diverse as vehicle manufacturing, media and finance. Considerable literature exists on the importance of ICTs for the global management of transnational companies (see for example Langdale, 1989; Howells, 1990; Howells and Wood, 1992; and Brunn and Leinbach, 1991 for more extensive literature reviews). These firms that are linked by and indeed increasingly dependent on ICT networks have been termed 'network firms', although there is no standard form of such organizations. Indeed that is the very nature of such firms: the organizational form is capable of adaptation to the needs of the external environment.

Bartlett and Ghoshal (1989) try to make sense of some of the changes in the structure of large firms with a four-fold classification: multinational, global, international and transnational. Each of these can be summarized briefly with a well-known example:

- The 'multinational' operates as a federation of relatively autonomous companies, in the form of a holding company which has grown by acquisition such as Hanson. Each national subsidiary is self sufficient and seeks to exploit local opportunities, and knowledge is developed and retained within each national unit.
- The 'global' firm is the classic Japanese firm with a strongly centralized approach, although with transplant factories around the world. Here the emphasis is on global scale of operation with overseas operations implementing the product strategy established at the centre.
- The 'international' firm is the typical American organizational form with a strong technology and control focus within the parent company, but with some decentralization of responsibility to the overseas divisions. Thus as in IBM in the 1970s, key technologies were developed centrally and transferred to production units around the world, but there was a move to decentralize some of these activities and to adapt to local markets. However, the US market and headquarters were still assumed to know best.
- Bartlett and Ghoshal argue that a new form of 'transnational' organization is emerging which takes the form of a more 'integrated network configuration', in which assets and capabilities are 'dispersed, interdependent, and specialized'. Thus different national subsidiaries contribute in their own distinctive way to the competence of the firm as a whole, and the knowledge gained is shared across the organization.

Although there is no detailed consideration by Bartlett and Ghoshal of the implications of ICTs for these organizational forms, we can suggest how the different forms might adopt different network architectures. The multinational model has only limited needs for formal networks, as the key controls are simply regular reporting of accounting data to the HQ, although some specialized bilateral links may exist between related subsidiaries. The global firm by contrast has intense demands for control information between the central hub and dispersed plants, with regular exchange of financial and production information, and even the downloading of design information to transplants. Use of ICT networks is a critical issue for such firms, but in a very centralized manner, of a star configuration. The international firms will also tend to use a star configuration with a central communications hub, but here the flow of information will tend to be more two-way. Thus instead of technical and control information being sent out, and reporting information returning, some of the subsidiaries will be able to feed in technology to the company as a whole, although still mediated and filtered by central corporate functions.

The contrasting case, however, is the transnational firm, where a true global communications network is required. If knowledge is to be developed jointly and shared across the firm then a complex series of connections is required, drawing on sophisticated data-sharing applications, multi-site video conferencing, corporate-wide e-mail and remote access to large-scale facilities such as supercomputers.

Hagstrom (1992) goes further in exploring the nature of the 'wired MNC', arguing that greater ease of control through the use of ICTs has led also to a greater tolerance of variations in organizational structure. The creation of corporate-wide networks and the growth of interdependency amongst subsidiaries has encouraged direct and spontaneous lateral communications, by-passing corporate management and further strengthening the autonomy of subsidiaries.

Focusing on the locational implications of the development of new patterns of ICTs in the large firm rather than the simple extension of global control, it is important to see ICTs as enabling the firm to reconfigure its organization on an almost continuous basis. Such reconfiguration may take many forms. The firm may, for example, seek to deliver a number of new services via an existing network of front offices rather than establish new specialized outlets. In a production system, products may be shifted between different manufacturing sites according to patterns of demand, site of customer, availability of spare production capacity, etc. (this depends on flexible production equipment as well as on the networking technologies). In project-based operations, new virtual teams or organizations can be created drawing upon knowledge resources in different groups of functional or product/market specialists.

In this sense, then, the geography of the firm can be reconstructed without physical relocation of staff. Keen terms this the 'location and structure-independent organization' in which 'location will no longer determine planning, control, reporting, function and communication, making the firm's tele-communications resources the real definer of structure'. This raises challenges for the firm's infrastructure also stimulating demand for new forms of telematic networks, such as ISDN, and workstation/software technology in multimedia, video conferencing, user interfaces and groupware. Thus, for example, European firms that have engaged in considerable merger activity in recent years often find themselves with a large number of sites at which some aspect of product development is taking place. The post-merger challenge is always to gain the benefits of integration, yet attempting to move staff is always risky. Companies such as SGS-Thomson or Alcatel are now using ICT networks instead as a means of providing the glue for the organization, thereby allowing a more dispersed form of organization than would otherwise be feasible (see Howells and Wood, 1992).

One of the most significant effects of these developments is not so much the location of different activities as the conjunction of those activities within particular places. Formerly the need to develop managerial hierarchies and process information locally meant that most large organizations operated via a set of sites with multiple but interlocking functions. A factory might have functional support on site from marketing, R&D, sales, etc. A service organization would have regional HQs that replicated many of the general HQ functions. Now, however, many of these specialized functions are more likely to be available over the network, and the crucial geographical issue is one of where the skills and human resources can be found.

Thus two main implications emerge. First ICTs permit firms to better exploit geographical difference, by allowing new and more flexible ways of bringing together different types of labour in places with different costs, availability and regulation. Thus for example the multinational, multitechnology R&D organization can seek the advantages of a set of national systems of innovation by carrying out, as Hitachi does, industrial design in Italy, engineering in Germany, solid state physics in the UK and software engineering in Ireland. At a national level too, firms such as ICL have various sites of expertise which are brought together in different ways to address specific project demands. In functions such as R&D, it is clear therefore that firms are able to tap into different specialized labour markets and indeed into national systems of innovation without dramatically reshaping their organizations.

Second and perhaps more interesting is what is beginning to happen in leading-edge firms at the site level. If an office or multifunctional site is connected to these corporate networks, and staff engage in new forms of space-independent virtual organizations, then the local interactions become weakened. Indeed the individual site would have a locational logic mainly in terms of shared overheads and a presence in a specific labour market. In this extreme case the integrated local subsidiary could become no more than a collection of unconnected activities, even though it may appear to have all the trappings of a stand-alone business in terms of different functional specialists. This development therefore continues the trend towards firms' local offices becoming detached from their local industrial environment, with decisions on supplier or partner selection being made by the firm as a whole rather than individual branches with knowledge of local firms. If certain regions lose key professional jobs as part of this process then the negative effects will be reinforced.

So far examples of this trend are very few, but they can be seen in leading-edge IT users such as Rolls-Royce or British Aerospace, and in some of the management consultancy companies. Such developments have important implications, however, for inward investment strategies, as received wisdom is that it is sensible to seek an upgrading of plants by adding new functions to the initial manufacturing investment. This generally implies a shift of work from another site, where the work is in support of the manufacturing operations and would benefit from closer links. If new IT infrastructures lead to a reduction in the degree of integration through co-location across the company, between manufacturing and sales for example, then the prospects of peripheral regions gaining such jobs will be determined less by their having the specific related activities and more by their having relevant skills available at an appropriate cost. Interregional competition for inward investment will increase in intensity as winning the initial investment will not guarantee further rounds of investment in related functions.

IT, LOGISTICS AND THE SUPPLY CHAIN

The previous sections have concentrated on the role of ICTs in the reshaping of information flows within organizations, and the reconstitution of those organizations across space. However, ICTs are also being used increasingly between firms as a means of controlling transactions.

A key area of application of ICTs to the management of linkages and flows of goods between firms is in the use of electronic data interchange (EDI), which is the replacement of paper transaction documents such as orders and invoices by electronic messages. Through EDI, internal ICT systems can generate orders, to replenish stocks or to match the demands of a production line, and instead of printing and posting these orders, with the added delays and errors from rekeying information at the recipient firm, an order can be entered into the ICT systems of the supplier within minutes. Such rapid exchange of data is an important element in emerging patterns of just-in-time (JIT) production as noted earlier, and can give rise to important economies of proximity. In other words if the order can be sent instantaneously, then time taken by the supplier to provide goods will be as fast as the physical transit time, with clear competitive advantages for localized suppliers.

The JIT supply chain, emerging from the lean production paradigm (Morris, 1989; Wells and Rawlinson, 1992) is typified by the Japanese automotive industry (e.g. Hill, 1989). Mair (1993) has characterized the focus on such developments as a just-in-time strategy for local economic development (JIT LED) in which economic development actors have placed hopes on the attraction of suppliers to major assembly plants, on the understanding that the JIT processes adopted will require supplier proximity. Thus based on a transplantation of a Toyota City model of development it was hoped that the tight, short lead time JIT purchasing patterns of new car and electronics plants would lead to a new spatial agglomeration of subcontractors and suppliers in those regions that were able to attract the main assembly plants. Whilst there is an emerging critical line on the potential for JIT LED growth, the phenomenon has stimulated renewed interest in the connections between large firm linkage studies and regional development. What is perhaps lacking is a greater understanding of the effects of innovation in the form of supply chain intermediation such as EDI.

An alternative perspective to this focus on the supply chain of the large firm or transplant is the industrial district perspective, drawing on the experiences of networks of small, flexibly specialized firms in regions of central and northern Italy and elsewhere (see Amin and Robins, 1990, for a critique). Here again inter-firm linkages are a vital element in processes of development, this time endogenously based, but distinctively the linkages within industrial districts are highly informal and flexible, based on individual trust and familial ties.

So if linkages are important to economic geography and to processes of regional development then how might EDI affect the nature and pattern of linkages, specifically with a spatial dimension? First is the general attendant need for EDI to be accompanied by closer inter-firm relations, longer-term power-dependent relations whereby customers exert control over suppliers but are themselves dependent on single sources and increasingly on the competitiveness of that supplier (Womack *et al.*, 1990). This may to some extent be a temporary process in that EDI implementation requires a scale of effort that is only justifiable for on-going trading relationships, and also that having adopted EDI, suppliers can better match non-cost requirements of supply such as response time.

Such closer and less transitory links may be accompanied by faster response times and this requirement may be added to the advantage of suppliers in immediate proximity to the customer. As will be explained shortly this may be further extended into cases where EDI is used to support extreme versions of JIT whereby localization of supply is imperative. This is not to say that EDI causes localization but that it is a mechanism in gaining maximum flexibility and benefit from such strategies. Without EDI, localized suppliers might have less advantage in cost and response terms than longer distance suppliers.

A third issue is the importance of better information links, more and better quality planning information flowing between supply chain partners. In this sense advantage is built into extant members of a supply chain locking out new or marginal participants. Thus EDI use may preserve existing links and alter patterns of transaction costs in such a way as to create advantage for localized suppliers. Against this, however, it will be argued that there are countervailing tendencies to weaken local supply requirements which may act in opposition to this.

Referring back to our two earlier models of JIT-based development and industrial districts, it is clear that EDI may be far more relevant to the former. The ability for large firms to use EDI to speed up the logistics chain and tie in suppliers more closely is clear. This will be explored more closely below with one example. However, in the industrial district case the benefits of EDI are less clear. EDI is a rigid and hierarchical technology; it depends on strict product codes, communications standards, and predetermined contractual conditions, all of which are inimical to the supposed symmetry of trading relations in industrial districts. Furthermore it is unclear from where the impetus for adoption of EDI would come, given that in most cases it is driven by large customers back up their supply chain. Thus only an industrial district organized by a large customer might be expected to see the rapid adoption of EDI.

Overall, then, EDI has the potential to change the economic base of transactions in such a way that their geography might be affected and, therefore, patterns of local sourcing changed. In terms of regional development any such development presents challenges for less favoured regions in terms of how to capture some advantage or more likely to eliminate possible peripheralization.

As firms target inventory levels and various forms of production flexibility as prime strategies for competitiveness, so the nature of the information exchange with suppliers and its effect on patterns of delivery becomes a vital concern. Following the lean production paradigm, effort has focused on both reduction of inventory to a minimum, but with a fast response to cope with volume flexibility, combined with the flexible supply of type variants so that the customer can source a varying mix of a product to meet specific patterns as well as volume of demand.

LOCALIZATION IN THE AUTOMOTIVE INDUSTRY

This is particularly well developed in the case of automotive assembly but can also be seen within the electronics sector. In general there is a limiting factor in the form of the technological sophistication, economies of scale and degrees of concentration in the source industries. However, for simple products and styling-sensitive components such as car seats, external shells, packaging and so on JIT is becoming a priority. As an example of this we can look at the localization of suppliers to the Nissan car plant in north-east England.

Nissan has been required by the need to establish European producer status to achieve a high level of local value added and hence European sourcing of components. In this the company has sought to minimize stock levels and reduce lead times to an extent that local (i.e. same region) supply has become essential for some components. The Nissan approach to lean production links concerns over work organization, quality and logistics extremely closely. The company follows a strict single source policy covering type of commodity rather than a single design of component (thus all seats are sourced from the same supplier rather than simply seats for one model). The company insists on high levels of quality on incoming components as well as in the assembly process, and this is implicit in the work organization of the assembly line. Hence it is intended that the assembly worker will be able to pick up the next component to be fitted on the next car without taking more than one step backwards, and without having to make a selection of the appropriate part. For standard parts which are identical for every car on the line this is not problematic, but for other parts there will be a high degree of variety, such that every car will have a different requirement, and there is no repetition in the pattern of production. Large parts also present problems in terms of storage close to the line.

Nissan's approach to this problem has been to insist that for some parts only local (within 25 miles) supply is tolerable, so that the supply of parts, on a multiple daily delivery, is synchronized with the pattern of production of cars. This is best illustrated with car seats or carpets, where each car will need a different colour depending on the body colour, different styling/material depending on the variation within a model, and a different shape/type depending on three-door or five-door variants. In both cases the company uses an EDI system to transmit final orders at very short lead times so that the suppliers can deliver the components in the right variations in the order in which they will be required. The lead times for seats are of the order of 40 minutes whilst for carpets they are still shorter. Although the companies are given production planning information with a somewhat longer timescale, the final EDI order is a confirmation that basically the relevant car is still on the production line and has not been removed because of problems. The companies are only expected to ship the goods once the order is received and hence proximity to the plant is essential.

The importance of the localized suppliers to Nissan can be seen in their share of the total purchasing bill. Although in 1993 there were a mere 25 out of a total of 180 European suppliers based in the north-east, these accounted for almost half of its UK spend, and one-third of EC purchasing. The products may not be particularly sophisticated, but they tend to be large, bulky, and styling sensitive.

Turning from the localization issue to the effect of EDI on long-distance interactions, the key question is whether EDI enables firms in peripheral regions to gain better access to markets elsewhere, or whether it is the core region firms that benefit most. Here Nissan has been using EDI and logistics innovation to enable multiple daily deliveries without the need for separate lorries from each supplier. Since a large number of car component suppliers have been historically concentrated in the West Midlands region, a solution was developed by Nissan in collaboration with a third-party logistics services supplier: the development of a 'cross dock' system in December 1991 (see Figure 6.1). The 'cross dock' is a vehicle consolidation ('groupage') centre,[2] which was set up by Ryder at a location in the Midlands which was just close enough to the Nissan factory for a driver to make a return journey in a single working shift. Currently, components from 35 suppliers are delivered to the cross dock, where they are unloaded and mixed with components from other suppliers and re-loaded onto larger lorries. Eighteen dedicated lorries constantly shift components from the cross dock to Nissan allowing an even flow of materials to and from NMUK.

Ryder collects the parts from suppliers one to four times per day and takes considerable responsibility for matching supply to Nissan's quantity requirements. Nissan produces a production schedule which gives the supply requirements. Via EDI, these are sent to suppliers and at the same time to Ryder. Ryder calculates the loads needed by Nissan such that one lorry per unloading bay is

---

[2] The cross dock is owned and managed by Ryder. It is not a warehouse or a stockholding place, but a groupage centre where no stock will stay for longer than eight hours.

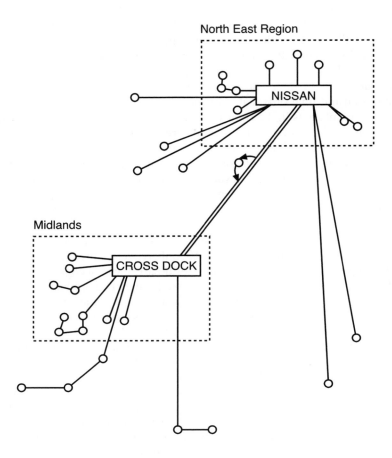

Figure 6.1   Nissan's UK just-in-time supply network

sent to Nissan with a fixed proportion of production time requirements on board. These loads then provide a target for Ryder to bring in sufficient stock to the cross dock to be able to assemble that combination in time to send the load to Nissan. Ryder informs Nissan of the mixture of parts on each lorry, and gives each lorryload a bar code number. At Nissan the driver unloads the lorry with a forklift truck to a setdown area and books in the whole load with the swipe of one bar code, after which the parts are moved directly to the assembly line. Nissan tends to keep the pattern of pickup and delivery times fairly constant, which reflects the limited fluctuation of production volumes.

Although the capacity utilization of the vehicles from the suppliers to the cross dock (short distance) is not high, that between the cross dock and Sunderland (long distance) is significantly improved. The annual saving on vehicle mileage was in the order of several millions, which – contrary to the expectation that JIT would create more traffic on the road – reduces the pressure on the road infrastructure and on the environment. Although delivery frequencies have increased threefold, mileage has been reduced and total freight costs have remained virtually the same through consolidation. There are some congestion effects at the local scale around the cross dock, but the major benefits have been found in long-distance efficiencies and in preventing congestion at the Nissan site.

This example thus shows the potential for the remote supply using EDI, in this case where Nissan has insufficient power over a set of suppliers to force them to locate production facilities near to its plant. Put alongside the earlier comments on Nissan, this perhaps illustrates an interesting balance in the localization process of component supply to inward investments. The inward investor or other large plant located in a peripheral region can use EDI and its purchasing power to develop a local supply base for those components where economies of scale are such that the company can justify a dedicated plant. However, for more technically specialized components and where purchasing volumes are low, the company will have to creatively use EDI to enable it to bring in supplies from the core regions, where suppliers are typically based. Thus there are limited opportunities for the regions, and EDI may permit the most competitive firms to retain an advantage despite geographical separation.

IT AND GLOBALIZATION

The analysis and examples discussed so far show some of the dynamics between globalization and localization arising from the application of ICTs. Globalization, however, is normally only considered within the context of the so-called Triad regional groupings of developed economies, although the newly industrializing countries of south-east Asia have been promoted into this context. The real challenge facing the world currently is not the competitiveness of individual Triad economies, but the development paths open to countries in the Third World, and the consequences of those paths. IT may have a substantial impact on these processes, although so far it has tended to remain outside the literature.

As the major firms controlling the majority of world trade increasingly use ICTs as the means of coordinating that flow, so the barriers presented by poor quality and lack of access to communications technology in the Third World become more important. Already retailers in the industrialized economies are rolling out EDI for purchasing across national barriers, initially between developed economies, but with a clear desire to apply the technologies to all purchasing wherever the supplier. For suppliers in the Third World, one solution is simply to bypass the national infrastructures, and indeed many multinationals operating in the Third World are keen to encourage the entry of global communications companies, or even shift to wireless communications. However, this behaviour potentially exacerbates the enclave development trend, as areas of good infrastructure become a focus for development, further increasing disparities within Third World societies.

Some organizations have tried to develop electronic links with Third World traders in order to improve access to markets and to improve trading policy, notably through the UNCTAD Tradepoint policy, but such policies are ultimately hindered by the combination of a lack of ICT infrastructure and the low level of awareness of telematic applications.

More fundamental, perhaps, is the possibility of a partial reversal of some of the patterns of subcontracting which have developed in recent years as multinationals try to use increased automation to reduce the cost of labour in order to repatriate work that might have been moved offshore to Third World locations. Increased attention to control, quality and logistics also favours manufacture close to markets. Conversely where local production is established in the Third World, MNEs adopt the same approaches as in developed markets, thereby reducing the employment potential.

However, the one area where opportunities are suggested arising from IT being a critical element in global production systems is in the supply of high-value software services not only to MNEs operating in these regions, but also exporting back to the Triad. Examples of these activities include the growth of an export-oriented software industry in India and value added data services in Puerto Rico. We may face a new scenario of the labour-intensive elements of production being informational, formerly that regarded as high value added. If production is highly automated and close to the market then software may be commoditized and located offshore – with low costs of transport and labour as a result of telecommunications networks.

MNEs are using IT to selectively tap the assets of all countries, including the Third World. These strategies are not fixed but are evolving over time as technology constantly changes the balance of factors required for production. Consequently we may be seeing ICTs assisting in the further integration of some elements of the Third World into the production networks of the multinationals, but at the same time seeing wider disparities opening up within Third World countries and between the advanced economies and the mass of Third World industry.

It should be stressed, however, that this is not an argument for technological determinism. Innovations in ICTs increase the range of options and possibilities for MNEs to adopt new organizational forms, to increase their global scope, and to exploit selectively a greater range of different local production environments (Gillespie, 1993). The firms themselves, though, are part of the innovation process, and this process goes beyond the developments in new technologies. A key underlying development, without which many of these ICT innovations could not be exploited, is the liberalization of the telecommunications environment. Given that much of the advantage to networking ICT applications derives from the network itself, it is important to note that until relatively recently such networks were highly constrained by national telecommunications regulations. Here the MNEs have been important lobbyists for liberalization, especially in terms of the ability to lease lines for private networks, and for new private competitors to offer high-quality business-oriented services in addition to the main public telecoms operators. Thus as an intermediate step towards fully liberalized and competitive telecoms markets we have seen initiatives such as teleports, where localized digital optical fibre networks with satellite connections bypass the national communications infrastructures completely. The areas served by teleports have been seen as attractive locations for high-volume information-processing centres for MNEs where preferential charges for international networking can be obtained. Some developed to serve existing demands (e.g. New York), some to cope with problems of existing network capacity (in the former Soviet bloc, for example) whilst others have been purely promotional devices to attract industry to new sites. All such initiatives can be seen as a transitional phenomenon however, as liberalized public telecoms operators and their new competitors scramble to provide premium services to large inter-national customers.

CONCLUSIONS

In this chapter we have examined the potential for information and communica-tion technologies to influence the nature of international production systems. It has been stressed that it is only in the communication of information between discrete IT applications that real transformative potential can be achieved, although as yet the effects have been somewhat limited in the production environment to those large leading-edge firms that have been able to make significant investments.

ICTs are being used to assist firms to increase their degree of flexibility within a given array of physical locations, not so much abolishing geography as assisting its more efficient exploitation. Whilst firms have traditionally been shaped by their historical evolution and the environments in which they operate, now the application of ICTs gives firms the opportunity to redesign their organizations to take advantage of changing conditions, and to alter the balances in capital and labour factors used across the corporation. As Hepworth (1989) has pointed out, capital can be separated from labour and located in a different region yet still be accessed via communications networks. But in addition to a simple delocalization effect, ICTs also enable an increased speed of economic activity with a reduction in the time of response to changes in market requirements and a move to just-in-time methods.

With the quickening of the pace of response and the restructuring of relations between parts of the organization, firms are seeking to adopt new organizational forms that enable them to manage in more turbulent markets, often with a decentralization of decision making, even if power itself is more firmly centralized. One of the prime contradictions within ICT systems is the apparent decentralization effects as responsibility is passed down the hierarchy to national operating units and lower-tier managers, precisely because the ICT systems allow top management to see what are the effects of those decisions, and to exercise power less frequently but when required. At the local level within subsidiaries of global firms what may be emerging is a collection of activities that have responsibility, and all the appearances of being locally embedded, but where integration is achieved via the computer network on a global rather than local basis.

As a specific example of the effects of ICT networks, we examined the effect on logistics and supply chains and the use of ICTs within just-in-time production systems. Here again we found the dualistic effects of the use of technology, with electronic data interchange being used both to maximize the advantages of proximity through the quasi-integration of suppliers with assembly plants, and also to underpin the long-term competitiveness of existing distant suppliers by bringing some of the advantages of proximity.

The prospects for the coming years are of a continuation of these trends, with multinational firms using ICTs as a means of further reinforcing their ability to exploit geography, moving increasingly into new and emerging markets with enclave-based developments where the firm can even be independent of local communications services, using satellite or teleport services as a way of bypassing poor infrastructures. Whatever happens within the production workplace itself, and IT is increasingly important here, the bigger picture is of the mobility of work, and it is the hypermobility between existing facilities that will be the feature of globalization of production in the next decade.

FURTHER READING

Bakis, H. 1987 Telecommunications and the global firm. In Hamilton, F.E.I. (ed.) *Industrial change in advanced economies*. Croom Helm, London: 130–60.

Brunn, S.D., Leinback, T.R. 1991 *Collapsing space and time: geographic aspects of communication and information*. Harper Collins, London.

Capello, R. 1994 Toward new industrial and spatial systems: the role of new technologies. *Papers in Regional Science* **73**: 189–208.

Gillespie, A. 1993 Telematics and its implications for industrial and spatial organisation. *Regional Development Dialogue* **14**(2): 138–50.

Hagstrom, P. 1992 Inside the wired MNC. In Antonelli, C. *The economics of information networks*. Elsevier: 325–45.

Hepworth, M. 1989 *The geography of the information economy*. Belhaven, London.

Howells, J., Wood, M. 1993 *The globalisation of production and technology*. Belhaven, London.

Linge, G.J.R. 1992 Just-in-time: more or less flexible. *Economic Geography* **68**: 316–32.

Mair, A. 1993 New growth poles? Just-in-time manufacturing and local economic development strategy. *Regional Studies* **27**: 207–22.

Womack, J.P., Jones, D.T., Roos, D. 1990 *The machine that changed the world*. Rawson Associates, New York.

CHAPTER 7

THE DEVELOPMENT OF MULTINATIONAL ENTERPRISES

Jeremy Clegg

INTRODUCTION

This chapter aims to shed light on the significance of multinational firms as agents in the global economy. It begins with an overview of the trends in aggregate multinational involvement, an assessment of the national origins of multinational enterprises (MNEs),[1] and an appraisal of the importance of these firms' activity for host and home countries. The industrial type of multinational activity has long been recognized to be crucial to understanding its development. Subsequent sections examine the recent pattern and shifts in investment from manufacturing to services, and the significance of the geographical dispersion of production stages.

Multinational activity has an increasingly regional dimension, and this is overviewed along with the leading home and host countries. The role of MNEs in less developed economies has been a matter of controversy for many years. The evidence presented challenges the tendency to treat these countries as a homogeneous group. Indeed, the widespread polarization of regions of the world into enclaves of dynamism and backwaters in FDI activity is highlighted in this chapter.

The developed countries, represented principally by the membership of the OECD,[2] are now the centre of gravity for world foreign direct investment (FDI) and multinational activity (see also Chapters 10 and 14). Through the 1980s, the developed countries accounted for 97 per cent of world outflows of FDI and 75 per cent of inflows. In particular, within the developed economies, the countries of the 'Triad' (the European Union, the United States and Japan) accounted for 81 per cent of world FDI outflows and 71 per cent of world inflows (UNCTAD, 1993b, p. 1).

---

[1] The term 'multinational enterprise' is interchangeable with the alternative term 'transnational corporation' (TNC), which is favoured in publications originating from the United Nations (see Hoogvelt, 1987).

[2] The Developed Countries are defined by the United Nations as all 24 member countries of the Organization for Economic Cooperation and Development (OECD) plus Israel, Singapore and South Africa, although for statistical purposes Israel does not appear in the developed country tables (see UNCTAD, 1993b, Note 4, p. 61).

The current development of multinational firms is progressing in two key directions. Firstly, developed country multinational enterprises are becoming global in a more comprehensive manner than ever before. This involves spanning mainly the developed and the advanced newly industrializing economies (NIEs), but in addition the opening up of new markets, such as those of China and central and eastern Europe, offers additional scope for higher levels of geographical diversification (see Chapter 13). Secondly, the number of firms qualifying as multinationals has risen considerably. Multinationals originating in the fourteen leading industrial countries of the world numbered just 7000 in 1969, but in the early 1990s they reached a figure of around 24000 (UNCTAD, 1993b). The world as a whole is estimated to hold a total of 37000 multinational firms, which control in total (that is, within their home plus host economies) around one-third of all private sector capital. These capital assets generate a sales value of approximately $US5.5 trillion (million million), a figure only slightly less than that of the US in 1993.

MULTINATIONAL ENTERPRISES AND THEIR ROLE IN FOREIGN DIRECT INVESTMENT CAPITAL FLOWS

There have been many attempts at a definition of a multinational enterprise (see Hoogvelt, 1987). The most practical is that an MNE is a firm that produces (adds value) in more than one country (Dunning, 1993). However, only very few firms actually operate abroad in the form of branches, i.e., through extensions of the parent enterprise itself. The preponderance of firms work through foreign affiliates incorporated according to local law. The parent firm in the home country will normally own significant equity in the foreign affiliate. Customarily, it has been understood that an MNE should have an equity ownership stake of a size adequate to ensure influence over the foreign affiliate (International Monetary Fund, 1977). However, some researchers have argued that, especially in the service sector, it is possible for the high degree of international coordination associated with equity ownership to be effected through contracts, e.g. via international franchising. In this chapter the orthodox view of multinational operations (based on an equity relationship) is retained, although it should be borne in mind that the internationalization of both services and manufacturing operations has often been through the medium of contracts between firms that are not significantly related by ownership.

The near-universal collection of statistics on foreign direct investment has enabled it to become the premier means of gauging the activities of MNEs, particularly when the objective is to make international comparisons. It does, however, have its drawbacks. Foreign direct investment is the financial value of the interest of a firm in an affiliate located abroad. There is general agreement that it is necessary for a parent firm to have an equity shareholding in a foreign firm of at least 10 per cent for the latter to be considered an affiliate. Even so, some countries set this threshold higher (e.g. the UK at 20 per cent). As most FDI occurs at higher equity levels, international comparability is not significantly affected by these national deviations in the practice of inferring the existence of an affiliate.

The flow of foreign direct investment consists of net capital flows (which may be positive or negative) plus reinvested earnings. The difference between annual values of the FDI stock is equivalent to flows of FDI plus (or minus) valuation adjustments. In the case of those countries which do not conduct surveys of the FDI stock, the cumulation of FDI flows over a reasonable period is an acceptable substitute measure of the extent of MNE activity. Both stock and flow figures are commonly employed in evaluating the pattern and development of multinational activity.

The determinants of FDI fall into two distinct categories: those real factors that determine the level of MNE activity and the financial factors that influence the financing of FDI. Real factors have received the most attention in the literature on the MNE, and are treated in Chapters 12, 13 and 17 of this volume. Financial factors have often been overlooked, but are dealt with thoroughly in Gilman (1981), while some basic applications to US FDI in the European Community are explored by Clegg (1995).

TRENDS IN THE PATTERN OF MULTINATIONAL ACTIVITY

In the early days of multinational enterprise, during the nineteenth and early twentieth centuries, the normal pattern of international organization was to allow foreign affiliates a very high degree of autonomy within a hierarchical multinational structure. This fitted the relatively stable international business environment. The degree of operational coordination between parent and affiliates was typically not high. Such coordination as existed was effected through the appointment of managers with common educational and cultural backgrounds in order to secure common objectives despite geographical remoteness, a strategy exemplified in early multinational banking (Jones, 1993).

Innovation in communication and transport, coupled with increased turbulence in the international business environment, has generated both the means and the incentive for increased coordination between parent firms and foreign affiliates. The progressively tighter control of key functional areas and integrated decision making now characterizes many multinational operations. These developments have enabled firms to reap further economies of firm size and scope.

The recent history of the evolution of foreign direct investment gives a flavour of the macroeconomic factors that shape its development. During the 1960s FDI grew at twice the rate of GNP in the countries of the OECD. There has clearly been a tendency for economies to become progressively more internationalized through multinational activity. Although no formal estimates have been made, the growth of multinational activity appears to be highly elastic with respect to national (and world) income, being strongly linked to the international business cycle and macroeconomic shocks (Clegg, 1995). Accordingly, the growth of FDI was particularly curtailed by the impact of the oil price rises of 1973 and 1979. The rate of growth of FDI resumed again with strength from the mid-1980s, and in the period 1983 to 1990 FDI outflows increased at an unprecedented annual average rate of 27 per cent, which is three times faster than the growth of exports and almost four times faster than the growth of world output. In 1990 outflows were valued at $US234 billion (UNCTAD, 1993b, p. 1).

The acceleration of FDI in the 1980s can be attributed to the effects of a number of factors. The rise of Japanese multinational enterprises added considerably to the world growth of FDI (see Strange, 1993, pp. 64–71). Japanese FDI doubled between 1975–77 and 1981–83, and then increased by a factor of eight between 1981–83 and 1987–90. Next, developing countries' attitudes towards inward FDI changed (see Buckley and Clegg, 1991). During the 1960s and the 1970s there was a general disposition on the part of developing countries to employ restrictive policies on the entry, ownership and operations of foreign affiliate firms. However, apart from political changes, the worldwide recession of the 1980s spurred a shift in attitude by these countries away from debt as a source of capital in favour of equity.[3] It became common practice for developing countries to pursue novel FDI-promoting policies, especially certain of those in south-east Asia (UNCTC, 1992, pp. 1–15; Lecraw, 1991).

Another factor is that the sectoral composition of FDI flows has moved from natural resource-oriented FDI into the less developed countries and import-substituting FDI in the developed markets towards integrated methods of international production. It would appear that trade liberalization and market growth in services has resulted in the share of services in total FDI flows into the EU (both extra- and intra-EU) generally exceeding 60 per cent in the period 1984–88 (UNCTC, 1991).

Historically low tariff rates and improved transport and communications technology have meant that the different stages of production in manufacturing processes can be separated and located in their least cost location. This is known as 'vertical disintegration' and is discussed later. The effect has been an expansion of multinational operations in those industries in which communications and transportation technology enables production stages to be coordinated in spite of considerable distance. These industries include many services, as international information flows are often all that is required to integrate services' production internationally. The deregulation of service industries has added considerable impetus to the move to internationalize.

---

[3] During recession equity is favoured by developing countries as a source of finance because its value varies with the fortunes of the host country, whereas debt maintains its value irrespective of the debtors' ability to pay.

THE SCALE OF MULTINATIONAL ENTERPRISE

United States multinational firms' sales revenues from operations outside the US stand at around twice their earnings from exports from the US – a figure which demonstrates how far the performance of leading multinationals is linked to the organization of production on a global scale. Although it will not concern us here, this spanning of national boundaries, and the progressive disengagement of the fortunes of the firm from the fortunes of any particular country, is the origin of host country versus MNE conflicts over employment, the balance of payments, technology and fiscal issues, and so on. The interesting point is that when MNEs become highly multinational, the position of home countries becomes not dissimilar to that of just another host. For an excellent discussion of these wider issues, which feed back to government attempts to control the activities of MNEs and the flow of FDI, see Dunning (1993).

While the creation of new technology is usually quite centralized, its application within a multinational is widespread, and in many ways the MNE can be seen as a conduit to speed up the adoption of new production methods in remote locations (Pearce, 1990; see also Chapter 9). Technology-intensive multinationals traditionally have favoured affiliates reporting to product group headquarters, while marketing-intensive MNEs have generally given precedence to country or regional headquarters. Most of the larger MNEs, however, have moved towards the adoption of a matrix structure, which involves simultaneous reporting to each type of headquarters – a structure that facilitates responsiveness to national markets and the efficient employment of technology and organization of production at the international level.

The sizes of the leading 50 multinationals in the world and their countries of origin can be seen in Table 7.1. The most frequent nationality out of the leading 100 firms is Japanese, with 26 firms. MNEs of US origin number 19, and then there is a considerable hiatus. Then follow two nations with eight MNEs (the UK and Germany), four with seven (the Netherlands, Switzerland, Italy and France), Sweden with six firms, Spain with three, and Norway and Canada with one apiece. All in all the top 100 multinationals are accounted for by just twelve advanced industrial nations.

The sales figures of Table 7.1 are in respect of worldwide sales, that is they include both domestic sales and sales abroad, whether by foreign production or export. This is quite representative of the available data: it is all too infrequent that even large firms disclose their foreign production or employment figures. The effect is, as here, to make countries with the largest internal economies appear to spawn the largest multinationals. The US and Japan certainly are source countries to many of the world's leading multinationals, but including domestic sales as well as sales abroad clearly tends to overstate their presence. A country like the UK, by contrast, has a far more modest internal economy, but the degree of commitment of its eight leading multinationals to international operations will certainly be above the average. This argument applies with even greater force to small home countries such as Sweden.

Table 7.1   The largest multinational enterprises from the developed countries, percentage distribution, 1988

Firm	Industry	Home country	Percentage
1. Resource-intensive industries			
Exxon Corp.	Petroleum	US	27.26
Royal Dutch Petroleum Co.	Petroleum	Netherlands	26.77
Mobil Corp.	Petroleum	US	16.51
British Petroleum Co. Plc.	Petroleum	UK	15.82
Shell Transport and Trading Co.	Petroleum	UK	13.63
Total			100.00
Value $US million			291 848
2. Motor vehicle industry			
General Motors		US	34.96
Ford Motor Co.		US	26.69
Toyota Motor Co.		Japan	15.35
Daimler Benz AG		Germany	12.08
Ente Nazionale Idrocarburi (E.N.I.)		Italy	10.92
Total			100.00
Value $US million			346 359
3. Electrical equipment industry			
IBM Corp.		US	30.25
General Electric Co.		US	25.04
Siemens AG		Germany	17.13
Philips N.V.		Netherlands	14.38
Matsushita Electrical Industrial Co.		Japan	13.20
Total			100.00
Value $US million			197 318
4. Chemicals industry			
Dainippon Ink & Chemicals Inc.		Japan	28.08
BASF AG		Germany	19.02
Hoechst AG		Germany	18.36
Bayer AG		Germany	18.14
Imperial Chemical Industries Plc.		UK	16.40
Total			100.00
Value $US million			127 054
5. Distributive Trade			
C. Itoh & Co. Ltd.		Japan	22.58
Mitsui & Co. Ltd.		Japan	21.38
Sumitomo Corp.		Japan	20.72
Marubeni Corp.		Japan	19.99
Nissho Iwai Corp.		Japan	15.34
Total			100.00
Value $US million			525 186

Firm	Industry	Home country	Percentage
6. Communication			
Nippon Telephone and Telegraph Co.		Japan	26.93
American Telephone and Telegraph Co.		US	21.08
Bell South Corp.		US	17.04
NYNEX Corp.		US	15.18
British Telecommunications Plc.		UK	11.81
Finanziaria Telefonica S.p.a.(STET)		Italy	7.96
Total			100.00
Value $US million			167049
7. Transport			
United Parcels Service of America Inc.		US	27.90
United Airlines		US	22.80
A.M.R. Corp.		US	22.32
Compagnie Nationale Air France S.A.		France	15.05
Danzas A.G.		Switzerland	11.93
Total			100.00
Value $US million			39538
8. Construction			
Kansai Electric Power Co.		Japan	38.25
B.T.R. Plc.		UK	23.32
Bouygues S.A.		France	20.08
Italiana per Infrastrutture a l'Assetto del Territorio S.p.a.(Italstat)		Italy	9.34
Skanska A.B.		Sweden	9.01
Total			100.00
Value $US million			41809
9. Finance and Insurance			
A. Finance			
Dai Ichi Kangyo Bank Ltd.		Japan	21.43
Sumitomo Bank Ltd.		Japan	20.91
Fuji Bank Ltd.		Japan	20.22
Sanwa Bank Ltd.		Japan	19.03
Mitsubishi Bank Ltd.		Japan	18.40
Total			100.00
Value $US million			2012732
B. Insurance			
Prudential Insurance Co. of America		US	34.51
Metropolitan Life		US	27.99
Prudential Corp.		UK	16.32
Nationale-Nederlanden N.V.		Netherlands	12.32
Norwich Union Life Insurance Society		UK	8.86
Total			100.00
Value $US million			336677

Adapted from:
United Nations Transnational Corporations and Management Division (1993). Table 21.

In order to discern the extent of the multinational dimension to operations it is often necessary to turn to statistics on foreign direct investment. These more accurately reflect the direct involvement of MNEs outside their country of origin than do worldwide sales figures. Table 7.2 presents statistics for available years on multinational enterprises' FDI capital stock and employment (both outward and inward) in respect of the developed countries. The main caveat with these data concerns the valuation of the capital stock, which does not necessary align with the IMF definition. As a consequence, the comparability between countries is impaired to an unknown extent. However, this does not bias the ratio of outward to inward investment for each country. The employment figures, by their nature, are not open to pronounced valuation bias, and so give a true reflection of the magnitudes across countries.

As a group, developed countries are net outward investors, and it is clear that the most developed countries have ratios of outward to inward multinational activity greater than one. Countries unequivocally in this group include Germany, the Netherlands, the UK, Finland, Sweden, and the US. It has been suggested that countries follow an investment development path with respect to net outward investment (gross outward minus gross inward FDI). In particular, such a notion suggests that during the early stages in the internationalization of economies the net FDI position is negative, later rising to a positive value, but then perhaps falling back (Dunning, 1986a, 1986b; Dunning and Narula, 1994). Working in terms of the ratio of outward to inward FDI, this argument certainly appears to apply in the cases of pre-eminent foreign investing countries such as the US and the UK, whose ratios have been higher in the past. Their decline would appear to be partly a result of other countries catching up over a number of decades.

The differences between the FDI and the employment-based ratios are largely attributable to industry composition differences between outward and inward activity. For example, if most inward activity were in capital-intensive industries while most outward activity were in labour-intensive industries, it would follow that the outward to inward FDI ratio would be lower than the employment ratio. This situation would appear to be the case for the Netherlands, the UK, Finland, Sweden, and the US. Interestingly it is certainly not the case for Japan, which testifies to the high volume of capital-intensive outward FDI by Japanese firms in the developed countries in more recent years. During the 1960s and the 1970s Japanese multinational firms were characteristically labour-intensive foreign investors, investing predominantly in the economies of south-east Asia. This pattern of activity was dignified by a theoretical account put forward by Kojima (1978, 1990), to the effect that Japanese FDI was more beneficial than Western FDI as it better respected the law of comparative advantage, owing to its orientation towards labour-abundant host countries. Japan was characterized as the capital-abundant source country. Early Japanese FDI certainly did fit this account and did generate much employment in labour-intensive production. However, in the 1980s and 1990s new Japanese FDI clearly shows that this earlier pattern has been supplanted.

THE MULTINATIONALIZATION OF ECONOMIES

In the discussion so far it has been very difficult to gauge the actual importance of multinational activity either for home countries or for host countries. The magnitudes involved are undoubtedly large, but then so are the economies of the countries concerned. One solution is to look at the importance of FDI capital in relation to the total capital formation of economies, in effect to ask 'how multinationalized' they are. Table 7.3 studies the period 1976 to 1990, grouped into three sub-periods. Because there are too few countries with accurate estimates of domestic capital stock, the table is constructed in terms of average annual gross fixed capital formation, and the proportion that, on average, outward and inward FDI flows constitute of this. In general, FDI capital flows are strongly linked to the size of the FDI stock because of the importance of reinvested earnings. A few ratios are negative, which probably reflects disinvestment over the period studied. However, it is worth recalling that, over a short time span, negative figures may result from the refinancing of FDI rather than from the real liquidation of the capital stock. In looking at these figures, contrasts will be seen with the picture gleaned from Tables 7.1 and 7.2. For instance, the US appears to have more inward than outward FDI. This is because inflows have come to dominate outflows in recent years as the US has become more attractive as a host economy, and the stock positions will accordingly be slowly adjusting in the same direction.

The most multinationalized economies are the UK, Belgium and Luxembourg ('Bleu'), and the Netherlands. It is generally true that small economies are the most open in terms of both trade and investment (FDI often follows trade patterns). In the case of the UK its island geography, sizeable internal market, and extensive history in international trade and investment account for its leading position in both inward and outward multinational activity. The United States might appear at first sight to have unduly low indices, but in fact the size of the US economy means that it has a tendency towards being a closed rather than an open economy. Quite simply, the vast internal economic area of the US means that most economic resources and production conditions can be found within its borders, thereby causing extensive internal trade and cutting the need for international trade and investment. The fact that the US in absolute terms is a leading source country can be attributed theoretically to the absolute size of the US, as in the Product Cycle Model (PCM) of trade and investment, which is discussed later (see Vernon, 1966, 1979).

Japan clearly is more active in outward multinational activity than it is as a host, a fact which has caused concern for firms facing difficulty in entering the Japanese market. Small developed economies such as Denmark, Finland, Norway, Sweden and Switzerland have become net outward investing countries from a relatively small base, while the larger economies of France and Germany have built up extensive multinational activities abroad that exceed inward multinational activity. Portugal and Spain at present host more multinational activity than their firms engage in abroad, as foreign firms seek low-cost

Table 7.2 Foreign direct investment stock and employment of multinational enterprises, by country for available years, $US million, and numbers employed

| Developed countries | Years | FDI Stock | | Employment | | Outward/Inward | |
		Inward	Outward	Inward	Outward	FDI	Employment
Europe; EU							
Bleu	1990; 1978	28588	22651	348900	—	0.79	—
Denmark	1990; 1985	9192	10441	86685	78000	1.14	0.90
France	1990; 1981	51121	74833	4473000	791000	1.46	0.18
FRG	1990; 1989	93456	155133	1768000	2154000	1.66	1.22
Greece	1990; 1977	13011	—	75744	—	—	—
Ireland	1990; 1987	5405	—	84761	—	—	—
Italy	1990; 1988	57985	56105	504205	373726	0.97	0.74
Netherlands	1990; 1987	54982	87325	196000	783000	1.59	3.99
Portugal	1990; 1981	2019	199	136620	—	0.10	—
Spain	1990; 1977	41951	14987	1244724	231245	0.36	0.19
UK	1990; 1988	205618	244753	635200	1390000	1.19	2.19
Other Europe							
Austria	1990	6816	1360	26200	60871	0.20	0.23
Finland	1990; 1987	4112	8188	59800	131400	1.99	2.20
Norway	1990; 1987	2450	2757	106879	—	1.13	—
Sweden	1990; 1987	7309	24850	131254	487707	3.40	3.72
Switzerland	1990; 1989	25946	52613	940641	—	2.03	—
North America							
US	1990; 1988	403735	423183	3844200	6403500	1.05	1.67
Canada	1990; 1976	108023	74703	778915	—	0.69	—

Other developed

Australia	1990; 1987	74451	27357	200183	—	0.37	—
Japan	1990	18432	310808	182299	1549669	16.86	8.50
New Zealand	1990; 1989	3242	2322	218242	—	0.72	—
Turkey	1990; 1987	1320	154	120000	—	0.12	—

Notes:
— Signifies that data are not available or are not applicable.
Dates given for each country refer to FDI and employment, where applicable.

Adapted from:
United Nations Transnational Corporations and Management Division (1993), tables 1 of country chapters, and United Nations Conference on Trade and Development (1993b), Annex Table 2.

Table 7.3   Percentage share of FDI flows in gross domestic capital formation, annual averages, 1976–90

Country	1976–1980 Outward	Inward	1981–1985 Outward	Inward	1986–1990 Outward	Inward
Europe: EU						
Bleu	2.7	5.8	1.3	7.7	14.2	15.5
Denmark	0.8	0.3	1.7	0.9	5.2	2.9
France	1.7	2	2.5	2	8.1	3.9
Germany	2.7	1.1	3.4	1.1	6.2	1.7
Greece	—	6.5	—	7.1	—	7.9
Ireland	—	6.9	—	4.1	—	1
Italy	0.6	0.7	1.9	1.2	2.3	2.2
Netherlands	14.5	4.5	15.4	6	19.3	12.2
Portugal	0.1	1.7	0.3	3.4	0.5	9.7
Spain	0.5	3.2	0.9	5.4	1.6	8.8
UK	11.6	8.2	12.4	5.6	18.4	13.2
Other Europe						
Austria	0.5	1	0.9	1.7	2.3	2
Finland	0.9	0.4	1.9	0.7	8.1	1.9
Iceland	—	1.6	—	3.7	0.4	−0.5
Norway	1	3.1	3.9	1.2	5.3	3.3
Sweden	2.8	0.5	5.8	1.2	21.2	3.5
Switzerland[a]	—	—	9.2	4	10.2	5
North America						
Canada	4.5	1.8	5.4	−0.7	5.1	3.6
United States	4	2	1.6	2.9	2.5	6
Other developed countries						
Australia	1.1	5.1	2.6	5.1	5.9	9.9
Israel	0.1	1.5	2.8	2.4	1.5	2.9
Japan	0.8	0.05	1.4	0.1	3.9	0.04
New Zealand	1.6	6.3	1.9	5.5	9.6	9.9
South Africa[b]	1.6	−1	1.2	0.6	0.3	−0.01
Turkey[c]	—	0.3	—	0.9	−0.01	2.5
Total	3	1.9	2.7	2.1	5.2	4.1

Notes:
— Signifies that data are not available or are not applicable.
[a] Outward data for the middle period are for the years 1983–1985.
[b] Outward data for the middle period are for the years 1986–1989.
[c] Outward data for the middle period are for the years 1987–1990.

Adapted from:
United Nations Transnational Corporations and Management Division (1983), Tables 7 and 15.

production bases within the European Union. Eventually, even these countries are likely to become net outward investors in their own right. One final observation is that, as a group, the developed economies have a higher outward than inward ratio, reflecting their collective net investment position *vis-à-vis* the rest of the world.

THE SECTORAL PICTURE

In the last 15–20 years there has been an important modification to the factors that are seen as the determinants of FDI. The predominant notion in the 1960s and the early 1970s was based on the US model of manufacturing investment in Europe, as encapsulated by the Product Cycle Model (PCM) initiated by Raymond Vernon (Vernon, 1966). This school of thought saw the superiority of source country firms' technology (i.e., the US) as the driving factor in explaining FDI. Foreign direct investment was primarily a medium for the transfer of technology. This wisdom was challenged as technological prowess became less concentrated in the US and, during the 1980s, as service industries became increasingly significant in multinational activity – industries in which firms do not rely on scientific technology for their competitiveness. It is now argued that firms may actually invest in countries where the native industry has either a technological advantage (in manufacturing activities) or a critical mass (e.g., external economies in financial services) (see also Chapter 12). Accordingly, inward investment can be linked to host country economic structural strength, in addition to the more obvious motive of local market servicing via FDI to reduce spatial costs (e.g., as in Buckley and Casson, 1981).

From Table 7.4 it is evident that industrial activities generally form a minority of inward multinational activity. The averages for the developed regions as a whole are not too dissimilar, being within the range 34–47 per cent. The variation between countries largely reflects the character of their economic structure. The countries with higher proportions in these activities are those with either strong manufacturing bases, large internal markets, or specific natural resources. The economies with the most extensive inward investment in finance and insurance are, in order of importance, Belgium and Luxembourg (Bleu), New Zealand, the Netherlands, Switzerland, Ireland, and France. While this gives a picture of the relative importance for these countries, percentage shares by their nature abstract from the absolute size of the multinational activity itself. This is why it is quite possible for small countries to have impressively large shares – but in narrow activities. This said, clearly these activities are important in Switzerland as well as France. Tertiary activities other than finance and insurance are highly variable between countries, and no particular pattern emerges.

A comparison of the sectoral breakdown of leading multinational outward sales with inward sales presents a quandary. How can the proportion of outward MNE sales in the industrial sector on a regional and country-by-country basis

Table 7.4 Sales of the largest foreign affiliates in the host economy and the largest multinational enterprises abroad, by country, 1988

Country/region	Inward				Outward			
	Industrial	Tertiary	Finance and insurance	Total $US million	Industrial	Tertiary	Finance and insurance	Total $US million
Western Europe	37.33	13.38	49.29	748648	16.93	6.29	76.78	7120858
EU	36.86	12.53	50.60	635505	16.76	5.47	77.77	5786352
Bleu	12.31	4.27	83.42	137143	13.99	5.54	80.47	340780
Denmark	61.85	30.14	8.01	8126	9.73	7.30	82.98	123074
France	35.05	14.67	50.29	106777	10.60	5.28	84.12	1341611
FRG	58.15	8.54	33.31	99003	20.09	2.41	77.50	1246867
Greece[a]	65.12	5.70	29.19	12	1.31	—	98.69	327
Ireland	29.60	17.49	52.91	15949	13.56	6.77	79.66	49514
Italy	42.35	18.83	38.82	40497	20.55	6.37	73.08	640089
Netherlands	31.51	11.25	57.24	59771	25.30	4.64	70.06	653276
Portugal	31.79	37.72	30.49	6492	6.86	0.64	92.49	54950
Spain	45.50	10.05	44.45	43978	7.60	2.94	89.47	272566
UK	46.33	19.73	33.93	117756	17.79	9.88	72.33	1063298
Other Europe								
Austria	34.87	24.82	40.31	19633	6.49	3.28	90.23	182905
Finland	20.09	55.17	24.74	6424	18.62	8.19	73.19	161504
Norway	64.58	26.70	8.72	12358	19.55	4.42	76.03	136050
Sweden	46.12	33.26	20.62	13448	28.26	12.50	59.23	276424
Switzerland	37.37	7.10	55.53	61280	15.48	12.41	72.11	577622
North America	47.54	16.09	36.37	352968	25.49	11.38	63.13	2412068
US	42.32	16.13	41.56	258518	30.46	11.80	57.74	1872811
Canada	61.82	16.00	22.17	94450	8.23	9.91	81.85	539257

Other developed	34.82	28.23	36.95	84426	14.75	8.72	76.53	481596
Australia	36.87	35.57	27.57	64314	13.60	6.90	79.49	343590
Japan	32.68	25.15	42.17	926	6.60	16.78	76.62	31993
New Zealand	21.03	4.00	74.97	15035	18.40	37.75	43.85	34247
Turkey[a]	53.59	2.96	43.45	4152	22.14	—	77.86	71766

Notes:
Figures may not sum precisely to 100 due to rounding.
— Signifies that data are not available or are not applicable.
[a] Finance and Insurance includes all Tertiary Sector for Greece and Turkey.

Adapted from:
United Nations Transnational Corporations and Management Division (1993), country tables 17 and 18.

systematically be so much lower than the inward proportion, especially given the well-known fact that developed country MNEs invest mainly in other developed countries? For western Europe, the EU, North America and 'Other Developed' the shares of the industrial sector in outward sales are, respectively, 37 per cent, again 37 per cent, 47 per cent, and 35 per cent, while in inward sales the figures are as low as 17 per cent, 17 per cent, 25 per cent, and 15 per cent. It is possible to argue that some of the difference represents developed country MNE sales in the developing countries, but this cannot account for such a wide gap. There is no simple explanation, but rather a combination of several.

Firstly, while inward data (for both sales and FDI) are generally classified by the activity of the affiliate, outward data are usually classified by the main activity of the parent, which may differ considerably from that of the foreign affiliate. Secondly, the use of sales as the measure of multinational involvement imparts a bias in favour of service, particularly finance and insurance, firms. Were FDI (more closely associated with capital intensity) to be used, the picture would look very different. This links into the possibility of size bias between the inward and outward samples, where the largest outward investors happen to be in finance and insurance for the majority of source countries, while the largest foreign affiliates are in industrial activities. Some credibility is lent to this view by the fact that service firms have tended to grow large domestically, and have only comparatively recently been significant foreign investors. Each of these arguments is likely to be valid to some extent, but each of them testifies to how cautiously one must interpret any statistics on the operations of MNEs.

THE MOVEMENT FROM FDI IN MANUFACTURING TO SERVICES

There are a number of reasons why a redirection towards multinational activity in services should have occurred in recent years. Generally they relate to the fact that many service activities are best conducted in some degree of proximity to the customer (see Clegg, 1993). In contrast, manufacturing activities can often be quite remote from the ultimate customer, with the output traded across extensive geographical space. In the scheme of international trade theory, the tradability of most manufactures is high while that of services (especially manpower-intensive services) is low (see also Chapter 10).

Firstly, it is commonly argued that service firms follow manufacturing firms into the multinational arena. As the scale of manufacturing FDI reaches a critical size it becomes economic for service firms that cater for manufacturing clients to themselves become multinational, to better service their multinational clients. The second point is a corollary of the argument in the foregoing paragraph: that trade barriers against service firms within their potential foreign markets have traditionally been in the form of the control of their rights of establishment. In the manufacturing sector, it is often a sufficient form of protection for domestic industry that governments apply trade barriers (mainly tariffs and quotas) to imports of the traded outputs of foreign firms. As trade barriers of this type are either impossible or prohibitively costly in the case of services trade, and given that service firms have a preference for local production, the most effective form of protection against competitive foreign firms is to deny or limit severely their right of establishment. It follows that the liberalization of international business in the manufacturing sector has relied on tariff barrier reduction. However, in the service sector the counterpart is liberalization through deregulation.

A third leading factor has been that many manufacturing firms have increasingly engaged in the provision of services, notably in marketing and distributive activities, in foreign markets in order to increase their competitive presence. There has been a tendency for manufacturing firms to diversify into services provision domestically, and this proclivity has been to some extent evident internationally. As noted above, inward FDI is commonly classified according to the industry of the foreign affiliate (rather than the industry of the parent enterprise), therefore taking snapshots of affiliates over time highlights the growth in multinational activity in service activities.

Table 7.5 looks at the sectoral distribution of developed countries' outward FDI stocks, for a selection of available years, in order to gain an impression of recent trends. Over the period from 1975 to the late 1980s the share of the manufacturing sector in outward FDI has tended to decline or remain roughly static. There is one notable exception in the case of Austria, where the proportion of secondary sector FDI has risen. However, foreign direct investment in the tertiary sector has almost universally risen over the period, notwithstanding some temporary reductions in shares around 1980. The two countries not to show an overall shift towards services are Austria and Norway though, as noted in the table, the separation of the tertiary sector from other activities is incomplete for these two countries and consequently the data should not be relied upon.

By the late 1980s the outward FDI of four developed countries was either above or in the region of 70 per cent: Portugal (78), Denmark (74), Spain (73), and Japan (68). Portugal and Spain are relative newcomers to extensive outward FDI; as a result their sectoral pattern reflects most vividly the new directions in foreign investment patterns. Japan has built up outward FDI at a tremendous rate, and so also exhibits the same shift, while Denmark, as a small country, has effected a sizeable shift, though from a comparatively small base. The most compelling redirection of FDI towards services in percentage terms over the period has been recorded by Finland and Japan (28), the Netherlands (27), Australia (24), and Spain (23). Denmark's difference of 17 per cent from 1982 to 1990 is equally noteworthy. The more mature foreign investing countries, such as the US, UK, and France, record among the more modest redirections towards services, though in absolute terms their shifts will outweigh those of the smaller and newer foreign investors.

According to Table 7.6, countries that host the highest percentage shares of inward FDI in the tertiary sector are Denmark (68), France (67), Germany (64), Italy, Norway and Sweden (58). Again the UK has a more modest proportion at 35 per cent, and Japan has just 36 per cent inward FDI in the tertiary sector,

Table 7.5   The sectoral distribution of developed countries' outward FDI stock, by major source region, percentage distribution for available years

Country	Year	Primary	Secondary	Tertiary
Western Europe: EU				
Denmark	1990	0.8	25.4	73.8
	1982	0.4	43.1	56.5
France	1989	13.4	39.9	46.7
	1980	15	41.2	43.8
	1975	22.1	38.2	39.7
Germany	1990	2.3	39.1	58.6
	1980	4.4	47.6	48
	1976	4.5	48.3	47.2
Italy	1990	8.2	33.6	58.2
	1980	19.2	50.2	30.6
	1975	31	28.9	40.1
Netherlands	1989	35.1	23.9	41
	1980	51.6	29.4	19
	1975	46.8	38.6	14.6
Portugal	1988	1.3	21.2	77.5
	1985	1.8	24.4	73.8
Spain	1990	8.9	18.7	72.4
	1980	11.2	40.5	48.3
	1975	13.1	37.4	49.5
UK	1987	27	34.4	38.6
	1981	27.9	35.9	36.2
	1974	23	50.4	26.6
Other Western Europe				
Austria[a]	1988	—	67.2	32.8
	1980	—	43.3	56.7
Finland	1989	—	58.9	41.1
	1980	0.4	64.9	34.7
	1975	—	86.4	13.6
Norway[b]	1988	11.6	33.5	54.9
	1980	2.5	40.4	57.1
	1975	0.1	32.7	67.2
Sweden	1988	0.2	75.8	24
	1986	0.32	76.8	22.9
Switzerland	1989	—	58.7	41.3
	1986	—	69.6	30.4
North America				
Canada	1990	6.6	53.1	40.3
	1980	9.9	64.2	25.9
	1975	9.2	62.3	28.4
US	1990	8.3	44.3	47.4
	1980	12.1	49	38.9
	1977	12.7	47.6	39.7

Other developed countries

Australia	1990	14.5	28.2	57.3
	1980	19.6	33.3	44.9
	1975	25.6	40.9	33.4
Japan	1991	5.7	26.7	67.6
	1980	21.9	34.4	43.7
	1975	28.1	32.4	39.5

Notes:

Figures may not sum precisely to 100 due to rounding.

— Signifies that data are not available or are not applicable.

[a]Data on tertiary sector include all sectors other than the secondary sector.

[b]Includes portfolio investments.

Adapted from:

United Nations Transnational Corporations and Management Division (1993), Table 18.

reflecting factors such as the size of domestic markets for manufactures coupled with host industry structure. Despite the significant variation between host countries, the trend towards a higher proportion of FDI in services is apparent in the inward statistics. Apart from those countries where there is a question over the sectoral allocation of the data, only Greece, Portugal, Sweden and South Africa show a decline in the domestic share of FDI in the tertiary sector. The unduly short period for comparison for Sweden raises doubts over the accuracy of the data (based on cumulated balance of payments flows), while the movement in South Africa's share is minuscule.

The decreased shares in Greece and Portugal are the result of these countries increasingly acting as production bases for low-cost manufactures within the European Union, i.e., the relocation of investment to maintain competitiveness (considered further below). Hosts which record the largest percentage shifts towards services are Turkey (32), Germany (30), Italy (29), Spain (24), the Netherlands (19), and Japan (18). Again it must be said that the percentage shifts in the US and UK (13 and 8) if viewed in absolute terms will be considerably more important than absolute shifts seen in smaller host economies. It is therefore clearly borne out by the data that the shift towards service activities is both widespread and substantial. This lends credence to the arguments made out above both that service sector multinationals are in the ascendancy and that multinationals from other sectors are also increasingly engaged in FDI in services. The implications of this are that the world is set for a more pronounced interpenetration and comprehensive integration of economies than has ever been witnessed before.

Table 7.6 The sectoral distribution of developed countries' inward FDI stock, percentage distribution for available years

Country	Year	Primary	Secondary	Tertiary
Western Europe: EU				
Bleu	1980	—	83.4	16.6
	1975	—	88	12
Denmark	1990	1.9	29.7	68.4
	1982	13	29.7	57.2
France	1989	1.4	32	66.7
	1980	2.6	35.8	61.6
	1975	3	37.4	59.6
Germany	1990	0.1	36.3	63.6
	1980	0.5	59.3	40.2
	1976	0.4	66.1	33.5
Greece	1984	7.2	72.7	20.1
	1981	2.4	63.4	34.2
	1976	2.9	70.6	26.5
Ireland	1986	2.2	65	32.8
	1981	3.4	74.8	21.7
Italy	1990	3.5	38.2	58.3
	1980	10.2	58.7	31.1
	1975	11	60	29
Netherlands	1989	30.9	22.9	46.2
	1980	32.4	28.1	39.5
	1975	41.9	30.7	27.4
Portugal	1988	7.2	38.2	54.6
	1980	10	42.5	47.5
	1975	11.4	29.9	58.7
Spain	1989	3.6	50.4	46
	1980	2	72.8	25.2
	1975	1.9	76.3	21.9
UK	1987	29.1	36.2	34.7
	1981	34.3	40.6	25.1
	1974	28.2	45.6	26.2
Other Western Europe				
Austria[a]	1988	—	256.3	43.7
	1980	—	57.2	42.8
	1975	—	48.8	51.2
Finland	1989	—	45.3	54.7
	1980	—	30.2	69.8
	1975	—	24.6	75.4
Norway[b]	1988	13.2	28.6	58.2
	1980	0.9	40.2	59
	1975	1.5	45.3	53.2
Sweden	1988	0.1	41.9	58
	1986	0.1	29.9	70

North America

Canada	1990	4	63.3	32.7
	1980	7.5	67.5	25
	1975	9.3	66.2	24.5
US^c	1990	3.5	46.8	49.7
	1980	4.4	51	44.6
	1975	22.5	41.2	36.4

Other developed countries

Australia	1991	14.5	29.1	56.3
	1980	21.7	31.1	45
	1975	22.3	34.4	43.4
Japan	1990	—	63.9	36.1
	1980	—	77.7	22.3
	1975	—	81.6	18.4
South Africa	1986	5.9	36.8	57.3
	1984	5.5	36.3	58.2
Turkey	1990	3.1	52.2	44.7
	1979	0.8	79.4	19.8
	1975	1.1	86.3	12.6

Notes:
Figures may not sum precisely to 100 due to rounding and unallocated industries.
— Signifies that data are not available or are not applicable.
^{a}Data on tertiary sector include primary sector.
^{b}Sectoral distribution includes portfolio investment.
^{c}Data on the primary sector include all activities of the petroleum industry from extraction to processing and distribution. These activities cannot be delineated in the original data source.

Adapted from:
United Nations Transnational Corporations and Management Division (1993), Table 10.

LOCATIONAL SHIFTS IN GLOBAL MULTINATIONAL ACTIVITY AND THE THREAT OF VERTICAL DISINTEGRATION

The notion of vertical integration is well known in economic theory. It refers to the combined administration of separate stages of production (see also Chapter 3). It is most frequently applied to bringing adjacent upstream and downstream stages under common ownership. It does not necessarily imply the geographical centralization of stages although, other things being equal, this would occur where it reduces total communication and transport costs. In contrast, vertical disintegration is taken to mean the geographical separation of stages of production, frequently while under unified ownership by a multinational enterprise.

In fact, this blurring of national boundaries for the purposes of production, marketing and (to a lesser extent) research and development has been a progressive feature. A corollary of this is increased trade in both intermediate and final goods and services between countries, but within the internal economies of MNEs. On account of the increased specialization between parts of the multinational, the ratio of intermediate trade relative to final trade tends to rise. Trade between firms within a group of companies (the multinational enterprise) is often known as intra-group or intra-firm trade.

The logic behind these developments is to reduce unnecessary duplication in production, thereby increasing productive efficiency and competitiveness, and to maximize the exploitation of comparative advantage. This represents a dramatic movement away from the servicing of foreign markets via small foreign facilities, often of sub-optimal scale, confined to selling only within the local host market. This pattern was common in the 1950s and 1960s, when trade barriers between countries were relatively high and markets were effectively segmented. With the progressive reduction in trade barriers on industrial products under successive General Agreement on Tariffs and Trade (GATT) rounds (and latterly in services), firms were moved to treat markets in a more unified manner, and to reorganize production between countries. This reorganization of FDI has been given further impetus between countries pursuing market integration, such as the European Union, and new flows of FDI increasingly treat markets at the regional rather than national level. Parallel with the freeing of trade in both intermediate and final goods has been the rise in intra-firm international trade in services and in technology. Multinationals which have gone furthest along this route are closest to becoming 'borderless firms'.

This vertical disintegration has accounted for much of the relocation of production stages away from traditional centres of business activity. The desire to maintain cost competitiveness first drove Western MNEs to locate production in Asia and the Pacific, thereby reducing home country employment in gross terms. Vertical disintegration means that a near-full complement of production stages no longer follows with foreign investment, i.e., investment is 'pared down'. This also makes it less likely that the smallest and least developed countries will secure large-scale inward FDI. Although they may succeed in attracting just the labour-intensive stages, these may have less permanence and commensurately fewer spillover benefits.

The regional trends in multinational activity encapsulate many of these current issues in international studies (Table 7.7). One of the foremost problems is the relative stagnation or decline in the share of multinational business involving the less developed countries as a group – a fact which severely hinders their prospects for integration within the world trading system. In the less developed countries, MNEs seek high wage-bill productivity, not simply low labour costs, so skills and the work ethic are important locational attractants. With already modest shares of FDI certain regions risk further diminishing shares of world inward multinational activity. Only Asia and the Pacific reveals any clear growth in inward FDI. The picture otherwise consists of a steeply declining share for Africa in inward FDI, a more gradual decline for Latin America and the Caribbean, and the absence of any clear trend for western Asia. This is a direct outcome of world recession in the 1980s and of the international debt crisis, which severely reduced the motive for inward market-seeking FDI

Table 7.7 Foreign direct investment stock, percentage distribution for the leading regions of the world, 1980–90

Regions	Inward stock			Outward stock		
	1980	1985	1990	1980	1985	1990
Western Europe	40.72	31.80	40.77	43.81	43.10	46.88
EU	37.39	28.82	37.65	37.73	36.85	41.32
Other Western Europe	3.33	2.97	3.12	6.08	6.25	5.57
North America	30.05	36.05	34.21	47.09	41.98	30.87
Other developed countries	7.84	6.53	7.25	8.68	14.14	21.58
Developed countries total	78.61	74.38	82.23	99.58	99.22	99.33
Africa	5.20	3.28	1.30	0.08	0.06	0.03
Asia and the Pacific	7.59	9.54	8.08	0.18	0.30	0.38
Western Asia	0.77	4.01	1.90	0.21	0.17	0.00
Latin America and the Caribbean	8.81	8.78	6.49	0.16	0.27	0.19
Less developed and industrializing countries total	22.36	25.62	17.77	0.42	0.78	0.67
Total	100.00	100.00	100.00	100.00	100.00	100.00
Value $US million	448248	685293	1496114	515537	690227	1612980

Notes:

Figures may not sum precisely to 100 due to rounding.

Adapted from:
United Nations Transnational Corporations and Management Division (1993b), Annex Table 2.

into developing countries. Countries that fared better in attracting inward FDI were those that pursued an export-based strategy.

The sum of the less developed countries' investment abroad is under 1 per cent of the world total. Even the newly industrializing countries of Asia and the Pacific are unable to muster more than 0.03 per cent between them, which highlights the fact that the established home countries at present have an across-the-board dominance. However, the strategy of the new multinationals from these countries will, like that of Japanese firms before them, be to extend abroad in key industries linked to existing trade advantage, from which later diversification can occur (see the penultimate section).

While there are few clear trends in the pattern of multinational activity in the developed regions, since the mid-1980s there has been an upward surge in inward FDI into western Europe, and particularly into the EU. Assuming that the effects of market integration are confirmed as a leading cause (Clegg, 1995), this would suggest the later emergence of a surge in inward investment into the North American continent.

The quasi-regional analysis masks important sub-trends that can only be addressed at the country level, for instance, how to interpret the rather unsatisfactory category of 'other developed countries', whose outward multi-national activity has mushroomed. Table 7.8 confirms that this particular phenomenon is almost entirely due to the growth of Japanese investment abroad, to 19 per cent of the developed country total by 1990. However, a word of

Table 7.8 Foreign direct investment stock, percentage distribution for developed countries and regions, 1980–90

Developed countries and regions	Inward stock			Outward stock		
	1980	1985	1990	1980	1985	1990
Western Europe	51.80	42.75	49.58	44.00	43.44	47.20
EU	47.57	38.76	45.79	37.89	37.14	41.59
Bleu	2.07	1.73	2.32	1.18	0.68	1.41
Denmark	1.19	0.71	0.75	0.40	0.32	0.65
France	4.39	3.77	4.16	2.38	2.96	4.67
Germany	10.40	7.24	7.60	8.40	8.75	9.68
Greece	1.28	1.63	1.06	—	—	—
Ireland	0.77	0.90	0.44	—	—	—
Italy	2.52	3.72	4.71	1.36	2.38	3.50
Netherlands	5.44	4.86	4.47	8.20	6.96	5.45
Spain	1.46	1.75	3.41	0.24	0.30	0.94
Portugal	0.16	0.16	0.16	0.00	0.01	0.01
United Kingdom	17.88	12.27	16.71	15.73	14.78	15.28
Other Western Europe	4.23	4.00	3.79	6.11	6.30	5.60
Austria	0.90	0.70	0.55	0.10	0.16	0.08
Finland	0.13	0.26	0.33	0.14	0.27	0.51
Norway	0.22	0.19	0.20	0.11	0.16	0.17
Sweden	0.58	0.86	0.59	1.57	2.02	1.55
Switzerland	2.41	1.97	2.11	4.19	3.69	3.28
North America	38.23	48.46	41.60	47.29	42.31	31.08
Canada	14.66	12.25	8.78	4.40	5.65	4.66
United States	23.57	36.22	32.82	42.89	36.66	26.41
Other developed countries	9.97	8.78	8.82	8.72	14.25	21.73
Australia	3.74	4.91	6.05	0.44	0.97	1.71
Japan	0.85	1.26	1.50	7.11	12.21	19.40
New Zealand	0.67	0.40	0.26	0.05	0.12	0.14
South Africa	4.69	2.14	0.90	1.11	0.95	0.48
Turkey	0.03	0.07	0.11	—	—	—
Total	100.00	100.00	100.00	100.00	100.00	100.00
Value US$M (current prices)	352369	509719	1230215	513346	684856	1602199

Notes:
Figures may not sum precisely to 100 due to rounding.
— denotes data are not available.

Adapted from:
United Nations Conference on Trade and Development (1993b), Annex Table 2.

caution is necessary, as Japanese multinational activity abroad is customarily measured using the cumulation of Ministry of Finance balance of payments flow data. This means that the FDI stock estimate can diverge significantly from the true figure. Historically this has tended to be an underestimate, but as profits are reinvested abroad and investments mature the position becomes more uncertain. However, there is no argument over the direction of the Japanese trajectory.

The leading host and home countries to multinationals are France, Germany, the Netherlands, the UK, Canada and the US. The retention of its share of inward stock by the UK testifies to the attraction of the UK market itself, and of the UK as a profitable production base within the EU. A telling comparison is that of the US and the UK as outward investing nations: while the US has lost share consistently (from owning over 40 per cent of the developed country total to just over 26 per cent), the UK has virtually maintained its share of 15 per cent over the period. This suggests that UK firms abroad are highly competitive, notwithstanding a declining trade performance in key sectors.

The deregulation of markets has had a perceptible impact on inward investment flows. Beginning at first as a set of national initiatives to reduce the scope of the public sector and to promote competition, as in the USA and the UK, the momentum towards deregulation as a means of eliminating trade barriers in key (frequently service) sectors will be maintained by the provisions of the Uruguay round, the completion of the Single European Market (SEM) of the European Union (EU), and the North American Free Trade Agreement (NAFTA) (see also Chapter 14). The independent effect of regional market integration on FDI inflows is notoriously difficult to disentangle from the effects of market growth and size. The literature on the European Community is inconclusive, although a critical review of the overall statistical evidence for the US supports the conclusion that historically the EC Common Customs Tariff wall has increased FDI inflows, i.e., a net substitution of FDI inflows for trade. This is to be expected for FDI and trade between areas that are separated by considerable distance. The reduction of internal EC tariff barriers appears to have promoted inward US FDI, and by extension it should be expected that the SEM programme will have a similar effect (Clegg, 1995).

There is no coherent information on the regional or metropolitan distribution of multinational activity within national economies. For an insight into what is likely to be happening, one has to have recourse to theory. Recent research suggests that multinationals' locational strategy is to seek out locationally immobile scarce factors. In the light of the discussion of vertical disintegration, these factors are those in which a separable stage (of the entire production process) is intensive. This means, for example, that research and development activity, which is intensive in professional scientists and engineers, will locate in or near metropolitan centres, where a pool of appropriate manpower already exists. Specific scarce factors such as these will therefore not only draw FDI to a country, but to a particular location within that country, and are crucial to national competitiveness (Casson, 1991).

In activities such as research and development, high value added manufacturing, and banking and finance, critical mass in professional manpower is crucial in securing investment – by both native MNEs and those from abroad. Foreign direct investment in production stages intensive in lower cost labour, for which labour costs are a high proportion of total costs, are more footloose. Such FDI is attracted to the industrial centres of lower income countries, which enjoy a comparative trade advantage in routine production. The output of these production units is then mainly exported to the higher income markets, or to the developed countries for further processing. As multinationals continually seek further economies of integrated production, and as trade barriers fall, the divorce of the location of production and the location of the market will tend to become more marked.

Market integration between countries in one sense constitutes an attempt to increase the locational attraction of member states, by reducing the cost of locating production close to the market. A large and integrated internal market is a key source of bargaining power in securing an enhanced share of economic activity. Within such areas, investment incentives can play a role in tipping the balance in favour of a particular location, if all other things are equal. However, there is, quite understandably, a rise in the competitive offering of such incentives by local governmental bodies, or the relaxation of regulations (as in, for instance, export processing zones in the lower income countries). These can be crucial in developing an industrial base, which in turn attracts further inward investment through the generation of external economies.

MULTINATIONAL ENTERPRISES AND THE LESS DEVELOPED COUNTRIES

Research suggests that the less developed host country should pursue a cautiously liberal inward investment policy (with controls on only the most sensitive industries) to encourage the inflow of knowledge, coupled with an equally liberal outward regime (see Dunning, 1993; see also Chapters 11 and 12). This enables firms to develop competitive foreign market servicing strategies, thereby promoting export sales via sales and production affiliates abroad (see Buckley and Ghauri, 1993; Young *et al.*, 1989). While the foregoing reasons from the experience mainly of developed-country multinationals, the principles of choosing an appropriate strategy apply to all firms engaged in international business.

The leading host countries amongst this group in 1990 are clearly to be found in the Asian and Pacific regions: Indonesia, Singapore, Hong Kong, China, Malaysia, Thailand and Taiwan. Even a cursory glance at the somewhat patchy data suggests that those countries that have recorded the most inward activity have in turn become the leading outward investors of their region. The role of absolute market size in drawing inward investment is highlighted by China. At the same time China, within a remarkably short period, has grown to be second only to Malaysia as a source country.

Within the other regions there is evidence of declining or stagnating inward shares. This is true even among the leading host countries of Latin America, Argentina and Brazil, the latter being also the region's leading outward investor. Largely because of its proximity to and increasing economic integration with the US, Mexico stands out as the only major host with an enhanced share by the end of 1990 – conditions which are sadly not reproducible by other countries, but which testify to the role of geography in determining economic fortune.

Multinational enterprise seeks out host countries with stable political and economic environments with large markets and those with the potential for production for export. In the last 10–15 years Africa has been lacking in these ingredients relative to other hosts, to the extent that even its leading hosts for which data are available, Nigeria and Zimbabwe, have lost share to end up with under 1 per cent in 1990 from previously commanding positions (7 per cent each in 1980). Within western Asia only Saudi Arabia stands out as a host country; not surprisingly this is based on its extensive domestic market resulting from oil wealth.

The notion of multinational enterprises from less developed countries began to attract attention in the 1980s (for example, see Lall, 1983). That firms from such countries should be capable of FDI was one of the earliest test cases to the ruling dogma that the stereotypical MNE needed to be based on some technological advantage. Since then, there has been a growth of understanding that the creation of multinationals can be based on the establishment of international internal markets within firms for a wide variety of intermediate assets (Casson, 1982, 1987). Knowledge of neighbouring markets can be enough to generate small multinationals, which then grow further. Many of the leading multinationals from Asia and the Pacific have developed following the spur delivered to domestic enterprise from extensive inward investment and technology transfer (Table 7.9). China's outward multinational stock is already very substantial at 15 per cent of the developing world's total, and is sure to grow still further.

Although comparative share of multinational activity is informative, because relative growth rates mirror the evaluations and competencies of investing firms, it is necessary to focus on the importance of multinational enterprise for economies to assess the impact of the development of multinational enterprise. Table 7.10 employs the yardstick of FDI inflows normalized for domestic capital formation. The economically small countries of Africa have been among the most dominated by inward capital, a factor that has been important in the literature on economic dependency, centring on the destructive effects of inward investment on domestic enterprise when the host industry is too weak to benefit from pro-competitive effects (Jenkins, 1991b). Countries which do not appear as having significant overall share of inward FDI show up as heavily reliant on foreign capital. Liberia is an exception in that, as a tax haven, much of the inward investment then goes on to finance outward investment. There are three countries which recorded inflows over 20 per cent at some point between 1971 and 1990:

Table 7.9 Foreign direct investment stock, percentage distribution for less developed and industrializing countries and regions, 1980–90

Developing and industrializing countries and regions	Inward stock			Outward stock		
	1980	1985	1990	1980	1985	1990
Africa	24.31	12.81	7.30	19.13	7.26	4.09
Algeria	0.77	0.33	0.14	4.52	2.59	0.98
Cameroon	0.07	0.07	0.04	8.95	1.12	0.57
Egypt	1.98	3.04	1.68	1.23	1.47	0.60
Gabon	0.84	0.44	0.55	3.61	1.32	—
Kenya	0.70	0.21	0.14	0.82	0.78	0.32
Liberia	1.28	0.76	0.51	—	—	—
Nigeria	6.93	3.88	0.80	—	—	—
Tunisia	0.57	0.81	0.96	—	—	—
Zimbabwe	7.04	1.69	0.80	—	—	—
Other	4.13	1.58	1.68	0.00	0.00	1.61
Asia and the Pacific	35.47	37.25	45.47	42.83	38.43	56.46
China	0.70	1.96	4.00	1.78	2.44	15.39
Hong Kong	1.80	2.00	4.39	—	—	—
India	1.23	0.61	0.44	—	1.79	0.70
Indonesia	10.72	14.22	14.62	—	—	—
Malaysia	6.34	4.85	3.80	18.54	15.38	17.42
Papua New Guinea	0.78	0.39	0.51	1.14	0.41	0.08
Philippines	1.28	0.74	0.59	7.81	3.13	1.43
Republic of Korea	1.19	1.03	1.49	6.48	8.86	10.38
Singapore	6.47	7.41	10.07	—	—	—
Taiwan	2.51	1.67	2.56	4.66	3.80	6.54
Thailand	1.02	1.14	2.08	0.59	0.26	2.39
Other	1.44	1.22	0.90	1.83	2.36	2.12
Western Asia	3.59	15.65	10.70	—	20.01	11.03
Iran	1.27	0.49	0.25	—	—	—
Iraq	0.16	0.08	0.06	—	—	—
Israel	0.04	0.24	0.51	—	9.76	5.10
Oman	0.28	0.56	0.53	—	—	—
Saudi Arabia	—	12.77	7.88	—	9.46	5.11
Other	1.85	1.51	1.46	—	0.80	0.82
Latin America and the Caribbean	41.19	34.29	36.54	38.04	34.28	28.42
Argentina	5.57	3.74	2.61	—	—	—
Brazil	18.23	14.62	13.97	29.77	26.07	22.23
Chile	0.92	1.32	2.32	1.92	1.90	1.86
Colombia	1.11	1.27	1.32	6.26	5.60	3.73
Ecuador	0.75	0.56	0.52	—	—	—
Mexico	8.82	8.33	11.40	—	—	—
Peru	0.94	0.66	0.47	0.14	0.71	0.58
Trinidad and Tobago	1.13	0.98	0.79	—	—	—

Venezuela	1.67	0.88	1.45	—	—	—
Other	2.04	1.93	1.69	0.00	0.00	0.01
Total	100.00	100.00	100.00	100.00	100.00	100.00
Value US$M (current prices)	95878	175574	265899	2190	5371	10781

Notes:
Figures may not sum precisely to 100 due to rounding.
— denotes data are not available.

Adapted from:
United Nations Conference on Trade and Development (1993b), Annex Table 2.

Table 7.10 Percentage share of FDI inflows in less developed countries' gross domestic capital formation, annual averages, 1971–90

Country/region	1971–75	1976–80	1981–85	1986–90
Africa				
Botswana[a]	24.3	24.1	16.1	15.9
Congo	31.6	3.9	4	3.5
Côte d'Ivoire	5.4	2.5	2.3	5.3
Egypt	—	7.1	6.9	7.8
Gabon	10.8	3.2	5	7.6
Liberia	37.3	18.7	13.8	—
Nigeria	4.9	0.5	3.6	16.3
Seychelles[a]	3.6	8.9	6.4	6.9
Swaziland[a]	16.1	18.8	4.3	31.3
Zimbabwe	—	0.02	0.02	-0.8
Asia and the Pacific				
China	0	0.08	0.9	2.3
Fiji[a]	12.2	6.7	10.7	11.4
Hong Kong[b]	5.9	4.2	6.9	12.1
India	0.3	0.1	0.1	0.3
Indonesia	4.6	2.4	1	2.4
Malaysia	15.2	11.9	10.8	9.7
Pakistan	0.5	0.9	1.3	2.3
Papua New Guinea	—	8.7	15.1	16
Philippines	1	0.9	0.7	5.7
Republic of Korea	1.9	0.4	0.5	1.1
Singapore	15	16.6	17.4	29.4
Sri Lanka	0.1	2.6	2.9	3
Taiwan	1.4	1.2	1.5	3.5
Thailand	3	1.5	3.1	6.3
Western Asia				
Cyprus	13.8	11.1	9.3	6.1
Jordan	4.6	2.9	4.5	1.7
Oman[a]	3.6	8.9	6.4	6.9

Table 7.10 (*cont*)

Country/region	1971–75	1976–80	1981–85	1986–90
Latin America and the Caribbean				
Argentina[a]	0.1	2.1	5	14.5
Barbados	20.4	4.1	2.5	3.3
Brazil[a]	4.2	3.9	4.3	1.7
Chile	–7.3	4.2	6.3	5.7
Colombia	1.7	2.2	7.7	6.1
Costa Rica	11.3	6	7.1	8.8
Dominican Republic	9.4	5	2.8	9.6
Ecuador	13.6	1.8	1.9	3.5
Guatemala	10	7.9	5.7	12.2
Jamaica	12.9	1.6	–1.4	6.6
Mexico	3.5	3.6	2.7	7
Trinidad and Tobago	22.3	10.7	7.3	9.4
Uruguay	—	15.7	1.5	4.1
Venezuela	–0.9	0.9	1	4.3

Notes:
[a] Indicates that data are for 1987–90.
[b] Indicates that data are for 1986–89.

Adapted from:
United Nations Conference on Trade and Development (1993b), Annex Table 3.

Botswana, Congo and Swaziland, while there are several others that reached in the region of 10 per cent or over.

Multinationals in Asia and the Pacific countries have sizeable normalized FDI inflows, but their economies are not too dominated because the domestic economic bases are that much more developed. Even so, Singapore reached a figure of over 29 per cent in 1986–90. The still small figure for China in 1990 is mainly a reflection of the immensity of its internal economy, from which it is clear that inward FDI flows are still a long way from their potential. While multinationals have had a consistent presence in the Latin American and Caribbean region, the clear pole of growth is Argentina, with investment in Guatemala, Mexico and the stable Costa Rica holding up. On the other hand, there is a decline of flows to the smaller economies, such as Barbados and Trinidad and Tobago.

CONCLUSIONS

The portrait of multinational activity has changed substantially in the last fifty years. There has been the emergence of a greater diversity of countries from which multinationals spring, and an increasing range of countries which receive the affiliates of foreign firms. Most importantly, the list of host countries has recently been extended and deepened. Notable here is the economic liberalization of China, and the economic and political liberalization of markets in central and eastern Europe, from which foreign multinational activity had been barred or strictly controlled for much of the twentieth century.

In this chapter there is evidence of a continual relocation of production at work, with increasing FDI into the lower-cost members of the EU and into the economies of Asia and the Pacific. The threat that this poses is clear: the developed countries from which production is relocating have then to adjust their economic structures towards activities in which their dynamic comparative advantage lies. The extent to which they fail in this will be measured in their balance of payments position and partly in their level of structural unemployment. The movement towards market integration is itself partly a response to the growth of production, particularly in the countries of Asia and the Pacific. Therefore it is not surprising that, more recently, multinationals have been directing their activity and investment flows towards the large economic areas, whether these are natural (such as China) or constructed, such as the EU and the integrating market of the North American continent. The losers in this game are the countries on the periphery, especially those in Africa, the Caribbean, and west Asia. To this extent, there is evidence of the polarization of the world into areas of international dynamism and areas of relative stagnation. Foreign direct investment is still inextricably linked to market growth and size. Given the existence of external economies in location, there is a pressure for economies to integrate, to better exploit these economies.

While multinationals have played a central role in speeding the international relocation of capital, they do not bear the main responsibility for initiating changes in comparative advantage. This lies with governments. However, it is true that multinationals do accelerate the pace of structural change that is required of economies, and sometimes their location decisions can appear arbitrary, especially when MNEs' private goals diverge from the social goals of the countries in which they operate. Even so, the relocation of production between countries via non-FDI routes, such as international subcontracting (and even imitation), shows that MNEs are not unique in presenting a challenge to the existing pattern of production. They are, however, the most efficient generic form that has yet evolved for the international organization of production.

FURTHER READING.

Brooke, M.Z., Buckley, P.J. (eds) 1988 *Handbook of international trade*. Macmillan, London.

Buckley, P.J. 1985 A critical view of theories of the multinational enterprise. In Buckley, P.J. and Casson, M.C. *The economic theory of the multinational enterprise*. Macmillan, London: Chapter 1.

Buckley, P.J., Casson, M.C. 1976 *The future of the multinational enterprise*. Macmillan, London.

Buckley, P.J., Casson, M.C. (eds) 1992 *Multinational enterprises in the world economy:*

essays in honour of John Dunning. Edward Elgar Publishing, Aldershot, Hants.

Buckley, P.J., Ghauri, P.N. (eds) 1993 *The internationalisation of the firm: a reader.* Academic Press, London.

Buckley, P.J., Ghauri, P.N. (eds) 1994 *The economics of change in East and Central Europe: its impact on international business.* Academic Press, London.

Chandler, A.D. Jr 1986 The evolution of modern global competition. In Porter, J.E. (ed.) *Competition in global industries.* Harvard Business School Press, Boston, MA: Chapter 13.

Clegg, J. 1990 Intra-industry foreign direct investment: a study of recent evidence. In Webster, A.D., Dunning, J.H. (eds) *Structural change in the world economy.* Routledge, London: Chapter 7, 114–42.

Dunning, J.H. 1983 Changes in the level and structure of international production: the last one hundred years. In Casson, M.C. (ed.) 1983 *The growth of international business.* Allen and Unwin, London: Chapter 5.

Dunning, J.H. 1993 *The globalization of business.* Routledge, London.

Dunning, J.H., Cantwell, J.A. 1987 *IRM directory of statistics of international investment and production.* Macmillan, London

Dunning, J.H., Pearce, R.D. 1981 *The world's largest industrial enterprises 1962–1977.* Gower Press, Farnham, Surrey.

Dunning, J.H., Pearce, R.D. 1985 *The world's largest industrial enterprises 1962–1983.* Gower, Farnborough, Hants.

Grimwade, N. 1989 *International trade: new patterns of trade, protection and investment.* Routledge, London.

Ietto-Gillies, G. 1992 *International production: trends, theories, effects.* Polity Press, Oxford.

McMillan, C.H. 1987 *Multinationals from the Second World.* Macmillan, London.

Preston, J. (ed.) 1993 *International business: text and cases.* Pitman, London.

United Nations Centre on Transnational Corporations (UNCTC) 1988 *Transnational corporations in world development: trends and prospects.* United Nations, New York.

United Nations Centre on Transnational Corporations (UNCTC) 1989 *Foreign direct investment and transnational corporations in services.* United Nations, New York.

CHAPTER 8

PRODUCING FUTURES:
Global finance as a geographical project
Erik Swyngedouw

Speculative movements in the international financial markets are the AIDS of our economies

Jacques Chirac, June 1995

MONEY, MONEY, MONEY

The financial system as a geographical project

Today, just as any other day, well over one trillion US dollars will whizz around the globe from one place to another. Only about 10 per cent of this money flow will be used for settling foreign trade transactions. The bulk concerns purely financial movements in the currency or stock exchange markets, in securities or in an ever-proliferating market for 'new' financial arrangements such as swaps, futures, options and other, often very complex, derivative instruments. These flows rampage around the earth in search of security, collateral, safe tax havens and speculative gain. The sums involved outweigh many times the total value of goods and services produced worldwide. For example, in the foreign exchange markets alone, the daily net turnover of $US900 billion in 1992 is around 12 times the combined GDP of OECD countries on an annualized basis. Underlying transactions in international portfolio capital markets varied between 135 per cent of GDP in the US to over 1000 per cent in the UK (BIS, 1994, pp. 174–175).

From a geographical perspective, these flows are of course eminently spatial (see also Chapter 5). They move from somewhere to somewhere else and, in the process, shape 'local' conditions at both the emitting and receiving ends of the flow. The moments and instances of these 'spaces of flows', which Castells (1989) makes so much of, create particular and distinct geographies. In addition, they give a geographical shape and configuration to the network of tele-communication lines and information freeways that link the financial markets together in a dense and complex web of 24-hour dealing systems (Thrift, 1986; Warf, 1989).

135

Needless to say, therefore, the global economy is heavily affected by such spiralling growth in the international financial markets. But evidently, not only are the global geographical configurations and political–economic tensions wrought from these conditions of the international financial system, but they also shape and affect everyday life environments and prospects for each of us. Investment portfolios, such as pension funds, for example (see Clark, 1993b), are deeply caught up in this 'casino' economy as Strange (1986) quite aptly called it.

Devaluations and revaluations of currencies, often resulting from frenzied speculative activity such as, for example, in September 1992 when sterling was forced to abandon the European Exchange Rate Mechanism, also affect daily life in important ways, sometimes wiping out sizeable amounts of potential value and wealth at the stroke of a few computer keyboard keys. The spectacular virtual bankruptcy of Orange County in December 1994 (the county with the highest mean income in the US), when it failed to refinance its highly leveraged investment fund with which its portfolio managers had gambled on the wrong side in the interest futures market, will cost the taxpayer an estimated $US2 billion and years of declining service provision and cutbacks in social, environmental and educational services (*The Orange County Register*, 7 December 1994).

Indeed, places are, of course, not passive recipients which adjust to the whims of money flows. On the contrary, specific local configurations of social empowerment and disempowerment and their dynamics play a decisive role. National regulatory policies, the characteristics of local financial centres, national economic performance and so on partake in important ways in shaping the geography of global finance (see also Chapter 5).

But while places act as (temporary) depositories of money and other forms of value, it is the flows of money over space that define and circumscribe money's meaning as value. I wish to unravel this thing (place)/process (space) character of money in the light of changes in the global financial economy over the past few decades. In this chapter, I seek to explore how tensions and contradictions unfold in and through the spatial organization and geographical restructuring of global finance. This is a deeply historical–geographical process, in which socio-spatial contradictions, tensions and differences work themselves out through a profound reworking and restructuring of geographical landscapes, through the destruction and devaluation of vast reservoirs of value and, most disturbingly, at the expense of often chilling human suffering.

'Money makes the world go round'

Money is a very strange thing. Some observers doubt whether it is actually a thing at all. Altvater (1993), for example, shows how money makes sense only in terms of it being part of a continuous circulation and transformation process. It is the flow and the transformations taking place along the way that give meaning and content to this thing called money.

Money seems to contain or symbolize many things and processes. In fact, some would argue that these many meanings of money are central to its functioning in a capitalist society (Harvey, 1982). First, money is clearly a container of some sort of value. One can buy popcorn, houses, sex and other more or less desirable things with it. Second, money is, of course, also a universal sort of measure in the sense that most things can be expressed in, and exchanged for, money. These characteristics give money a somewhat relative quality. The worth of things does not remain the same over time and varies over space. But surely, at a given time in a given place, money must also represent an absolute value as well. Thirdly, there is also the thing called money. Today in New York, a hundred dollars will buy me a series of desirable things, but Russian roubles would buy me nothing at all in Times Square. This alerts us already to an interesting paradox. Money seems to be relative and absolute at the same time; its meaning derives from the process of money/commodity exchanges while, undoubtedly, different sorts of money exist as things in themselves as well.

However, money is not just the thing that lubricates the economy by facilitating the buying and selling of goods. We are all acutely aware of the power and the value of these paper or metal things in our wallets. Indeed, money allows us to store value and to accumulate wealth. You start with money and intend to end up with more stored value. This intricate, almost mystical process can only be achieved by turning money into something else, into a series of other commodities, although, of course, this exchange can just mean an exchange into another sort of money (for example, gold for dollars or dollars for pounds). This transformation shows the link between the circulation of money and the circulation of labour, means of production such as machinery, roads and the like, resources and nature (see Cronon, 1991).

Moreover, money is much more than just this instrument of circulation, store of value and mediator of the interaction between society and nature. While representing some sort of value, facilitating exchange and permitting accumulation, it is ultimately, at least in our times, just a particular piece of paper, of metal or, in recent years, increasingly a string of bits and bytes rushing through information highways. This, of course, gives money a quintessentially fictitious character and makes it intrinsically speculative (Harvey, 1982). Whenever we store it or, for that matter, whenever it is 'on the move', we just bank on the fact that tomorrow or next year we can still exchange it for something desirable or that it still expresses the same value (or preferably more) when it surfaces again at the end of the flow-line. This is quite a gamble we take; very often this gamble is entirely unwarranted as, for example, the collapse of Barings, Britain's oldest merchant bank, so vividly illustrated (*The Economist*, 4 March 1995; Tickell, 1995). Such whims in money markets, then, suggest that money is perhaps not such a reliable container of value as we often imagine it to be.

Money is also closely related to credit. Banks provide credit (to states, companies and individuals), speculating on some successful future venture. That is exactly what the financial sector has traditionally done. Banks assemble large sums of money and provide credit, expecting the lender to pay it back with interest. This of course depends on successful future use, something that is also by no means guaranteed. Recent growth in Ponzi financing and the 1980s junk bond megalomania combined highly speculative and risky ventures with the prospect of quick gain. But when the debt built up, money devalued or interest rates shot up, this speculative bubble burst open with dramatic social and political consequences.

All this suggests yet another paradox. We cannot imagine living without money and, surely, an integrated global market economy is unthinkable without money to grease the endless transactions that give some sort of coherence to a market-based society. Production, trade, exchange and investments rely fundamentally on the existence of some sort of reliable money. Moreover, future growth depends crucially on money in the form of credit. Yet all these forms of money circulation are often uncertain, volatile and highly unpredictable. What will buy us food and provide the basis for further growth today may be worthless tomorrow.

We have still not exhausted the many and, as we can already tell, conflicting characteristics of money. Money also constitutes a relationship between people. The many (often contested) meanings of money as well as the determination of its value are shaped by and, ultimately, transformed through social relations. Money, therefore, is expressive of the relationships that are constituted by passing from hand to hand. There is no doubt that social power is related to the amount of money in one's bank account. Also, of course, the success of credit depends on performing some future form of activity and of labour. Money, it seems, lies at the heart of the 'power geometry' of socio-spatial relations and its complex web of relations of domination and subordination (Harvey, 1989; but see also Massey, 1992, 1993).

Finally, money is always stored somewhere and moving from one place to another. In fact, all the above characteristics derive from the incessant flow of money from place to place: from production to consumption, from investment to circulation, from the capitalist to the worker, from London to Kathmandu, from now to tomorrow. It is this socio-spatial constitution of money that makes it one of the most powerful signs in a world of almost complete commodification (Simmel, 1979; Harvey, 1985). But surely, it is not just a sign and a metaphor ready for deconstructive enquiry. Money incorporates also, and arguably foremost, direct bodily power (Shilling, 1993). Starvation in Sudan or in the homeless shelter of London's South Bank, the plight of the unemployed or the summits of economic and political power show the powers of money in their most repressive, violent, subordinating or, as the case may be, empowering and emancipatory capabilities. Yet another paradox emerges. The social character of money turns it into an instrument of oppression for some and into one of great power and control for others. Yet again, this hinges on the spatiality and the social geography of the money process.

The excavation of this inevitable spatiality of money would already take us quite a long way in grappling with the choreography of the world economy and its dynamics. We would, however, end up talking about money in the abstract and the global economy as structured in and through the inter-place flows of some abstract quality.

We have, indeed, not yet completed our inquiry into the 'nature(s)' of money. In fact we should rather talk about moneys rather than just money. For the time being, at least, there is no universal money in the abstract sense referred to above. Not so long ago, we were deluded into the possibility of some 'World Money'. Now we know that even the making of a European currency is not easy. In fact, money is still in important ways irrevocably caught up with the (national) state (see Altvater, 1993; Martin, 1994). This gives it an added twist and yet another tension emerges. Not all moneys are the same and, quite clearly, could not be the same if we take the idea of the socio-spatial constructedness of money seriously. National moneys take on different values. This turns money itself into a commodity, into something that can be bought and sold on the basis of the real, imagined or expected value difference between different units of money. Quite simply, the buying and selling of money is predicated upon geographical differences in the socio-spatial construction of different moneys. This, in turn, is related to the geographical geometry of trade and international exchange and the process of uneven global development.

The national constitution of money (while nevertheless operating at a much higher geographical scale as well) is also the source of considerable confusion. It is space and 'socio-spatial distanciation' that necessitates the introduction of money to make a market economy function. In particular credit and credit formation, which is now largely a private activity, is increasingly globally organized by private capital and operating independently from specific national interests (Lash and Urry, 1994). Of course, at the end of the day, the operation of the system is still largely grounded in the local (national) provision and regulation of money. We should, indeed, not confuse the national territorial basis of moneys with the inevitable spatiality of money. This is what O'Brien (1991) seems to do in his book *Global Financial Integration: The End of Geography*. He argues that the globalization of money funds irrevocably leads to the end of geography as a result of the (highly questionable) demise of the nation-state as the single most important institution in regulating the value of money. Later on in his book, O'Brien has to acknowledge that money is always 'on the move', has to go somewhere, but, unfortunately, he fails to point out that this observation reasserts the inevitable spatiality in defining what money is all about. Clearly, the state's role is quite central, if only to restrict the amount of money around. Indeed, the intrinsic value of paper money is virtually zero. In a capitalist market economy, based on the production of scarcity amidst real or imagined abundance, it is imperative that money scarcity is constructed and maintained. The state's role is crucial, therefore, in limiting the amount of circulating money through its monopoly over the money-printing machines. As an increasing amount of money takes the form of money on account (in electronic databases, for example), this task is notoriously difficult to manage as the state's monopoly over money's circulation and the necessary scarcity are never absolute.

All this is relevant for setting the framework of what is going to come in the remainder of this chapter. Particularly in a context of considering the global order, global trends and global restructuring, there is often a tendency to see the world as a purely global place. This is particularly acute when considering themes such as the international economy, global finance, debt, trade and other similarly important issues. I shall focus on money and much will be made of global processes. However, it needs to be reiterated that this global (dis)order discussed below is, at the end of the day, inevitably and necessarily constructed in and through particular places (Swyngedouw, 1992). The flows of moneys in all their forms that pass through these places are, in fact, predicated upon and made possible through the variability between places and, thus, in the end, through geography. Money makes the world go round, precisely because space is deeply heterogeneous and variegated. It is the differences (and the tensions engendered through this differentiation process) between places, among moneys and between money and other things that provide such vital energy that it can move the world. And it is exactly the condition exemplified earlier of the gigantic sums of money that circulate around space and the socio-spatial tensions arising out of this that I attempt to unravel in the remainder of this chapter.

THE ABORTED ATTEMPT TO CREATE WORLD MONEY

The contradictory geo-politics of post-war 'global?' financial regulation

In this section, I want to focus on how the global (capitalist) financial markets moved from a situation of relative stability to a condition in which money began to circulate as a seemingly almost purely fictitious asset. Indeed, the geo-politics of money and the particular harnessing of the world's financial system during the third quarter of this century was nothing short of remarkable. While we saw a spiralling growth of the number of 'independent' nation-states (with their own currencies) after 1945 as the decolonization process accelerated, world economic integration speeded up. This was led by US expansionism (which was geographically rather limited by the consolidation of a then impressive socialist bloc), followed by a recovering Europe and completed by the remarkable 'catching-up' of south-east Asia under Japan's leadership. The Western hegemony of the US, albeit by no means uncontested, anchored the dollar as the world's foremost currency. In fact, the latter was already anticipated by and reinforced through the Bretton Woods agreement, concluded in 1944 by the main Western allies.

This agreement would try to reconcile the impossible by homogenizing the world's financial space in a context of soon well over a hundred competing national territories each with its own money and regulatory context. The Bretton Woods blueprint, and its ensuing institutional framework, would become a masterpiece of social and economic engineering and geo-political strategic thinking (Triffin, 1961; Gowa, 1983; Walter, 1993; Leyshon and Tickell, 1994).

Until the First World War, most of the world's money operated on the basis of some kind of standard, usually silver or gold. With the internationalization of investment and trade in the second half of the nineteenth century, the sterling gold standard *de facto* operated as some proto-World Money (Ingham, 1994). The gold standard refers to nothing more than that governments issuing paper money guaranteed its free convertibility into gold. The mounting interstate rivalry and competition during the first few decades of this century would create massive tensions in the financial system which would eventually force the anchoring currencies, mainly sterling and later the dollar, off the gold standard. The subsequent volatility in currency markets, combined with rising protectionism to defend national territories against competitive devaluations, broke the backbone of international trade and accelerated the downward cascading of the world economy into its longest and deepest recession. The ensuing human suffering and discontent brought the capitalist system to the verge of total collapse. Particularly at a time when the promise of the dawning of a socialist Utopia loomed large, it seemed that the age of capitalism was nearing its end.

At Bretton Woods, these legacies crystallized around a global compromise that would confirm and further propel the US to a hegemonic leadership position in a geographically shrunk capitalist world economy (Van der Pijl, 1984). This leadership role would, so the belief went, remain relatively uncontested if growth would accelerate and spread geographically. This could only be achieved by promoting trade, global exchange and internationalization of investment and production. This, in turn, demanded a stable financial system, an end to pre-war beggar-thy-neighbour policies and a retreat from the anarchic and often fictitious nature of pre-war money circulation. The anchor of the system would be the US dollar. This turned the US and its Federal Reserve into the arbitrator of the world's financial matters (Parboni, 1981). Although actual policing would be delegated to and organized by the newly established International Monetary Fund (IMF) and further supported by the Bank for International Reconstruction and Development (better known as the World Bank), the US had a *de facto* veto right in these institutions. The American quota in the IMF largely outweighed those of other contributors. The gold convertibility of the dollar was reinstated (at a fixed value of $US35 per ounce) and other currencies had to pledge to peg the value of their currencies to the dollar. Competitive devaluations and protective changes in currency values would be impossible unless sanctioned by the IMF (Glyn *et al.*, 1988; Strange, 1994). Fluctuations in exchange rates were no longer left to the whims of the market or to the 'bulls' and the 'bears' in the game of speculation. Temporary disequilibria and balance of payment problems could be alleviated through drawing rights that countries had on the IMF's monetary resources. Moreover, it was thought that the expansion of international trade would be fairly homogeneous and that, therefore, structural imbalances would be, at best, exceptional. Finally, it was agreed that the world's moneys would gradually be liberated and freely convertible.

This system would shape a particular post-war global geographical configuration, but the unfolding of this process would also gradually erode the very conditions and premises on which the regulation of the world market was predicated by multiplying the tensions and conflicts that riddled the system from its inception. These socio-spatial tensions can be summarized as follows:

1. The dollar and, by implication, all other currencies were given a fixed (in time and over space) value in terms of gold. The dollar became a truly remarkable container of absolute value. We have argued before that this stability is, from a dynamic perspective, a mere illusion. Things do (and have to) vary in value over time.

2. The Bretton Woods agreement as an instrument of regulation was an international compromise (as all regulatory forms are compromises indicative of relative power positions) reflecting the spatial power geometry at the time. However, during the subsequent decades, the hegemony of the US would gradually erode as the global power geometry changed (Glyn *et al.*, 1988). In addition, the compromise was at best partial in the sense that national governments and national socio-economic regulations and compromises remained at the level of the nation-state. The different geographical scales of socio-economic regulation would soon show massive tensions (see Aglietta and Orléan, 1982; Aglietta, 1986). Different national economies and, by implication, their currencies began to sit uncomfortably in the imposed cocoon of fixed exchange rates as domestic conditions and practices changed the relative position of one national economy *vis-à-vis* the others. Moreover, the intended liberalization of world trade proved to be rather difficult to achieve. Although the Bretton Woods agreement implied the establishment of an International Trade Organization alongside the IMF and the World Bank, it would take seven difficult rounds of GATT negotiations before this could be agreed (Bhagwati, 1991).

3. Perhaps even more importantly, the dollar itself, with its fixed gold value, functioned differently according to the geographical scale in which it circulated. These scales became, moreover, increasingly more permeable. Indeed, the value over time of a currency, expressed in interest rates, was determined, or at least seriously influenced, by domestic socio-economic, fiscal and monetary policies. On the one hand, governments, including that of the US, tried to keep interest rates down to boost investment, productivity and growth in the 'real' economy and pursued national interests. On the other hand, the dollar quickly became world currency. In that global environment where dollars would soon circulate in ever greater quantities, the Federal Reserve and the American regulators had, of course, no direct sway or say.

4. The US Federal Reserve was put in a unique position. In Bretton Woods they had finally found the alchemist's stone by the stroke of a pen. Paper would be turned into gold. And the Federal Reserve acquired the Midas touch. Every $US35 running off the printing machines, in fact, theoretically

equalled an ounce of gold. As long as the demand for dollars remained high, this was sustainable. However, when the shortage turned into glut and the printing mills continued to operate at full capacity, the iron (rather than the golden) disciplining force of the market would overtake the divine powers of the emperor.

5.   The assumption of a relatively homogeneous (over space) expansion of the world economy on which the stability was predicated defied the self-assigned leadership role of the US. The spatial power geometry under which the compromise was negotiated, in fact, reinforced the hold of the US over the world economy, and structural geographical imbalances (although switched around in the 'inconstant geography' of a spatially perpetually changing world economic map: see Storper and Walker, 1989) would become engraved through the geography of the world's unequal trading system.

These eminently spatial tensions that were captured by and integrated in the mechanisms and operation of the post-war financial system would soon take their toll as the ensuing choreography of global integration would multiply and intensify the contradictions that had been embryonically engineered in 1944. Also, the power geometry cemented into the system would be reworked in important new directions.

Multiplying tensions: the disturbing choreography of global integration

The geographical configuration and regulation of national and world money set the scene for the post-war global integration process. This process would change the mosaic of uneven development and reshuffle the relationships between places, regions and countries. Inevitably, the cocoon of financial regulation at both the national and international scale through which a particular form of globalization was supported would soon show a series of tensions. In this section, these multiple tensions that gradually rippled through the world's economic web will be briefly summarized.

During the post-war period, the US dollar would become simultaneously a national currency, subject to all the forces, conflicts and power struggles that unfold within the US, *and* a world currency, linking fundamentally different political, social and cultural systems together under the homogenizing process of trade and international exchange. The post-war globalization of the economy was clearly led by the US as the hegemonic capitalist power in the world economy. Facilitated by the fixed exchange rate system and supported by the rapid accumulation of capital, the frontiers of capital investment were pushed outwards (Swyngedouw, 1989). The internationalization of productive capital, usually within the organizational structure of companies, generated an outflow of capital from the US. This Direct Foreign Investment was further supported by the Marshall Plan dollars in an attempt to recreate the devastated war spaces and to accelerate their integration in a US-led expansion of the world economy

(Lipietz, 1987). Clearly, during the early years (until about the mid-sixties), the US balance of payments was positive. However, by the end of the sixties, this very internationalization process had begun to turn the geography of global uneven development around. The reconstruction, first in Europe and later in Japan and other countries in east Asia, increased global competition while the US national economy began to gradually lose its competitive edge. This is illustrated by the fact that, after 1966, the US balance of payments began to show important deficits which rose enormously over the next few decades (Armstrong *et al.*, 1991; Corbridge, 1993).

The political and economic hegemony of the US was of course highly contested and sometimes militarily challenged (Frank, 1994). In particular, the Cold War and the regionalization of this global conflict demanded significant political, military and financial commitments from all sides (Cox, 1987). While it may have announced the sound of the death-knell for existing Communism, it also proved to be a massive drain on US resources. The financing of the political and military control over the Western world, the military build-up and the engagements in places where its hegemony was seriously contested (Korea and Vietnam, for example, among many other 'local' conflicts), further expanded the flow of dollars outside the US. The financing of this geo-political strategy, particularly as the costs spiralled out of proportion in the later sixties, was maintained by printing more dollars/gold.

The recovery of Europe and the gradual abolition of currency controls further fuelled the outflow of US dollars. Indeed, for individual states, hoarding dollars became a way to supplement gold reserves as dollars were as good as or better than gold (Swyngedouw, 1992).

This internationalization of the US dollar was further accentuated by the emergence of the dollar as the *de facto* world currency. As the Bretton Woods negotiators had anticipated, the fixed value of the dollar would turn the currency into the preferred intermediary for world trade exchanges. Not only did this process fuel demand for dollars, but perhaps more importantly and contrary to the IMF's expectations and hopes, some of the trade balances remained or became structurally out of balance in either the positive or the negative sense. A number of countries began to run a sizeable trade surplus (for example, the oil exporters) which resulted in the accumulation of dollars outside the US itself. This petro-dollar boom, which emerged in the sixties and expanded enormously during the seventies, would lay part of the foundations for a buoyant Eurodollar market. The other reasons for the expansion of a 'global' dollar were associated with the above processes of internationalization. Indeed, even some American fund holders decided to keep dollars out of the US in order to avoid domestic fiscal and monetary measures, while the Soviet Union and other socialist states kept their dollar accounts outside the US out of fear of potential action from the US government (see Strange, 1971; Wood, 1986; Roddick, 1988; Pilbeam, 1992).

These socio-spatial tensions and conflicts intensified gradually during the 1950s and 1960s and altered the geometry of power in the world economy. The sharpening of tensions can be summarized as follows. First, the double geographical scale at which money was regulated became internally more contradictory. As the competitive position of the US economy on the world stage changed, domestic pressures to align monetary policy more closely with domestic conditions demanded an increased monetary flexibility. The emergence of a balance of payment deficit, however, necessitated a growing call from the US on international dollar holdings.

In addition, the demands for a stable medium of exchange and a world currency became even more important as global trade expanded. However, the negotiation of a global trade agreement (GATT) – which was in principle agreed at Bretton Woods – proved extremely difficult as individual states considered some forms of protectionism inevitable to remain competitive in an integrating world, particularly under conditions in which currency realignments and competitive devaluations were no longer easily tolerated (see also Chapter 10).

Second, the rise of the Eurodollar market resulted, *de facto*, in two distinct but related markets for the same currency. On the one hand, there was the US dollar market, which was under the regulatory umbrella of the Federal Reserve and, thus, the state, and on the other there was a non-US market where different rules were in play. For example, from a modest $US11 billion in 1964, the Eurocurrency market grew to $US1 trillion in 1984 and to almost $US3 trillion by the early 1990s (Martin, 1994, pp. 257–258). We are faced here with an extraordinary condition. Two geographically distinct markets in terms of regulatory conditions existed (but socio-economically were intimately related), in which the same dollar sign operated and was freely exchangeable between these 'continents' and for gold.

Third, the ailing competitive position of the US and growing domestic pressure to deal with this condition, combined with the need for greater access to global dollars to finance its deficit (printing more money became increasingly more inflationary as the dollar shortage of the late fifties had turned into a glut by the late sixties), put serious pressures on the system of fixed exchange rates and guaranteed convertibility. In addition, the different returns on Eurodollars and US-based dollars *de facto* forced the dollar back from an absolute measure of value to a more relational, relative value definition. The combination of these opposing tendencies could no longer be contained by the cocoon woven by the Bretton Woods system and its institutions. The first cracks appeared in 1968 when the gold convertibility of the dollar was temporarily suspended, followed in September 1968 by the German announcement to let the deutschmark float for one month. The axe came down terminally when Nixon unilaterally announced in 1971 that the US would abandon the guaranteed gold convertibility of the dollar. Other states decided to delink their currencies from the dollar in order not to be sucked into the devaluationary spiral in which the dollar was trapped during the 1970s. Between 1971 and 1973, then, the Bretton Woods agreement further unravelled as currencies began to float against each other and against gold (or other commodities) (Reszat, 1993) (see Figure 8.1).

In sum, these geographical dynamics and their power relations unleashed a

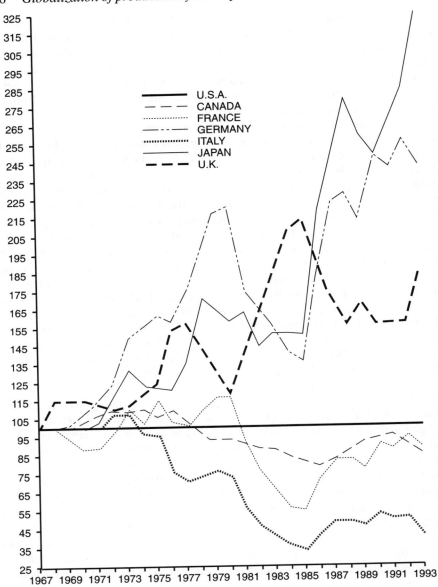

Source: IMF (International Financial Statistics, 1991)

Figure 8.1   Exchange rates of major currencies against the US dollar, 1967–93 (period averages; 1967 US dollar parity = 100)

series of tensions and processes that, in the end, undermined the relative coherence of this particular historical–geographical configuration of the capitalist world economy. The internal geographical contradictions that render a capitalist economy dynamic and creative also continuously undermine the very foundations on which it rests.

Spatial fragmentation and financial integration: money's new 'glocal' chequerboard

The prospect of a stable global capitalist order promised in the post-war era proved to be no more than a mirage. The *de facto* implication of the demise of Bretton Woods was that the dollar began to float freely against gold, re-establishing a relative measurement of value, but abandoning the principle of money as a stable container of absolute value. The imposed homogenization of the world's monetary order was in tatters. The global order was shattered, but in the interstices of this mosaic, new global–local ('glocal') arrangements, new money flows and new geographical configurations would emerge.

The ailing competitive position of the US, its balance of payments problems and the rising budget deficit (which would become particularly dramatic during the Reagan arms build-up) made the US much more inward looking. Monetary policy was increasingly targeted towards domestic objectives. Of course, the build-up of 'xenodollars' also meant that the global order would be affected by this process. In an attempt to put the devaluationary crunch on to others, Carter tried to balance the books by printing dollars. This resulted in a rapid devaluation of the dollar *vis-à-vis* gold, but also unleashed an inflationary spiral which would push up inflation well into double figures. When the dollar reached an all-time low by the end of the seventies and inflation was spiralling out of control, Reagan's monetarism applied the brakes on the money supply. The value of the dollar and real interest rates shot up, sending shock waves throughout the world economy and, in particular, negatively affecting debtor states (Corbridge, 1993).

However, given the fact that the dollar was still world currency and a global means of exchange, commodity exporters were faced with the danger of being sucked into a devaluationary spiral. Several commodity cartels were formed in an attempt to safeguard commodity prices against a dollar sliding downwards. OPEC was most successful, for a series of political–economic reasons. Each time the dollar went down, with an all-time low registered in the late seventies, oil prices rose spectacularly. In addition, the rush for a safe value haven resulted in a scramble for gold and a rapid increase in its price. Clearly, these upheavals in commodity markets affected trade relations as well as price structures and contributed to the emerging global economic crisis running riot. The monetary value uncertainties negatively affected international trade and reinforced structural spatial imbalances. For example, the oil price hikes alone resulted in a massive outpouring of dollars from mainly the advanced economies and to the creation of a vast pool of petro-dollars, which further fuelled the Eurodollar markets. Matters were, of course, considerably worse for those Third World economies that were faced with increasingly unstable export prices while import prices (and certainly oil) kept rising. While some countries were running enormous trade balance surpluses, others suffered from revenues leaking away. The West and in particular the US, but also the UK and other European countries, were faced with deteriorating trade balances and skyrocketing budget deficits. The latter were the result of declining competitive positions combined with growing demands put on the state to keep some form of social cohesion. Some countries tried to inflate the debt away (inflation levels of almost 20 per cent at the turn of the decade were no exception) by printing more money. This, of course, further undermined whatever was left of monetary stability. In addition to exchange-rate instability, interest rates also began to fluctuate rapidly and erratically (see Figure 8.2).

Japan, whose industrial renovation was now completed, managed to further grow and take over some of the territory lost by Europe and the US. In this context of rapidly changing geographical configurations, calls for protectionism, and *de facto* protectionist measures to shield the domestic economy from importing devaluations, gave rise to the emergence of a number of trade blocs (Thurow, 1992). Although by no means hermetically sealed off from the world economy – on the contrary, one objective of protectionism is to reinforce competitive positions in the world market (see Hilferding, 1981) – there was the emergence of a Triad bloc centring respectively around Japan, the US and the German–French axis in Europe. Of course, increased intraregional cooperation did not lead to heightened interbloc protectionism, but rather to a rescaling of competitive mechanisms. Improved regional cooperation and trade facilitates achieving an improved competitive position in the world market (Anderson and Blackhurst, 1993; Borrman and Koopmann, 1994).

Evidently, not only trade was affected, but the spatial and temporal choreography of actual production of goods was profoundly shaken. As Jeelof (1989) has pointed out, the volatility in the money markets made production planning extremely risky and uncertain. The internationalization of production and world planning of production chains and input/output flows which characterized much of the post-war international division of labour became a high-risk strategy. Different centres of production and commerce were located in different currency zones and subject to often rapid and dramatic relative exchange-rate fluctuations. This made a shambles of long-term corporate strategic locational planning. Globalizing companies trying to deal with rapidly changing relative locational conditions launched a series of strategies, which I have earlier defined as 'glocalization' strategies (Swyngedouw, 1992), involving subcontracting, strategic alliances, networking, and flexible organizational arrangements. These strategies allow for rapid temporal and spatial adjustments in production, distribution and marketing arrangements (Cooke *et al.*, 1992).

In short, spatial and temporal horizons shrank considerably as the monetary order unravelled and success began to depend increasingly on shorter transaction times, condensed time–space distances and an accelerated turnover time of capital (Harvey, 1989). A new mosaic of uneven development emerged in which

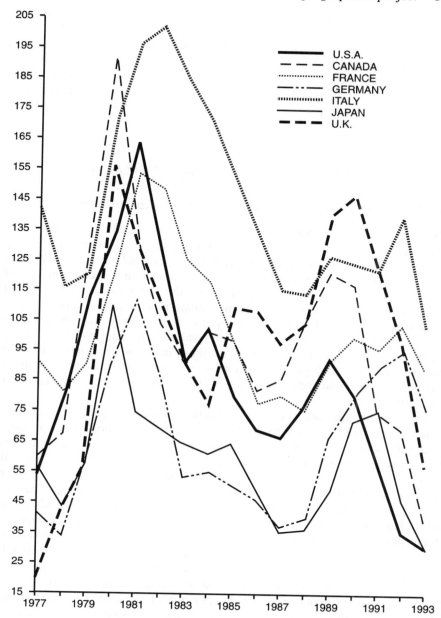

Source: IMF

Figure 8.2 Interest rates for selected countries, 1977–93 (money market rates; period averages in per cent per annum)

the financial sector, now liberated from the cocoon of fixed exchange rates and absolute values, would itself become a key arena for capital accumulation and feverish expansion. It is exactly this global choreography of money and its historical–geographical dimensions which will shape much of the contemporary global economic shifts and transformations. In the next section, we shall turn to the analysis of how money itself (and not just as medium and means of exchange) is becoming part and parcel of geographical strategizing and profound spatial restructuring processes.

MAKING MONEY THROUGH TIME/SPACE DISPLACEMENT

Credit and the currency exchange market: creating space/buying time

The 'liberalization' of the global financial system signalled the end of an integrated monetary world space and, consequently, the reaffirmation of a mosaic of different national moneys. Most currencies would fluctuate in relative value *vis-à-vis* each other, depending on the combination and confrontation of national economic and monetary policies on the one hand and international money flows on the other. Attempts to regulate money at new supranational, subglobal, geographical scale levels proved to be extremely difficult and riven with geo-strategic tensions and interstate rivalries. The bumpy history of the European Monetary Union, for example, illustrates how the confrontation of national demands and global financial integration and strategies result in perpetual tensions and continuous friction (Gros and Thygesen, 1992; Leyshon and Thrift, 1992).

A geo-politically and geo-economically 'glocally' organized monetary system arose out of this perpetual tension and negotiation between local (national) money spaces and global money flows. The growth of global 'hot' money was paralleled by an equally important expansion of offshore financial centres (Roberts, 1994). Johns (1994, p. 32) reports that 'as much as half of the world's stock of money either resides in, or is passing through, tax havens making them an essential catalyst for world trade.' These towering places in the global chequerboard of ballooning stateless money combine limited or absent domestic regulation of and control over foreign currencies with global integration which permits round-the-clock trading. More regulated markets felt increasingly the sting of these emerging competitors and, combined with a monetarist free-market ideology, decided to liberate their domestic capital markets (see also Chapter 17). The deregulation of the money markets in the US in the early eighties and London's 'Big Bang' in 1986 lifted many controls and allowed for a further opening up and expansion of global financial markets. By the end of 1993, the Bank for International Settlements reported that total gross international bank liabilities amounted to $US7.3 trillion (BIS, 1994, p. 97).

The exchange and interest rate fluctuations in Figures 8.1 and 8.2 illustrate the volatility of the financial system and summarize the effects of the last two decades of monetary deregulation. These fluctuations result from the interplay between national monetary and socio-economic conditions and policies and international currency movements. Of course, national monetary and economic policies matter, but in ways that are profoundly different from the mechanisms that operated during the Bretton Woods era. The often announced death of the national state is surely premature, although its position and role in this 'glocal' mosaic has changed. In particular, monetary policy began to figure as a key vehicle in economic growth policies as Keynesian domestic demand-based expansion policies began to give way to strategies aimed at expanding international trade and at achieving an improved competitive position in the global marketplace (Drache and Gertler, 1991).

More importantly, perhaps, the liberated money markets and the volatility of the international money markets created a new market environment. Contrary to the Bretton Woods era, buying and selling currencies and speculating on exchange rate fluctuations allowed for the development and rapid growth of a speculative foreign exchange (forex) market. Interestingly enough, making money by buying and selling money and speculating on future currency values (how ever near this future may be) became a prime vehicle for accumulation. Money as expressions of value-in-motion and capital as claims to future (labour-) time established an arena for frenzied financial activities. Speculating on future values and the buying of time proceeded through the creation of new spaces and spatial relations. Figure 8.3 shows that the forex market grew from a modest

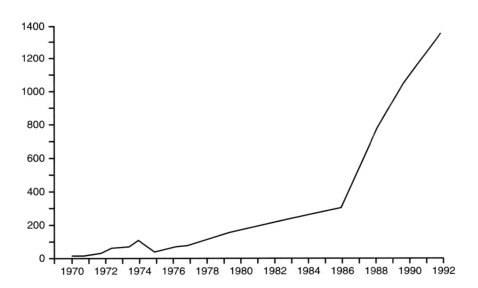

Source: UNCTAD, Trade and Development Report, 1981, p. 72; BIS (1980, 1984, 1987)

Figure 8.3 Gross daily turnover in the world foreign exchange market, 1970–92 ($US billion per average day)

$US15 billion in 1970, when most deals were directly related to settling trade, to well over $US1 trillion today. The bulk is driven by constant hedging, arbitrage and speculative position-taking in the international financial markets. The UK, the US and Japan, the leading centres in the European, American and Asian time zones, account for about 60 per cent of total trading. The three next most important centres (Switzerland, Singapore and Hong Kong) account for 20 per cent of all deals. The US dollar is still the main currency in the forex market. It was on one side of about 90 per cent of all transactions; the yen and the deutschmark, the next most important, are involved in almost one quarter of all deals (BIS, 1990a, pp. 209–210).

Almost all deals involve spatial transfers of money as well as changes in the relative positions of states' currency values (which, in turn, influence interest rates, buying capacity, monetary and fiscal policy and so forth). The short-term fluctuations on which these transfers are predicated and which also contribute to creating this volatility are summarized in Figure 8.4. This figure shows the daily variation in the exchange rate of the US dollar against most other important global currencies during an average month (8 November to 8 December 1994). This volatility enables speculative gain, while the flows of money further contribute to reaffirming these fluctuations. Let us assume, for example, that a trader exchanges £1 billion for the equivalent amount of US dollars on 8 November 1994 at an exchange rate of 62 pence to the dollar. Four days later, with an exchange rate at 63 pence, reversing the transaction would yield a net profit of over £16 million!

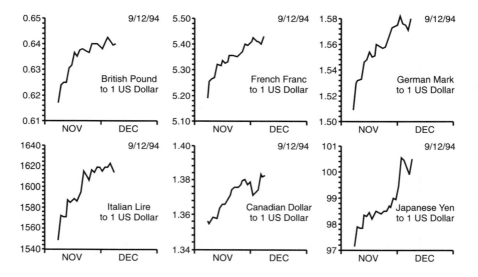

Source: Datastream

Figure 8.4   Daily variation in exchange rate of the $US against six major currencies (period 8 November to 8 December 1994)

These speculative geographical flows and the accumulation of financial assets unleashed a frenzy of activity, not only in the financial markets but also in the money/commodity/investment nexus. Credit-based financing, Ponzi financing schemes and risky paper issues such as junk bonds and Third World debt, combined with over-exposed company lending and spiralling consumer debt, brought the global financial system both fame and instability.

The volatility in the financial system necessitated that traders, companies and others involved in global interactions hedged against rapid devaluations or revaluations of currencies, commodity price fluctuations or changes in interest rates. The ensuing demand for new financial instruments generated an internal dynamic which spun off an increasing array of financial products and services. Telecommunication networks, sophisticated computer-assisted dealing infra-structure and software, the City's financial services, the restructuring of the internal socio-economic conditions of finance capitals and the deregulation of markets developed in tandem as the build-up of fictitious capital proceeded (see, among others, Sassen, 1991; Budd and Whimster, 1992).

However, with these developments, moving money around geographically to bank on interspatial differences and expected temporal variation accelerated to such an extent that time–space transactions through information and tele-communications systems permitted a virtually on-the-spot market equilibrium. It takes no more than about ten seconds to conclude a transaction between two partners. Again, the mastering of time in these (spatial) transactions is of paramount importance.

Until the late seventies, almost all transactions took place in the 'spot' market. The spot market consists of that part of the market in which two economic agents agree to exchange amounts of two currencies within the space of two business days. By 1989, the share of the spot market, in contrast to a variety of 'derivative markets' (see below), had fallen to 57 per cent (BIS, 1990b). Between 1989 and 1992, this figure fell further to 47 per cent (BIS, 1993b, p. 16). In terms of market expansion, daily turnover in the periods 1986–89 and 1989–92 grew respectively 104 per cent and (only) 18 per cent for the spot forex market, but respectively 134 per cent and 77 per cent for the non-spot market (BIS, 1990b, 1993b). Indeed, producing new volatility, new uncertainties and new disequilibria (in the future) became important strategies to maintain the accumulation rhythm of the financial sector. Creating an uncertain and volatile future through spatial transactions of money would become increasingly important. Moreover, other rapidly changing money values, such as interest rates and stock markets, also provided increasingly lucrative market niches in addition to the forex market.

The new financial instruments and the derivatives market: buying space/creating time

Since the early eighties, and growing rapidly over the subsequent years, a whole host of new financial instruments have been introduced. They are usually referred to as 'derivatives' and vary from rather simple options and futures to very complex multi-process tools. They constitute the pinnacle of the contemporary financial markets and capture the time/space dynamics of the 'glocal' order in a most telling fashion.

Of course, the derivatives market is not new. Futures and options were introduced more than a century ago on the Chicago commodities exchange. The first reports date back to 1848 and the Chicago futures market was first formally regulated by the mid-1860s (Cronon, 1991, pp. 120–125). Commodities futures and options have never really gone away. What is new is the spectacular rise in purely financial derivatives that operate on the same principle as commodities futures and options and the introduction of new, but related, financial instruments (see Box 8.1).

BOX 8.1   'New' financial arrangements and the derivatives market

Financial derivatives

'Derivatives' is a general term for a whole series of financial assets that are 'derived' from other 'underlying' assets, such as foreign exchange, bonds, equities or commodities. Derivatives take the form of contracts which give one party a claim on the underlying asset (or its money value) at some point in the future and bind the other party to meet a corresponding liability. They can bind both parties equally or offer one party an option to exercise it or not. For example, a currency exchange option allows you to buy or sell a given currency at some time in the future. The value of the option (a financial asset) is derived from the currency value itself (the underlying financial asset). Derivatives are useful for hedging, speculating, arbitraging and low-cost adjustments to investment portfolios. They can also be combined in complex operations. Some derivatives are traded on open exchanges, others can be bought and sold 'over-the-counter' (OTC). Their market price depends in part on the movement of the price of the underlying asset since the contract was created.

Origin of derivatives

Many derivative instruments are not particularly new. For example, commodity futures and options have been around since about the mid-1860s (see Cronon, 1991). The first swap deal was concluded in 1962. However, the growing uncertainties in the financial markets since the mid-seventies have given rise to a proliferation of new instruments to hedge against risks associated with volatile forex markets, rapidly fluctuating interest rates and so forth. The derivatives market permits better risk management. However, derivatives also allow and are used for purely speculative activities. In this sense, their proliferation further reinforces market volatility and uncertainty. Their rapid growth has been accelerated by the globalization of capital markets, by technological advances in computers and telecommunications, by market deregulation and by increasingly fierce competition among financial institutions to devise and sell new products.

Definitions of the most important derivatives

Option: The right to buy or sell a specific number of securities (currency, stock, commodity, etc.) at a specific price within a specified period of time. This right (the option) can be bought and sold as well (on the options market), but if the right is not exercised within the specified period, it expires and the purchaser of the option loses his or her money.

Future: A contract to buy or sell something in the future at a price agreed in the present. Contrary to an option, a future has to be exercised at the end of the contract. However, this rarely happens in practice as traders generally agree to settle only the difference between the agreed price of the contract and the effective price at the time the contract is exercised. There are futures in a whole range of assets, varying from pork bellies to stock market indexes.

Swap: A transaction in which two parties exchange financial assets. There can be a whole host of swap types, for example currency swaps or interest-rate swaps. In the latter case, for example, a borrower who has raised, say, a loan in deutschmarks swaps the interest payments on this loan with those of another borrower who has raised a loan in, say, UK pounds.

Combined derivatives: In recent years a series of new instruments which combine one or more of the above basic transactions have been introduced (floors, caps, collars, swaptions, etc.). The management of these sophisticated instruments can become very complex and demands advanced software and computer systems.

Problems

The derivatives market is currently virtually unregulated. National and international regulators are very worried about the potentially catastrophic consequences the proliferation and expansion of the derivatives market may have on the stability of the international financial system. Investors often take great risks, generally operating with highly leveraged assets in a very volatile market. Many examples are known of investment funds losing millions of dollars (see Table 8.1). As the derivatives market operates with only a fraction of the value of the underlying assets, things could go badly wrong (*cf.* the collapse of Barings Bank). Given the dense relations in the international financial system, a crash at one place can ripple quickly throughout the international system like a domino effect (Group of Thirty, 1993; Basle Committee, 1994).

For more details, see Becketti (1993), Group of Thirty (1993), Hindle (1994), United States General Accounting Office (1994), *The Economist* (18 May 1994).

Clearly, the very volatility of the forex markets and the uncertainties in the capital markets necessitated that commodity producers and bankers operating on an international scale took action to safeguard (as far as possible) against rapid changes in currency values or interest rate changes. In addition to new organizational and locational strategies (see Swyngedouw, 1992), new financial instruments (in particular options and futures as well as a variety of swaps) were introduced. They allow hedging against currency and interest rate fluctuations.

However, the same instruments, by betting on future currency exchange and interest rate values, introduced a new set of uncertainties and future volatility that provided a breeding ground for speculative time/space transactions and money flows. The spot market with its instantaneous access, combined with near-perfect information flows, adjusts virtually immediately to near-perfect market conditions. The new financial instruments, on the other hand, allow the purchase of national moneys, interest rates, stocks, bonds, etc., and bank on the development of their future value. These instruments, therefore, partially create uncertainty, volatility and market disequilibria (Thrift and Leyshon, 1994). The perpetual production of such market uncertainty is central to maintaining a profitable derivatives market. While the forex market involves a spatial displacement of money, the derivatives market creates a future in real time through time/space displacements of future values of financial assets. These time/space displacements produce their own instability and further reinforce the stronghold of the financial sector over the 'glocal' dynamics of contemporary socio-spatial change. The best available data suggest that the total volume of worldwide derivatives oustanding at the end of 1992 was at least $US12.1 trillion in terms of the notional, or principal, amount of derivatives contracts out-standing, a 145 per cent increase since 1989 (United States General Accounting Office, 1994, p. 34). Figure 8.5 illustrates the spectacular rise of the derivatives market between 1986 and 1993.

In the early years, the derivatives market was highly concentrated in the traditional financial capitals, but recent expansion of the derivatives industry in Latin America, Asia and eastern Europe has been spectacular, growing from $US15 billion in 1992 to $US57 billion in 1993, a 275 per cent increase (Westlake, 1993; Locke, 1994). The constant chase of traders and investors for new high-yield markets has resulted in a geographically expanding and more diverse pattern. This spatial expansion is itself predicated upon an extension and densification of the technological carriers and telecommunication networks and more sophisticated computer-based information exchange (Kredietbank, 1992, p. 3; *Risk Technology Supplement*, 1994). But surely, the spatial spread of this financial chequerboard generalizes risk and further expands an already shaky speculative bubble. Not surprisingly, the world's financial watchdogs are deeply worried about the potentially disruptive consequences of a breakdown of the system (McDonough, 1993; United States General Accounting Office, 1994; Group of Thirty, 1993). The amount of money lost through over-exposure to risky investments, wrong speculation and unexpected changes in the market, etc., is growing rapidly. As mentioned before, the bankruptcy of Orange County may cost the taxpayer as much as $US2 billion. A few years ago, the London borough of Hammersmith and Fulham lost $US600 million in similarly speculative activities. About 130 other British local authorities entered into interest-rate swaps throughout the 1980s. When in January 1991, the House of Lords ruled that the use of swaps by local authorities was *ultra vires* and that all such transactions were null and void, the local authorities' counterparties were left with potential losses of £600 million (Moody's, 1991, pp. 4–5). Table 8.1

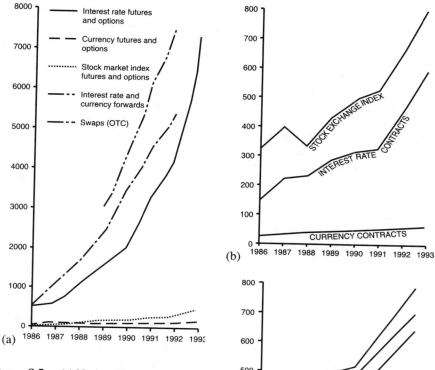

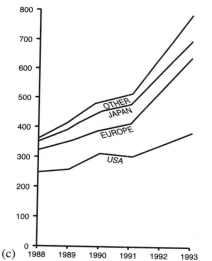

Figure 8.5 (a) Notional/contract amounts for selected derivatives worldwide (in $US billion) (end of fiscal year, 1986–93); (b) Annual turnover of derivatives contracts on organized exchanges by type of product (in millions of contracts) (1986–93); (c) Annual turnover of derivatives contracts on organized exchanges by region (in millions of contracts); (d) Notional/contract amounts for derivatives worldwide by individual product (in US$ billion) (end of fiscal year, 1986–93)

(d)

Derivative	1986	1987	1988	1989	1990	1991	1992	1993
Futures	{ 583	724 }	935	1259	1540	2254	3154	5109
Options			371	953	1305	1841	2263	2729
Swaps	500	867	1330	1952	2890	3872	4711	—
Swap-related	—	180	300	450	561	577	635	—
Total	—	1771	2936	4614	6296	8544	10763	—
Forwards	—	—	—	3034	4437	6061	7515	—
Total	—	—	—	7648	10733	14605	18278	—

Sources: United States General Accounting Office (1994), p. 187; Hindle (1994), p. 210; BIS (1991, 1992, 1993a, 1994); Group of Thirty (1993), pp. 55–58; Remolona (1993), pp. 30–32.

lists some of the most notorious derivatives losses up to 1994. Until now, these individual disaster stories have not yet sent major shockwaves through the financial and economic system, although the local effects have often been dramatic.

However, it is not inconceivable that such failures ripple over space and result in panic, financial disintegration and collapse of the international financial system. When Barings Bank collapsed on 26 February 1995 in the wake of a bout of disastrous trading on the Nikkei Stock Index Option market which exposed the bank to an estimated £900 million loss, the British regulatory authorities and the Chancellor of the Exchequer moved briskly to restore confidence in the stability of the markets and the reputation of the regulators (Tickell, 1995). As the scale and the scope of the damage was difficult to gauge, the uncertainty made the markets extremely nervous and the National Bank had to launch on a path of damage limitation.

Particularly as the geography of the derivatives market expands and different national regulatory systems become involved, the danger of a spectacular collapse of over-accumulated capital in this sector looms large. Very little information is available about risk exposure from derivatives. First, it is difficult to assess credit risk because the very volatility of derivatives instruments continuously alters credit exposure rates (contrary to, for example, exposure from loans). Second, the regulators collect few data about the derivatives market and exposure rates. Finally, the systematic assessment of risk permitted by derivatives generates new forms of risk, increases time/space volatility and, arguably, creates the potential for new forms of systemic risk (Thrift and Leyshon, 1994). Figure 8.6 shows derivatives-related credit exposures of ten major US over-the-counter derivatives dealers in 1992 for which information was available. Their gross credit exposure is more than 100 per cent of equity capital. Sizeable losses in the derivatives market would, therefore, affect their financial condition in important ways (United States General Accounting Office, 1994, pp. 53–55). Of course, exposure to loans is, on the whole, much larger, but the intrinsic risk of derivatives instruments makes the risk many times greater.

More problematic, however, than such a doom scenario of global collapse is that billions of dollars or yen or pounds are devalued, annihilated and wiped out, while human suffering, poverty and socio-economic polarization are on the increase and many basic human needs remain unfulfilled for a growing number of people. For example, when the German oil and metal company Metall-gesellschaft lost over $US1.3 billion as a result of engagements in the derivatives market that ran out of control, the company needed to restructure its operations to cover the loss, resulting in about 10000 job losses (Verbraeken, 1994, p. 34). During the first half of October 1994, the rouble fell from 2000 roubles per dollar to 5000 per dollar. Of the 2300 commercial banks in Russia, many do little more than gamble on such changes. There is no need to dwell on the effects that such volatility has on energy and food prices for Russia's poor (Higgins, 1994).

Table 8.1   Some famous derivatives losses

Loss	Company	Transaction
The first ten years		
$ 25m	General Reinsurance	Caps
$ 377m	Merrill Lynch	PO mortgage-backed securities
$ 125m	Société des Bourse Françaises	Financial futures
$ 600m	London borough of Hammersmith and Fulham	Various
$ 380m	Klockner	Commodities hedging
$ 275m	Allied Lyons	Forex options
$ 70m	ABN AMRO	MTM valuation
$1456m	Kashima Oil	Currency derivatives
$ 130m	Nippon Steel	Forex derivatives
September 1993 to February 1995		
$ 50m	Medani	Structured notes
$ 90m	AIG	Derivatives revaluation
$1340m	Metallgesellschaft Corp.	Energy derivatives
$ 200m	Codelco Chile	Commodity futures
$ 100m	Cargill	Mortgage derivatives
$ 600m	Askin Securities	MBS model
$ 157m	P&G	Leveraged DM/USD spread
$ 121m	Mead Corp.	Leveraged swaps
$ 100m	Florida State & Florida League of Cities	Mortgage derivatives
$ 10m	Kidder Peabody	Amortizing swap pricing
$1450m	Kashima Oil	Currency derivatives
$ 20m	Gibson Greetings	Leveraged swaps
$ 10m	CIBC	Financial futures
$ 8m	Caterpillar Financial	Caps and swaptions
$ 22m	ARCO (pension fund)	Structured notes
$ 35m	Dell Computer	Leveraged swaps and options
$ 113m	Air Products	Leveraged and currency swaps
$ 51m	Harris Trust Savings Bank	Mortgage derivatives
$ 68m	Pacific Horizon Funds	Structured notes
$ 20m	Paramount Communications	Interest rate swaps
$ 10m	Kidder Peabody	Bond options
$ 40m	CS First Boston Investment Management	Currency linked derivatives
$ 90m	Investors Equity Life Insurance Co.	Bond futures
$2000m	Orange County (Dec. 1994)	Interest rate futures
$1400m (est.)	Barings Bank	Nikkei Index options

Sources: Wilson (1994), p. 22, Moody's (1991), *The Economist* (4 March 1995).

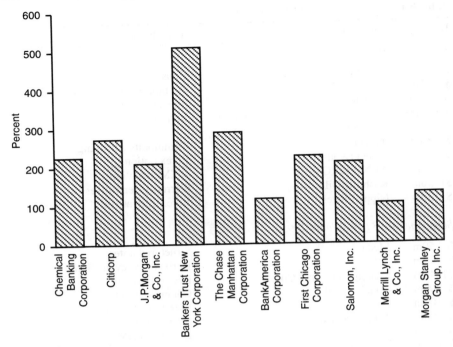

Source: United States General Accounting Office (1994)

Figure 8.6   Derivatives gross credit exposures of ten US OTC derivatives dealers as a percentage of equity, 1992

RESCALING/RETIMING MONEY: TRIAD POWER AND CAPITAL CIRCULATION

Money movements rule the world in ways until recently thought impossible. While increasing uncertainty and volatility, these burgeoning flows also reinforce the emerging new political spatial order and socio-spatial fragmentation. In fact, this very flux is predicated upon fragmentation and geographical differentiation.

The overwhelming majority of financial transactions take place in dollars, yen or German marks. This reinforces the Triad geometry of world money power in which none of the regions can impose a world hegemonic project. However, the fluctuations and volatility between each of the anchoring Asian, American and European currencies define the dynamics of the world's financial system. As already discussed above, this has profound implications for investment flows and the geography of production as well as on geo-political relations. There have been concerted actions in each of the 'blocs' to strengthen intraregional cooperation and to stabilize intraregional trade and money flows. The examples of the European Union and NAFTA are cases in point.

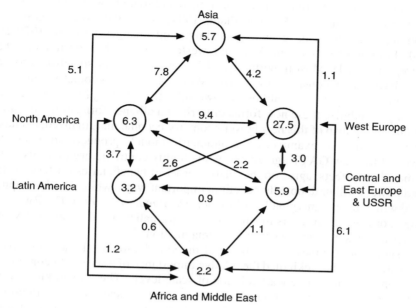

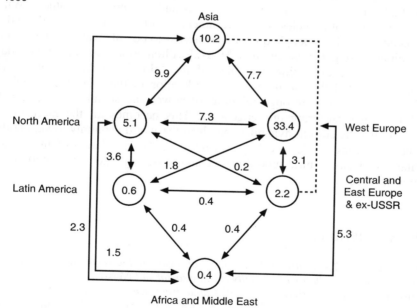

Source: The Group of Lisbon (1994), p. 111.

Figure 8.7 Regional trade flows (in percentages of total world commodity trade), 1970 and 1990

It is no surprise, therefore, that world trade and trade flows reflect these new geo-political conditions (Randzio-Plath, 1994). As Figure 8.7 suggests, for example, trade flows have undergone important changes between 1970 and 1990. Intraregional trade in Asia and western Europe has risen more than interregional trade. Most importantly, Africa and the former socialist European states have fared considerably worse. While the Triad geometry reinforces intraregional cooperation – although powerful differentiating forces are at work that may destabilize these new forms of territorial alliance formation – the areas that fall off the map of this new power geometry become marginalized, excluded and left to rot. For example, all econometric models produced to assess the impact of the new GATT agreement, while highly contradictory in terms of the estimated net effects, agree on the relative order of beneficiaries (or losers). The Triad powers will undoubtedly benefit in important ways, while the 'developing' world will gain only marginally or lose out (*De Standaard*, 1994). The Rwandan, Zairean or Russian disasters illustrate these marginalizing and exclusionary geo-politics in ways that are beyond human imagination.

In short, the complex restructuring of the world's financial and trade spaces and spatial flows has rekindled the relative importance of a series of geographical scales and produced a new articulation of scale levels. These reworkings of the relative importance of and relations between geographical scales are in no way neutral in their social content. On the contrary, this new power geometry has propelled some to new commanding heights and disempowered others. While many thousands of homeless roam the streets of London and New York, and an estimated 800 million people do not have access to potable water in the world's great cities, City gamblers circulate $US1.3 trillion around the globe each day! Better and more disturbing examples of the 'glocal' world we inhabit are difficult to find. This also urges a reconsideration of the role of geographical scale, its construction through relations of power and social struggle and the chilling human suffering this engenders. This becomes all the more urgent knowing that the current dynamics may lead the world economy to yet another moment of crisis, while rescaling and retiming the circulation of money and capital could easily turn subordination and suffering into emancipation and empowerment.

FURTHER READING

Altvater, E. 1993 *The future of the market – an essay on the regulation of money and nature after the collapse of 'actually existing socialism'*. Verso, London.

Armstrong, P., Glyn, A., Harrison, J. 1991 *Capitalism since 1945*. Blackwell, Oxford.

Cooke, P., Moulaert, F., Swyngedouw, E., Weinstein, O., Wells, P. 1992 *Towards global localisation*. University College Press, London.

Corbridge, S. 1993 *Debt and development*. Blackwell, Oxford.

Corbridge, S., Martin, R., Thrift, N. (eds) *Money, power and space*. Blackwell, Oxford.

O'Brien, R. 1992 *Global financial integration: the end of geography*. Pinter, London.

Simmel, G. 1979 *The philosophy of money.* Routledge, London.

Strange, S. 1986 *Casino capitalism.* Blackwell, Oxford.

Swyngedouw, E. 1992 The mammon quest. 'Glocalization', interspatial competition and the monetary order: the construction of new scales. In Dunford, M., Kafkalas, G. (eds) *Cities and regions in the new Europe.* Belhaven Press, London: 39–67.

Walter, A. 1993 *World power and world money.* Harvester Wheatsheaf, London.

CHAPTER 9

RESEARCH AND DEVELOPMENT
Roger Hayter

This chapter discusses the changing motivations, organization and geography of research and development (R&D) during the past two decades of deep-seated structural changes in the global economy. It is widely recognized, particularly among industrially advanced countries, that R&D is critical to technological innovation, which in turn is a major, indeed dominant, engine of national economic growth and development (Boskin and Lau, 1992; Freeman, 1982). In this view, the starting point for the interpretation of the comparative advantage of nations is not 'given' endowments of land, labour and capital, as assumed in conventional theory, but the manner in which technological change is dynamically and socially constructed. R&D is the heart of this social construction (Freeman, 1982, p. 5; Forey and Freeman, 1993).

Technological innovation as a basis for global competitiveness, whether considered from the perspective of firms or countries, is not simply a function of the scale of R&D. IBM, a technological flagship among multinational enterprises (MNEs), for example, spent $US6.5 billion and $US5.6 billion on R&D in 1992 and 1993 respectively while simultaneously incurring unprecedented corporate losses of $US17.8 billion (IBM, 1993). Throughout the 1980s and 1990s, the United States (US) as a whole has maintained high levels of R&D expenditure while continuing to see its economic performance challenged and even surpassed by the European Union (EU) and especially Japan. In the United Kingdom (UK), deindustrialization has maintained its inexorable march in apparent disdain of substantial R&D programmes and high-quality supplies of scientists and engineers. Yet economic supremacy, with respect to the UK in the nineteenth century, the US in the twentieth century, Japan in recent decades, and indeed advanced (and long-established) capitalist countries as a whole in relation to the rest of the world, has unquestionable foundations in inventiveness and superior patterns of technological innovation. In contemporary contexts, in addition to the scale of effort, the key to understanding the effectiveness of R&D relates to how it is organized as a system of related processes and how it is linked to broader systems of production and marketing (Dosi *et al.*, 1988; Freeman, 1982). Traditionally, geographical variations in R&D systems and related production system linkages have reflected distinctive 'national' models of innovation (Freeman, 1988; Lundvall, 1988), as well as the international fissures among the capitalist, (former) Communist and developing country worlds. These systems also change over time. Indeed, it is widely argued that recent, profound changes in the global economy intimately implicate R&D and related linkages, including with respect to its geography (Howells and Wood, 1992; Pearce and Singh, 1992).

According to Freeman and Perez (1988), since the late 1970s the restructuring of the global economy involves a shift in 'techno-economic paradigm' from that based on 'Fordist mass production' to a new one based on 'information and communication'. This new paradigm comprises numerous combinations of radical and incremental innovations in technology and organization which have already fundamentally altered the conditions underlying production and distribution and created new industries in microelectronics, biotechnology, the new materials, telecommunications and computers plus software, robots and machine tools. Thurow (1992, p. 45) labels the latter 'brainpower industries' to emphasize the importance of R&D to their competitive advantage. Furthermore, during this same period, the pace of technological change has quickened in many industrial sectors and R&D has created possibilities to consolidate and even rejuvenate existing industries, such as iron and steel, forest products and automobiles (Chapman and Humphrys, 1987). This increased role for R&D has potentially paradoxical effects, however. On the one hand, R&D imparts to nations, industries and firms competitiveness and flexibility to cope with a dynamic and globalizing economy which is posing a continually changing mosaic of differentiated market demands and sources of supply. On the other hand, R&D is itself a costly and uncertain process which generates innovations which further contribute to change and uncertainty. For firms, industries and nations, investment in R&D serves both to resolve and to complicate the implications of globalization.

The thesis that the global economy is in a period of transition from a Fordist to an information–communication techno-economic (IT) paradigm asserts that the economic impacts of the new information technologies are so pervasive that institutional innovations with respect to industrial organization, labour relations and training, education and even forms of international cooperation are required (Freeman and Perez, 1988; see also Chapter 6). For nations and their constituent governments, firms and labour organizations, the challenge is to 'match' the new technology with new institutions to provide the conditions for stable investment behaviour which best serves community interests. Any 'mismatches' in the relationships among R&D, educational, managerial, labour and design capability represent competitive disadvantages and sources of instability. In a comparision of 'brainpower industries' in the US and Japan, for example, Florida and Kenney (1990) demonstrate the skewed US emphasis on R&D and innovation, with much less interest in developing manufacturing potentials once initial super-profits have been claimed, in contrast to Japan where R&D, innovation and manufacturing are closely integrated and profit (and employment) possibilities more fully pursued. In the case of the UK, it has long been argued that an outstanding supply of scientists (research expertise) has not been 'matched' by equivalent engineering and managerial competence (development and organizational expertise), neatly symbolized by the fact that Nobel prizes in science have not meant economic success (Rosenberg, 1992, p. 92). In fact, this kind of mismatch is more deeply felt by the former centrally planned economies of Europe where elaborate R&D networks have been compromised by ineffective mechanisms of technological innovation and adaptation and in meeting consumer demands, the scale of the failure underlined by *glasnost* and *perestroika*. In many parts of the developing world such as Africa, on the other hand, imported technology often occurs without reference to indigenous R&D and technological capability, a mismatch seriously restricting long-run development (Ofori-Amoah, 1994).

In practice, governments and firms have choices regarding the organization, size and geography of R&D and how R&D processes are related to broader patterns of innovation and production. This chapter examines the changing nature of these characteristics and relationships on a global scale in the present period of global transition. There are three main parts to the chapter. First, R&D is defined and the key conceptual building block, specifically the R&D system, is explored, based on the experience of advanced capitalist countries, as an interlocking set of organizations in the public and private sectors that provide competitive and complementary roles in the R&D process. The second part focuses on the transition in the nature of the R&D system from the Fordist to the IT paradigm, including with respect to the internationalization of R&D activities. Finally, R&D is contemplated more broadly as part of national innovation systems, particularly with reference to the nature of technology strategies and technological transfer.

It should be noted that any evaluation of R&D on a global scale faces considerable difficulties in terms of information availability. Attempts to define the size and scope of R&D on an international scale are relatively recent, and reflect trends occurring since the 1960s. The most globally comprehensive and periodically available of these data sets are provided by the OECD (1971, 1981a, 1981b, 1990) and they primarily measure R&D in terms of (a) inputs such as size of employment and budgets; (b) the formal R&D programmes of large industrial corporations; and (c) activities located in advanced industrial countries. Even among these countries, information on R&D outputs, notably innovations, has been much more painstaking to construct (Freeman, 1982). A similar point may be made regarding the R&D activities of small and medium-sized enterprises (SMEs), with respect to inputs as well as outputs. In addition, the very core of R&D and related processes comprises a bewildering and complex variety of 'technological liaisons' or information exchanges which occur within and across organizational boundaries and which are extremely difficult to assess in a systematic, comparative way (Pearce and Singh, 1992). Moreover, in periods of dynamic change, in which long-term trends are complicated by short-term fluctuations and idiosyncratic behaviour, such assessments are particularly difficult.

RESEARCH AND DEVELOPMENT SYSTEMS

According to the OECD (1981a, p. 25), R&D comprises 'creative work undertaken on a systematic basis in order to increase the stock of knowledge ... and the use of this stock of knowledge to devise new applications.' Conventionally, R&D is interpreted as a continuum of activities involving basic research, applied research, development and technology transfer (Furness, 1958; see also Freeman, 1982, pp. 225–233; OECD, 1981a, pp. 25–37). Basic research is the search for fundamental laws and the study of natural and social phenomena for their own sake, while applied research uses the results of basic research to a specific process, material, device or product, on an industrial scale, to meet a commercial objective. Applied research typically involves the construction of working models (in the case of electrical or mechanical devices) or through the glassware stage in chemical analysis. The development stage involves further improvement, testing and evaluation of products or processes including the design, building and running of pilot plants. Technology transfer, which often requires major capital investment in new facilities, occurs when technology is installed and started up at specific industrial sites.

Historically, the roots of contemporary R&D activities were established in the last quarter of the nineteenth century when, as arguably the most important institutional innovation of the new 'electrical and heavy engineering' techno-economic paradigm (Freeman and Perez, 1988, p. 51), in-house research laboratories were established by a few firms in the new electrical and heavy chemical industries, especially in the US and Germany (Malecki, 1991, p. 161). An early 'model' of an in-house laboratory is provided by the German chemical manufacturer, Bayer AG, which began contracting university scientists in the late 1870s before opening up its own research laboratory in 1891 (Graham and Pruitt, 1990). In Freeman's (1982, pp. 10–15) terms, this development marked the onset of large scale, scientific and 'professionalized' R&D as individual inventors, often working directly in the production process, were increasingly replaced by teams of university-trained and highly specialized scientists and engineers working under the sponsorship and control of individual firms in expensive laboratories in which the R&D process involved the application of formally learned scientific principles to whole systems.

The pioneers of professionalized R&D, Germany and the US, surpassed the UK in terms of technical innovativeness and industrial production by 1900. Germany and the US, however, innovated totally different labour market institutions in articulating the link between R&D and production. While both countries, especially Germany, through universities and technical institutes provided high-level education for professional engineers of a scale and quality not hitherto available (Freeman, 1987, p. 3), Germany emphasized skill development throughout the workforce, particularly through large-scale and demanding apprenticeship schemes. In the US, on the other hand, Taylorism or scientific management became the basis for mass production in which job tasks were demarcated as narrowly as possible to permit high levels of productivity by essentially unskilled workers (Urry, 1986). While Germany's approach encouraged contributions to incremental technical change by workers, Taylorism deliberately restricted such tendencies.

Given German and US leadership, after 1900 R&D networks or systems were soon established by industry, government and the universities among the leading industrialized countries. After 1945, these systems were significantly enlarged and elaborated, including by Japan, and professional R&D increasingly became the most important source of innovation (and the term 'R&D', rather than 'industrial science', became widely used). The most sophisticated, successful R&D systems were developed in the capitalist countries and featured a diversity of organizations in which in-house R&D played a special role and which typically became a locationally distinct function within the firm.

The diversity of R&D organizations

The dominant organizations of professional R&D systems are the large-scale laboratories of corporations, governments, universities, industrial associations (funded by groups of firms) and cooperatives (funded by government and firms). According to Nelson (1988), the rationale for the diversity of R&D organizations is twofold. First, such diversity ensures competition in how, why and when technology is developed. Although at times wasteful and inefficient, as frequent failures both before and after commercialization attest, the offsetting benefits of technological competition relate to the inherent technical and economic uncertainty of R&D and innovation. While technical risk typically declines during the R&D process, the economic uncertainty of rival behaviour and consumer demand remains until after technology transfer. According to Nelson (1988), technical and economic uncertainty undermines *ex ante* consensus regarding the future direction of technological change even among experts. In this view, the economically superior performance of capitalist economies results from the extensive privatization of technology, the multiple, often rivalrous sources of new technology, and reliance on *ex post* market forces to determine success.

The second rationale for the diversity of R&D organizations relates to the complementary roles played by each type of organization within the R&D process. The most basic distinction is that between public and private sector organizations. At this level, the complementarity between public and private sector organizations rests on the relative merits and demerits of the 'public and private facets of technology' (Nelson, 1988, p. 314). Thus, private control of R&D is important partly for its competitive aspects and partly because it links the profit motive, and market opportunities, to the innovation process. In turn, such privatization depends upon the ability of individual firms to appropriate sufficient return on investments in R&D. If the 'appropriability regime' is too weak, which might well be the case in highly competitive industries comprising many small firms, there will be little incentive for an individual firm to engage in R&D. If the appropriability regime is too strong the potential for monopoly increases, the impacts of innovations in terms of spurring further innovations are reduced and users of technology are placed at a serious disadvantage. In this regard, publicly available technology offsets the disadvantages of private sector R&D in that widespread access to generic knowledge broadens the understanding of technical possibilities. That is, 'The public aspect of technology helps to control the inefficiencies associated with the private rivalrous aspect' (Nelson, 1988, p. 314). On the other hand, public sector technology cannot duplicate the advantages of private sector technology creation.

Traditionally, it has been argued that different organizations enjoy different advantages in the R&D system (Forgacs, 1979). A model based on the experience of the forest product industries, for example, suggests that basic research is best performed by universities, applied research is best performed by universities and association laboratories, while the in-house laboratories of forest product firms and equipment suppliers have comparative advantages in the development and technology transfer stages (Table 9.1). In practice, R&D systems have always varied considerably around this particular model. Thus, in industries dominated by small firms, including agriculture, the risks and costs of R&D may encourage association or government laboratories to invest in development R&D and technology transfer as well as applied R&D. On the other hand, in technologically dynamic sectors, the search for competitive advantage may push in-house groups to engage in applied and in-house R&D.

Whatever the precise configuration, the comparative advantages of different organizations in the R&D system are realized through networks of technological liaisons, or technologically based information exchanges. These liaisons may be public or private, formal or informal, hierarchical or lateral, unidirectional or multidirectional, long term or short term, intra- or interdepartmental, intra- or interorganizational and local or non-local. The liaisons may also be 'free' or involve an explicit price. In broad terms, these liaisons evolve according to the comparative advantages of each organization within the R&D system. Thus, during the

Table 9.1　The comparative advantages of alternative agencies in the forestry sector R&D process

	Basic research	Applied research	Process development	New product development	Technology transfer
Universities	A	A	B	C	C
Research cooperatives	B	A	B	B	C
Industry R&D	C	B	B	A	A
Equipment suppliers	C	C	A	C	A

Note: A is strong comparative advantage; B is moderate comparative advantage; C is weak comparative advantage. Note that if government-run laboratories were to be included they would enjoy moderate comparative advantages in basic and applied R&D but would not be effective in developmental and technology transfer work.

Source: Hayter (1988), p. 30.

twentieth century, as part of the overall growth of R&D, universities have expanded to supply labour to the system, introduce new programmes, supply the results of research activities in publicly available lectures, journals and meetings and offer sources of scientific and engineering expertise for contract.

As Nelson (1988) notes, there are no mechanical rules to resolve 'the institutional assignment problem' with respect to the allocation of resources among different R&D types, or to the most appropriate forms of technological liaisons. In practice, there are variations among nations in the relative size and functions of different types of organization within R&D systems, even within the same sector. In the R&D system underlying the North American forest product sector, for example, traditionally the US has given greater relative emphasis to in-house and university R&D while Canada has favoured government and association R&D (Hayter, 1981, 1985, 1988). Notwithstanding such differences, Nelson (1988, p. 325) judges that capitalist countries have 'solved the institutional assignment problem not optimally, but tolerably well.' In this context, in most industries, it is in-house R&D that plays a distinguishing and leading role.

In-house R&D

In-house R&D exists because it offers firm-specific advantages. Firms invest in R&D because they believe they can appropriate at least part of the benefits of this investment for themselves in terms of profits and market share. In-house R&D also provides firms with flexibility as to when R&D is conducted and technology transferred. These benefits cannot be derived easily, if at all, from other forms of R&D, especially that by governments and universities, whose mandates are to extend publicly available knowledge, although military R&D is one notable exception to this observation. Within the context of civilian R&D, however, only in-house R&D is oriented towards providing individual firms with the market advantages to be derived from product innovation, including those product innovations by equipment suppliers and subcontractors which represent new processes or component parts to user firms. In addition, firms, especially in resource sectors, may have to conduct in-house R&D to generate process innovations which are peculiar to their specific operations and resource endowments (Hayter, 1988).

Moreover, technology know-how is cumulative so that the probability of technological advance is to some extent a function of existing levels of technological knowledge (Dosi, 1988, p. 223). Over time, in-house R&D therefore potentially provides a dynamic source of advantage which adds to a firm's 'unique technological and organizational abilities' (Cohen and Mowery, 1984, p. 118) or 'tacit knowledge' (Teece, 1988, p. 263). For Cohen and Mowery (1984) and Teece (1988), as an alternative to in-house R&D, reliance on other firms ('the market') for technology is limited in practice by the costs and uncertainties involved in identifying specifications, the timing of supply, pricing formulas and secrecy considerations.

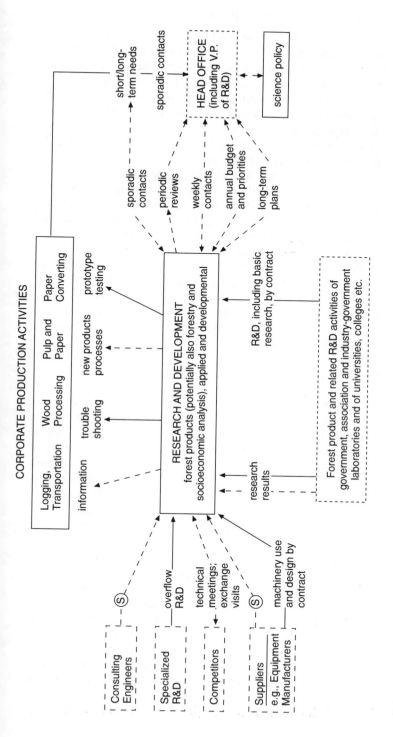

Figure 9.1 Technological liaisons and in-house R&D: the case of a forest product firm

In general, the importance of in-house R&D lies in its distinctive role in realizing the benefits of the 'private facets of technology', which includes focusing the 'public facets of technology' to suit the particular needs of the firm. A model of the technological liaisons organized around in-house R&D, based on experience within the forest industry, summarizes this role (Figure 9.1). On the one hand, through a plethora of technological liaisons, in-house R&D links its firm to the scientific and technological expertise of a wide variety of external organizations, including public sector sources, literally located throughout the globe. Given its intimate knowledge of the firm's production activities and associated marketing networks, in-house R&D is able to monitor, absorb and use information from the 'outside' world of science and technology to meet the specific needs of the firm, particularly those pertaining to long-run strategies which are directed by the head office. In this regard, the innovations generated by in-house R&D provide the firm with a set of investment opportunities whose timing, location and scale ultimately depend upon head-office priorities. Moreover, in-house R&D enhances the ability of firms to access and negotiate technological liaisons of varying degrees of complexity and sophistication, for example with university scientists (to access 'public' knowledge) or other in-house R&D groups (to exchange 'private' knowledge). Indeed, in-house groups contribute not only towards a firm's knowledge base and technology strategy but also to its bargaining power.

Location requirements

With gathering momentum throughout the twentieth century an increasing number of large firms established large, specialized R&D laboratories in new locations. Frequently, the origins of these centres are found in the consolidation of small-scale, scattered research and engineering groups established as part of manufacturing operations. The new centres, however, were typically located away from factories, often in a suburban area in the same metropolitan area as the corporate head office. While some firms have built several R&D centres, including in a few cases some in foreign countries, large (corporate) R&D centres locationally separate from production are an important theme in the professionalization of R&D.

The rationale underlying the trend towards the assembly of groups of scientists and engineers in a few large-scale operations is partly based on the advantages of a division of labour which assumes that there are significant productivity gains ('problem solving' benefits) by hiring and coordinating a large number of highly specialized professionals rather than a smaller number of individuals with more general skills (Vernon, 1970; Howells and Wood, 1992, p. 34). Such larger groups can be expected to generate benefits in terms of a more sophisticated knowledge base (and associated larger networks of technological liaisons) and more effective brainstorming, and in spreading the cost of equipment and support staff, which in turn allows specialists to concentrate on their speciality. In addition, there is an insurance principle which states that among a large group of projects a few are bound to be successful. Centralized laboratories also offer security advantages and, by offering technological expertise to the rest of the firm, a way in which the parent company can control and integrate increasingly dispersed operations.

Historically, in-house R&D has been dominated by large firms, especially multinational firms based in advanced capitalist countries, which have concentrated R&D overwhelming in home (donor) economies (Mansfield *et al.*, 1979). Such locational preferences reflect corporate concerns for effective communication, security of the R&D process itself, and the sophisticated infrastructure available in advanced countries including universities which supply basic and applied research and a supply of scientists and engineers. Indeed, in-house R&D continues to be strongly concentrated in the Triad of the US, Japan and the EU (Malecki, 1991). Within advanced nations, the tendency towards the locational concentration of R&D in particular regions and even metropolitan areas has long been noted, including the US (Ullman, 1958; Malecki, 1979, 1980), throughout Europe (Hall *et al.*, 1987; Molle *et al.*, 1989) and Japan (Edgington, 1994; Nishioka and Takeuchi, 1989). In these countries, the concentration of R&D tends to favour established, dominant regions which are also political, corporate and cultural control centres. At metropolitan and community scales, numerous locational surveys point to the importance of access to good communications, universities, availability of scientists and engineers, nearness to head offices and urban and recreational amenities thought conducive to attracting such professionals (Malecki and Bradbury, 1992).

The explanation for the locational separation of R&D from manufacturing activities is a matter of some debate. Three main reasons, not necessarily mutually exclusive, are made in this context. First, the conventional argument, often discussed within the terms of reference of the product cycle model, is that R&D, activities require different inputs from manufacturing activities and these different inputs are found in different locations (Vernon, 1966; Erickson, 1976). The model predicts locational change as labour requirements shift from the need to access professional scientists and engineers to the need to access manufacturing workers. A second argument emphasizes the long-run 'strategic' nature of R&D, which requires that R&D groups do not become embroiled in short-run troubleshooting activities at particular manufacturing plants. A related point is that some distance between head office and R&D centre reduces disruptions by too frequent personal contact. A third argument is based on labour relations considerations, and stresses that the locational separation of R&D workers from manufacturing workers facilitates managerial preferences to 'segment' the two groups according to different employment policies (Clark, 1981). In this view, because R&D professionals are expensive to recruit and train, and they contribute towards the firm's core expertise, firms wish to provide them with high wages, relatively autonomous employment conditions and job stability through minor recessions. In contrast, if firms wish to strictly control the employment conditions and costs of production workers, geographic separation of R&D and manufacturing activities can help the formulation of different labour market agreements and reduce chances of spillover effects from one labour agreement to another. This thinking is also consistent with the legacy of scientific management, which stresses sharp dividing lines between managers, who do the thinking, from highly specialized and deskilled workers, who do the operating (Marshall and Tucker, 1992; Urry, 1986). In this philosophy, R&D workers are a part of management.

Whatever the relative importance or mix of locational factors, the geography of R&D is important for local development. Thus, R&D offers high-income jobs and associated multiplier benefits while in a more fundamental way the nature of R&D itself, and related innovative performance, is intimately interrelated with geographical context. As R&D systems evolve, these interrelationships are becoming even more important.

R&D IN TRANSITION

The shift from the Fordist techno-economic paradigm to the IT techno-economic paradigm has reinforced the role of R&D and innovation as a source of competitive advantage. Among OECD countries, for example, the high R&D intensity ('high-tech') industries spent at least 4.4 per cent of their revenues on R&D, and in the case of aerospace, office machines and computers, electronics and components, and drugs (pharmaceuticals) this proportion was significantly greater (Table 9.2). In general, the more research-intensive industries have grown much faster. In contrast, the low R&D intensity ('low-tech') industries spent less than 1.0 per cent of revenues on R&D. Even so, technological change has been important in these industries, and perhaps to an unexpected degree competitiveness and even survival have depended upon innovation and creating products which have more value (Chapman and Humphrys, 1987).

Table 9.2 Gross Domestic Expenditure on R&D (GERD) as a percentage of GNP: selected countries, 1961–90

	1961		1969		1979		1990	
	All	Civilian	All	Civilian	All	Civilian	All	Civilian
United States	2.73	1.20	2.72	1.49	2.28	1.59	2.77	1.75[c]
Japan	1.39	1.37	1.64	1.61	1.97	n/a	2.88	2.86[c]
Germany	1.25	1.14[a]	2.05	1.81	2.34	2.16	2.73	2.40[c]
United Kingdom	2.46	1.48	2.22	1.66	2.13	1.49[b]	2.19	1.65[c]
France	1.38	0.97	1.94	1.52	1.81	1.38	2.42	1.75[c]

[a] Data for 1962.
[b] Data for 1978.
[c] Data for civilian R&D in 1990 are estimated because they are inferred from a graph.

Source: Adapted from Pianta (1988), p. 66; *Research Technology Management*, **37**(1) (1994) 6.

Table 9.3 Industries classified according to R&D intensity[a]

Industries (high intensity)	Intensity 1980	Industries (medium intensity)	Intensity 1980	Industries (low intensity)	Intensity 1980
Aerospace	22.7	Motor cars	2.7	Stone, clay and glass	0.9
Office machines, computers	17.5	Chemicals	2.3	Food, beverages, tobacco	0.8
Electronics and components	10.4	Other manufacturing	1.8	Shipbuilding	0.6
Drugs	8.7	Rubber, plastics	1.2	Petroleum	0.6
Instrument	4.8	Non-ferrous metals	1.0	Ferrous metals	0.6
Electric machinery	4.4			Fabricated metal products	0.4
				Paper, printing	0.3
				Wood, cork, furniture	0.3
				Textiles, footwear, leather	0.2

[a]Intensity is the ratio of R&D expenditure/sales.

Source: OECD (1986), p. 59.

Geographically, the transition from the Fordist to the IT paradigm has been driven largely by the technology generated by the OECD countries which continued to fund large-scale R&D activities (Table 9.3). Thus, among these countries, gross domestic expenditures on R&D (GERD) have never fallen below 1.25 of GNP since at least 1961. For these and other OECD countries, including Sweden, the Netherlands and Switzerland, GERDs have consistently increased, at least as regards civilian R&D. In 1990 GERDs for civilian R&D for the US, Japan, Germany, the UK and France were all higher than in 1961 and, with some exceptions, have increased steadily over this period. The increase in the GERD for civilian R&D in the UK, however, is relatively modest. Among this group of countries the US and the UK, and to a lesser extent France, are exceptional in the importance attached to military R&D and for both these countries (but not for France) the relative role of military R&D in relation to civilian R&D declined from 1961 to 1990. As a result, in overall terms, the UK's GERD has declined significantly while that for the US in 1990 was more or less the same as in 1961. In contrast, Germany and Japan have significantly increased their GERDs over the last several decades and the relative importance they attach to civilian R&D by 1990 was much greater than for the US. Indeed, even in absolute terms, by 1990 when the US spent $US104.6 billion on civilian R&D, Japan spent almost as much on this type of R&D. Freeman (1987) also argues that Japan was organizing its R&D differently and more effectively than in the Fordist model so that by 1980 Japan had emerged as the globe's leading national innovation system.

Under Fordism, R&D developed as a linear process which provided the technological underpinnings for highly structured and rigid production, employment and marketing activities. In the IT paradigm, R&D is developed as a loopy process to provide the underpinnings for more flexible production, employment and marketing activities. This transition is by no means clear-cut in chronological or geographical terms. Outside the leading industrial sectors in the US, where Fordist features were most fully developed in the 1950s and 1960s, there are questions as to the extent of Fordism (Storper and Scott, 1992). Indeed, at this time Japan's R&D and related production systems were developing in distinctive ways that culminated in its emergence as a leading proponent of loopy R&D interconnected to flexible manufacturing within the IT paradigm (Freeman, 1988). Moreover, in the present period of transition, there are inevitably variations in the speed and extent to which established Fordist R&D systems are adjusting while new, loopy models, because they explicitly celebrate flexibility and the 'blurring' of boundaries, are inherently diverse. Within the context of complex practice, however, the shift from linear to loopy R&D is a powerful impulse which resonates globally.

From linear to loopy R&D systems

Fordism was most elaborately refined during the 1950s and 1960s in the US, specifically among the leading industrial sectors dominated by giant corporations and supported by 'big' government and labour (Galbraith, 1967). The core of Fordist production refers to large-scale, capital-intensive factories mass-producing standard products for mass consumption and employing a unionized workforce organized according to the structured discipline of Taylorism (see also Chapter 3). Technological dynamism is provided by extensive commitments to R&D, organized around in-house laboratories whose responsibility is to supply a stream of product and process innovations to highly specialized factories.

Fordism fundamentally organized technological change, from beginning to end, as a linear process in which ideas are progressively researched, developed, transferred to factories and incorporated within the productive process. The labour process is arranged in an equivalent way with the highest level and most abstract intellectual skills found in basic and applied research gradually giving way to more practical problem-solving skills and ultimately to the minimally skilled manual ('machine minding') workers on the factory floor. This Fordist linear approach to technological change emphasizes the specialization and compartmentalization throughout the entire process. On the one hand, there is the basic distinction between the 'thinkers', the professional scientists, engineers and managers, and the 'doers' or operators who perform simple, sharply demarcated tasks within factories and within areas of factories, as required by scientific management (Urry, 1986). At the same time, Fordism stresses the principles of specialization ('demarcation') within R&D groups. Thus scientists and engineers are recruited because of their particular specialisms, which define the nature of their subsequent contributions within a particular R&D department such as basic, applied or development research (Table 9.1). Each R&D department constitutes its own compartmentalized speciality and any planned interaction between these departments, and indeed between the R&D group and production, is constrained to times when a task of one department is completed and is passed (forward) to the next department in the linear line of progression.

As a graphic illustration of technological change as a linear process under Fordism, specifically with reference to the practice of American auto manufacturers, following Lutz (1994), in-house R&D may be represented as a set of 'chimneys' (Figure 9.2). Within the R&D system, each chimney represents a separate functional department, such as basic research, while beyond R&D there are additional chimneys representing other functions, notably procurement and supply and production activities in home and foreign countries. In this model, technology moves progressively forward between these specialized, semi-autonomous chimneys so that, for example, 'the design department, working more or less in a vacuum, would design a car and then "shove it out the door" to the engineering department' which in turn would behave in a similar manner (Lutz, 1994, p. 14). Planned interaction between chimneys is limited to these points of exchange. In practice, some decentralization of R&D occurs, such as an R&D unit in support of foreign-based manufacturing operations, but under Fordism these units are typically small in scale and limited to short-run adaptations of mature products to meet any distinctive requirements of the local market (Mansfield *et al.*, 1979; Britton and Gilmour, 1978).

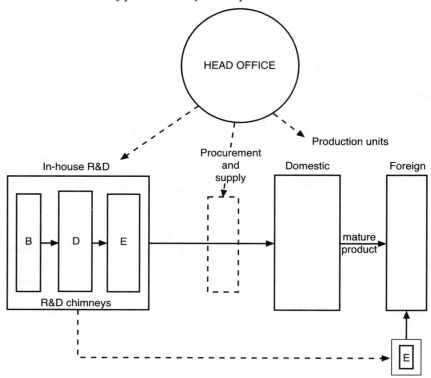

B: basic research
D: applied research and product design
E: engineering development and technology transfer

Figure 9.2   Innovation as a linear process (adapted from Lutz, 1994)

The problem underlying the Fordist linear model of technological change is its rigidity, a characteristic often associated with Fordism as a whole (Storper and Scott, 1992). In this model, R&D occurs within largely separate and highly specialized departments and technology is assumed to flow only one way. Yet, even if linearity is important, the R&D process also exhibits some decidedly non-linear features. The inherent uncertainty of R&D means that it is a messy process which does not, and cannot, always unfold in simple, linear terms. Thus documentary evidence typically, if not invariably, points to the occurrence of rethinking, redesign, re-experimentation and reassessments during the R&D process, as well as the need for the creation of interdisciplinary and inter-departmental groups to deal with special problems (Freeman, 1982). While in Fordist models such feedback and integrative mechanisms necessarily occur, they are treated as *ad hoc* responses to unanticipated problems and are not systematically incorporated into the planning of the R&D and innovation process. Based on experience within the US auto industry, Lutz (1994, p. 14) notes that reassessments and corrections, which he labels 're-do loops', were constantly required and led to high costs and long development times. In this industry, as in others, these problems were often compounded by a workforce, with minimal responsibilities and rarely even meeting R&D members, increasingly disinterested in contributing to technical change or quality control.

The Fordist model nevertheless performed successfully, if not optimally, during the 'long boom' following 1945, especially in the US, where US corporate giants dominated domestic markets. With gathering momentum, however, signalled by the energy crisis of 1974, the increasing intensity of technological change, differentiation of markets, severity of recessions and global competition exposed the limitations of the Fordist mass production paradigm and its linear model of technological change (Kenney and Florida, 1993). These same trends also emphasized the growing primacy of production systems based on principles of flexibility, including R&D and innovation processes in which 'loopiness' is a built-in characteristic. The leading model of these principles is provided by Japanese industry.

As Freeman (1988, pp. 335–336) notes, in contrast to the strictures of Fordism, corporate policy and practice in Japan have encouraged (a) a commitment to 'reverse engineering' to comprehensively learn best practice technology as a basis for further innovation; (b) managers, engineers and workers to think in an integrated way about the entire production system including with respect to product and process design; (c) use of factories as laboratories which constantly bring together R&D professionals with production engineers and workers in a manner which facilitates collective learning processes; (d) an emphasis on increasing quality by constantly seeking to correct defects and upgrading products and processes; and (e) the involvement of suppliers and consumers in close and stable relationships at the core of which is the exchange of technological expertise (see Asanuma, 1989; Patchell, 1993a, 1993b). Recently, Fruin (1992) and Kenney and Florida (1993) have elaborated on these themes to stress the thoroughness of Japanese concern for innovation, the importance of interdependence and cooperation within and among Japanese firms, and the emphasis on skill formation and learning at all levels of operation.

In contrast to Fordist practice, Japanese firms have developed flexible production systems in which a loopy model of technological change is explicitly incorporated. As Kenney and Florida (1993, pp. 55–65) observe, while Japanese firms have invested in central laboratories to conduct long-term R&D they have also typically retained significant developmental R&D groups at factory sites. Moreover, narrowly based specialist education is less important to Japanese firms when hiring scientists and engineers, who are likely to be involved in more diverse tasks and be given more leeway to follow 'leads' than counterparts in a traditional Fordist laboratory. Thus, in Japan polyvalence or functional flexibility within the framework of teamwork is important among professionals as well as among factory floor workers. In addition, R&D professionals in central laboratories are typically relocated to factory sites over extensive periods, while factory floor experimentation involving worker cooperation is a normal and accepted activity. Moreover, in part, the loops that link R&D and production, and those linking groups within R&D, within the firm are complemented by extensive networking with other firms which features the looping and mutual development of expertise. For Fruin (1992, p. 21), this loopiness culminates in 'focal factories', which are multifunctional manufacturing sites which combine production of several products with planning, design, development and process engineering capabilities and a commitment to continuous improvement. In turn, focal factories are typically closely integrated with the activities of specialized SMEs to provide Japanese companies with 'a formidable range of complementary resources for potentially unending business activities' (Fruin, 1992, p. 26).

Loopy R&D and innovation processes are a crucial element in the transition from the Fordist to the IT techno-economic paradigm not only in Japan but elsewhere. In Germany, for example, a parallel trend is reflected in the development of 'diversified quality production' and the idea of firms as learning organizations (Streeck, 1989). Some US manufacturers steeped in Fordism are also adapting. Chrysler, for example, has 'toppled the old functional chimneys and replaced them with *cross-functional* product development teams' called platforms, each of which seeks to integrate research, design, engineering, procurement and supply, sales and manufacturing for one particular model of vehicle (Lutz, 1994, p. 14). Such platforms exemplify an explicitly loopy process in which boundaries between functions are designed to be permeable. The trend towards loopy R&D, now deemed a more efficient model than linear R&D in generating innovations and quality production, is also adding to the uncertainty of the R&D process.

Increasing uncertainty of the R&D process

There is increasing evidence that the life spans of new products are shortening. Among high tech industries, for example, Howells and Wood (1992, p. 43) report that in the UK the 20-year patent life of new drugs has been reduced to eight years while the time scale between generations of semiconductor devices has dropped from four to three years. In Japan, car companies have been planning on entirely new models every four years for some time, and in a mature industry Silversides (1984) reports that the life expectancies of innovations in Canadian forest harvesting operations have declined dramatically over the past 100 years. Such shortening product life cycles inevitably place more pressure on in-house R&D programmes to generate innovations, pressures which increase during recessions such as that of the early 1990s when even Japan-based MNEs trimmed R&D budgets, especially for basic research (Swinbanks, 1994, p. 6; Wolff, 1994, p. 22). At the same time, there is evidence that the ability of R&D to generate payoffs is becoming more difficult.

In the pharmaceutical industry, for example, it is argued that the 'easy' discoveries have been made and that the remaining diseases, such as cancer and Acquired Immune Deficiency Syndrome (AIDS), are extremely complex and pose considerable scientific difficulties in creating effective cures (Howells and Wood, 1992, p. 41). Indeed, the rate of innovation of new products in pharmaceuticals has dropped considerably from the 1960s to the 1980s while the length of time, the effort and the costs required to develop new products have increased. For example, one estimate has placed the average length of time to make a new medicine publicly available in 1970 at six years and in 1985 at 12 years. Similar evidence exists in aerospace and telecommunications (Grupp and Schnoring, 1992; Mowery and Rosenberg, 1989). Moreover, even if rates of return on R&D investments in mature industries are underestimated (Mansfield *et al.*, 1977), such R&D still faces considerable uncertainty (Hayter, 1988; Tillman, 1985).

To the extent that the rate of innovation is enhanced, the trend towards loopy R&D is a cause and effect of uncertainty. This trend is also associated with new developments in the internationalization of R&D facilities and of technological liaisons as firms seek to broaden bases for innovation and market growth.

The internationalization of R&D

MNEs have operated foreign-based R&D laboratories for a long time, some-times as a result of acquisition. International Paper (IP) of New York, for example, in the 1920s acquired a Canadian subsidiary which had an R&D centre which subsequently became the central facility of IP until 1969 when it was replaced by a new centre in New York state, after which the Canadian operation was gradually run down (Hayter, 1988). The Canadian centre was finally closed in the 1980s shortly after IP had sold its Canadian subsidiary to a Canadian firm. A condition of the sale required that any results from established R&D programmes in the Canadian laboratory were to be the intellectual property of IP, thus creating obvious difficulties for its maintenance.

In general terms, the impact of acquisition by foreign companies on indigenous R&D is not well documented. It is known, however, that MNEs have overwhelmingly preferred to consolidate R&D operations, particularly impor-tant longer term R&D, in donor or home economies. In 1966, for example, just 7.4 per cent of in-house R&D by US firms occurred in foreign countries, the lion's share of which was located in Canada, Germany and the UK. Moreover, there is considerable survey evidence, especially of US MNEs, that traditionally foreign R&D is largely oriented to short-run, 'adaptive' R&D designed to modify product innovations from parent laboratories for local markets (Britton and Gilmour, 1978; Firn, 1975; Hayter, 1988; Mansfield *et al.*, 1979; Thwaites, 1978).

In recent years, however, there are indications of a trend, albeit modest so far, towards an increase in the number of foreign-controlled R&D centres and of possible changes in the motives for such centres. Howells and Wood (1992, p. 23), for example, note that by 1990 9.3 per cent of US-owned in-house R&D

centres were in foreign countries, a slight but noticeable increase from the situation in the 1960s, and that foreign-owned R&D accounted for 11.3 per cent of R&D in the US in 1988, up from 4.8 per cent in 1977. Within the US, a recent survey counted 250 R&D facilities in 1992 that are owned by over 100 foreign companies, over 50 per cent of which had been established since 1987. In fact, 70 had been set up or acquired between 1990 and 1992 (Serapio and Dalton, 1993). Japanese companies have the most foreign-owned R&D facilities in the US (150 out of 250 in the Serapio and Dalton 1993 survey) and firms such as Sony, Matsushita and Fujitsu have at least eight such laboratories. European companies account for most of the remainder while South Korean conglomerates, including Samsung, Hyundai and Daewoo, operated 15 R&D facilites in the US by 1992.

There have been suggestions that new motives underlie this recent expansion of foreign R&D centres, notably related to accessing new sources of technological expertise by hiring 'foreign' scientists and engineers, establishing liaisons with organizations comprising the 'foreign' R&D system, facilitating collaboration in joint R&D projects and generally helping to keep abreast of technological developments (Howells and Wood, 1992; Serapio and Dalton, 1993, p. 37). In the US, for example, some Japanese auto companies and German pharmaceutical companies are conducting more sophisticated R&D than has been associated with foreign laboratories in the past. In the case of pharmaceuticals, German companies have established an unusually strong basis of R&D in the US as BASF AG is building a US$70 million genetic research facility in Massachusetts, Hoechst AG is constructing a molecular neurobiology laboratory in New Jersey, Bayer AG is building a US$130 million genetic research centre in Connecticut and Schering AG has acquired an existing gene technology specialist (Blau, 1994, p. 3). Indeed, according to Blau (1994), 75 per cent of Germany's genetic R&D is located outside the country, principally in the US, in part to escape extremely strict German regulations governing genetic R&D and partly to access internationally renowned US university-based expertise. Hoechst's new laboratory in New Jersey, for example, involves a cooperative agreement with Harvard University while Bayer has established strong liaisons between its Connecticut laboratory and Yale and the University of California at Berkeley.

The establishment of foreign-controlled 'leading edge' R&D centres is not limited to the US. Thus, US MNEs, such as Texas Instruments and IBM, have major R&D centres in Japan and Europe as well as the US. IBM, for example, has created an extensive global network of R&D centres anchored by three basic research laboratories in Ruschlikon, New York (IBM's headquarter location), San Jose ('Silicon Valley') and Zürich (Kelly and Keeble, 1990). These pools of basic research support IBM's global network of 23 R&D laboratories, which are engaged in various kinds of applied and development work for IBM as a whole rather than simply as a support to local manufacturing operations. As a Japanese example, Hitachi's nine corporate laboratories, employing 4500 people, include the Hitachi Cambridge laboratory, a cooperative venture with Cambridge

University, and the Hitachi Dublin laboratory, a cooperative venture with Trinity College, Dublin (Takeda, 1993, p. 9). According to Yamamoto (1994), more Japanese companies need to create such foreign-based R&D laboratories to facilitate 'cross-cultural exchanges' if they are to be in the forefront of radical technological change in the future.

The internationalization of R&D through strategic alliances among 'rival' R&D groups, to share costs and to promote 'synergistic' interactions among interdisciplinary research groups for expensive technologies, including those which promise pervasive effects, is also increasingly mooted. The four global alliances to promote RISC (reduced instruction-set computing) technology, for example, involve complex links although one company at the centre of each alliance (Sun, Hewlett Packard, IBM and MIPS) was primarily responsible for developing the RISC technology (Gomes-Casseres, 1994, p. 64). In this case, alliance relationships centred more on agreements, formal and otherwise, to use and market the technology and provide equity. An extremely ambitious proposal for strategic alliances has recently been made by Japan for an Intelligent Manufacturing Systems (IMS) programme to involve companies from Japan, the US, Europe, Canada and Australia over a ten-year period to develop global manufacturing techniques, environmentally friendly manufacturing technology and human and cultural aspects of manufacturing (Swinbanks, 1994). The initial idea of coordinating this programme through one large, centralized laboratory, mainly funded by Japan, was rejected in favour of a more decentralized organizational structure, and eventually 73 companies and 60 universities in five regions were involved in testing the feasibility of IMS during 1993. Examples of projects under consideration are 'Globeman 21', led by British Aerospace, to find the most effective ways of running global manufacturing operations; 'holonic manufacturing systems', led by Allen Bradley of the US, to develop technology for open, distributed, autonomous, cooperation systems in manu-facturing; and 'systematization of knowledge' led by Mitsubishi (Swinbanks, 1994).

Whether or not the IMS proposals become reality, during the transition from the Fordist to the IT techno-economic paradigm professional R&D has become more internationalized in the sense that foreign R&D centres have expanded in number, have more diverse national origins, are more involved in sophisticated research, and have stimulated new technological liaisons within R&D systems, while strategic R&D alliances which cross national boundaries have also occurred. Howells and Wood (1992, p. 36) argue that while the R&D efforts of most MNEs continue to be 'home market' based (that is, exclusively concen-trated in the home market) or 'host country' based (that is, R&D is still concentrated in home countries but is supplemented by R&D in foreign countries which adapts technology created in parent laboratories for local markets and conditions), the clear trend is towards 'world based' R&D (that is, R&D located in several countries which supply technology to international markets).

The scale of the internationalization of R&D, and whether this trend implies that MNEs are 'transforming themselves into "placeless" networks of economic power, shifting financial and intellectual power' (Howells and Wood, 1992, p. 4) lacking any national allegiance, however, may be questioned. Howells and Wood's data, for example, indicate that almost 90 per cent of in-house R&D in the US is still conducted by US firms and that over 90 per cent of R&D by American firms remains in the US. Pearce (1990) and Patel and Pavitt (1991) also emphasize that in-house R&D remains largely a domestic enterprise that is very much concentrated among advanced countries and typically in a few locations within these countries which give preferred access to established sources of expertise and labour. Many of the recently established foreign R&D centres represent the 'host country' (adaptive R&D) model and in some cases represent the relatively recent growth of Japanese and European MNEs, which are catching up with the established presence of US MNEs. Typically, the various forms of 'world based' R&D (Howells and Wood, 1992, p. 145) have occurred within MNEs in research-intensive industries characterized by loopy R&D and under considerable pressure to maintain high rates of innovation. Even among these firms, foreign R&D laboratories are not randomly located but contribute to the strategies and structures of MNEs, which have distinct geographies, including control and ownership bases which have distinct national roots. Moreover, formal, long-term R&D collaborations among MNEs remain rare.

From spatial to flexible divisions of labour

Under Fordism, it was argued that MNEs, especially US MNEs, locationally arrange functions so as to produce a distinct spatial division of labour, whether at global (Hymer, 1972b) or national (Clark, 1981; Erickson, 1976) scales (see also Chapter 4). Simply stated, at the global scale, this thesis predicts that MNEs tend to concentrate head-office and R&D centres (and high-paying jobs) in industrialized countries (and in a hierarchy of centres within these countries) while decentralizing the least skilled, manual work (and low-paying jobs) among poor countries. The linear model of R&D helped underpin this thesis by associating the locational requirements for R&D and innovative manufacturing with industrialized countries and of standardized manufacturing of mature products with poor countries.

With the transition to the IT techno-economic paradigm, however, the 'simple' spatial division of labour thesis has been complicated by the tendency towards flexible manufacturing and loopy R&D. Flexible production and loopy R&D generate far more varied predictions about the geography of the division of labour both within large corporations (the internal division of labour) and among firms (the social division of labour). On the one hand, tendencies towards the integration of R&D and production and inter-firm collaborations, especially in research-intensive industries marked by rapid innovation, imply strong tendencies towards geographic concentration. In this context, production systems throughout Japan (Patchell, 1993a) and selected high-tech centres in the US, notably Silicon Valley (Saxenian, 1983), represent quintessential, albeit different examples. On the other hand, flexible manufacturing can imply the exploitation of a peripheral workforce in a manner consistent with the spatial division of labour thesis. For governments wishing to 'clone' Silicon Valley or Toyota City, understanding the conditions underlying their evolution is a prerequisite.

NATIONAL INNOVATION SYSTEMS IN TRANSITION

The purpose of R&D is to generate innovations of one kind or another and commercially oriented R&D is designed specifically to generate product and process innovations for commercial advantage. Indeed, for Freeman (1987, p. 1) R&D systems are part of more broadly conceived national innovation systems which comprise interlocking public and private sector organizations that exist within a nation to import, adapt and diffuse, as well as to research and develop, new technologies (see also Lundvall, 1988; Nelson, 1988, 1993). It is argued that the transition in techno-economic paradigm from Fordism to IT features powerful globalizing tendencies, for example in the form of declining barriers to trade, more mobile financial capital, the growth of trade and foreign investment, which are increasing the 'openness' of nations to outside influences and rendering them less viable as political and economic entities (Storper, 1994). A parallel suggestion is that regions (subdivisions of nations) are more relevant territorial units in the face of such globalizing pressures. According to Freeman (1987), however, the contemporary shift in paradigm, and associated global-ization pressures, are placing even more stress on nations to effectively organize R&D and innovation systems and to cooperate with other nations to deal with international problems exacerbated by globalization, such as Third World debt and environmental issues. In addition, Freeman's focus on national innovation systems does not preclude a greater role for regions.

National innovation systems are deeply embedded and are cemented, not only by expensive and extensive physical infrastructure, but also by systems of education and training, information networks and associated established values and customs, including those of business itself. In this latter regard, for example, business culture, that is established beliefs and microeconomic practices and attitudes towards government–business relations, have varied historically among nations, even if these variations are becoming blurred (Atkinson and Coleman, 1989; Dyson, 1983). For Freeman (1987), the policy challenge posed by the paradigmatic shift from Fordism to IT is whether industrialized countries, including former centrally planned ones, have the ability to reorganize or adjust established innovation systems in appropriate ways and whether developing countries can create appropriate innovation systems. In this context, a variety of options for technology strategy can be recognized.

Technology strategy options

To emphasize the range of options available to individual firms, Freeman (1982, pp. 169–186) classifies technology strategies as 'traditional', 'dependent', 'imitative', 'defensive' and 'offensive'. In turn, this framework has been applied to countries at different stages of industrialization comprising different bundles of technical skills, capabilities and policy needs (Britton and Gilmour, 1978, pp. 134–140). According to this framework, non-industrialized countries are in a 'traditional' stage in which the basic policy need is the creation of basic educational and technical skills; industrializing countries are 'dependent' upon the adoption of 'mature' technology developed elsewhere and technology policy concerns involve the development of management and technical skills to properly evaluate this technology; and semi-industrial countries pursue 'imitative' technology strategies which involve the deliberate adaptation of foreign technology and stress the creation of development and design engineering skills. At the other end of the continuum, industrial and post-industrial countries respectively emphasize defensive and offensive technology strategies. In both cases, countries have developed sophisticated R&D systems. Defensive strategies, however, imply an emphasis on secondary innovation or innovative copying of high-value and differentiated products; the policy need is to develop the leading edge R&D and the original innovative capacity associated with offensive strategies.

It is not easy to classify countries according to these admittedly crudely defined stages, especially given the dynamic nature of technology strategies and of sectoral and regional variations within countries. Nevertheless, this framework does underline the real differences in technical sophistication and innovative potential that exist among countries. As of the early 1990s, for example, the poorest African countries probably remain in the traditional strategy stage while Japan, the US and Germany constitute the three most important countries pursuing offensive technology strategies. Most countries probably straddle or represent combinations of the stages outlined. Many developing countries, for example, reveal dependent and imitative technology strategies and South Korea may well illustrate a country contemplating a defensive technology strategy. Some formerly centrally planned economies of eastern Europe may have the ability to move rapidly beyond defensive and imitative strategies to pursue defensive technology strategies.

Regardless of how individual countries are classified in these technological terms, historically and to the present, there have been strong causal relationships between R&D, innovativeness and industrial development. These relationships do not evolve on an inevitable evolutionary trajectory, however, so that distinctions between traditional, dependent, imitative, defensive and offensive strategies (or some related scheme) represent only a continuum of possibilities. If Japan has moved rapidly through these possibilities to establish the world's leading innovation system, the technology levels of some African countries may have declined as adoption of foreign technology has not been equated with improvement in indigenous skills, with respect to either adapting foreign technology or creating more appropriate technology (Ofori-Amoah, 1994). According to Britton and Gilmour (1978), primarily because of unusually high levels of foreign control, Canada represents a country that is 'frozen' in the imitative stage as most branch plants chose to adapt the technology supplied by parents (Britton, 1980). The UK may even be moving backwards to the extent that the deindustrialization of many parts of its economy is associated with a withdrawal from offensive strategies to defensive and even imitative ones. Moreover, the UK, once the world's leading industrial innovator, is itself increasingly relying on foreign investment to establish 'best practice' models of technology and organization. There are, however, important dilemmas facing such a strategy, not only for the UK but for all countries.

Technology transfer and the international firm: the paradox for host country development

Once the industrial revolution had begun in the UK in the late eighteenth century, countries have been forced to consider how to respond to technological change elsewhere. Technology can be copied, imitated or adapted, by purchase or theft, or it can be imported in the form of finished goods or as a branch plant operation of an international firm. With gathering momentum since the 1860s, the transfer of technology within foreign-controlled branch plants has been a seductive and insistently offered option. It has also posed a complex paradox for host country development.

As the theory of the multinational firm attests, firms expand internationally because they seek some distinct resource or know-how, such as technological know-how, which they can readily transfer to host economies within the context of branch plant operations (Dicken, 1992b). In effect, MNEs enjoy 'entry advantages', which are the costs and uncertainties facing local firms in duplicating the expertise the MNE already has (Hayter, 1981). For host economies, the MNE potentially offers formidable advantages in strategies of economic growth. In particular, by offering an established bundle of know-how and resources in the form of access to markets and financing which are locally scarce, foreign investment can substantially speed up rates of growth. Whether or not foreign investment acts as a catalyst for wider structural changes in the host economy, however, is debatable. Indeed, MNEs may have little interest in transferring expertise to a local economy if such a strategy potentially serves to reduce entry advantages and create new sources of competition. Rather, in such instances, MNEs seek to internalize transactions and maintain control of their know-how within the firm as far as possible.

Thus, the paradox for host economies of relying on MNEs for technology transfer exists when know-how, which is embodied in plant and equipment and internalized within international intracorporate networks, cannot be readily disaggregated and communicated within the host economy, beyond the knowledge associated with operating skills. Moreover, the traditional tendency of

MNEs to concentrate R&D groups in donor economies reinforces constraints on effective technology transfer and reduces the chance of similar activities in the host economy. In this way, high levels of foreign control in the long run, such as that experienced by Canada, may lead to 'technological truncation' in which potentially viable R&D and innovative activity is undermined (Hayter, 1982). That is, the catalytic contributions of branch plants in host economies may be complicated by their truncating effects. Historically, the powerful paradoxical forces generated by MNEs in transferring technology help explain why countries have differed so radically in their attitudes to foreign investment.

Among industrial countries in contrast to the UK and especially Canada, Japan and Sweden are countries which have long emphasized the need to 'reverse engineer' leading-edge technology as the basis for effective technology transfer which can be subsequently built upon to develop advantages based on indigenous technology. Kudo (1994), for example, carefully documents how the production, managerial and technical skills of one of the leading chemical manufacturers of the time, I G Farben of Germany, were transferred to Japan's chemical industry in the 1920s and 1930s in sometimes difficult negotiations through direct investment (including with respect to German plant and equipment), exports, licensing arrangements and training provided by I G Farben engineers and managers. Similarly, in another 'high-tech' activity of the period, automobiles, Japan obtained know-how from US firms, notably Ford (but less successfully from General Motors), using the same methods of technology transfer (Takeuchi, 1990). Moreover, in both these key industries (as in others), Japan achieved a comprehensive understanding of leading-edge technology from foreign corporations without relinquishing any noteworthy degree of control. In fact, these and related critical features of the Japanese innovation system, which evolved so rapidly after the Second World War, were evident in the late nineteenth century (Fruin, 1992).

Apart from any social or political motives, the explicit concern of Japan, and several other countries, for promoting indigenous R&D systems and associated technological capabilities is economically rooted in the need to have control over the most important source of economic growth, technological change. Indigenous scientific and engineering know-how itself is a source of high-income jobs and more importantly potentially allows nations (and regions) to develop their own industrial priorities and to provide progressive sources of competitive advantage which are consistent with progressively increasing wages. The innovations foreigners are willing to supply a country are unlikely to be the same, or to have the same structural impacts, as innovations generated through indigenous R&D and other means. Moreover, the cumulative nature of technological advances applies to countries as well as to firms (Dosi, 1988, p. 223). As a corollary, the ability of nations and firms to negotiate technical exchanges, interpret technical advances and participate in joint R&D is also a function of existing levels of know-how. For these reasons, it is not surprising that recent statistical evidence, for example from the UK and the US, broadly correlates geographical patterns of innovativeness with (commercially oriented)

R&D efforts (Glasmeier, 1986; Malecki, 1985; Oakey *et al.*, 1980, 1982). Such results confirm what countries such as Japan, Germany and Sweden knew last century.

International technological transfer by MNEs is then a problematical process. Effective transfer requires that host countries not only attract branch plant operations but also learn in minute detail the science, engineering and organization embodied in these operations in order to further develop technological and related skills. For many developing countries, however, there remains a huge gap ('mismatch') between the technology embodied in the branch plants of MNEs and local levels of education and training. Indeed, this gap partly underlies Ofori-Amoah's (1988a, 1988b, 1994) eloquent pleas, rooted in Ghanaian experience, for Africa to rethink its technological strategy and to give greater consideration to appropriate technologies deliberately aimed at promoting indigenous technological and economic progress.

For their part, the formerly centrally planned economies of eastern Europe and Russia, as well as China, are currently engaging in a massive global experiment in technology transfer which features attracting investments by MNEs (Ho and Huenemann, 1984; Michalak, 1993). Moreover, these countries, including China, are seeking to ensure that these investments generate enhanced industrial know-how as well as industrial activities. Such aspirations will inevitably require institutional innovation, including the restructuring of existing R&D systems to incorporate organizations motivated to exploit the 'private facets of technology'.

CONCLUSION: R&D AND UNEVEN DEVELOPMENT

The global economy is characterized by intense geographical unevenness of development. The geographical structure of R&D systems and of related innovative behaviour is an important basis for this unevenness. Thus R&D systems and innovative behaviour remain highly concentrated in industrial countries, especially the US, EU and Japan, and global technology gaps may increase. At the same time, R&D and innovation may help reduce uneven development. However, R&D and related know-how are not inevitably transferred by the branch plant operations of MNEs, while investment in R&D does not inevitably imply innovative behaviour. Rather, R&D, innovation and production are an interrelated set of processes which have to be 'matched' by appropriate institutional arrangements which relate to the process themselves, such as the R&D system, the liaisons that exist between them, and society as a whole such as the education and training system. In a period of increasing global competition and during a shift in techno-economic paradigm from Fordism to IT, the matching of technical and institutional and social change is not easy. Each country faces distinct problems of adjustment. Moreover, among different groups, for example the OECD countries or formerly centrally planned countries or developing countries, the ability to make the necessary institutional and social changes can be expected to vary (Freeman and Perez, 1988, p. 64). This differential ability to effectively organize innovation systems will itself contribute to further geographical unevenness in the future. Simply put, those societies that comprehensively organize themselves for learning and innovation will do better than those which do not.

At the present stage of global development, the problems of uneven development also need to be placed in the context of growing environmental problems. Economic growth increases environmental demands, and just how developing countries, including China, can achieve their economic goals without exerting significant, possibly devastating impact on the environment is unclear. R&D will probably continue to play a paradoxical role in this regard as innovations come on stream which mitigate or worsen the problem. Effective solutions to this increasingly global problem will require substantial international cooperation and the introduction of appropriate and matching institutional as well as technological innovations.

FURTHER READING

Britton, J.N.H. 1980 Industrial dependence and technological under-development: Canadian consequences of foreign direct investment. *Regional Studies* **14**: 181–99.

Chapman, K., Humphrys, G. (eds) 1987 *Technical change and industrial policy*. Basil Blackwell, Oxford.

Florida, R., Kenney, M. 1990 High-technology restructuring in the USA and Japan. *Environment and Planning A* **22**: 233–52.

Freeman, C. 1982 *The economics of industrial innovation*. Frances Pinter, London.

Freeman, C., Perez, C. 1988 Structural crises of adjustment, business cycles and investment behaviour. In Dosi, G., Freeman, C., Nelson, R. Silverberg, G. (eds) *Technical change and economic theory*. Frances Pinter, London: 38–66.

Hayter, R. 1988 *Technology and the Canadian forest-product industries: a policy perspective*. Background Study 54, Science Council of Canada, Ottawa, Ministry of Supply and Services.

Howells, J., Wood, M. 1992 *The globalisation of production and technology*. Belhaven Press, London.

Malecki, E.J., Bradbury, S. 1992 R&D facilities and professional labor: labor force dynamics in high technology. *Regional Studies* **26**: 123–36.

Ofori-Amoah, B. 1994 Technological change strategy for economic development in Africa. In Ezeala-Harrison, F., Adjibolosoo, S.B-S-K. (eds) *Perspectives of economic development in Africa*. Praeger, Westport: 85–102.

GLOBALIZATION OF PRODUCTION SYSTEMS: RESPONSE

PART 3
GLOBALIZATION OF
PRODUCTION SYSTEMS
RESPONSE

CHAPTER 10

THE LEAD ROLE OF DEVELOPED ECONOMIES

Peter Daniels

INTRODUCTION

'Globalization' is an elusive concept. It is pervasive, however, in current thought about the organization of production and trade that involves increasing interdependence between nations both near and far (see for example Porter, 1990; Amin and Thrift, 1994; Chapter 8). Reich (1990) suggested that in the late twentieth century we are witnessing a process of transformation that will rearrange the economic landscape of the next century; indeed, one interpretation is that national economies and governments will cease to be important arbiters in development and trade as we move towards a borderless world (Ohmae, 1990). On the other hand, Porter (1990) advocates the growing significance of the nation-state as an accompaniment to the globalization of competition. The reliance on market forces and the involvement of the private sector in the day-to-day operation of the world economy is increasing as more countries, such as those comprising the formerly centrally planned economies of eastern Europe and the USSR, Latin America and to some extent China, have adopted economic policies that involve much more participation in the global economic system. These changes have been stimulated by the Uruguay Round of the General Agreement on Tariffs and Trade (GATT), which has led many countries to liberalize their trade policies with respect to both merchandise and service transactions. The effects are especially marked amongst those industries, mainly services such as transport and telecommunications, that in many countries have until very recently been in public ownership. Innovations in technology, especially telecommunications, have also allowed economic activities to con-template international expansion based on the management of information and organizational structures that were hardly conceivable even ten years ago (see for example Forester, 1987). Shared or common-access international telecommuni-cations networks are increasingly complemented by private networks owned and operated by individual multinational firms (Langdale, 1989). The interaction of ideological, regulatory and technological changes has had the effect of enabling the value-adding activities of firms to be located or distributed to numerous cities, regions or countries in all corners of the globe. The prospect of the organization of global space along industry lines can now be realistically contemplated (Kapstein, 1994).

The reality rather than the prospect suggests that as nations have become disenfranchised from the global economy they have sought to regulate or deregulate their institutional and other apparatus either to attract or to protect those economic activities that add value or competitiveness to their position in the new economic order. But even here they are acknowledging the dilution of their sovereignty by joining up with contiguous nations to form trade blocs such as the European Union (EU), the North American Free Trade Agreement (NAFTA), the Association of South East Asian Nations (ASEAN), the Latin American Free Trade Area (LAFTA) or the Central American Common Market (CACM). These are powerful alliances with common economic interests (as well as social, political or cultural agenda) and it is in the context of these blocs rather than nation-states that multinational enterprises (MNEs) must increasingly take their strategic and other decisions (see Chapters 7 and 14). Spanning these blocs is the interlinked economy of the so-called Triad (Ohmae, 1990; United Nations, 1991a) of leading developed economies: Europe, Japan and the United States. These dominate the volume, pattern and value of the transactions that that are contributing to the globalized economy; they are also the 'home base' of the MNEs that are viewed as the key players in the globalization of production systems.

It will be evident from other contributions to this volume (Chapters 7, 9, 16 and 17, for example) that many of the processes shaping the outcomes of economic globalization have originated from the developed economies. These were the cradles of industrial capitalism where the search for growth (profit) was the compelling motivation (Johnstone, 1980; Knox and Agnew, 1989) and as national markets inevitably became saturated producers needed to identify new strategies to accommodate this imperative. Apart from developing new products, an obvious way forward was to identify and enter new (geographical) markets, to find ways of deploying labour or raw materials in ways that would reduce production costs, and this would often involve looking outside the national space economy. The result has been increasing internationalization of economic activity, which Dicken (1992a) characterizes as a 'global shift'. The momentum of this shift has been sustained and accelerated by the transition of the developed economies from industrial to post-industrial capitalism, especially duing the last 30 years (Knox and Agnew, 1989). This has been brought about as a result, for example, of the dramatic diversification and increasing penetration of technology (information and transport) into the processes of production *and* consumption, the rise of flexible production as markets for standardized products have become saturated and customers or clients more discerning, and a shift from agriculture and manufacturing towards services as the focus of employment growth and investment. The purpose of this chapter is to examine some of the indicators that can be used to illustrate the shift to post-industrial capitalism and its global expression, including the dominant but changing role of the developed economies.

MULTINATIONAL CORPORATIONS AND FOREIGN DIRECT INVESTMENT

Global economic relations are not easy to unravel because of the variable quality of the available statistics but amongst the most common measures used are foreign direct investment (FDI) stocks and flows, global patterns of trade, financial flows and technology transfer. Data on global trends in FDI show that outflows increased by approximately 155 per cent between 1985 and 1990, equivalent to an average annual growth rate of 27 per cent (United Nations, 1992a). A slowdown in the economic growth of a number of the leading developed economies after 1988 was followed by a reduction in the annual rate to 7 per cent in 1990 and the possibility of a further decline in 1991. The lead agents in FDI activity have been multinational corporations (MNEs), which have their roots in the economic milieu of the developed economies and which have subsequently extended their operational capacity into the newly industrialized countries (NICs) as well as into the less developed countries (LDCs) (United Nations, 1991b). It remains debatable whether the MNEs are all-powerful in shaping change in the global economy (Dicken, 1994) but there is no doubt that not only are they one of the key agents of economic globalization but also the determinants of the process and the outcomes. According to the United Nations,

> ... in a world in which the sales of foreign affiliates are more important than exports in serving international markets, and in which technology and other flows are associated with foreign direct investment, international economic transactions must be seen from the perspective of international production by multinational corporations. Foreign direct investment, as managed by multinational corporations, is increasingly the driving force of international economic transactions (United Nations, 1992a, p. 6)

The determinants of FDI have been extensively scrutinized (see for example Aharoni, 1966; Dunning, 1988; Casson, 1991; United Nations, 1992b). The accumulated evidence indicates that universal generalizations about the process are elusive. Dunning (1988) advocates the use of an eclectic analytical framework that recognizes this difficulty as well as the need to avoid any restrictions imposed by the use of specific theoretical models. The eclectic approach to the FDI decision suggests that it should be approached with three advantages in mind: first, ownership advantages that favour the foreign firm over the local firm in the host country; second, location advantages reflecting variations in factor costs, though host country policies dictate whether ownership advantages need to be capitalized via a presence in the target overseas market; and third, internationalization advantages which determine whether foreign firms with ownership and location advantages need to keep these advantages under their control or are able to allow indigenous firms in the host market to produce the product or service on their behalf. The latter may involve higher transaction costs or compromise the ability of the foreign firm to control the quality of the service provided or to protect the specialist knowledge or research incorporated in its product or service.

A global strategy implies an integrated worldwide approach to corporate strategy formulation which replaces a strategy based on a country-by-country or world region-by-region approach (Prahalad and Doz, 1987). Globalization drivers (Levitt, 1983; Yip, 1989, 1992) have been used to explain differences between industries in the extent to which they have exploited the potential for adopting the strategy. There are four groups of globalization drivers: market (including common customer needs, transferable marketing, global channels); cost (including sourcing efficiencies, global scale economies, differences in country costs); competition (including competitors globalized, competititors from other continents, growing interdependence of countries); and government (including favourable trade policies, common marketing regulations, compatibility of technical standards). Recent research by Johansson and Yip (1994) suggests that market and cost drivers were most significant for the globalization of manufacturing enterprises while for service industries government and market drivers are more relevant.

It has recently been estimated that there are 35 000 parent MNEs in the world (Table 10.1). Because of variations in data collection between countries this total (and that for the number of foreign affiliates) is almost certainly an underestimate. The home countries of almost all MNEs are advanced economies, which are also the principal origins of foreign direct investment (FDI) (see below). The distribution of affiliates is more evenly balanced between developed and developing economies, with most being small or medium-sized firms given that less than 20 per cent of world FDI flows during the 1980s were directed towards developing countries. The geographical pattern of FDI is largely shaped by just seven countries (Table 10.2), which are also the places which demonstrate a very clear sectoral shift from primary and secondary sectors to the service (tertiary) sector. Thus, the 'new world economy is increasingly a service economy' (United Nations, 1992a, p. 105). Technology has greatly increased the tradability of services (Daniels, 1993), which comprised about 25 per cent of the total world stock of FDI at the beginning of the 1970s. By the late 1980s the proportion was nearer 50 per cent and represented some 55–60 per cent of annual flows (United Nations, 1991a, 1992a). The sectoral shift in the distribution of FDI mirrors economic restructuring in the originating countries and at the destinations of the investment. Especially in developed economies, but also in developing countries, the share of the primary sector in GNP has been falling steadily while ownership of natural gas and non-fuel resources, for example, has been nationalized in many developing countries to the detriment of any interest by MNEs in investing in those economies. Meanwhile the share of services in GNP has increased significantly, especially in the advanced economies, and this has raised the profile of services into a component of FDI at least as large as, and in most cases larger than, that of manufacturing.

The factors contributing to the rise of services in FDI are manifold (see also Chapters 6 and 7). As real per capita incomes in the advanced economies have

Table 10.1 Transnational corporations and foreign affiliates, by region and selected country

Country (year)	Number of parent MNEs	Number of foreign affiliates[a]
France (1984)	2000	3671[b]
Germany (1990)	6984	10978[c]
Japan (1990)	3331	2884
Switzerland (1992)	3000	—
United Kingdom (1981)	1533	3411[d]
United States (1989)	3712	13582
All developed countries (1989)	30900	73400
Brazil (1986)	576	7110
China (1988)	553	15966
India (1988)	176	926
Republic of Korea (1988)	668	2821
Taiwan (1988)	405	4764
All developing countries (1989)	3800	62900
Commonwealth of Independent States (1991)	68	2296
Czechoslovakia (1991)	26	592
Poland (1991)	58	2168
All central and eastern Europe (1991)	300	10900
World total (1990)	35000	147200

[a] As reported by host countries.
[b] For 1971.
[c] For 1989.
[d] For 1988.

Source: United Nations (1992a), extracted from data in Box I.1, p. 12.

Table 10.2 The changing sectoral composition of FDI: leading advanced economies, 1975–90

Country	Period	Sectors			Total
		Primary	Secondary	Tertiary	
Canada	1975	9	62	29	100
	1990	6	51	43	100
France	1975	22	38	40	100
	1990	13	38	49	100
Germany	1975	5	48	47	100
	1990	2	49	49	100
Japan	1976	28	32	40	100
	1990	6	27	67	100
United Kingdom	1984	33	32	35	100
	1988	25	38	37	100
United States	1975	26	45	29	100
	1990	8	44	47	100

Source: United Nations (1992a), extracted from Table I.3, p. 18.

increased the demand for consumer services such as retailing, tourism and passenger transport such as air travel has increased. The demand for services used by primary and manufacturing enterprises, the producer or intermediate services, has expanded as advances in technology and improvements in quality have placed a premium on information, specialist advice and knowledge. The fusion of computing and telecommunications into a seamless network of information technology has created opportunities for the creation of new services and changed the form and frequency of interaction between producers and consumers. Best placed to take advantage of these opportunities are the MNEs which, provided that the regulatory environment in the host economy is 'friendly', are able to deploy information technology to achieve competitive advantage over domestic enterprises. However, it is service MNEs that have most to gain since many services are not tradeable; manufacturing MNEs can serve foreign markets by exporting from the home country while service MNEs must acquire domestic enterprises or seek direct representation via the establishment of new branches if they are to be able to operate effectively in new markets. Financial, banking, business and professional services, advertising and hotels are just some of the services that are really only able to strengthen their position in international markets via some form of FDI. Thus, services FDI has been taking place from an increasingly diverse range of countries but in view of their initial comparative advantage a large proportion emanates from the developed economies within the EC, from Japan and from the United States. In the case of the EC, for example, during the period 1984–88 some 37 per cent of the outward flow of investment was by services and 60 per cent of inward investment, in addition to intra-EC services FDI, which amounted to 57 per cent of reported flows (United Nations, 1991a). Some of the NICs have increasingly turned their attention from manufacturing to services FDI in industries such as banking and hotels, but almost 85 per cent of stock of FDI in services by the mid-1980s was located in the developed countries. This reflects the locational advantages of the advanced economies with their diverse and dynamic markets for consumer and producer services, their sophisticated telecommunications and associated infrastructures and their invariably more open and deregulated environments, which make them attractive to service MNEs.

Although the sectoral balance of FDI has been changing during the last 15 years, the dominance of the Triad countries (the EC, United States and Japan) remains unchallenged. The formation of the Triad has only really become clear in the late 1980s as Japan has emerged as a major source of outward flows of investment. Between them, the countries comprising the Triad accounted for some 80 per cent of outward FDI flows in the world whereas they accounted for less than 50 per cent of world trade. However, outward FDI for the Triad has declined from 84 per cent to 81 per cent during the 1980s (Table 10.3) as the NICs have begun to produce goods and services that can command market share amongst competitor countries or MNEs that comprise the advanced economies. On the other hand a growing share of inward FDI is concentrated in the Triad, up from 50 per cent of the world total in 1980 to 55 per cent in 1988. The position

Table 10.3   Outward and inward FDI: EC, United States and Japan, 1980–88

Country	Stock							
	Outward FDI[a]				Inward FDI[a]			
	1980	%[b]	1988	%	1980	%	1988	%
EC[c]	153	33	332	34	143	31	239	23
US	220	46	345	35	83	18	329	31
Japan	20	4	111	11	3	1	10	1
Triad	398	84	788	81	230	50	579	55
World	474	100	974	100	464	100	1059	100

[a] Billion $US.
[b] Per cent of world total FDI.
[c] Excludes intra-EC FDI.

Source: United Nations (1991a), extracted from Table 10, p. 32.

of the US as the principal source of outward investment to a point where it is almost matched by the EC is balanced by its significant expansion as the leading host location by the end of the 1980s. In the case of the EC there are significant flows of FDI between the member states, encouraged by the 1992 Single European Market Programme, which has enabled MNEs, especially those in the service sector, to rationalize their operations at the scale of the EC as the home market rather than home nation.

One of the key ownership advantages that has been shown to underpin the ability of MNEs to engage in production and marketing in a wide range of countries is research and development (R&D) intensity (Howells, 1990; Pearce, 1990; United Nations, 1992b; see also Chapter 9). MNEs have recognized the importance of differentiating products and achieving optimum production capacity in different foreign markets; this requires the creation or adaptation of the appropriate technology. This makes it difficult for developing countries to attract FDI (or indeed to generate outflows) unless they provide incentives for MNEs to establish R&D facilities that will enable product or process adaptation to local conditions. Another significant ownership advantage, which also favours MNEs from the advanced economies, is advertising intensity since marketing and product differentiation are an important feature of their competitiveness. The number and quality of managerial workers within MNEs is another ownership advantage, especially if they are required to front or develop the operations in new overseas markets. The principal location advantages are host country market size and the supply of cost-effective labour. But size of market must be complemented by the prospects for growth of the host economy in a way that will stimulate further demand for MNE outputs. This may actually divert FDI towards other developed economy markets or the NICs rather than the developing countries unless MNEs and the host countries can work together to achieve a mutually compatible commitment to sustained growth (United Nations, 1992b).

While this could be interpreted to mean that national distinctions in most of the activities of MNEs have become increasingly blurred, research and technology development have remained relatively centralized in the home countries of MNEs, however extensive their international activities (Office of Technology Assessment, 1994). Since most of the major MNEs originate from Europe, Japan and North America this means that the specialized, high-skill and high-wage jobs associated with research and technology development and any spin-off technology-intensive industries will tend to be retained by the 'home' developed countries. Only some 13 per cent of the manufacturing R&D of US-based multinationals is undertaken by their affiliates overseas and the share is probably comparable for European and Japanese multinationals (Office of Technology Assessment, 1994). The domestic concentration of research and technology development is also attractive to foreign firm affiliates in the US or in Europe which, either by establishing their own facilities or by acquisition of host country firms, now account for more than 15 per cent of the total spent on research. The principal exception to this trend is Japanese affiliates, which show the lowest R&D intensity (ratio of R&D spending to sales). Another consequence of the retention by MNEs of research and related activities in their home countries, especially in the US, is the impact on the technology trade balance: according to the OECD, for example, whereas Japan imported ($US2480m) more technology than it exported ($US1956m) in 1988, the US had receipts of $US10858m and payments of only $US2054m (United States Information Service, 1993). Most of this trade in technology takes place within multinational corporations. Between 1983 and 1992 intra-firm trade between European and US multinationals was approximately 43 per cent of all merchandise trade between them.

DEVELOPED ECONOMIES AND WORLD TRADE

A second indicator that can be used to demonstrate the pivotal role of the developed economies is trade. Trade has played a critical part in global economic growth and integration (GATT, 1993; United Nations, 1992a; Armstrong *et al.*, 1991). This has been especially the case since 1945 when, during the 1960s for example, merchandise trade grew in real terms at an average annual rate of 9 per cent. A strong performance in export markets is associated with a high average level of income and therefore the expectation that there will be a reciprocal demand for imports. Such imports may compete with similar domestic products and services, replace products and services that are more profitable to export or be used to enhance the competitive advantage of goods and services that are ultimately exported. In a perfect market the income generated by exports would be balanced by expenditure on imports but it is clear that because of differences in factor endowments or variations in the cost or efficiency of producing similar products or services in different countries, for example, there is scope for considerable imbalance in the trading characteristics of the advanced economies. Thus, US merchandise imports far exceed its exports to produce a very large negative trade balance (Figure 10.1), which is partially compensated for by its positive balance on trade in services, which has been steadily growing throughout the 1980s. Contrast that pattern with Japan, which is in a converse position to the US (Figure 10.1); a growing positive balance of trade in merchandise is matched by a growing negative balance in commercial services trade. These and similar contrasts amongst the leading trading countries also, of course, result from different attitudes to trade. The US and most of the European countries have adopted a relatively liberal attitude towards the use of tariff barriers, for example, to protect home country manufactures or commercial services on the grounds that the benefits of increased trade and competition outweigh the costs.

World exports of merchandise[1] had an estimated value of $US3731 billion in 1992 and commercial services[2] an estimated value of $US1000 billion (GATT, 1993) (Table 10.4). The value of exports grew by 12 per cent in 1994 and exceeded a total value of $US4000 billion for the first time (World Trade Organization, cited in Serjeant, 1995). The share of commercial services in total world exports has increased slightly from 19 per cent in 1970 to 21 per cent in 1992. Manufactures comprised almost 73 per cent of world exports in 1992 (with almost half arising from exports of machinery and transport equipment) with mining products (12 per cent) and agricultural products (12 per cent) making up the balance of merchandise trade. In 1994 office machinery and telecommunications equipment (including computers and semiconductors) accounted for 11 per cent of world trade and was growing more strongly than the average. The World Trade Organization estimates that trade in these goods is now larger than the trade in food, fuel or cars (Serjeant, 1995).

The regional pattern of exports and imports (Figure 10.2) reveals the pivotal role of western Europe, North America and Asia between 1982 and 1992. These are the engines of the expanding volume of both exports and imports clearly

[1] Exports are valued at transactions value (including transportation and insurance) to bring the merchandise to the frontier of the exporting country. Imports are valued at transaction (plus transportation and insurance) costs to the frontier of the importing country. Customs data are the preferred source for the statistics. Merchandise is defined as agricultural products, mining products and manufactures (Standard International Trade Classification, 1988, sections 5, 6, 7, 8 excluding division 68 and group 891). Because of the lack of market-determined exchange rates the valuation of merchandise trade of central and eastern Europe and the former USSR is particularly difficult. Comparability of trade values is at best indicative (see GATT, 1993).

[2] Commercial services are defined as transportation, travel and other private services and income. Balance of payments statistics (compiled by the International Monetary Fund) are currently the only source of comparable data on international service transactions. The statistics significantly underestimate services trade because: (i) a number of important economies are not members of the IMF, (ii) many service transactions are not recorded, especially those using electronic media and those between the affiliates etc. of multinational firms, (iii) some countries do not provide statistics of certain service items, (iv) statistics are sometimes reported on a net basis, i.e. exports minus imports, and (v) transactions may be misclassified, for example, as trade in merchandise rather than in services (see GATT, 1993 for full details).

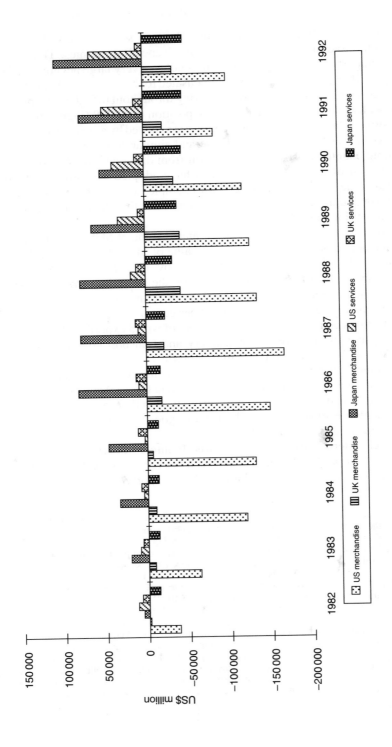

Figure 10.1 Balance of merchandise and commercial services trade, US, UK and Japan, 1982–92

Table 10.4   Leading exporters and importers of merchandise and commercial services, 1992

Country	Exports ($US billion)			Imports ($US billion)		
	Merchandise[a]	Services[b]	Share (%)	Merchandise	Services	Share (%)
Belgium & Luxembourg	123.0	35.0[c]	3.3	125.0	33.0[c]	3.3
Canada	134.1	15.9	3.2	129.2	27.2	3.2
China	85.0	9.1	2.0	80.6	9.2	1.9
France	235.8	102.3	7.1	239.6	84.2	6.7
Germany	430.0	64.4	10.4	408.6	111.9	10.7
Italy	178.2	65.2	5.1	188.5	67.2	5.3
Japan	339.9	49.6	8.2	233.2	97.6	6.8
Netherlands	139.9	36.1	3.7	133.8	35.7	3.5
United Kingdom	190.0	55.1	5.2	221.5	47.0	5.5
United States	448.2	162.3	12.9	553.9	107.7	13.6
Total of above	2304.1	595	61.1	2313.9	620.7	60.5
World total	3731	1000	100	3855	988	100

[a] Agricultural and mining products, manufactures.
[b] Commercial services: includes transportation, travel and other private services and income.
[c] Estimated by GATT.

Source: GATT (1993), extracted from Table I.4 and Table I.6, pp. 3–5.

shown in Figure 10.2. In 1994 the value of western European exports and imports grew by 11 per cent, giving the largest boost to overall world trade. While Asia's share of merchandise imports and exports has been growing, the share of Latin America, the Middle East, Africa and central and eastern Europe (and the former USSR) has remained very low and in some cases was even contracting during the early 1990s. More recently in 1994 the export volumes of central and eastern Europe increased by 11.5 per cent with only the Far East 'tigers' – Hong Kong, Singapore, Taiwan and South Korea – outpacing that region. The leading exporters and importers of merchandise and commercial services are shown in Table 10.4 (Hong Kong is not included because a large part of its export trade, 75 per cent, is comprised of re-exports). All the countries listed, apart from China, are developed economies with Germany, the United States and Japan dominating both exports and imports. The ratio of services to merchandise trade is approximately 1:4 but some countries, notably the US, France, Italy and the UK, achieve ratios nearer 1:3. Japan and Germany, on the other hand, are major exporters of merchandise but major importers of services.

Just five exporting countries dominate world merchandise trade (Figure 10.3). The value of this trade doubled between 1982 and 1992 from $US1.9 billion to $US3.7 billion in 1992 while that of the leading five exporters doubled from $US0.7 billion to $US1.6 billion. Thus, the US, France, Germany, the UK and

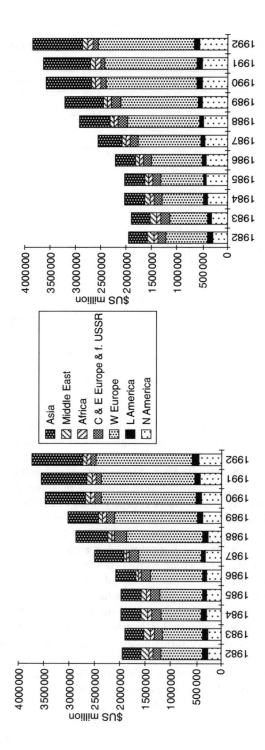

Figure 10.2 (a) World merchandise exports (million $US), by region, 1982–92; (b) World merchandise imports (million $US), by region, 1982–92 (data from GATT, 1993)

Japan have increased their aggregate share of merchandise exports in a steady upward trend from 38.5 per cent in 1982 to just over 44 per cent in 1992. Although a smaller economy, Germany has vied with the the US as the leading exporter for much of the 1980s because it specializes in the production of precision, high-technology and therefore high-value engineering and related merchandise. Japan and the UK have maintained a steady rather than expanding share of merchandise exports at around 9 per cent and 5 per cent respectively of the world total, while France has increased its share steadily from 5 to 6 per cent over the decade (see Figure 10.3). World exports of commercial services are also substantially dominated by five countries (Figure 10.4), which accounted for 43.4 per cent of the total by value in 1992, up from a share of 38.2 per cent in 1982. The group is essentially the same as for merchandise trade except that Italy is marginally ahead of Germany and has therefore been included. The dominant position of the US as a services exporter[3] is much clearer than for merchandise whereas for most of the other countries, except the UK, services exports have remained relatively stable throughout the period. Commercial services exports from the UK as a proportion of the world total have declined from just over 7 per cent to 5.5 per cent, placing it in a very similar position to Japan, which has always relied much more on domestic and imported services than most of its competitors in the leading group of economies.

An examination of the network of merchandise trade (Table 10.5) in 1992 demonstrates that the developed economies that are major importers and exporters are also the focus for significant intraregional trade. More than 73 per

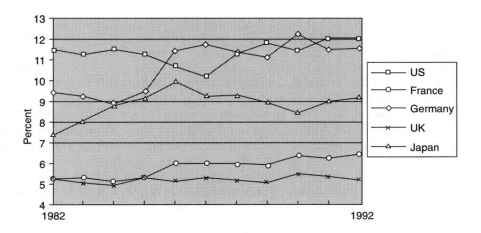

Figure 10.3   Share (per cent) of leading exporters in world merchandise trade, 1982–92 (data from GATT, 1993)

[3] There were changes in the recording of US services data in 1984 and 1986–88 which had the effect of increasing the figures for exports.

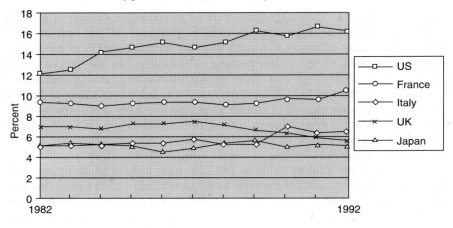

Figure 10.4   Share (per cent) of leading world exporters of commercial services, 1982–92

cent of the merchandise trade originating in western Europe (approximately 20 countries) remains within the region. It therefore has comparatively weak links with every other major region, especially for agricultural and mining products with approximately 80 per cent of the trade taking place within the region.[4] The Latin American region comprises a similar number of countries but only 15.6 per cent of its merchandise trade takes place within the region. Almost half of the trade originating in Latin America is destined for North America (48 per cent) and 21 per cent for western Europe. This suggests that the characteristics of the origin and destination regions help to shape the network of world trade: more than 60 per cent of Africa's already small share of world trade is destined for western Europe. The design and quality of the merchandise being traded is also significant. Almost 20 per cent of merchandise traded from Asia moves to western Europe but only 2 per cent of central/eastern Europe and former USSR trade is with the North American region. On the other hand almost half of the Middle East's trade, much of it in the form of oil, moves to Asia, especially Japan, which has much more limited oil resources than North America or western Europe. The network illustrated in aggregate form in Table 10.5 accords with international trade theory, which predicts that two-way trade in similar products tends to take place between similar countries (world regions) (Markusen, 1986; Helpman and Krugman, 1985). In those cases where countries vary in relation to their income levels or factor endowments the level of two-way trade in merchandise will be dictated by the traditional determinants of comparative advantage (Balassa and Bauwens, 1987).

[4] Data for the network of world commercial service trade are not available.

Table 10.5 Network of world merchandise trade, 1992[a]

Origin	Destination							
	North America	Latin America	Western Europe	C and E Europe, former USSR	Africa	Middle East	Asia	World total
North America	33.39[b]	13.54	21.80	1.16	1.81	2.98	25.33	551.54[c]
Latin America	48.12	17.53	20.59	1.53	1.41	1.62	9.21	146.07
Western Europe	7.46	2.13	73.06	3.36	3.13	3.33	7.53	1663.99
C. and E. Europe, former USSR	2.38	1.86	64.29	16.89	1.79	1.60	11.18	87.49
Africa	16.14	2.11	60.58	2.26	7.44	1.59	9.88	84.4
Middle East	13.03	2.95	26.79	2.13	4.95	7.79	42.36	122.12
Asia	26.63	2.47	19.56	1.11	1.57	3.64	45.02	858.96
World total	638.89[c]	164	1674.05	93.48	91.5	117.69	734.96	3514.57

[a] Agricultural and mining products, manufactures.
[b] Per cent of total by destination.
[c] Absolute total (billion $US).

Source: GATT (1993), calculated from data in Table A7, pp. 92–95.

The network of global trade has an important bearing on economic growth in that it provides countries or regions with opportunities for expanding and improving the production of goods and services. Inputs to economic growth such as natural resources, technology and merchandise are increased by countries exchanging goods and services that they can produce relatively cheaply for those they either cannot produce or can only produce at a cost that is relatively higher than other countries. Trade is therefore sometimes described as an autonomous engine of growth (Nurske *et al.*, 1961) although there is also the converse view that it is the by-product of growth. Thus, the human resources or the stock of technology within an economy stimulate growth of output which in turn stimulates faster growth of exports. Using this interpretation it is not hard to see why such a large proportion of global trade is between economies with a diverse stock of the mainsprings of growth. Active participants in international trade also benefit from externalities such as learning about new processes or technologies that improve the efficiency of production and boost aggregate economic growth. This is particularly important for the growth through exports of developing country economies. This might ultimately threaten the hegemony of the leading five countries. The UK, for example, has been experiencing steady economic decline relative to the rest of the world. Although services accounted for 50 per cent of the total in 1993, manufacturing exports were not holding up. A quarter of all exports were made by just 12 manufacturing companies[5] in areas of traditional strength such as chemicals, electronic equipment, mechanical engineering and pharmaceuticals. If the UK is to reverse the trend by winning an extra 1 per cent of world trade by the year 2000 (Confederation of British Industry, 1995) it will have to adjust its pattern of exports from a European and North American emphasis to a focus on the NICs such as Taiwan, China, Singapore and Hong Kong. These countries are no longer just a source of low-technology products such as toys, textiles or bicycles; they are starting to produce high-quality, competitively priced electronic products in which countries like the UK and the US have traditionally dominated production. Assuming that these can command a growing share of the market in the advanced economies, they will raise income and wealth and therefore purchasing power which will create new opportunities for UK exports. To succeed they will need competitive products based on core R&D and a sophisticated knowledge of the needs of the emerging markets. It will not be enough to export merchandise or services that are simply surplus to demand in the UK market.

[5] British Aerospace, BP, Shell, IBM, Rolls-Royce, GEC, Zeneca, Ford, ICI, British Steel, Guinness, Glaxo.

FACILITATING FDI AND WORLD TRADE

International trade should enhance the growth of national economies. By integrating into the world economy producers of merchandise or services are more likely to acquire knowledge of new techniques or the attributes of competing products. This should benefit productivity and stimulate innovation and further growth while also fostering competition amongst innovators in different countries. The latter may have the added benefit of more efficient innovation and technology development and this also assists the growth process. Development strategies based on import substitution, for example, which have been used by countries that have turned away from trade, are even less likely to succeed in a world economy that has become more open in the last 15 years. The ability of nations to succeed or to participate in world trade will therefore depend in part on individual national domestic policies and the degree to which they are designed to help or hinder participation in a liberal environment for world trade.

The mobility of enterprises, i.e. capital, information and human resources, is undermining the power of national governments. They must now become internationally competitive with respect to the economic policies that they devise; if in doing so they impose costs without compensating benefits they run the risk of undermining domestic enterprises. This can have the effect of loss of business to firms in other countries or the relocation of domestic enterprise resources and production activities to more favourable environments. Human resources are often seen as key components in corporate and national competition; those countries that will do well in the global marketplace are those that are able to generate and keep educated, skilled, knowledge-processing workers such as managers, research scientists and entrepreneurs. Clearly, some countries and especially the developed economies have already established considerable advantages in relation to factors of production of this kind and, in a context of growing world trade, it is usual to have a set of rules and protocols agreed by nations and designed to ensure trading efficiency and the distribution of benefits to countries which are at different points on the development trajectory.

Trade agreements may be bilateral (the US/Canada Free Trade Agreement), trilateral, such as the North American Free Trade Agreement (US, Canada, Mexico) or multilateral. The most recent example of the latter is the Uruguay Round global trade accord which was finally agreed in late 1993 and signed in Marrakech in January 1994 after 12 years of talks and seven years of negotiations. The accord came into operation on 1 January 1995. It was first discussed by members of the General Agreement on Tariffs and Trade (GATT) in 1982; it took until 1986 for the countries to agree to formal negotiations on a wide range of issues such as tariffs, sector-specific trade rules, intellectual property or services. Disputes were the cause of much delay to the progress of the accord with many of them between the countries comprising the developed economies and the less developed economies. In the case of services, for example, the main objective of the negotiations for the developed countries was to liberalize international trade in services and/or to expand such trade; for the developing countries the ultimate objective of the negotiations was the promotion of their economic and social development. The developing countries were conscious that they were not internationally competitive in transborder service flows (requiring little or no need for international mobility of FDI) or in the sales of the foreign affiliates of their (very few) services MNEs. Exceptions were traditional and labour-intensive services such as tourism, construction and engineering. With the developed countries seen as services exporters and some developing countries as manufacturing exporters there was a suspicion that the idea that comparative advantage would be working at its best was highly misleading. It overlooked the fact that an ability to integrate the production of goods and services was an increasingly important determinant of national export performance in both sectors. Thus, most of the developing countries are convinced that the developed countries will, in reality, continue to dominate the international market in services unless they are able to negotiate arrangements that will enhance the mix of services with knowledge and information services and occupations receiving priority over semi-skilled services and jobs or the opportunity to gain access to telecommunications and other technology that will underpin the development of such activities.

A response would be to suggest that the developing countries might be able to achieve their development goals by importing the services that they require. This assumes, however, that the developed country MNEs will make them available at a comparable quality and price to that in other developed countries. But as Krugman (1986) has observed, trade is shaped by the advantages conferred by large-scale production and cumulative experience. Take the case of the international airline industry, where 'it is clear that geography confers certain competitive advantages to those countries with an abundance of land and substantial domestic aviation markets' (Debagge, 1994). The US is the prime example where both these conditions apply, although in other instances such as the UK neither condition applies but there is substantial cumulative experience in providing international air services since it is the only way that British airline companies have been able to grow successfully since the 1930s. Liberalization of the US airline industry has stimulated the demand for domestic air travel even further as competition has driven fares down but this has taken place at the expense of small, regional airlines. It has also resulted in reduced services to smaller cities and the imposition of a hub-and-spoke system which has not necessarily improved the quality of service to customers (direct non-stop flights without routing via a hub, for example). Deregulation has created an oligopolistic market structure with the prospect, if not yet the reality, of rising air fares. If this scenario is replicated at the international level it will result in the disappearance of the inefficient domestic airlines of many countries, to be replaced by major international airlines (many of which are positioning themselves into global alliances; see for example Debagge, 1994; Oum *et al.*, 1993) providing more expensive services with frequency and quality not necessarily any better than the original local airlines. Whatever the outcome this process will reinforce the role of developed economy service MNEs (international airlines in this case) at the expense of the developing economies and the NICs.

The improvement of intellectual property right protection (IPR) was the focus for much multilateral trade discussion, and even though developing countries have a critical need for new technology it was a much higher priority for developed countries. Intellectual property includes diverse items such as medical processes, copyright on books, patents on inventions and software. These are items for which the developing countries rely on imports to gain access since they have little domestic capacity for technological innovations and product development. It is not surprising then that many developing countries considered that most of the gains from IPRs would go to the advanced economies since providing stronger patents to foreign firms and introducing laws against domestic imitation would raise prices for key inputs and consumer goods. At the same time profits would be transferred ouside the developing country. Differences in IPR policies have created disputes surrounding the sale of 'pirate' copies of tapes and films without royalty payments being made, infringements of patents on products with high development costs such as computer software and pharmaceuticals, or sales of counterfeit designer clothes, watches and other luxury goods. The differences also impose costs on the international trading system and on the firms engaged in trade. Thus, companies will make trade and investment decisions on the level of patent protection available in a country rather than their assessment of market demand for their product. In many instances this discriminates against emerging rather than developed economies. Variations in IPR policies and procedures between countries impose patent application and maintenance costs on firms that erode their potential sales and profits for ploughing back into innovation. Countries such as the US, the UK and France have supported the international harmonization of IPR since the beneficiaries will be innovative countries and firms with the poorer countries likely to experience losses. Under the terms of the current GATT accord an investor, writer, performer or developer of a creative work has a right to the financial gains subsequently accruing. This is achieved by providing copyright protection for books and computer programs, for example, by providing patent protection for all new and useful products, by clearly defining rules on trademarks and, for the first time, by protecting semiconductor layout designs and trade secrets. Developing countries are given a longer time to implement these rules with technical and financial assistance from the developed countries. Domestic competition policies will be upgraded to discipline any potential undesirable monopoly practices by firms owning IPRs.

In addition to IPRs the 1994 trade accord targets many other impediments to a more liberal environment for world trade in both goods and services. One of the most important is tariffs which, whether visible or invisible, are used by countries and trade blocs to protect the markets of domestic producers. The average cut in tariffs for manufactured goods is approximately one-third and for ten sectors – namely construction equipment, agricultural equipment, pharmaceuticals, medical equipment, beer, brown distilled spirits, paper, furniture, textiles and toys – the tariffs of major trading partners will disappear completely. In the case of textiles the system of bilateral textile and apparel quotas (the so-called Multifibre Agreement) will cease after 1 July 2005 with countries such as the US reducing tariffs on textiles by some 12 per cent over the transition period (in 1995 US tariffs on textiles averaged 16 per cent). The agreement defines more precisely and implements stricter rules on subsidies and provides a mechanism for relief for those countries injured by subsidies. Investment barriers that have an effect on trade are also restricted such as local content requirements that specify that some minimum level of local resources be used in operations at foreign-owned plants or trade balancing requirements that specify that an investor cannot import more than is exported.

For the first time the Uruguay Round sets out general international rules relating to trade in services. These are less comprehensive than was hoped, with negotiations on open markets in telecommunications, securities, shipping, insurance and banking inconclusive, although engineering, environmental services, tourism, computer services, accounting, law and advertising are now covered. These are just some of the many provisions within the 1994 accord, which is now monitored by the World Trade Organization (WTO), which has superseded the GATT to oversee trade relations between nations and cooperate with other international economic and financial institutions to enhance global economic policy making. One of the key principles for enhancing trade in services is national treatment, i.e. countries should treat foreign firms operating within their territories no less favourably than domestic firms. For services such as banking this principle is the exception rather than the rule with the developed economies generally being more open than less developed economies. More than 350 foreign banks operated agencies, branches and subsidiaries in the UK in 1994 and almost 300 operated in the US. But China, for example, prohibits foreign banks from participating in local currency business and confines branches to limited geographic areas; foreign banks in Singapore and Malaysia are not able to gain access to automatic teller machine networks of local banks and are prohibited from establishing their own networks; Brazil prohibits new entry of foreign banks and imposes a freeze on increases in foreign participation in the ownership of existing institutions, and Mexico and Canada prohibit entry of foreign banks via direct branches.

CONCLUSION

There is no question that the developed economies have initiated and sub-sequently performed a key role in shaping the geography of global production. They have achieved this in a number of ways. As national markets became saturated in countries that were at the centre of industrial capitalism it became necessary to identify opportunities beyond the national domain. This not only ensured continued domestic economic growth but also enabled these core economies to exert influence on the process and pace of development elsewhere.

Much of this has been achieved through the activities of MNEs engaged in FDI. The majority of the major MNEs originate from the leading developed economies, which are also the main source of FDI outflows, which have been growing steadily. The drive towards globalization of production is based on market, cost, competitive and government factors with the developed economies and their manufacturing and service MNEs generally better placed to exploit the opportunities or to create the conditions most favourable to achieving their objectives. Service industry FDI is largely driven by market and government factors while manufacturing FDI is shaped more by cost as well as by market factors. There are signs of a sectoral shift from manufacturing to services FDI but this has done little to change the dominance of the EC, Japan and the US in the pattern of inward and outward flows. The NICs and the less developed economies are struggling to sustain, let alone expand, their share of global FDI and as the appropriate technology is a necessary precondition, and this is one of the major ownership advantages of MNEs, their position will remain relatively weak.

Trade has also played an important part in global economic growth and integration. As with FDI, however, the pattern of flows is overwhelmingly dominated by the leading industrialized countries in western Europe, North America and parts of Asia. Merchandise accounts for most world trade although services, which are now estimated to be more than 20 per cent of the total, are becoming more significant, and for some countries such as the UK or the US the ratio of service to merchandise trade is now 1:3. Furthermore, these countries and associated regions such as western Europe are the focus for intraregional trade; in Africa or Latin America intraregional trade and its associated economic benefits amount to less than 20 per cent of total merchandise trade, for example. Whether it is a by-product or an autonomous engine of growth, a strong network of trading relationships creates opportunities for developing and expanding the production of goods and services. Through the knock-on effects on human resource quality and skills or the refinement of technological know-how the stranglehold of the developed economies on global development is further reinforced at the expense of the weaker, less developed economies.

There are ways in which national governments operating unilaterally or on the basis of multilateral agreements such as GATT or NAFTA can seek to modify the flows of global trade in order to generate economic benefits for the participants. It is argued that more liberalized trading arrangements will not only increase the total volume of world trade but also enable the less developed economies to capitalize upon comparative advantage more effectively. The difficulty for all the participants is to be seen to be committed to greater liberalization while at the same time ensuring that their own interests are either protected or enhanced. For the dominant developed economies this poses just as much of a threat as it does to the less developed economies, which see more open markets for merchandise and services as exposing them to increasing control and dependence on external actors at the cost of limited domestic economic improvement. While such uncertainties persist there is plenty of scope for the developed economies to consolidate their dominant position, even though that position is not totally secure as NICs such as Taiwan and South Korea, or newly emerging markets with massive potential such as China and the post-socialist countries of eastern Europe and the former Soviet Union, play a larger part in the ongoing process of global economic transition.

FURTHER READING

Dicken, P. 1992 *Global shift: the internationalization of economic activity* (2nd edition). Paul Chapman, London.

Dunning, J. 1993 *Multinational enterprises and the global economy*. Addison Wesley, New York.

Jones, R.W., Krueger, A.O. (eds) 1990 *The political economy of international trade*. Blackwell, Oxford.

Knox, P., Agnew, J. 1989 *The geography of the world economy*. Edward Arnold, London.

Ohmae, K. 1990 *The borderless world: power and strategy in the interlinked economy*. Harper, New York.

Porter, M. 1990 *The competitive advantage of nations*. Macmillan, London.

Reich, R.B. 1990 *The work of nations*. Random House, New York.

CHAPTER 11

LESS DEVELOPED ECONOMIES AND DEPENDENCE

David Drakakis-Smith

INTRODUCTION

Dependency is a flexible concept. It means different things to different people. What is seen as a generous, benevolent relationship by one country can be evaluated in quite a different, even resentful, light by another. The nature of dependency can also vary through time as political and economic fortunes ebb and flow. This review takes this theme of the different and changing interpretations of dependency across space and time as the basis of its structure. The remainder of the introduction will explore this question of definition in order to establish a framework for the chapter as a whole, identifying significant phases in the evolution of global relationships and examining in detail within these the changing nature of dependency and interdependency. Such an historical approach is essential if we are to understand fully the intricacies of dependency in the modern world since so many contemporary problems have their roots in the immediate and long-term past.

Definitions

Dependence in the context of less developed countries has a complex set of meanings. In a structuralist sense it implies that the development of societies so affected occurs as a consequence of their reliance on others for investment, markets, aid and political protection. There are a wide range of analytical concepts which have been constructed around this premise, such as core–periphery theory, dependency theory and world-system theory (see Roxborough (1979), Forbes (1984) and Hettne (1990) for reviews of development theory; see also Chapter 12). Most of these emerged in the 1970s and early 1980s as a response to earlier neo-classical or liberal models in which development was considered to be the inevitable end-product of the diffusion of *laissez-faire* capitalism – a linear process which was inhibited only by the initial state of underdevelopment in which Third World countries were immersed.

Dependency theories, in essence, argued that there was no initial state of underdevelopment and that the allegedly 'backward' condition of most Third

World countries was the consequence of an uninterrupted and steadily intensifying process of imperialist exploitation which began in the sixteenth century. Direct exploitation occurred within colonialism and indirect exploitation continues largely through the medium of the multinational enterprise (MNE). Much of this approach can be validated, as the following section will illustrate, but as an explanation of contemporary dependence it is too simple and over-emphasizes exogenous factors at the expense of specific indigenous historical, political, cultural and economic processes, which act in concert with external factors to produce a development process which may contain common denominators, but which is unique to each individual state. Indeed, it has been argued that the term 'underdeveloped' was a creation of President Truman who, in his inaugural address in 1949, sought to give some logic and legitimacy to the desire of the United States to become the world's economic powerhouse, replacing the European colonial powers which it was encouraging to decolonize (Sachs, 1992). Development thus became equated with the struggle to achieve the goal of economic growth to standards set by the United States. The new 'three-world' terminology, which was also becoming popular at the time, helped to identify those who were involved in this process, i.e. those promoting development (the First World), those opposing it (the Second World) and those who were the object of the exercise (the Third World). The First World thus became the dominant core of the world economy and the Third World became its dependent periphery (Drakakis-Smith, 1993).

However, the developmental context of 'dependence' is more complex than this. For example, the expansion of production within developed or core countries has, since the mid-nineteenth century, been based on expanding markets, cheap raw materials and, subsequently, cheap labour. In this sense 'the development of the core thus *depends* on the systematic underdevelopment of the periphery: it is a structural necessity' (Knox and Agnew, 1989, p. 79). In similar vein, Brookfield (1975) argued convincingly the case for interdependence within the world economy, a theme to which this chapter will return in its concluding section.

The notion of dependence, particularly that of a uniformly passive dependence to exploitation by the capitalist core of the world economy, has also been drawn into question by the diversity which has emerged in the Third World over the last 25 years. To a great extent this is the consequence of the clear differentials operating within the acceleration of neo-colonial or 'indirect' MNE exploitation, particularly the selectivity of core capital in the early search for low-cost, high-productivity locations. The emergence of the newly industrializing countries (NICs) was in part a consequence of such selectivity, in parallel with other, more spatially and temporally localized processes. In conjunction with similarly local benefits from oil price rises, industrialization began to stretch the economic and social contrasts between, as well as within, Third World countries. All of these changes have served to make simple concepts structured around dominant–dependent relationships rather crude as theoretical constructs. This situation has been rendered more complex by the rapid changes which have occurred over the last 50 years.

Prior to 1950 the great majority of Third World countries in Asia and Africa were still colonies and had very narrow, direct and intense relationships with their respective metropolitan powers. Over the next twenty years many of these states became politically independent but remained locked in an exploitative economic situation in which they continued to export primary commodities to and import manufactured goods from developed countries. Compared with the last quarter of the century, the third quarter was a relatively predictable world. Exchange rates were fixed, capitalism battled with Communism, and social life and work patterns in the West revolved around a spatially settled nuclear family and a lifetime job. The first signs of change emerged in the 1970s with the rapid growth of MNE investment in the Third World in the context of the new international division of labour (NIDL) (Thrift, 1986; see also Chapter 12). This has proceeded to develop into a fully globalized and interconnected economy in which the role of the MNE is said to be all-powerful. By the 1990s, however, even this radical interpretation has become constrained by its own orthodoxy. The world has changed again, at least in part, and whilst some forces or issues seem to be drawing countries even closer together, over environmental management for example, others are recasting North–South, or three-world, structures into new groupings which cut across old linkages. Clearly, historical processes have changed substantially over a relatively short period of time and have affected the nature of dependency considerably. The following section will review those phases in a little more detail.

COLONIALISM, IMPERIALISM AND DEPENDENCY

All too often terms such as colonialism and imperialism are employed very loosely in analyses of the development process. Although frequently used interchangeably, they are not the same. Colonialism did not begin in the nineteenth century but is a long-established process in which direct control is extended to another political area, usually inhabited by people of a different race or culture. The form of political control may vary and economic exploitation is usually involved. Imperialism, on the other hand, has been used in two distinct ways – in a technical sense, to define the latest stage in the evolution of capitalism, and in a colloquial sense, to describe the relationships between metropolitan centres and underdeveloped countries (Bell, 1980, p. 49). Imperialism is, therefore, a much broader concept than colonialism and refers to 'a general system of domination' (Bernstein *et al.*, 1992, p. 176) which is rooted in the political economy of capitalism as it has expanded since the sixteenth century. Taylor (1985) has used the terms 'formal imperialism' to describe the process whereby colonialism and imperialism coincided and reinforced one another, and 'informal imperialism' to describe the period following decolonization in the 1950s and 1960s.

This discussion is of more value than mere semantic clarification: it is also important for providing a framework in which to examine the evolution of dependency in all its forms. Basically this framework is structured around two sets of cycles of economic growth and stagnation. The larger of these comprises what is known as logistic waves and corresponds to the rise and fall of the major economic systems of feudalism, mercantilism and industrial capitalism. The smaller cycles, known as Kondratieff cycles, nest within these and are said to last for around 50 years and encompass two phases of growth and stagnation. Growth is curtailed by overproduction and stagnation impels a search for new conditions of production related to new technologies, new sources of material and new markets. Thus colonial expansion would be closely linked to these cycles. Useful discussions of the cyclical nature of the world economy may be found in Taylor (1985) and Knox and Agnew (1989), both of whom attempt to summarize the main processes in diagrammatic form. Figure 11.1 represents a simplified version of these diagrams.

What is clearly evident from the discussion above, as well as from Figure 11.1, is the complex chronological nature of economic change within the colonial era. Colonialism and imperialism changed markedly over time as capitalism changed and embraced larger territorial areas of the world. However, the territories being incorporated into capitalism also varied enormously. Far from being the simple subsistence economies that early colonizers characterized, others, particularly those involving Islam, were structured around extensive trading enterprises (see Bujra, 1992). Indeed, Blaut (1993) has claimed that many of the changes afoot in feudal Europe, which eventually gave rise to capitalism, were also underway elsewhere in the world and that it was only its geographical proximity to America that gave Europe its crucial boost to dominance. Whatever the reason, European dominance of emergent capitalism eventually ensued as did European overseeing of the gradual acceleration of its spread to the rest of the world. According to the radical development theorists of the 1980s, dominance is paralleled by dependence – so what form did this dependence, if that is what it was, take over the period from 1500 to 1950? It will help if we use Figure 11.1 to divide it into phases.

MERCANTILE COLONIALISM

Until the middle of the nineteenth century most colonial activities were dominated by trade. Commodities on which profits were made were obtained in a variety of ways that varied over space and time. Plunder, principally of precious metals, was the crudest way in which profit was extracted, being practised primarily in the Americas by Spain and Portugal and in India by the British. Elsewhere trading agreements were agreed with or forced upon various pre-capitalist states to obtain the luxury items, such as spices or fabrics, that were valued in Europe. Later, in the Americas, more productive enterprises were established in which plantation crops, such as sugar or tobacco, were grown using slave labour transported from Africa in the notorious triangular trade.

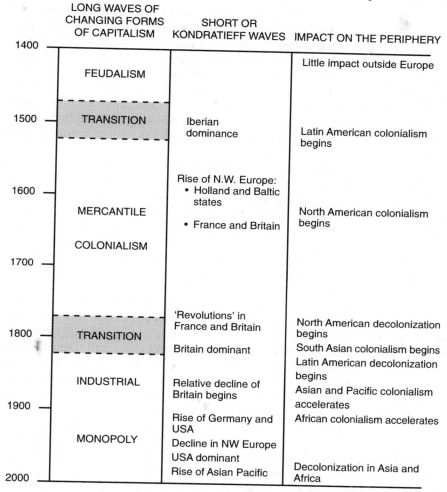

Figure 11.1 Phases of development in the world economy (after Taylor, 1985, and Bernstein *et al.*, 1992)

Enormous profits were made from this Atlantic trade for European merchants, eventually providing much of the capital that furnished the industrial revolution.

In this long and varied mercantile period, it was the trading company, often dominated by charismatic individuals, rather than the state which dominated colonial exploitation. Eventually, the escalating costs of the gradual shift into production, rather than commodity accumulation and circulation, forced many of the old merchant-adventurers into bankruptcy towards the end of the eighteenth century. Often the physical presence of Europeans, except in the settler colonies of North America, was quite limited and in the early years of trade in Asia and Africa, in particular, Europeans often constituted just another trading group living in their own sector of an established trading or capital city (Drakakis-Smith, 1992; Lowder, 1986). Even where Europeans assumed control, as did the Portuguese in Malacca in 1511, the fortress and church that were constructed on the hill above the city looked out over uninterrupted trade in the Chinese, Arab, Japanese and Indian trading quarters (McGee, 1967). Indeed, continuation of this trade and accumulation of regional products was precisely what the Portuguese wanted; they simply slipped into an existing regional trading economy and milked it for what they could (Dixon, 1991).

It is difficult to establish the extent to which 'dependence' existed during the mercantile colonial period. Commodity circulation certainly brought great profits, and some colonies in the Americas, in particular, were heavily exploited for commodity extraction or production. North America also became a major market for the products of England's growing manufacturing enterprises (Barratt-Brown, 1974). The American colonies were, therefore, subordinate to the growing dominance of Britain in political and economic terms but were not 'dependent' to the same extent as was clearly shown by the relative ease with which independence was obtained.

Elsewhere dependence on European colonial powers was even less marked, partly because of the relatively restricted amount of total trade that was with Europe, partly because of the limited presence of Europeans, and partly because the direct involvement of European governments was also small. Dependence, therefore, on European metropolitan powers was very limited, particularly so in the eyes of indigenous rulers who tolerated Europeans only because they were useful. And yet change was occurring. Many local rulers in Africa and Asia found that European technologies, in particular military technology, were not only useful but indispensable in helping overcome local rivals. In this sense, some degree of dependency was established. Trade agreements gradually became closely entwined with political and military alliances and gradually the economies of many Asian, and to a lesser extent African, states became increasingly part of an intensifying world economy, the focus of which lay firmly in Europe.

Yet towards the end of the eighteenth century, European interest in colonialism seemed to be waning somewhat. The loss of the American colonies was swiftly followed by the all-consuming Napoleonic Wars and European attentions, from adventurers to investors, turned inwards. Moreover, the growing profits from the expanding industrial revolution ensured the investments remained inwardly focused. In this context, it is not surprising that old-style adventurers, such as Francis Light, Stamford Raffles and Charles Elliot, found little initial enthusiasm for their acquisition of the islands of Penang, Singapore and Hong Kong, respectively.

INDUSTRIAL COLONIALISM

The inward-looking phase of British and European economic development was relatively short-lived; by the early decades of the nineteenth century rapid industrial growth had led to an expanded demand for raw materials and also for cheap food to feed the burgeoning urban workforce. This increased circulation of investment capital was more concerned with production *per se* than in the past. Accumulation of a tradeable commodity surplus was no longer sufficient. Both the quantity and quality of the commodities to be traded had become important. The import of raw materials and food, on the scale now required, needed more than trading toe-holds and reliance on agreements with local rulers; it was predicated on the acquisition and control of territory from which minerals and/or agricultural commodities could be extracted and production organized. Whilst such production was largely organized through commercial firms, the principal agent of colonialism was the state, which acquired territory and provided various facilitating structures, such as garrisons, administrators and communication links, thus itself investing directly and extensively in colonial development. Subsequently, both the colonial and indigenous populations became important markets for manufactured goods from Europe. From 1870 to 1915 around one-third of Britain's rising exports went to its empire (Barratt-Brown, 1974). Particularly pernicious in this context was the resale of basic commodities, such as tea, sugar and flour, that had been grown in the colonies, often to the poor who grew them, after processing and value addition in Europe. Thus, the colonial poor were exploited twice over, as labourers and as consumers.

For Britain, from the 1870s onwards, the colonies also became an important area for speculative investment (Figure 11.2). Barratt-Brown (1974) argues that as competition from other European manufacturers intensified, and periodic recessions set in, so Britain's investors sought to exploit the opportunities

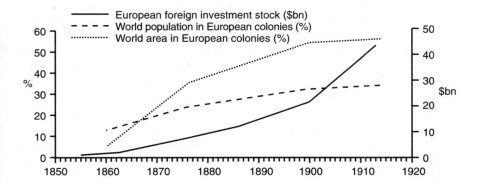

Figure 11.2   Colonialism and colonial investment, 1850–19

offered by its empire. By 1915 the stock of foreign investment capital held by Britain stood at almost $20 billion (Warren, 1980, p. 62), an 18-fold increase in real terms over the total in 1855 (Barratt-Brown, 1974, p. 171). Around 80 per cent of this investment was in what we would now call the Third World, the great majority being in the British Empire, although Latin America also attracted a sizeable share.

Direct colonialism impacted largely on Asia and Africa. Most Latin American countries had achieved political independence before Asia and Africa were carved up between the European powers. Although territorial acquisition occurred over a relatively short period of time, largely between 1850 and 1920, the form and structure of colonialism varied enormously in accordance with the metropolitan power itself, the rationale behind the acquisition of the colony, and the political, economic and cultural composition of the occupying power. Some European powers, like France or Holland, preferred direct rule. Others, such as Britain, opted for indirect control through traditional local rulers. Some colonies were acquired for their commodity assets; others were acquired simply to prevent another European country becoming too powerful in one region, or to safeguard other possessions, and had little economic value. Some states resisted colonial annexation vigorously, others even submitted willingly to one power to prevent occupation by another (see Dixon, 1991, for fuller discussion in the context of south-east Asia).

But whatever political form the colonies took, their economies, however vigorous and profitable, were restructured towards the needs of the colonial power. In terms of agricultural production this often meant a narrow concentration on those commodities that were needed by metropolitan manufacturers. Countries that had hitherto produced a wide range of produce found themselves covered in extensive plantations growing one or two export crops, such as rubber or coconuts. Figure 11.3 illustrates the situation for the Dutch East Indies during the nineteenth century and all over Asia and Africa there was a similar rise in the growth of primary exports. Of course not all of the colonial populations were directly affected by such changes. In most countries the peasantry remained outside the plantation system but gradually, as in Malaysia, they began to switch from subsistence to commercial crops, often with assistance from the authorities. Even the few politically independent states failed to resist this change in the structure of production. Dixon (1991) has revealed clearly how Thai exports were reduced from a wide range of products in 1850 to an overwhelming concentration on rice, later supplemented by rubber, teak and tin (Figure 11.4). Ironically most of the rice was exported to colonies throughout the region to feed plantation workers, thus reinforcing the exploitative economic structures.

Much of the labour for the large-scale production of export crops was created through the amalgamation of existing units into commercial plantations and the consequent creation of a large pool of landless labourers. In areas where local labour was in short supply, contract labour was brought in, either from elsewhere in the colony, as in French Indo-China, or from overseas. Thus the Chinese mine operators in Malaya imported large numbers of their compatriots whilst

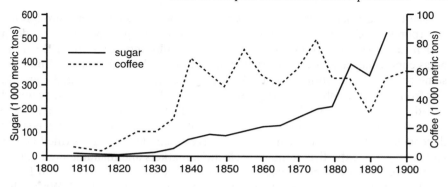

Figure 11.3   Dutch East Indies: the growth of primary exports, 1800–1900

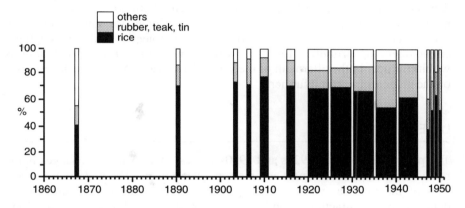

Figure 11.4   Thailand (Siam): increasing export concentration, 1860–1950

subsequent rubber plantations relied heavily on Tamil workers recruited from south India (Cho, 1990). As elsewhere, the evolution of such plural societies created enormous ethnic problems that continue to affect development today.

Overall, therefore, production during the industrial colonial phase was rural-based; there was little urban manufacturing, other than to meet local consumer needs. Colonial cities were essentially control points for the colonial economy rather than points of production *per se*. Indeed, where established local manufacturing industries posed a threat to imported goods, as happened with textile production in India, they were rapidly squeezed out of the market (see Habeeb, 1981). The pivotal role of such cities in controlling colonial economies was reinforced by new transport communication technologies. Railways, themselves a profitable investment, linked rural production points to ports; steamships linked these ports to their counterparts in Europe; the telegraph facilitated rapid decision making in both the political and economic spheres.

The consequence of the rapid expansion of the world economy through the incorporation of extensive territorial colonialism was a huge increase in trade in which Latin America, Asia and Africa played a substantial role. By 1913 these areas contributed a quarter of world exports and were the recipients of almost the same proportion of world imports. As Knox and Agnew (1989, p. 253) remark, 'far from being peripheral to the growth of the world economy, the undeveloped world (*sic*) ... was vital'. Of course, this involvement was very narrowly focused. Few colonies traded directly with one another and all were heavily dependent on the metropolitan power for investment, technology, skilled labour and managerial expertise, military protection, markets and manufactured goods. In this context, it can be argued that the settler colonies, i.e. those with larger numbers of expatriate emigrants, were in a less vulnerable position. Whilst this may have been true in a political sense, and to a certain extent with regard to investment and labour skills, economically the settler colonies were just as dependent on the metropole. Yet, dependence cuts both ways, and in turn the metropolitan countries were dependent on their colonies for supplies of cheap raw materials and food, for expanding market potential and for supplying employment opportunities for a growing number of 'surplus' middle-class within Europe. In the aftermath of the First World War, this reverse dependence on the colonies increased further.

LATE COLONIALISM

The period between the 1920s and 1950s witnessed a number of changes in the relationship between colonies and metropolitan powers. The widespread recession of the interwar years, which was the consequence of declining world demand for manufactured goods and overproduction of raw materials, sent profits tumbling and trade into decline. There was much less of the mutual interchange of commodities between periphery and core, with the multinational firm becoming more prominent and focusing on resource exploitation or provision of manufactured goods much more specifically. This shift was both a cause and a consequence of increased involvement in international trade by the United States. Between 1914 and 1938 North America increased its foreign direct investment from 20 per cent of the world total to more than 30 per cent: by 1960, following extensive decolonization, this share had risen to 55 per cent. As Agnew (1987, p. 62) observed, 'American governments could preach against colonialism while large American (and other) firms colonized the world.'

During the interwar years investment in the colonies was erratic, although helped to some extent by the expanding American interests noted above, but in comparison with previous decades the overall rise in investment slowed considerably. Indeed, in places it declined substantially. Dixon (1991, p. 118) reveals that from the mid-1920s to the mid-1930s French investment in Indo-China fell by 80 per cent (see also Havinden and Meredith, 1993). However, as a result of declining profits from primary exports, slow but steady diversification into secondary and tertiary activities was occurring, particularly in Asia. In part, this was the result of the need to satisfy growing political unease in the colonies, because the 1930s saw a steady politicization of colonial populations, partly as a result of increasing polarization within Europe. Both indigenous and non-European immigrant populations were encouraged to invest and became more involved in local manufacturing and service industries. In Java, for example, the number of textile mills increased by 600 per cent during the 1930s, almost all representing Chinese investment (Robison, 1994).

This economic diversification was both encouraged and made possible by another set of changes related much more to the European populations in the colonies. The first of these related to the increased European emigration to the colonies during the interwar years. Distressed by rising unemployment and poor prospects at home, many Europeans moved to what they perceived as better opportunities in the colonies. Some went into an expanding colonial administration which, in many colonies, was strongly influenced by Wilsonian principles of trusteeship and the responsibility of the colonial administrator to improve life for all colonial populations, not just Europeans. However, the great majority of European emigrants did not enter into colonial civil service; instead they took up a wide range of occupations, some not deemed suitable for Europeans in earlier years. Thus, although the number of settler farmers increased, so did the number of Europeans in a variety of urban-based businesses, including retailing and waged labour. In Rangoon in 1931 well over one-quarter of the European population could be classified as traders, shop assistants or unskilled/semi-skilled labour (McGee, 1967).

The nature of the links between colonies and the metropolitan powers thus changed subtly during the late colonial period. On the surface the narrow focus on a restricted range of exports persisted, even worsened (Figure 11.5), as did the reliance on the metropolitan countries for imported goods. But changes were afoot; manufacturing was rising slowly in the colonies, depressing the demand for European products, investment from Europe was declining, and the United States was becoming a more prominent player in the trading game. Fundamentally, the exploitative relationship between core and periphery remained the same but the narrow conduit of those links between colony and 'mother country' was being widened by the active intervention of other countries. Colonization was giving way to a broader-based imperialism as global capitalism continued to develop in depth.

In this context, the European colonial powers, affected as they were by global recession, were perhaps more dependent on their colonies than ever before. This is certainly evident in the 1950s and 1960s when European involvement in Africa, the last continent to decolonize, intensified enormously. Because of the weakened state of the European currencies, Britain and France were forced to look to the sterling and franc blocs for both imports and investment opportunities, whilst a new wave of migrants eager to escape a war-ravaged Europe were encouraged to leave by state-assisted passages. Certainly the 'development' of African resources was seen as a crucial part of the post-war recovery process in Britain, not least

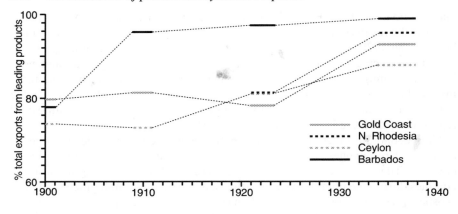

Figure 11.5   The narrowing of exports in late colonialism

because exports to the United States could earn for Britain the dollars which its balance of payments deficit desperately needed (Havinden and Meredith, 1993). Until the late 1950s and the rise of European economic unity, therefore, the colonies had considerable advantages and there was a stronger sense of dependency of the European metropolitan powers on the resources of their colonies to keep them afloat. Of course, these improved terms of trade brought relatively little improvement in the quality of life for most indigenous people, although some infrastructural investments were made. Indeed, the 'good times' of the 1950s served largely to entrench the colonies in their role as providers of primary resources, a role which was maintained after independence and under-pinned the resurgence of different forms of dependency which were to emerge.

INDEPENDENCE OR INTERDEPENDENCE: THE POST-COLONIAL SITUATION

1945 to 1970: illusion and delusion

As indicated above, the years immediately following the Second World War were characterized by sustained demand for primary products, partly linked to post-war reconstruction of developed economies. In contrast to the 1920s, the philosophy behind the political process was to give the defeated nations every opportunity to rebuild their economies. These policies were reinforced by the Bretton Woods agreement and the subsequent establishment of institutions, such as GATT, the IMF and the World Bank, to help encourage development globally. In conceptual terms this has been characterized as 'the long boom', a period of sustained expansion in production and trade which lasted until the late 1960s (Gwynne, 1990).

The role of the developing countries within the 'long boom' experienced considerable change during this period. The prevailing development philosophies of the period to the mid- to late 1950s were based on the long-established theory of comparative advantage, with the developing world producing the raw materials and the developed countries processing these into manufactured items for export. However, commodity prices had continued to fall in real terms and the newly independent states found themselves producing more but receiving less. The overall quality of life in many countries was declining, particularly in the cities to which so many had migrated after independence in the anticipation of work. The late 1950s and early 1960s, therefore, witnessed another surge in socialist political success in Cuba and south-east Asia.

The response to this was twofold. First, there was an enhanced aid programme as the United States in particular sought to prop up those countries vulnerable to socialism – Iran, Laos and South Vietnam began to rise to the top of the aid list. Second, there was a switch in development strategy in favour of more diversified economies in the developing world, following in particular import-substitution industries (ISI) (Gwynne, 1990; Sandhu and Wheatley, 1989). Industrialization began to feature more prominently in the development strategies recommended for the Third World, as it was increasingly coming to be known (Drakakis-Smith, 1993), as exemplified by Rostow (1960) and Gerschenkron (1962). At the same time the new technologies of the 'green revolution' were being hailed as a new, sure way to help developing countries become more self-sufficient in basic food production (Chapman, 1992).

These new directions did not have immediate or widespread impact in the developing world. Although the green revolution seemed to be designed to reduce the dependency of the Third World by making it more self-sufficient in food production, its initial success was spatially and socially patchy, particularly in Africa, which was more reliant on maize than on wheat or rice. Moreover, many of the technological inputs were Western in origin and could be said to have increased dependency. Others have alleged that in many parts of the world the self-reliance of agricultural reforms was blunted by a deliberate US policy of selling very cheap wheat to Third World countries in order to bring about an increased dependence which could later be used for political ends.

Import-substitution industrialization also had mixed success. In Latin America, where ISI had been underway since the 1930s and had been further encouraged by loss of imports during the Second World War, those states with large domestic markets, such as Brazil, had developed sizeable manufacturing capacities (Dickenson, 1987; Gilbert, 1990) and had already begun to attract investment from MNEs (Corbridge, 1993). In Africa and even in Asia, however, despite the encouragement of cheap oil, ISI proved to be a hollow strategy because of limited domestic markets in size and/or purchasing power.

The consequences of these changes on the development process were slow to filter through to trading relations. There were still considerable colonial ties in the trading patterns of south-east Asia, although the neo-colonial influences of the United States were also apparent, as was the importance of Japan, which had revived its fortunes very rapidly by means of an aggressive export-oriented development strategy – an early harbinger of things to come. In the rest of the Third World trading ties to advanced capitalist states were even greater than in south-east Asia. All in all the early decades of independence produced no great changes in the relations between the former colonizers and the colonized, the First and Third Worlds. Despite a commitment by the former to promote development in the latter, there was little change in the dominant–subordinate relations between the two, at least in economic terms. In political terms, there was a hope that the Third World would emerge, after independence, into a genuinely non-aligned bloc with the potential to mediate between East and West in the Cold War and then to convert this political independence to economic advantage. As we will see, this did not happen. However, as we have noted earlier in this narrative, a dominant–subordinate relationship does not always mean complete dependence of the latter on the former. Nowhere was this clearer than in the process of labour relations between developed and less developed states.

In the immediate post-war years, the industrial economies of north-west Europe suffered a considerable labour shortage. The loss of manpower as a result of the war was accentuated by the expansion of the European industrial economy. The response was to import labour from former colonies. Much of this labour had accumulated in the cities of newly independent countries, mainly migrants in search of work that was not there. It is no coincidence that it was during this period that the informal sector became a much more noticeable element of the urban economy and began to feature more prominently in development theories. Governments in both sending and recipient countries saw benefits in encouraging an international migration of labour, usually male, to perceived sources of employment in the former metropolitan powers. Thus Britain opened its doors to migrants from the new Commonwealth, France to north and west Africans, Japan to Koreans and West Germany to workers from Turkey (long a close ally of Germany). The flows to Europe were supplemented by migrants from around the Mediterranean in general: initially Italians, Yugoslavs or Portuguese, later from central and eastern Mediterranean sources, such as Malta or the Lebanon. The United States began similarly to receive migrant workers from the Caribbean and Mexico.

The number involved was extensive. At its peak in the early 1970s, some 3.5 million migrant workers were in France and another 2.5 million in West Germany. Most were employed in menial, repetitive low-paid work, had few if any civil rights and were herded together in dormitory accommodation. Trade union membership was discouraged and work permits revoked at the slightest sign of protest. The post-war miracle of the industrial economies of north-west Europe, and to a certain extent of the USA and Japan, was firmly built on the back of such exploited workers and clearly indicates that, although many of the sending countries were very reliant on remittances from migrant workers, the advanced economies could be said to have been very dependent on such labour for their early economic success.

1970s to 1990s: polarization of the global economy

Warwick Armstrong and Terry McGee (1988) have characterized the last 20 years as a period in which two contradictory yet mutually reinforcing processes have been in operation, viz. convergence and divergence. Convergence refers to the ways in which the developing countries were being drawn along those paths experienced by the West towards the current lifestyles and political economic structure of developed countries. Divergence encompasses the fact that each country has a unique history and culture which draws it into the world economy in its own way. Such ideas have emerged in recent years because of an apparent increase in involvement by developing countries in the global economy. However, as we have seen, the interlinkages between the First and Third Worlds have always been considerable. What has changed is the nature of those links, together with the impact this has had on developing countries as a whole.

The most investigated aspect of these changes has been the increasing investment in developing countries from developed countries. This acceleration of globalization is examined in more detail in several of the other chapters in this volume; in essence it stemmed from decreasing profitability within Europe and North America, itself the consequence of a variety of causes, such as increased costs for labour and environmental management, and stagnant markets associated with the recession in the developed world. Some, such as Weiss (1990) and Dicken (1986a), have placed these events in the larger context of the downswing of a Kondratieff wave, the end of a long boom which in turn stimulates restructuring of production, technologies and markets. Whatever the cyclical impetus to change in the late 1960s and early 1970s, substantial acceleration followed the rise in oil prices in 1973–74 and again in 1979.

The response on the part of many individual firms was to internationalize their production process, either by investing in new plant in major market areas or by investing in new plant in cheaper production areas (see also Chapter 7). Dicken (1986a) and Gwynne (1990), amongst others, have examined this process in detail and it is clearly linked to changes in the product life cycle, new transport and communication technologies, as well as to the role of recipient states in offering incentives to induce incoming investment. The focus for almost all of this type of change is the multinational corporation. And yet Corbridge (1993) has indicated that at the very time that MNEs seemed to be emerging as the cutting edge of investment in the Third World, their relative role was declining (Figure 11.6). Moreover, by far the great majority of FDI was invested in other developed countries, searching for improved market opportunities, although the relatively insignificant amount of total FDI that went to the Third World was very significant for certain types of firm and also for the developing countries themselves.

The major area of expansion in terms of overseas investment was through the medium of commercial banks (Figure 11.7). The funds for investment had come from two main sources, recycled petro-dollars and the balance of payments deficit run by the USA (Corbridge, 1993). As the recession had reduced the

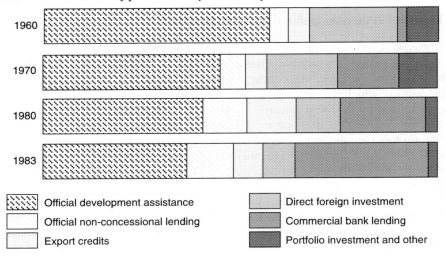

Figure 11.6 Financial flows to developing countries, 1960–83

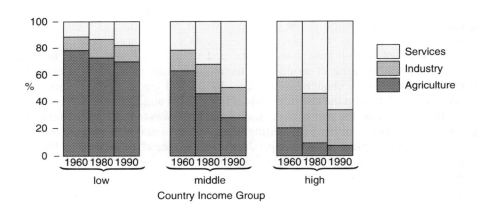

Figure 11.7 Changing employment structure, 1960–90 (from World Bank, 1982, and UNDP, 1993)

potential for borrowing by firms in developed countries, so the Third World became a more attractive and feasible alternative. At the same time rekindled enthusiasm for neo-liberal development had begun to erode ODA and to favour private funding for more market-oriented development. Essentially, therefore, the banks began to lend to governments, confident in the assurance that 'countries never go bankrupt' (Wriston, 1986), to promote infrastructural and industrial development. Overwhelmingly, these loans in the 1970s favoured Latin American countries and substantial debts began to accumulate. In part, indebtedness was exacerbated by the increased role played by the World Bank

BOX 11.1   From Southern Rhodesia to Zimbabwe: a case study of dependence

The initial European incursions into what is now Zimbabwe occurred in the early 1890s under the auspices of the British South Africa Company (BSAC). Early disappointments in the search for precious metals resulted in the BSAC encouraging white settlement in order to promote agricultural production for both African and British markets. From the 1920s onwards the land began to be formally designated for white or black economic activity and this persisted until the 1980s. White settlers and companies controlled 18 million hectares of the richest land; approximately the same area of poor-quality land was distributed amongst the various tribal groups who made up 95 per cent of the population.

The economy was similarly divided with most of the African population of Rhodesia living and working within a previous subsistence economy, whilst the expatriates were involved primarily in production for export markets. However, the latter were not independent of the former since the mines and commercial firms relied heavily on local labour, which was continuously reproduced at low cost in the tribal areas. In their turn most African families were forced into wage labour because of the poverty of their land. At the same time the scale of the commercial farming and mining operations in the rural areas required large amounts of capital, most of which came from Britain channelled through large companies. However, the management of these large-scale enterprises was largely in the hands of the long-term resident settler population.Until the 1940s, therefore, Southern Rhodesia was caught in a double layer of dependency. The colony itself was dependent on British investment capital and émigré managers or settlers but it was also dependent on the continued subordination and exploitation of its black population.

This situation changed substantially as a result of the Second World War, which saw the rise of manufacturing in the African colonies, partly as a result of reduced import opportunities. Southern Rhodesia joined the short-lived Central African Federation to take advantage of this trend using Northern Rhodesian resources and Nyasaland labour to establish a range of manufacturing plants, largely producing for the European and African export markets. Capital for these new ventures came from both South Africa and the UK, often via large multinational companies such as Lonrho. Such activity was looked upon particularly favourably by Britain after the war because it made the metropolitan power less dependent, in its turn, on the United States and the escalating dollar debt.

The introduction of industrial capital, however, had another effect as it also brought into Southern Africa a new type of colonialism, one with quite different values from the old settler community. Industrial capital needed an urban labour force and was positive in its encouragement of Africans to move into town, a phenomenon quite antithetical to pre-existing norms. Eventually, the settler colonialists were pushed too far by this move to 'liberalization' and reacted by staging a *coup d'état* through a unilateral declaration of independence (UDI) in 1965 which lasted for 13 years. During this period sanctions were applied to trade with Southern Rhodesia and effectively cut the state off from its traditional dependence upon Britain. In effect, however, South Africa stepped into the breach and dependency continued.

In 1980 the independent state Zimbabwe was established under a socialist government with the express aim of creating an independent country which would, in effect, be an equal partner in a coalition of anti-South African states (SADCC). Internally, land and wealth were to be redistributed from white to black, rich to poor. Whilst many of the achievements of the Zimbabwean state have been impressive, particularly in social welfare provision, in effect the economic situation has changed very little. The economy is still dependent on the export of primary commodities, which in turn are still produced, for the most part, by white commercial farmers or multinational companies. Attempts to break away from this double dependence have foundered on the indebtedness that Zimbabwe found itself experiencing by the late 1980s. The response from the main creditors, led by the World Bank, has been to impose an economic structural adjustment programme (ESAP) on Zimbabwe which emphasizes increased export earnings in traditional commodities and open-door policies to imported manufactured goods. Zimbabwe has, therefore, found it almost impossible to break away from a reliance on imports, investment funds and loans from the developed world and from an economy that is dependent on primary exports to those same countries.

The fate that has befallen Zimbabwe is not untypical of many African states, forced by indebtedness to adopt structural adjustment and maintain colonial forms of economic dependence. Clearly, however, the events of the last 100 years have been closely shaped by the individual character of the former colony, for example by the scale of settler colonialism and the proximity of the country to South Africa, both of which have enormously affected its political economy. In contrast to Taiwan, there have been no waves of refugee investment or United States aid or European multinational finance. And yet, like Taiwan, Zimbabwe has invested considerably in its infrastructure and its human capital, for example through health care and education. But the historical process of the incorporation of these two states into the world economy has been very different and this is clearly reflected in the nature of their dependent status.

and IMF in the recycling of petro-dollars and their harder attitudes towards debt servicing and recoverability, compared with softer bilateral lending between countries with historical colonial links. Debt accumulation occurred at a time when world commodity prices began to plummet, after a period of relative ease. Loan candidates began to tighten and the debt crisis burst in the early 1980s with a series of major defaults.

The responses to the debt crisis will be discussed below, as they play an important role in shaping the structure of development in the 1990s. However, it must be noted at this point that commercial bank lending, much more than FDI, has created increased dependency in the relationship between the First and Third Worlds. The old maxim that a small debt is a problem for the borrower, a large debt is a problem for the lender, has simply not been sustained in the real world, where international creditors, often syndicated and coordinated by global organizations such as the IMF or World Bank, have been able to dictate development programmes to so many developing countries that override the political leaning of their governments. Indeed, a shift to Western-style democracy has increasingly become a precondition of further loans, in addition to economic adjustment.

The impact of all these changes on the Third World in general has been a switch from agriculture to industry and services (Figure 11.7). Of course, such aggregate data tend to mask more localized trends, particularly as the categories themselves are so broad. Agriculture ranges from small semi-subsistence activities to huge commercialized factory farms to intensive production of high-value items, such as orchids; industry encompasses mining as well as manufacturing; whilst services incorporates traditional market selling, domestic service, or employment in a sophisticated financial institution. Nevertheless, it is possible to discern a shift towards manufacturing, one which is particularly noticeable in the upper-middle income range of countries. Here again, however, aggregated data on GDP conceal considerable differences. As Dicken (1986a) and Chandra (1992) indicate, most manufacturing output still occurs in the developed countries, just six of which account for some three-quarters of world production in terms of value added. Amongst the developing nations, the leading producers are those with the largest domestic markets, viz. China, India and Brazil. It is only when exports are specifically considered that the countries traditionally associated with manufacturing in the Third World come to the fore (Figure 11.8).

The remarkable point about Figure 11.8 is that the leading edge of manufacturing exporters in the developing world is still relatively small. The rapidly industrializing economies (RIEs) – it would surely be misleading to continue to refer to them as newly industrializing countries – still comprise Pacific Asia's 'four little dragons' of Singapore, Taiwan, South Korea and Hong Kong, together with Latin America's Mexico and Brazil. Admittedly a second wave of Pacific Asian producers, such as Thailand and Malaysia, are beginning to make their mark, and in conjunction with the four dragons are giving considerable impetus to regional development (see below), but their individual impact is as yet relatively limited.

The restricted number of RIEs has had a profound influence on the Third World as a whole, serving, in conjunction with rapid increases in revenue for some oil exports, to widen the differences between developing countries and reduce their group solidarity. Most African countries have experienced acute economic distress over the last ten years or so whilst Hong Kong and Singapore have joined the World Bank's first division of high-income nations. In the 1970s and 1980s this fragmentation led to a heated debate about the validity of the concept of the Third World, with some dividing the less developed nations into as many as nine groups (see Drakakis-Smith, 1993). These observations had some basis in reality with the average GNP per capita of the middle-income countries increasing from five to seven times greater than that of the low-income countries between 1976 and 1991. However, such figures tend to mask the even greater increase in income discrepancies which has occurred between developed

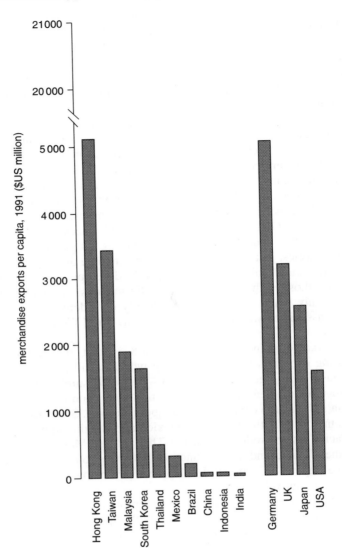

Figure 11.8   Leading exporters in the Third World, 1991

and developing centres. Thus, over the same period the ratio between the GNP per capita of high-income industrialized economies and that of low-income countries rose from 41 to over 60.

Despite or perhaps because of the recession, therefore, the high-income industrialized nations have drawn closer together over the last twenty years in terms of both investment and trade, a process reinforced by the consolidation of the European Union. As a result most of the world's trade is still between the advanced capitalist states, and the majority of imports into developed from developing countries still comprises primary products, with manufactured goods moving the other way. Indeed, in 1991 manufactured imports into OECD countries from non OECD states comprised less than 20 per cent of the total (World Bank, 1993). Nevertheless, this does represent a rapid growth since the early 1970s when the Pacific Asian RIEs provided only just over 2 per cent of OECD imports (Dicken, 1986a, p. 41). In 1991 the four dragons together with China provided more than 8 per cent, worth about US$150 billion.

The success of the Pacific Asian dragons in penetrating the world export trade in manufactured goods has prompted questions about why these states succeeded and others did not. There are basically two sets of arguments that have been put forward. The first relates to exogenous factors and emphasizes the importance of FDI and the role of MNEs in the generation of investment funds; the second group comprises a more indigenous rationale and has often been related to the *laissez-faire* free-market approach allegedly typical of the four governments. This latter argument has, in recent years, been effectively discussed in the light of evidence of a clear interventionist policy by the state. Political legitimacy in the RIEs of Pacific Asia has been sustained by economic success and full employment (Lubeck, 1992; Hsaio, 1992). Arguments related to exogenous influences similarly have been criticized, for only in Singapore has FDI played a substantial role *vis-à-vis* local capital. In the other three dragons exogenous capital was strongly linked to ODA, particularly from the USA, to help promote infrastructural development in the face of the Communist threat of the 1960s and 1970s. External capital was also brought into Hong Kong and Taiwan by refugees from China in even earlier periods. Indeed, many of the explorations of rapid economic growth in each of the Pacific Asian RIEs must be firmly placed in a particular mix of historical, cultural and geographical circumstances (Deyo, 1987; Hamilton, 1992; Yeung, 1994). Nevertheless, the search for the chimera of a Pacific Asian model of development continues: witness the recent World Bank research report on the east Asian miracle (World Bank, 1993), which looks back rather than forward and gives little emphasis to the social consequences of rapid growth. Substantial questions over the redistribution of wealth from rapid economic growth are still being asked about the RIEs (Booth, 1993), as well as over environmental deterioration and human rights (Bello, 1992; Drakakis-Smith, 1993; Loh, 1993).

CONCLUSION

What do all the complex changes outlined above mean for the dependency of the less developed countries, and what are the principal issues on which we must focus our attention in the 1990s and beyond? These are two quite separate questions and each will be addressed in turn.

It should be apparent from the discussion thus far that dependency and subordination are not necessarily coincidental. The dominant forces within the world economy lie primarily but not exclusively within developed countries, where private capital and state governments act in concert or independently, using both political and economic forces to safeguard and promote their own interests. To a certain extent this is mediated by international agencies seeking to encourage development within the Third World, but many of these agencies themselves are dominated by and operate on behalf of (directly or indirectly) core capital.

Dependency is a more ambiguous concept which can be interpreted in many different ways. John Weiss (1990, p. 42), one of the few analysts to try to identify the economic characteristics of dependence, summarizes the main characteristics of the literature as follows:

- a heavy penetration of foreign capital in the major sectors of the economy
- the use of capital-intensive imported technologies
- specialization in exports of primary commodities or labour-intensive manufactures
- consumption patterns of élites copied from the rich countries
- unequal exchange in trade (defined in various ways)
- growing inequalities in income distribution.

Weiss examines only the first of these in any detail, associating the penetration of foreign capital almost entirely with MNEs, and questioning associations between dependency and investment only in the context of the emergence of Third World multinationals. Much of the dependence within this investment process has been well debated (Taylor and Thrift, 1982; Peet, 1987; Dicken, 1986a), although there has been a tendency to overlook the fact that much of the FDI in developing countries is still associated with resource extraction rather than manufacturing (Dixon, 1991). The debate has also been strongly clouded by ideological rhetoric.

Clearly, countries or enterprises lacking in capital, technology, capital equipment, skilled white- and blue-collar labour and other aspects of production are going to be dependent on the suppliers of such inputs in order to initiate and sustain production. But, on the other hand, the recipients of the commodities produced will also be dependent on a continued supply at appropriate costs. As Knox and Agnew (1989, p. 169) conclude, 'quite simply the ascent of the core regions could not have taken place without the foodstuffs, raw materials and markets provided by the rest of the world.' In short, the components of the global economy are interdependent; but some are more dominant than others.

Another aspect of the assertion that dependency is related to capital penetration relates to the fact that much of the capital transferred over the last decade or so has not been directly invested in MNE plants but has been made available to Third World governments. The debt crisis which subsequently affected so many countries has proved to be a much more potent force in deepening dependent relationships. Once again, however, this dependency has become increasingly structured around global financial institutions controlled by and through core capital.

Further examination of Weiss's list reveals other contradictions, particularly the association of dependency with consumption patterns and with inequalities in income distribution. Adoption of Western lifestyles and the associated rise of imports occurs in a variety of forms, from the widespread consumption by the poor of bread made with imported wheat (see Andrae and Beckmann, 1985) to the status given to European cars. Similarly, inequalities in income distribution are as observable in Pacific Asia as they are in west Africa; indeed, the provision of basic needs, and human rights, show disturbingly little correlation with economic growth.

The conclusion of this review of dependency must be that the concept needs to be used very carefully. Most nations, if not most enterprises or individuals, are dependent upon others in some way. What is important, however, are the ways in which that dependence or interdependence is structured or manipulated by the dominant elements within the relationship. This can occur at any level, global, regional or local, and this chapter will conclude with two brief examples of how this is occurring, viz. structural adjustment in Africa and the emergence of regional divisions of labour in Pacific Asia.

The underlying rationale behind structural adjustment programmes (SAPs) is woven around the debt crises of the 1980s and the inability of many African states to meet repayment schedules because of persistent budget deficits. The World Bank (1994b) argument is that such deficits were caused by self-inflicted problems such as unrealistic exchange rates, overspending on social welfare, excessive subsidies, over-employment in government bureaucracies and inadequate export earnings. There was some truth in this but the debt crisis was also the consequence of shrinking commodity prices and very tight borrowing conditions. Most African economies have been stagnant or in decline for some time. Individually debts were small compared with those of Latin America or Asian states but collectively the continent posed a threat to international stability, economic and political.

More than 30 African states have been bullied into structural adjustment (Riddell, 1992; Gibbon *et al.*, 1992), the common denominators of which are increased private sector investment, liberalization of exchange rates and trade, reduction of government expenditure and deregulation of the economy in general. The World Bank has made great play in recent years of being seen to be trying to ameliorate the worst effects of SAPs through what it calls 'adjustment with a human face'. As Gibbon (1992) has noted, this has produced virtually nothing in practical terms and the social consequences have been substantial – increased unemployment, drastically reduced investment in housing and education programmes, rampant inflation and stagnant wages. Most of this burden has fallen on the urban poor and the consequence has been widespread unrest. Even in Harare, normally a relatively stable city, riots recently followed the removal of subsidies from wheat flour and a rapid trebling in bread prices (Drakakis-Smith *et al.*, 1995).

Far from increasing the economic independence of developing countries, SAPs have made them more dependent on the capitalist world economy, inducing not only great economic dependence on its major financial institutions but also a political switch away from socialism or state capitalism to the liberal democracy favoured by the West. The consequence has been a return to ethnic politics and further distortions to the development process.

In contrast to the increased dependency and economic hardships and distortions brought about in Africa, Pacific Asia would seem to have lessened its dependence on the developed core substantially over the last two decades. The region has become an increasingly important trading partner for other parts of the Pacific Rim, such as North America or Australasia, but their importance to Pacific Asia has diminished as its global role has broadened (Dixon and Drakakis-Smith, 1993). Within the region, too, the very dominant role of Japan as a source of investment has lessened as the four dragons themselves have begun to invest in production in the region's new low-cost production sites in Thailand or Malaysia. In turn, these ASEAN states are looking towards the emerging socialist economies, such as Vietnam, for even newer opportunities (Dixon and Drakakis-Smith, forthcoming). In short a clear regional division of labour has emerged but this does not mean that dominant–subordinate relationships have diminished or that dependency on MNE investment has lessened. It is simply that the chain of command has lengthened and become more complicated, giving hope to governments in the region that at some point the dominant–subordinate balance in their interdependent relationships may eventually turn in their favour. This is the essence of capitalism, to get someone else dependent on you in order to make a profit. For this reason dependency and underdevelopment, like the poor, will always be with us – capitalism could not survive without them.

FURTHER READING.

Chandra, R. 1992 *Industrialisation and development in the Third World*. Routledge, London.

Dicken, P. 1986 *Global shift*. Paul Chapman, London.

Dixon, C., Drakakis-Smith, D. (eds) 1993 *Economic and social development in Pacific Asia*. Routledge, London.

Havinden, M., Meredith, D. 1993 *Colonialism and development*. Routledge, London.

Knox, P., Agnew, J. 1989 *The geography of the world economy*. Edward Arnold, London.

Sachs, G. (ed.) 1992 *The development dictionary*. Zed Books, London.

World Bank 1993 *The East Asian miracle*. OUP, Oxford.

World Bank 1994 *Structural adjustment programmes in Africa*. Harper Row, New York.

CHAPTER 12

TRADE AND DEVELOPING COUNTRIES

Robert N. Gwynne

Any discussion of trade in developing countries must be linked to the wider debate concerning the role of trade in development. Drakakis-Smith (see Chapter 11) has noted that, historically, involvement in trade has not always benefited poorer countries. However, the increasing integration of the world economy during the second half of the twentieth century has made the promotion of export trade an economic strategy that has become increasingly necessary for the governments of developing countries to follow. Indeed, the principle that developing countries should promote trade in order to facilitate economic growth has become widely accepted during the 1980s and 1990s, particularly since the 'conversion' of the centrally planned economies of eastern Europe and the former Soviet Union to the importance of markets in allocating resources and of trade in constituting the engine of growth. However, just as this principle is becoming more widely accepted, the practical difficulties of achieving economic growth through trade seem to be increasing, particularly for the world's poorer countries.

For some of the world's poorest countries in sub-Saharan Africa, it has been foreign aid and not trade that has been the most important external factor in their economies. Furthermore, growth in trade for these very poor countries can often create a strongly dualistic economy. A dichotomy can develop (as in Sierra Leone) between a small export enclave based on mineral exploitation and an impoverished agricultural sector in which the great majority of the population survives. Growth in the export sector holds few benefits for the great mass of the population, who are more dependent on foreign aid than on trade.

However, dependence on foreign aid, whilst providing a strategy for survival, does not provide the basis for achieving economic growth, a necessity for all poor countries. Standards of living in developing countries cannot be improved unless increases are achieved in economic production. Increases in production should be primarily geared to national demand, particularly in the agricultural sector, but increased export of production should also be encouraged in those sectors in which countries have a comparative advantage in world trade. Increasing exports are vital for poor developing countries as such an increase gives them greater flexibility to import both essential goods (such as food) and investment goods (machinery, technology). A sustained growth in exports normally brings a sustained growth in production for developing countries.

Nevertheless, most developing countries are faced with the option of concentrating on the export of primary commodities, whether agricultural or mineral (or a combination of both). This chapter will first concentrate on some of the difficulties involved in developing agricultural exports in an increasingly competitive world economy. It is often presumed that countries rich in mineral and energy resources should have a relatively straightforward path of development. However, by exploring the resource curse thesis, (Auty, 1994), the following section demonstrates that this is rarely the case.

In concentrating on agricultural or mineral exports, national governments are attempting to exploit their comparative advantage in factors of production and resource ownership in international trade. National governments can also promote early stages of manufacturing based on principles of comparative advantage through emphasizing labour-intensive industrialization (with such sectors as textiles, footwear and clothing prominent). However, for developing countries to achieve sustained growth in industrialization, it would appear that the process of manufacturing must not only be export-oriented but also closely involve government in creating new advantages for manufacturing firms. It is argued that the concept of governments creating competitive advantages for manufacturing firms (and particularly national firms) lies at the heart of the success of the east Asian model of development and this is examined in the second half of the chapter.

DEVELOPING COUNTRIES AND THE WORLD ECONOMY

It is first necessary to make some meaningful links between the term 'developing countries' and the world economy. In this chapter, 'developing countries' refers to the countries of what has been and is still called the 'Third World'; thus, the countries of the former Soviet Union and eastern Europe are excluded despite the fact that the World Bank classifies these latter countries as 'developing'. However, such a definition involves about 90 countries in three continents or five World Bank regions – sub-Saharan Africa, East Asia and Pacific, South Asia, Middle East and North Africa, Latin America and Caribbean (World Bank, 1994a); 75 per cent of the world's population lives in these countries.

These countries present vast differences in terms of society, culture, religion and economy. In terms of general economic criteria, there are huge differences in per capita income, geographical size of country, population totals and resources. Physical resources are distributed in a most haphazard fashion over the surface of developing countries. Some countries have huge populations and limited mineral resources (such as Bangladesh) whereas others have small populations and a rich array of resources (such as Venezuela).

When poor developing countries start to promote export trade, they normally have to specialize in primary products and raw materials. It should be remembered, for example, that in the early phase of Japan's promotion of export trade in the late nineteenth century (before manufacturing became important), over 50 per cent of exports were raw materials, including foodstuffs (Lehmann, 1982). However, at this early stage of trading growth, the geographical distribution of mineral and energy resources significantly affects the options available for countries. In rather stark terms, those countries with limited mineral and energy resources have to specialize in agricultural exports. Meanwhile, those countries fortunate to enjoy 'the gifts of nature' have the potential to develop mineral/energy exports as well as those from agriculture.

With such great variety in the economies of developing countries, it is worthwhile to attempt a classification of developing countries. Given that there are over 90 developing countries, classification becomes a useful contextual tool even if only a limited number of variables can be inserted in the classification. Table 12.1 provides a classification that owes much to Auty (1990). Three of his variables (income, size of country, and the relationship between population and resources) have been maintained without change. However, the fourth variable (export option) introduces the all-important trading strategy into the debate. Specialization in agriculture is the export option for a very large number of developing countries, although the promotion of manufacturing exports can constitute a subsequent phase of trade growth. Mineral- and oil-exporting countries are seen to have surprisingly restricted export options, a theme that will be returned to later in the chapter. Indeed, the trade dynamics behind this country classification will be discussed throughout this chapter.

The Third World still relies on primary products for over 70 per cent of its export earnings (Todaro, 1994). However, in the latter half of the twentieth century, the expansion of most primary-product exports (excluding oil) has been less than that of total world trade. Moreover, the developing country share of these exports has been falling (Teitel, 1989). Furthermore, throughout the twentieth century prices for primary products have fluctuated greatly and in general have been declining in real terms. Real prices for agricultural and mineral products declined from 1950 until 1986 within a pattern of considerable cyclical fluctuations. Since 1986, real prices have crept up in some primary products.

FOOD AND NON-FOOD AGRICULTURALS

The agricultural sector constitutes the key economic sector for the poorer developing countries. First of all, the population economically active in agriculture in developing countries is still very high. According to 1993 FAO data, about 60 per cent of the total economically active population in all developing countries is involved in agriculture (see Table 12.2) – about 1039 million people. South and east Asia account for 823 million but the highest percentage of the economically active in agriculture (71.2 per cent) is found in sub-Saharan Africa; Latin America and the Caribbean, in contrast, have only 26.3 per cent.

Table 12.1 A resource-based classification of developing countries

Type	Income[a]	Size[b]	Population/resources	Export option	Examples
Large low-income Asian	Low	Large	Overpopulated	Agriculture, manufacturing	India, China, Pakistan
Small low-income sub-Saharan African	Low	Small	Underpopulated	Agriculture	Ghana, Kenya, Malawi
Small middle-income	Middle	Small	Underpopulated	Agriculture	Guatemala, Costa Rica, Uruguay
Latin American	Middle	Small	Underpopulated	Agriculture	Malaysia, Thailand
Small middle-income south-east Asian	Varied	Small	Overpopulated	Limited agriculture	Mauritius, Haiti, El Salvador, Cuba
Small overpopulated microstates	Varied	Varied	Varied	Minerals[c]	Zaire, Suriname, Chile, Bolivia
Mineral economies	Varied	Varied	Varied	Oil	Saudi Arabia
Oil economies	Middle	Large	Underpopulated	Agriculture, manufacturing	Brazil, Mexico (Argentina)
Newly industrializing Latin American countries	Middle/high	Varied	Overpopulated	Manufacturing	Taiwan, South Korea, Singapore
Newly industrializing Asian countries					

[a]Middle-income is defined as more than $500 per capita GDP in 1987.
[b]Large countries have more than 30 million people, more than $30 billion GDP, and areas in excess of 800000 km^2.
[c]Unless 'Dutch disease' avoided.

Table 12.2   Population economically active in agriculture in developing countries

	Population economically active in agriculture (millions)	Per cent of total population economically active
Sub-Saharan Africa	140	71.2
South Asia	274	64.7
East Asia	549	63.3
Near East/North Africa	35	37.2
Latin America/Caribbean	41	26.3
All developing countries	1039	59.8

Source: FAO (1993), *Agriculture: Towards 2010.*

Boosting agricultural exports should therefore affect large numbers of people. However, the price behaviour of agricultural exports in the latter half of the twentieth century has not assisted developing countries, with both a real decline in prices and major cyclical fluctuations recorded. By far the worst price performance since the Second World War corresponds to non-food agricultural commodities. The 1979/80 price for this group of commodities was nearly one third of the 1951 price in real terms, and the 1986 price was nearly half of the 1979/80 price. The concrete reality of such a decline can be seen in the behaviour of the sisal price from 1950 to 1987 (see Figure 12.1).

Sisal is a plant of the agave family renowned for its fibrous qualities. It constituted the main raw material source for low-cost twine until synthetic substitutes began to compete successfully with it in the latter half of the twentieth century. Between 1951 and 1987, there was a 75 per cent real reduction in its price (see Figure 12.1). Such huge reductions in the real price of sisal (along with numerous endogenous problems) caused sisal production in Tanzania to drop from 230000 tons a year in the mid-1960s to 30000 tons by 1990 and contribute to that country's large trade deficit of the 1980s.

Food prices have not demonstrated such major decline but they have been highly fluctuating since the mid-1950s. From 1977 to 1986, the real price of food commodities nearly halved in value. Because food and non-food agriculturals make up almost 40 per cent of developing country exports and constitute the main source of foreign exchange earnings for the great majority of Third World countries, it is necessary to examine the factors affecting the international demand for agricultural exports.

On the demand side there appear to be at least five factors working against the rapid expansion of agricultural exports from developing to developed countries, which constitute the main markets. First, population growth in most developed countries is now very small and hence market growth is limited. Market growth can, however, come from diversification of products and of markets: the Central American broccoli producer carving out markets in Europe and Japan as well as the United States (Barham *et al.*, 1992); production of okra

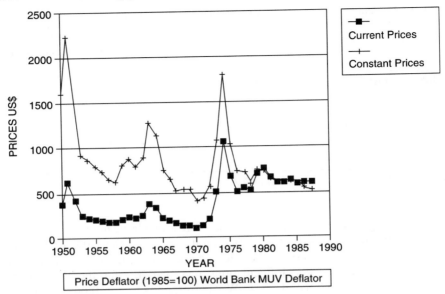

Figure 12.1   World sisal prices (c.i.f. London), 1950–90 (US$ per ton) (from *FAO Commodity Review and Outlook*)

or ladyfingers in Kenya for European markets; table grape producers in Chile carving out northern hemisphere markets between November and April (Gwynne, 1994).

Second, the per capita income elasticities of demand for agricultural products are relatively low compared with those for fuels and manufactures. As incomes rise, consumers spend a smaller proportion on food. There are some differences here between agricultural products; high-income consumers do demand more of some food products, such as fruit, than others, such as sugar and butter. However, overall, this means that only a high rate of per capita income growth in the developed countries can lead to even modest increases in agricultural exports from developing countries.

A third factor relates to the argument that the price elasticity of demand for most agricultural commodities is relatively low. Again there are differences between agricultural products. Price elasticities for speciality fruits and vegetables are much higher than for basic food staples (wheat, sugar) and beverages (tea, coffee). This meant that during the decline in food prices of the 1980s and early 1990s, demand for most basic products did not increase – causing a decline in total revenue for exporting nations. Developing countries have been relatively powerless to alter this tendency for primary-product prices to decline relative to other traded goods. In the case of coffee, an international commodity agreement was established in order to set overall output levels, to stabilize world prices, and to assign quota shares to various producing nations. However, the International Coffee Agreement was, in reality, ignored by producers (most countries did not keep to prearranged quotas) and such agreements did not even materialize for most other agricultural commodities.

The prices for non-food agriculturals have declined even more than those for food since the Second World War. A fourth factor has been at work here – the development of synthetic substitutes. Synthetic substitutes for cotton, rubber, sisal, jute, hide and skins operate to reduce commodity prices and act as a direct source of competition in world markets. In the latter half of the twentieth century, the synthetic share of world market export earnings has steadily risen over time while the share of natural products has fallen.

A fifth factor concerns the growth of agricultural protection in the developed countries through tariffs, quotas and non-tariff barriers such as sanitary laws regulating food imports. The agricultural policies of industrial countries have been particularly disruptive for agricultural exports from developing countries. Domestic price support programmes in industrial countries have caused large surpluses of production – most notably from the Common Agricultural Policy of the European Community. In order to 'solve' the short-term problem of large surpluses, the governments of developed countries have frequently sold surpluses at a fraction of their domestic prices on world markets. As a result, a huge anomaly has emerged, particularly in terms of the principles of inter-national trade theory. Most of the world's food exports are now grown in industrial countries, where the costs of food production are high, and consumed in developing countries, where the costs are lower. Between the early 1960s and the mid-1980s, the industrial countries' share of world food exports increased from 46 to 63 per cent, whilst the share of the developing countries fell from 45 to 34 per cent (World Bank, 1986).

During the 1990s, international agreements (such as the 'Blair House Accord' between the United States and the European Community and the completion of GATT's Uruguay Round) are likely to reduce agricultural protection in developed countries. The European Community launched a comprehensive reform of its Common Agricultural Policy in 1992, with an extensive shift from price support to direct income support policies as the mainstay of the reforms (FAO, 1993). This should gradually reduce the large agricultural surpluses of the European Union that enter world trade; hence, the distortions of world trade in agriculture should diminish.

There are numerous factors working against the rapid expansion of agricul-tural exports from the supply side. The most important are the structural rigidities and environmental problems of rural production systems in developing countries – limited resources, traditional rural institutions and economic structures, adverse systems of land tenure, vulnerable climatic conditions and poor soils. However, in countries as diverse as South Korea, Chile and China, pragmatic policies based on agrarian reform and market orientation have transformed the agricultural sector, particularly in terms of land productivity (Hodder, 1992). Chile, for example, has been transformed from a net importer of food in the early 1970s to a country with an agricultural trading surplus of over $US1 billion by the early 1990s (Gwynne, 1994).

The world economy in general and the developed countries in particular provide difficult and highly competitive markets for the farmers and agricultural exporters of developing countries. The 1990s should witness a relaxation of the extreme agricultural protectionism that has characterized most developed countries during the latter half of the twentieth century. However, the problems of limited demand growth in those markets, particularly for basic food products, make it essential for the agricultural exports of developing countries to be highly diversified; the reliance on one or two basic agricultural sectors for export is no longer a tenable option. The highly diversified nature of Chilean agricultural exports provides an example. In 1993, when agricultural exports were over $US1 billion, there were 20 food categories with over US$5 million in exports – mainly fruits (grapes, apples, pears, plums, kiwi, nectarines, peaches, raspberries, cherries) but also vegetables (beans, maize, onions, garlic, asparagus), avocados, seeds, walnuts, wool, oregano and rose hips (Banco Central de Chile, 1994).

The agricultural exporters of the Third World can be divided into three groups given the nature of their products in terms of supply and demand in world trade:

1. Countries exporting tropical products, such as coffee, tea, cocoa and bananas. There is normally no competition from producers in advanced economies (the notable exception is sugar) but world demand is normally lower than supply, and hence prices are kept down. There are some possibilities for diversification into tropical fruits (mango), vegetables (okra) and nuts.
2. Countries exporting staple temperate products in which there is substantial competition from producers in advanced economies. Products include wheat, rice, corn and sugar. World oversupply of these products and trade distortions provoked by protectionist policies in advanced economies signify very low prices and few opportunities for export growth.
3. Southern hemisphere countries exporting temperate products with a marked seasonality and limited storage capacity, such as table grapes, plums, cherries, peaches and nectarines. For these products, there has been a substantial increase in demand from advanced economies in the northern hemisphere. Good prices and high volume growth have frequently occurred; exceptions include trade in kiwi fruit and apples.

Overall, the strategy of promoting diversified agricultural exports provides the basis for gradual rather than fast growth in trade due to the constraints of poor world prices and slow growth in world demand. Compared with these limitations of agricultural trade, boosting export trade in minerals and energy resources has often seemed to be a much more attractive basis for achieving sustained economic growth in developing countries. This was seen as particularly apt in the 1970s and early 1980s as the spot market price for oil increased nearly 20 times and the price of some minerals remained relatively buoyant.

MINERAL ECONOMIES

Mineral economies can be defined as those developing countries that generate at least 40% of their exports and 10% of their gross domestic product from minerals (Auty, 1991). They comprise about one quarter of all developing countries and possess theoretical advantages for development that agricultural exporters lack. Their mineral exports have the potential to provide a large source of foreign exchange and government revenues. Mineral processing or resource-based industrialization offers an alternative strategy to import substitution and competitive exports. However, despite these potential advantages, the mineral economies have seldom outperformed other groups of developing countries (Auty, 1991).

During the 1950s, 1960s and early 1970s, prices for metals and minerals were relatively buoyant (*cf.* Figure 12.1). There were major fluctuations with real price increases in the mid-1950s, mid-1960s and mid-1970s. However, between 1974 and 1986, prices more than halved in value. Why have mineral prices declined in such an exaggerated fashion since the mid-1970s? Since the mid-1970s, the demand for minerals and metals in the industrialized countries has been weak. There has been a change in the ratio between consumption of metals and gross domestic product (GDP) in the OECD countries; between the mid-1970s and late-1980s, there was a 30 per cent fall in nickel used per unit of GDP, a 20 per cent fall in copper and a 40 per cent fall in tin.

However, whilst international demand for metals and minerals was weak, production (and supply) tended to increase. This was partly because the high prices of the mid-1970s led to overexpansion of supply in metals and minerals in the 1980s due to the lag effect of investments generated by the 1973–74 commodity price boom. Many mineral resource projects operate on a time horizon of five to ten years between initial decision making and full-scale production of the mine – particularly for mines in developing countries. In addition, the high prices of the 1970s encouraged greater use of recycled scrap metals and the development of synthetic alternatives, such as fibre optics (competing with copper wire). Thus, according to Manners (1986), the pattern of the 1980s could be described as balancing global supply and demand along lines of price and quality within a framework of world overproduction. However, the consequent low metal prices and concomitant lack of investment in new mines led to supply shortages in the late 1980s and the cyclical upturn in prices in the early 1990s.

This introduces the important issue of price stability in international metal markets. For mineral economies, it could be argued that modest but steady international prices for minerals should be welcomed. However, the harsh reality is that prices fluctuate strongly and that the real price of minerals declines alongside this cyclical pattern. The evidence of this for one commodity can be seen in Table 12.3, where the behaviour of the real copper price can be seen since 1966. In the 20 years from the 1966 cyclical high of the copper price to the 1986 cyclical low, the real price of copper declined by 71 per cent. Since 1986, there

Table 12.3   Average annual real price of copper, 1966–1993 (1987 dollars)

	$US per lb
1966	2.16
1969	1.94
1973/74	1.84
1986	0.63
1987	0.81
1988	1.11
1989	1.18
1990	1.03
1991	0.88
1992	0.83
1993	0.68

Source: El Mercurio 7/1/88; author's database.

has been a further cyclical rise and fall of the price. However, as Table 12.3 shows and using constant 1987 dollars, the cycle took the price of copper to only $US1.18 per lb in the peak year of 1989 (in real terms, 45.4 and 35.9 per cent less than the price peaks of 1966 and 1973–4 respectively). When the next cyclical low arrived in 1993, however, the real copper price nearly reached the very low levels of 1986.

In this respect, the international structure and vertical integration of mining industries are crucial factors to be taken into account. Manners (1986) argues that copper experiences significant price fluctuations because of a lack of vertical integration in the industry. Much of the copper production directed towards international trade is in the hands of state resource corporations of developing countries (such as CODELCO of Chile) and relatively small amounts are in the hands of multinational resource corporations (such as Phelps Dodge and Broken Hill). As a result, the majority of internationally traded copper is transacted between producers, consumers and intermediaries on the world metal exchanges (most notably London and New York). The operations of these world metal markets tend to accentuate the cyclical fluctuations of supply and demand; the influence of speculators tends to further reduce prices in times of oversupply although often further increasing them when global demand outstretches that of supply.

Copper multinationals have attempted to boost vertical integration (O hUallachain and Matthews, 1994) but their overall impact on the global stage is much less than that of their equivalents in the aluminium sector (Manners, 1986). In this vertically integrated industry, six aluminium multinationals dominate production, trade and consumption – Alcan, Alcoa, Reynolds, Kaiser, Alusuisse and Pechiney. Trade is organized through long-term contracts between the subsidiaries of the multinationals. Prices are therefore much more stable although the developing countries themselves do not necessarily benefit. First, raw material (bauxite) and intermediate product (alumina) prices are kept at low levels by the multinationals. Second, in order to maintain firm control over the industry and prevent nationalization by the governments of developing countries, the aluminium multinationals locate the three stages of aluminium production (bauxite into alumina; alumina into aluminium; aluminium into aluminium products) in different countries. Thus, bauxite producers in developing countries (such as Jamaica, Guyana and Guinea) have few processing facilities located near the mines (Auty, 1991) – unlike the copper industry where state resource corporations have invested in concentrate and smelting plants adjacent to mines (Gwynne, 1992).

The relationship between developing countries and mineral multinationals can often be fraught. If multinationals control production, trade and consumption in a global industry, raw material prices can be stable but are also relatively low, and few processing activities are located near to the mines. If multinationals do not control the global industry, trade is concentrated in world exchanges and prices can fluctuate widely. However, prices can sometimes be relatively high and the investment strategies of state resource corporations can create a substantial amount of refining and processing plants. In the 1970s, if the governments of developing countries had the opportunity, they tended to nationalize mining activities (Newfarmer, 1985).

The nationalization of mining activities has, in itself, not led to sustained economic growth in mineral or even oil economies. The fundamental problem concerns the existence of substantial rents (revenues in excess of production costs and a normal return on capital) being generated in mineral economies and their cyclical evolution; rents are substantial during periods of high world commodity prices but much more modest during the downswing in prices. When mining or oil sectors are controlled by foreign corporations, much of these rents flow overseas to boost the profitability of the mineral or oil multinationals. When these same sectors are controlled by national governments, rents do stay in the developing country but they are largely controlled by government. Furthermore, due to their cyclical pattern, the rise and fall of government rents create numerous problems for economic management in mineral and oil economies.

Gelb (1988) identified at least three critical problems in the management of oil economies, which Auty (1993) argued apply equally well to mineral economies. First, Gelb emphasized the insufficiency of savings during booms. The accumulation of savings during booms performs two important functions: it slows the rate of domestic windfall absorption through investment in overseas financial instruments and it provides a cushion to ease adjustment through any subsequent downswings. However, both consumption and investment tend to grow rapidly (sometimes uncontrollably) during booms. Gelb (1988) plotted the absorption of oil windfalls in six countries with large populations after the oil price rise of 1973–74 and showed that only the unexpected second oil shock of 1979–80 saved them from moving deeply into deficit. Some countries, most notably Venezuela, built up sizeable debts during the booms by using their oil reserves as collateral for foreign loans. Auty (1993, p. 21) saw the same pattern affecting mineral economies due to 'the persistent tendency towards overoptimism concerning future mineral prices', particularly during the 1979–81 mineral boom.

A second problem concerns the patterns of consumption and investment during the oil and mineral booms. Consumption tends to be boosted due to low personal taxation and price controls (particularly on food and energy) – as in the case of Venezuela, where the retail price of gasolene was lower than even the costs of production from the mid-1970s until the mid-1990s. Furthermore, import prices tend to decline due to the appreciation of the exchange rate, thereby increasing the capacity of the local population to consume imported goods – unless imports are prevented in order to protect domestic industry and agriculture. The quantity of investment does increase during boom periods but the quality is often questionable. Auty (1990) has been particularly critical of the large amounts invested in resource-based industrialization (RBI) and infra-structure. 'In the case of RBI ... cost overruns along with chronic overmanning ... turned the projects into resource sinks which lost money rather than generated new foreign exchange, taxes and capital.'

The third crucial problem concerned the neglect of what are called non-mining tradeable sectors – basically agriculture and manufacturing – during boom periods. The problem has become known as 'Dutch disease'. During oil and mineral booms, the exchange rate of the oil/mineral economy strengthens and appreciates. Exports become more expensive in international trade and imports much cheaper. 'Dutch disease' does not affect the mineral or oil sectors but it seriously affects the international competitiveness of agriculture and manufacturing industry. Due to an overvalued exchange rate, agricultural and manufacturing enterprises not only find it virtually impossible to compete internationally but also find it difficult to hold on to their home markets. Governments of mineral/oil economies frequently intervene to protect them from foreign competition but this reduces such enterprises to producing only for the restricted local market. Import-substituting industrial enterprises result which rely for their survival more on good political contacts with government than on developing competitive strategies for home and foreign markets. Furthermore, the competitive activity lost during exchange rate appreciation in the boom period is not easily restored during the exchange rate devaluations of the downswings.

Auty (1993, p. 1) suggests that a favourable natural resource endowment may be less beneficial to countries at low- and mid-income levels of development than the conventional wisdom might suppose. This is the basis of the resource curse thesis: that not only may resource-rich countries fail to benefit from a favourable endowment, they may actually perform worse than less well-endowed countries. Resource-rich developing countries are easily and adversely affected by 'Dutch disease' whereby all productive activities unrelated to the mineral export either decline or stagnate. The agricultural and manufacturing sectors suffer in particular; their export potential is severely curtailed by adverse exchange rates. Rentist economies emerge where economic rewards are given to those with the best political contacts rather than those with the most productive enterprises.

Good economic management can certainly alleviate the problems but few governments of resource-rich countries have ever managed it. Auty (1993) sees Chile as one of the countries characterized by 'best practice' economic management, particularly since the mid-1980s. Two policy developments stand out. First, the establishment of a Copper Stabilization Fund in 1987 meant that revenue from the high copper prices of the period 1987–92 was saved in order to supplement the fiscal budget for when copper prices fell (1993–94). Thus, Chile experienced a mineral boom and downswing between 1987 and 1994 but suffered no fiscal effects due to the early implementation of a mineral stabilization fund (Gwynne, 1994). Secondly, from the mid-1980s, a policy of competitive exchange rates promoted cheap exports and allowed for a substantial degree of diversification into resources other than that of copper. By 1993, copper accounted for only 35.5 per cent of total Chilean exports; in the mid-1970s, the figure had reached over 80 per cent.

Mineral economies can thus enjoy huge increases in revenue in a short space of time. However, there is a big problem of how to manage these booms. There tends to be an emphasis on consumption rather than production; production and productivity suffer particularly in agriculture and manufacturing. Investment may increase but it is often of poor quality. In poorly managed economies, the shift from boom to downswing normally brings economic crisis, with rapid reductions in production. Thus, it has been notoriously difficult for oil and mineral economies to achieve sustained economic growth.

Overall, then, countries specializing in the production and export of primary products have fared rather poorly in achieving sustained economic growth during the latter half of the twentieth century. One crucial question has concerned the role of manufacturing in the economic growth of developing countries. Throughout the latter half of the twentieth century, there have been some Third World governments that have promoted industrialization and others that have resisted it. It has always been difficult to generalize about the political context of industrialization. Kitching (1982) made an interesting distinction between those governments favouring modernization and seeking scale economies in economic planning (such as China) and those governments promoting small-scale and more decentralized modes of economic growth (Tanzania). The former category gave priority to industrialization whereas the latter did not. Industrialization has therefore been associated with governments that have been prepared to promote rapid economic change and face the institutional and social consequences.

THE CHALLENGE OF MANUFACTURING

The promotion of manufacturing by the governments of developing countries in the 1950s had much to do with their interpretation of the world economic system at that time (Storper and Walker, 1989). This was strongly influenced by the work of Prebisch (1950) and the United Nations Economic Commission for

Latin America (UNECLA) based in Santiago. Prebisch produced 'statistical evidence' to show that the terms of trade between primary products and manufactured goods had changed in favour of the latter during the twentieth century. The statistical work of Prebisch has since been criticized widely due partly to the inability to account adequately for quality improvements in the traded items; manufactured goods imported into developing countries have improved in quality much more during the twentieth century than that of the primary products exported from these countries.

However, despite these statistical flaws, Prebisch had some influence on the evolution of economic policy in developing countries due to his elaboration of what later became described as a core–periphery model. The core consisted of the manufacturing exporters of the developed world and the periphery of primary product exporters, and the trading relationship between them was not beneficial to the developing countries.

The argument was framed within the temporal context of economic cycles and can be summarized as follows. During the recessionary period of an economic cycle, the large-scale manufacturers in the developed countries reduced production rather than prices. In the prosperous period of the economic cycle, these manufacturers not only increased output but also raised wages under the bargaining pressures of well-organized labour unions; prices of manufactured products rose after being relatively static during the recessionary period. In contrast, neither producers nor workers in the primary-producing developing countries possessed the power to influence the world prices of their products. In direct response to world demand, the prices of their primary products fell in recessionary periods and rose again in the more prosperous phase of the economic cycle. The net long-term result of these trends, according to Prebisch, was to increase the prices of manufactured items relative to the prices of primary products through the economic cycle. The prices of manufactured imports into the developing countries increased relative to the prices of primary-product exports from those countries. This effectively meant that the developing countries were able to purchase fewer and fewer manufactured goods with a given quantity of primary-product exports.

Such a core–periphery model had a very obvious policy implication. The governments of developing countries should actively promote industrialization and shift their export profile from primary products to manufacturing. In order to do this, UNECLA implied that governments should withdraw somewhat from trading in the world economy in order to protect infant national industries, which would otherwise be unable to resist the competition from producers in developed countries.

This proved the origins of the policy of import substitution industrialization (ISI) that was popular throughout the developing world in the 1950s and early 1960s. The policy came to be formulated in terms of four stages (Gwynne, 1990). The first saw the production of basic non-durable consumer goods and the second of consumer durable products. The third stage had to promote 'intermediate' industries producing inputs for companies set up during the first and second stages – both strategic inputs (steel, chemicals) and the wide array of components required. The final stage of the process promoted the development of the capital goods industry which would manufacture machinery and plant installations. It was the task of government to plan and synchronize each stage in the process.

However, as ISI progressed through the 1950s and 1960s, it became evident that despite its theoretical attraction (one of the few policies that emerged from a core–periphery model of the world economy), high-cost industry normally resulted, particularly in the smaller countries where market size was limited (Gwynne, 1985, p. 25). One key structural problem was the lack of economies of scale that small markets permitted, particularly in the critical second and third stages of the import substitution process. ISI policies developed an inward-oriented pattern of industrial development, dominated by consumer goods production and lacking technological dynamism. Subsequent analysis (Schmitz, 1984) of the policy has identified at least seven major failings:

1. **Intrinsic problems of government interference**. Excessive administrative regulations gave rise to bureaucratization, corruption, uncertainty and delays. These discouraged both productive private investment and foreign trade initiatives.
2. **Bias against exports**. The existence of import restrictions led to a higher exchange rate than would have prevailed under a free trade regime, reducing the relative gains obtained from exporting.
3. **Bias against agriculture**. The protection of local industry raised the prices of manufactured goods relative to agricultural products in the home market and the overvalued exchange rate reduced the domestic currency receipts for agricultural exports.
4. **Underutilization of installed capacity**. Since import controls did not apply equally to capital goods and since credit for installing machinery was relatively cheap, factories were overequipped with imported machinery. At the same time, protection in domestic product markets made it possible to earn good profits even at low capacity utilization.
5. **Underutilization of labour**. Imported capital goods could be obtained relatively cheaply due to the combined effect of overvalued exchange rates, low import restrictions for such goods and subsidized financing conditions. ISI thus became characterized by the location of capital-intensive plant within countries whose labour markets had large numbers of underemployed and low-skilled workers.
6. **Import intensity of ISI**. Although consumer goods imports were reduced substantially under ISI, this was achieved at the expense of increased imports of equipment and materals, resulting in an even more rigid dependence on foreign supplies.
7. **The slowing down of ISI**. Although initially industry can grow fast under ISI, developing countries soon run out of import substitution possibilities. After that growth rates can be maintained only by a growth in domestic

demand or in exports. However, by then, the structure and inefficiency of industry stand in the way of conquering export markets.

Industrial strategies based on ISI are thus not appropriate for achieving sustained economic growth. Industrial growth is apparent in the early stages of ISI but slow growth and even stagnation rapidly ensues, particularly in small countries, where lack of economies of scale in industrial production can constitute a fundamental problem. These features of ISI caused some east Asian countries (most notably Taiwan and South Korea) to turn away from ISI policies in the 1960s. They began to promote exports (initially by a series of devaluations) and shifted their policies towards trade liberalization and closer integration with the world economy – what has become known as outward-oriented industrialization.

THE MOVE TO OUTWARD-ORIENTED INDUSTRIALIZATION

The process of outward-oriented industrialization that started in Taiwan and South Korea in the 1960s has now become the focus of study for numerous writers and development 'specialists'. This does not mean that there is any unanimity concerning the reasons behind the success of the process. However, the process has transformed both Taiwan and South Korea from impoverished developing countries to the rank of industrialized and developed countries. Furthermore, this has been achieved in a matter of 30–40 years, from the 1950s to the 1980s/1990s.

Taking the example of Taiwan (Wade, 1990), its per capita income in 1962 was still only $US170; as such it was classified as a poor developing country (85th world ranking between Zaire at 84th and Congo at 86th). By 1986, Taiwan's per capita income had risen to $US3580, making it into the higher ranks of the middle-income countries (38th world ranking between Greece at 37th and Malta at 39th). For end-1994, Taiwan's per capita income had soared to $US11 300, making it a high-income country according to the definitions of the World Bank (22nd world ranking between Israel and Ireland). Many of the institutional bases of Taiwan's rapid economic growth, such as agrarian and educational reform, were laid in the 1950s (Wade, 1990). But one of the key decisions taken by the Taiwanese government was to switch from policies of import substitution industrialization to export promotion in the late 1950s (Lin, 1989, p. 17). As Table 12.4 shows, it was a most opportune shift. Between 1952 and 1960, substantial economic reform allied to inward-oriented policies had permitted good rates of economic growth alongside very modest export growth. However, after the shift to outward orientation, export growth took off (increasing from an average of 4.3 per cent a year in the 1950s to 28.7 per cent a year in the 1960s) and became closely intertwined with a *sustained and high* rate of economic growth.

The cases of Taiwan and South Korea have provided the basis for euphoric

Table 12.4 Stages in the competitive development of east Asian industrialization

Stage	Source of competitive advantage	Relationships with global economy				Technology
		Trade exports	Imports	DFI/capital		
Labour-intensive (LI)	Low labour costs Low wages with high productivity	LI products	Resources	Limited unless exceptional circumstances (US aid)		Government stresses basic skills
Capital-intensive raw-material intensive (CIRMI)	Strong government involvement especially in investment Search for economies of scale	LI products Surplus CIRMI products	Resources, machinery	Strong reliance on government – direct or indirect		Imported CIRMI technology – ability to adapt imported technology
Capital-intensive machinery-intensive (CIMI)	Firm strategies and structural rivalry Skilled, cheap labour force	LI products CIMI products	Resources, machinery	Direct foreign investment important in joint ventures Domestic firm investment		Development of research institutes and research nodes in firms
Knowledge-intensive (KI)	Highly skilled labour force Firms creating new technologies	KI and CIMI products dominate	Resources dominate	Domestic capital plentiful		Some new technologies being created

analyses. Harris (1986) titled his book *The End of the Third World*, arguing that the cases of Taiwan and South Korea provided the way out of poverty for all Third World countries. However, the two cases have provided the grist for two very different interpretations of economic success. Writers such as Harris (1986), Jenkins (1991a) and Wade (1990) have stressed the role of government planning in both cases. Meanwhile, highly influential organizations such as the World Bank (through its 1987 report) and writers such as Krueger (1985), Balassa *et al.* (1982) and Harberger (1988) have emphasized the impact of trade liberalization and free market policies. The ideological underpinnings of the Taiwan and South Korean cases have thus been much argued about; the issue is the importance of unrestrained market economics versus the strategic role of government in economic management. In many ways, such ideological debate conceals the fact that both interpretations are indeed valid and not mutually exclusive.

In some ways, the recent work by Porter (1990) and his work on the competitive development of national economies broaches the gap. According to Porter (1990, p. 545), 'national economies exhibit a number of stages of competitive development reflecting the characteristic sources of advantage of a nation's firms in international competition and the nature and extent of internationally successful industries and clusters.' Porter stresses that it is not inevitable that nations pass through the stages. However, the first three stages that he elaborates are able to interpret some of the essential features of the industrialization of Taiwan and South Korea since the 1950s.

1. **Factor-driven stage**. In nations at this initial stage, virtually all internationally successful industries in the nation draw their advantage almost solely from basic factors of production, whether they are natural resources, favourable growing conditions for certain crops, or an abundant and inexpensive semi-skilled labour pool. A nation's indigenous firms in such an economy compete solely on the basis of price in industries that require either little product or process technology or technology that is inexpensive and widely available. In this stage, an economy is sensitive to world economic cycles and exchange rates, which drive demand and relative prices. It is also vulnerable to the loss of factor advantage to other nations and to rapidly shifting industry leadership. As a result, it could be argued that a factor-driven economy is one with a poor foundation for sustained productivity growth. However, Porter argues that few nations ever go beyond the factor-driven stage, due in particular to problems of capital and human resource development.

2. **Investment-driven stage**. In this stage, national competitive advantage is based on the willingness and ability of a nation and its firms to invest aggressively. Firms invest to construct modern, efficient, and often large-scale facilities equipped with the best technology available on global markets. They also invest to acquire more complex, foreign product and process technology through licences and joint ventures, which allows

competing in more sophisticated industries and industry segments. However, it is important that foreign technology and methods are not just applied but improved upon.

3. **Innovation-driven stage**. Firms not only appropriate and improve technology and methods from other nations but create them. A nation's indigenous firms push the state of the art in product and process technology, marketing, and other aspects of competing. Favourable demand conditions, a supplier base, specialized factors and the presence of related industries in the nation allow firms to innovate and to sustain innovation. The capacity to innovate opens up yet more new industries.

Ettlinger (1991, 1994) emphasizes the importance of using the concept of 'competitive advantage' in the study of production systems rather than 'comparative advantage', a concept rooted in neo-classical economics. Ettlinger argues that in world trade, local advantages are created and are not given. This is particularly the case at the national scale of analysis, due to the vital importance of national characteristics and government policy in institutional development. Table 12.4 attempts to generalize from the Taiwanese and South Korean case studies about the stages in the competitive development of east Asian industrialization. It envisages the following four stages in the evolution of east Asian industrialization.

1. **Labour-intensive (LI) stage**. This very much equates with the factor-driven stage of the Porter analysis. Both South Korea and Taiwan were characterized in the 1950s and 1960s by both scarce resources and low labour costs. Their only 'comparative advantage' thus lay in low labour costs. Labour was thus the factor that drove economic growth; the combination of low wages and high labour productivity was crucial. As both countries were resource-poor, resources provided the main imports. Capital for firms was limited, although the role of US aid in both countries was important. Government policy towards developing a national technological capability focused on basic skills.

2. **Capital-intensive raw-material intensive (CIRMI) stage**. Whereas the first stage of east Asian industrialization was factor-driven, the second stage was very much investment-driven *and* orchestrated by government. It is this stage that defeats the simple, factor-driven neo-classical interpretation of east Asian growth. Neo-classical trade theory states that countries with no resources do not have a comparative advantage in processing and refining those resources and therefore should import the refined products and not the resources. However, both South Korea and Taiwan in the late 1960s and early 1970s embarked on massive investment programmes in heavy industry – steel mills, chemical plants, petrochemicals, wood pulp, shipyards. Enos and Park (1988, pp. 48–50) record the worries of the South Korean government going into such a venture. They hired American consultants to help them but the American consultants were of neo-classical bent and

'concluded that the domestic market was far too small to support (petro-chemical) plants capable of producing at low unit costs, relative to plants abroad' (Enos and Park, 1988). However, despite these warnings, both the South Korean and Taiwanese governments pushed ahead with creating a wide range of intermediate industries that would be the feedstock for consumer-oriented manufacturing. The massive investment required was organized either directly (case of Taiwan) or indirectly (case of South Korea) through government, and the commitment of both governments to creating a heavy industrial base was not put off course by the oil and mineral price rises of 1973–74 and 1979–80. Sustained growth in factor-driven or labour-intensive exports (most notably textiles) was required in order to balance the substantial growth in resource, machinery and technology imports.

3. **Capital-intensive machinery-intensive (CIMI) stage**. This could also be seen to constitute part of Porter's investment-driven stage and very much overlaps with the CIRMI stage. However, unlike the CIRMI stage, investment comes largely from private corporations, with direct foreign investment (as in Taiwan) potentially important. Porter's competitive advantage is drawn from improving factor conditions as well as firm strategy, structure and rivalry. Firms invest continually to increase economies of scale, push down costs, improve product quality, introduce new models and modernize processes. Advantages in labour costs still occur, but competitive advantages widen to include low-cost university-trained engineers and research institutes. The development of research institutes (normally funded by government) is particularly important in order to enhance national technological capability. The export of CIMI products complements LI products but an outward-oriented strategy is now firmly in place due to the high level of resource and capital goods imports required by the industrialization process.

4. **Knowledge-intensive (KI) stage**. This very much corresponds to the innovation-driven stage of Porter (1990). In this stage, firms not only appropriate and improve technology and methods from other nations but also create them. Favourable demand conditions, a supplier base, specialized factors, and the presence of related industries in the nation allow firms to innovate and to sustain innovation. These become the main sources of competitive advantage. Although writing in the late 1980s, Porter (1990, p. 556) did not regard either Taiwan or South Korea as having attained this stage. However, during the 1990s, it could be argued that both countries have an economy increasingly driven by innovation due to the substantial amount of investment made in technology and technological research (and orchestrated through government) during the 1980s. Competitive advantage at the global level has thus been attained by investment in human resources. It is the highly skilled labour force, effectively organized, that has become the key to economic success. KI and CIMI products dominate exports, whilst resources now dominate imports. Domestic capital is now plentiful to finance innovation-driven developments.

Thus, it could be argued that the explanation for the success of east Asian industrialization lies both in the application of outward-oriented and market-economy policies and in the strong role of government in directing and managing the process. Wade (1990, pp. 155–157) refers to the process as 'governing the market' and identifies three characteristics in the exercise of leadership by governments in east Asia:

1. Interventions were aimed at promoting competitive production; 'the Korean definition of competitiveness emphasized export success to an unusual degree. The Taiwan government . . . relied more on the threat of allowing in imports if the prices of domestic substitutes moved much above inter-national prices.'
2. Interventions have been selective; the axis of discrimination has been between well-established and infant industries – the former face a neutral policy regime, the latter enjoy positive industry bias (as with heavy industry in the 1970s).
3. Interventions have a high degree of coherence and are cumulative in impact; firms that receive help through trade controls are also assisted through preferential investment finance and fiscal incentives.

One crucial question concerning the east Asian model of industrialization and rapid economic growth is whether this model can be applied to developing countries in other regions of the world. One problem is that the 'marketing' of the east Asian model by the World Bank and its large number of attached 'consultants' and 'advisers' has become intimately linked with trade reform (Rodrik, 1992) and deregulation, particularly in terms of the Latin American conception of the model. In terms of the previous analysis, trade reform and deregulation can very much assist with a rapid and substantial factor-driven stage of development, as has been fully demonstrated by the case of Chile from 1984 to 1994 (Gwynne, 1994). However, as Dornbusch (1992) observes, 'deregulation and trade reform can shake an economy out of a slow-growth trap, toward an acceleration of growth which then develops its own dynamics and financing. Of course, there is no basis here for a *sustained* increase in growth.'

The emphasis on trade reform and deregulation in recent policy shifts in Latin America has been linked to what Dornbusch (1992) calls the intellectual swing to anti-statism in the 1980s. The problem with this swing is that state involvement in economic issues has become characterized as counterproductive. However, the east Asian model (as we have described it) relies on the strong intervention of government in the investment-driven phase of industrialization. In Latin America, this phase now has to occur within the context of firms producing and competing in a highly competitive global economy, with minimal assistance from government. This is tending to reduce the potential for firms to invest in and increase their technological and organizational capability. In Chile, the lack of government involvement has led to Chilean firms preferring 'soft option' strategies, heavily based on the exploitation of the given factor endowment (low wages, significant natural resources). Messner (1993, p. 126) argues that this tendency will prolong the 'factor-driven' phase and slow the 'investment-driven sequence' in which it is essential to both optimize existing competitive advantages *and create new ones.*

CONCLUSIONS

In the increasingly competitive world economy, developing countries face great obstacles to achieve sustained economic growth. Rapid and sustained economic growth in developing countries since the Second World War has been intimately linked to export growth in manufactures, as the Taiwanese example demonstrates. However, the exports of most developing countries are still dominated by primary commodities, whether agricultural or mineral/energy resources. Increasing agricultural exports provides a relatively easy option for developing countries, but low world prices and slow growth in global demand mean that relying on this option produces, at best, sustained but slow growth. Specializing in the export of mineral and energy resources can provide rapid economic growth in the short term, particularly if world commodity prices are enjoying one of their periodic booms. However, for rapid export growth in minerals and energy to be transferred into sustained economic growth requires efficient and careful economic management, which very few developing countries have managed to achieve. Hence the idea of the resource curse thesis – that the ownership of substantial natural resources can be counterproductive in achieving sustained economic growth.

The model of east Asian industrialization shows that it is the development of human rather than natural resources within the context of outward-oriented industrialization which lies at the heart of sustained economic growth in developing countries in the latter half of the twentieth century. However, it must be emphasized that achieving such sustained growth is difficult and ideological approaches have little value in the explanation. Using Messner's (1993) determinants of international competitiveness (see Figure 12.2), it reflects success at four different levels of analysis: the meta level (essentially reflecting the cultural values of society and the basic patterns of political organization); the macro level, which focuses in particular on macroeconomic policy organized at the national level; the meso level, of vital importance in terms of human resource development (social, education and technology policy); and the strategies of large and small firms at the micro level. Close examination of the Taiwanese example (as provided by Wade) demonstrates that the east Asian model managed to advance competitiveness coherently and cumulatively at all four levels of analysis. However, it must be emphasized that it will be very difficult for this to be achieved in other developing countries. However, it conveys the extent of change that is required for sustained economic growth to be achieved in the developing countries of the world.

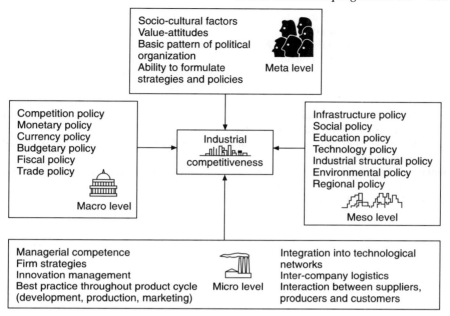

Figure 12.2   Determinants of international competitiveness (from Messner, 1993)

FURTHER READING

For the constraints and opportunities facing developing countries that wish to promote agricultural exports, a number of Latin American case studies are critically examined in:

Barham, B., Clark, M., Katz, E., Schurman, R. 1992 Nontraditional agricultural exports in Latin America. *Latin American Research Review* **27**(2): 43–82.

For the problems that constrain the successful management of mineral economies, including rentist economies and Dutch disease, the best analysis by an economic geographer is:

Auty, R.M. 1993 *Sustaining development in mineral economies: the resource curse thesis.* Routledge, London.

The development of manufacturing strategies with inward-oriented regimes (import substitution industrialization) and the spatial consequences of these is critically examined in:

Gwynne, R.N. 1985 *Industrialisation and urbanisation in Latin America.* Routledge and Johns Hopkins University Press, Baltimore, MD.
Schmitz, H. 1994 Industrialization strategies in less developed countries; some lessons of historical experience. *Journal of Development Studies* **21**: 1–21.

The successful process of manufacturing growth in east Asia and the various explanations for it can be referred to in:

Harris, N. 1986 *The end of the Third World: newly industrialising countries and the decline of an ideology*. Penguin.

Wade, R. 1992 *Governing the market: economic theory and the role of government in East Asian industrialisation*. Princeton University Press.

For comparisons of economic development and industrialization between east Asia and Latin America, the following are useful:

Gwynne, R.N. 1990 *New horizons; Third World industrialisation in an international framework*. Longman.

Jenkins, R.O. 1991 Learning from the Gang: are there lessons for Latin America from East Asia? *Bulletin of Latin American Research* **10**(1): 37–54.

Lin, C. 1989 *Latin America versus East Asia*. M.E. Sharpe, New York.

CHAPTER 13

THE PROSPECTS FOR THE POST-SOCIALIST ECONOMIES

Michael J. Bradshaw

INTRODUCTION

Mikhail Gorbachev's appointment as General Secretary of the Soviet Union in March 1985 marked the beginning of a period of political and economic transformation that will not be completed until well into the next century. The reforms introduced by Gorbachev, and the subsequent East–West rapprochement, brought the end of the Cold War and created a more liberal environment within the 'Soviet bloc'. The countries of eastern Europe seized upon this opportunity and the revolutions of 1989 saw the widespread rejection of Soviet state socialism as a model for political and economic development. Instead, the countries of east/central Europe (this term is used to define the countries of central Europe and the former Soviet Union) are now striving to establish democratic political institutions and market-type economic systems.

The revolutions of 1989 did not mark the end of political upheaval. In October 1990 East Germany was unified with West Germany. With this act the länder of the former East Germany joined the European Community. Events in central Europe (this term describes post-1989 eastern Europe) served as a catalyst for the republics of the Soviet Union; the Baltic republics sought to leave the Union, while the other republics demanded much greater control over their economic development. As Mikhail Gorbachev struggled to renegotiate the federal structure of the Union, conservative forces plotted to overthrow him and reinstate strong central authority. Instead, the failed coup of August 1991 caused the collapse of the Soviet Union and the emergence of 15 newly independent states. The three Baltic republics – Estonia, Latvia and Lithuania – rejected efforts to establish a post-Soviet economic union. However, the majority of the remaining republics became members of the Commonwealth of Independent States (CIS). By late 1993 all the post-Soviet republics, except the Baltic states, had joined the CIS. Unresolvable differences between the Czech and Slovak peoples resulted in the division of Czechoslovakia, on 1 January 1993, into two new states: the Czech and Slovak Republics. Thus, the seven states of the pre-1989 Soviet Union and eastern Europe (Figure 13.1) have become 21 post-socialist states (Figure 13.2).

263

Figure 13.1   European national boundaries, *c.* 1985

Clearly it is impossible to describe in any detail all the changes that have taken place in these states over the past five years (see Jefferies, 1993). Equally, given the individuality of each country, it is not possible to use a case study approach. Instead, this chapter examines the common legacies and challenges that face the post-socialist states of the former 'Soviet bloc'. The chapter is divided into two major sections. The first section examines their common heritage, the Soviet economic development strategy. The second section considers the challenge now facing the post-socialist states and identifies the key dimensions of economic transition. The second section ends by reviewing the current economic performance of the post-socialist states. The chapter concludes by evaluating the future prospects for the post-socialist economies and potential role of the 'transition' economies in the global economic system.

Figure 13.2 European national boundaries, 1995

LEGACIES OF THE SOVIET MODEL

The states of east/central Europe share a common post-war experience. Their economic development was shaped by the Stalinist development strategy and guided by a central planning system. The Soviet model has its origins in the industrialization debate that took place in the Soviet Union during the 1920s (see Nove, 1992, pp. 115–132; Gregory and Stuart, 1994, pp. 75–94). The Stalinist system that emerged dates back to 1928 when the First Five-Year Plan marked the onset of the industrialization drive and the collectivization of agriculture. In the Soviet Union, despite various attempts at reform, the Stalinist system remained essentially unchallenged until the late 1980s and the introduction of *perestroika*. *Perestroika* represented the last attempt to reform, rather than replace, the Soviet model. Following the failure of *perestroika*, the post-Soviet states (excluding the Baltic republics) have inherited an economic structure that is the product of nearly 60 years of Soviet central planning. By comparison, the states of central Europe and the Baltic are relative newcomers to the Soviet experience, 1948 marking the imposition of the Stalinist development strategy upon eastern Europe. This is an important distinction between central Europe and the CIS. Most of the states of central Europe have a recent memory of an independent political existence and an experience of market economic relations. This is also true of the Baltic states and may explain the relative ease with which they have left the former Soviet Union. This is not the case for the remaining twelve post-Soviet states, which must struggle with the dual challenges of state formation and economic transition (the same is also true for the Czech and Slovak Republics). Thus, while the emphasis of this chapter is upon common legacies and challenges, it recognizes that each of the post-Socialist states confronts a unique set of circumstances. This is a crucial factor shaping the reform strategies pursued by the individual states. The relationship between the general processes of economic transition and place-specific responses and outcomes is beyond the scope of this chapter. However, this issue is the fundamental challenge to economic geographers seeking to evaluate the prospects for individual post-socialist states (see Bradshaw, 1996).

The planned economy

To appreciate the scale of the change now taking place in the post-socialist states, it is necessary to understand the nature of the planned economy. Numerous terms have been used to describe the type of economic system that evolved in the Soviet Union: 'centrally planned economy', 'command economy' and 'administered economy', for example. Equally, many terms exist to describe its political system: 'totalitarian', 'state-socialist' and 'state-capitalist' are but a few. In reality, given the guiding role of the Communist Party and state ownership of the means of production, the Soviet system is best seen as a political–economic system. It was the political ideology of Marxism–Leninism that shaped the economic development of the Soviet Union and eastern Europe.

In combining the political and economic dimensions of the Soviet system, Gregory and Stuart (1992, p. 29) use the term 'planned socialism' to describe a system that is characterized by: 'public ownership of the factors of production. Decision-making is centralised and is co-ordinated by a central plan, which offers binding directives to the system's participants.' Campbell (1991, p. 9) maintains that the best way to understand the classical Soviet-type centrally planned economy is as an 'administered economy'. Such an economy is one in which 'the basic mechanism for making decisions about resource allocation is administration instead of the institutions of the market and price signalling.' Clearly, the centrally planned economy (hereafter CPE) was a very complex system, one very different from the market economies of the West (for further reading see Ericson, 1991; Grossman, 1963; Nove, 1987). In a CPE the state owned and controlled the vast majority of economic activity. This control even extended to a state monopoly over foreign trade. It was the state that determined the direction and strategy of economic development. Enterprises and their managers and workers were rewarded for achieving the goals set by the political leadership. The state bureaucracy was responsible for plan formation and implementation. In the Soviet Union the State Planning Committee, Gosplan, was responsible for the creation of the economic plans that guided development (see Pallot and Shaw, 1981). The responsibility for implementing these plans rested, primarily, with the industrial ministries which controlled the key sectors of the economy. Not all sectors of the economy were controlled by this central planning system and there were areas of the economy where market-type relations existed; however, the most important sectors were administered from Moscow.

Within this system, enterprises responded to production plans handed down from the industrial ministry to which they were subordinate. Clearly, it was in the enterprise's interest to obtain a plan target that was achievable. On the other hand, the central planners were well aware of this and set ever-increasing plan targets. This system of double-bluff was know as 'taut planning'. It placed the enterprise under continual pressure to meet its plan targets. In such an environment, when obtaining inputs, security of supply was often more important than cost of supply. This resulted in enterprises maintaining large stockpiles and developing their own service workshops to ensure uninterrupted production. Of course, in the contemporary world of just-in-time production and subcontracting, such practices are seen to be very costly. But, in a Soviet-type CPE, prices and profit were secondary to plan fulfilment. Prices were set centrally, and were often controlled for political and administrative purposes. The combination of centralized control and non-economic success indicators meant that price was no measure of value nor profits of success. The top-down decision-making structure and the pressures of taut planning meant that enterprises were unable to change their production profile or production techniques, since such changes, even though they may have increased productivity, would have endangered plan fulfilment. Thus the very nature of the system hindered innovation and technological change. That much of the capital stock of the post-socialist states is now obsolete is a direct result of a system that made no allowance for renewal. The in-built inability of the system to renovate and rejuvenate itself was eventually to prove its downfall.

The CPE was designed to meet the needs of the Soviet leadership in the 1930s. Hence, the emphasis was upon rapid mass-mobilization of resources to develop a heavy industrial base: energy, iron and steel and machine-building. At enormous human cost, the Soviet Union achieved rapid industrialization. The CPE subsequently proved itself adequate to the needs of heavy industry and the military–industrial complex. The economic policies that guided Soviet economic performance can be described as an 'extensive development strategy'. This Stalinist growth strategy achieved high rates of growth of output by maintaining high rates of growth of inputs. The nature of the system rewarded ever-increasing inputs regardless of cost and efficiency. In the post-war period, as the cost of inputs (capital and labour) started to increase, economic growth started to falter (Khanin, 1992). As the costs of sustaining extensive economic growth increased the Soviet economic system found itself introducing reforms to promote a more intensive development strategy (Aganbegyan, 1988), a development strategy that could sustain output by producing more output per unit of input (a change forced upon Western economies by the resource crisis of the 1970s). By the late 1960s the Soviet leadership was well aware of the need to intensify its economic development strategy. Brezhnev's 'Scientific–Technical Revolution' and later Gorbachev's 'Perestroika' were both campaigns aimed at improving the efficiency of the Soviet economy. The 1970s can be seen as an opportunity missed. Instead of facing up to the structural problems facing the Soviet economy, the Soviet leadership used windfall profits from energy exports to compensate for the shortcomings of the domestic economy. In the end, the very nature of the system made partial reform impossible (Ericson, 1991). The only means of ensuring long-term economic prosperity was to change the nature of the economic system itself; by the late 1980s talk was no longer of reforming the CPE, but of the introduction of a market-type economy. However, the state-socialist political system was untenable without the support of the political economy. Thus, economic failure sowed the seeds for the political revolution that was the prerequisite for the abandonment of the 'Soviet model' and the introduction of reforms to create a market-based economic system.

The structural consequences of extensive development

> ... there is the legacy of over 60 years where building physical capital and institutions has been largely an arbitrary, wilful political act, independent of economic consideration. The result is a capital stock that is massively obsolete, abuse and destruction of the resource base, and an environmental poisoning unmatched in history.

> Ericson (1991) p. 23

The Soviet development strategy has had a profound impact upon the economies of east/central Europe; this is most evident in the former Soviet Union, where the Stalinist system shaped the construction of a massive industrial base that supported a military superpower. In eastern Europe the Soviet model was imposed upon an already established economic fabric. Here the Soviet strategy served to exaggerate the development of heavy industry, at the expense of a more balanced economic structure (see Winiecki and Winiecki, 1992). Table 13.1 provides a general statistical survey of the socio-economic development of eastern Europe in 1988. From this table, two things are clear: first, the Soviet Union overshadowed its European satellites in all aspects of economic activity; and second, there was considerable variation in the levels of industrialization and urbanization across the states of eastern Europe: East Germany and Czechoslovakia appeared to be the most developed, followed by Poland and Hungary, with Romania and Bulgaria the least developed. Closer examination of the structure of industrial employment, Table 13.2, reveals a specialization upon the heavy industrial sectors of industry: energy, metallurgy, engineering and chemicals. The level of concentration in these sectors was greatest in the Soviet Union,

Table 13.1 Basic socio-economic indicators for the Soviet Union and eastern Europe, 1988

Indicator	Bulgaria	CSSR	DDR	Hungary	Poland	Romania	USSR
Area in 1000 km^2	110.9	127.9	108.3	93.0	312.7	237.5	22402
Population in 1000s	8986	15625	16675	10589	37775	23112	286700
Urban population (%)	67.0	75.6	76.8	59.4	61.2	54.3[a]	65.9
Population per km^2	81.0	122.2	154.0	113.9	120.8	97.3	12.8
Natural increase per 1000 population	1.1	2.4	0.1	−1.5	5.7	4.9[a]	8.7
NMP average annual change (%), 1981–88[b]	3.9	2.0	4.1	1.5	0.9	4.7	3.0
Contribution to NMP (%):							
Industry	59.5	60.6	67.3	50.1	49.1	62.1[a]	42.7
Agriculture and forestry	13.1	7.1	10.2	13.8	13.9	18.3[a]	22.8
Share of CMEA NMP	2.8	4.4	6.8	2.1	6.9	6.8	70.2
Share of employment (%):							
Industry	38.0	37.4	37.4	30.1	28.6	37.1[c]	39.0
Agriculture and forestry	19.3	11.8	10.8	20.5	28.5	28.9[c]	19.0

[a]Data are for 1987.
[b]Net Material Production at constant prices.
[c]Data are for 1985.

Source: Vienna Institute for Comparative Economic Studies (1990), pp. 42–43, 61–66.

Table 13.2 Employment by branches of industry, 1988 (per cent of total, annual average)

	Energy	Metallurgy	Engineering	Chemicals	Textiles	Food	Other
Bulgaria	2.4	2.7	17.6	7.0	8.4	12.1	49.8
CSSR	2.3	5.8	39.2	5.7	7.1	7.2	32.7
DDR	7.1	4.3	29.9	10.3	6.7	8.5	33.5
Hungary	3.0	5.6	32.7	7.8	6.8	14.4	29.7
Poland	2.9	3.6	32.5	6.7	8.0	10.0	36.3
Romania[a]	1.5	4.1	36.7	7.1	11.5	6.2	32.9
USSR	7.0	5.7	43.3	5.2	12.9	8.0	17.9

[a]Data are for 1985.

Source: Vienna Institute for Comparative Economic Studies (1990), pp. 93–97.

where they accounted for 74.1 per cent of industrial employment. These figures are unlikely to have accounted for the military–industrial complex, which serves to amplify the dominance of the engineering sector. This concentration upon the heavy industrial sector, at the expense of light manufacturing and the service sectors, resulted in high levels of energy consumption and led to widespread environmental degradation (Stewart, 1992).

The imposition of the Soviet model forced the resource-poor economies of eastern Europe to develop energy- and resource-intensive industrial structures. Regional variations in the levels of industrialization attest to the fact that some governments resisted the Soviet development strategy. The Soviet Union served as the provider of cheap, and seemingly inexhaustible, energy and raw materials. Thus the extensive development strategy aided Moscow's geopolitical goals by making the states of eastern Europe economically dependent upon the Soviet Union. In 1987 only Poland was close to energy self-reliance, meeting 97 per cent of its need; by comparison Bulgaria could meet only 29 per cent of its energy needs, Hungary 56 per cent and Czechoslovakia 68 per cent. Because the Soviet Union supplied energy and raw materials at well below world prices, there was little incentive to be energy efficient. Consequently, by international standards the states of eastern Europe have high levels of energy consumption. Table 13.3 provides recent data on the relationship between energy consumption and gross domestic product (GDP). These data reflect the impact of recent industrial decline upon energy consumption; in fact in 1987 the levels of consumption (in kg of oil equivalent) were considerably higher: Bulgaria 3833, Czechoslovakia 4908, Hungary 2888, Poland 3990, Romania 1958 and the Soviet Union 4990 (Vienna Institute, 1989, p. 397). The consequences of the extensive development strategy for the relationship between energy consumption and economic development are clearer when viewed in an international context. Figure 13.3 plots the relationship between Gross National Product (GNP) per capita and energy consumption per capita in 1992. The states of east/central Europe are compared with a sample of developed market economies, the world average, and the average for high- and middle-income countries, as defined by the World Bank. Although the majority of post-socialist states are defined as middle-income, their levels of GNP are for the most part lower than the average for the middle-income group, while their levels of energy consumption are much higher. That these economies have clearly been very poor at turning energy into economic growth is clear from the second column of Table 13.3, which shows the amount of GDP produced per unit of energy consumed. This is explained by their bias towards energy-intensive sectors of economic activity and the underpricing of energy resources. Another way of looking at it is that these economies were overindustrialized relative to their levels of economic development (Winiecki, 1994, p. 718). Thus, as the heavy industrial sectors experience decline and world prices force greater energy efficiency, one can expect the relationship between GNP and energy consumption in the post-socialist states to match international experience. This change in the relationship between energy and raw material consumption and economic growth will also bring with it

Table 13.3 Energy consumption in east/central Europe, 1992 (kg of oil equivalent)

Country	Per capita kg	$US GDP out per kg
Bulgaria	2422	0.5
Czech Republic	3873	0.7
Slovak Republic	3202	0.6
Hungary	2392	1.4
Poland	2407	0.9
Romania	1958	0.5
Russian Federation	5665	0.5
Ukraine	3885	0.5
Belarus	4154	0.7
Comparisons:		
China	1447	0.8
Germany	4358	5.5
United Kingdom	3743	4.8
Japan	3586	8.2
United States	7662	3.0
World average	1447	0.8
High-income	5101	4.4
Middle-income	1812	1.4
Low-income	338	1.1

Source: World Bank (1994a), pp. 170–171.

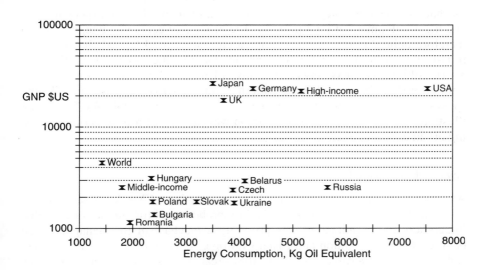

Figure 13.3 Relationship between GNP per capita and energy consumption per capita, 1992 (from World Bank, 1994a, pp. 162–163, 170–171)

improvements in environmental quality. Atmospheric emissions are already down right across east/central Europe. The polluting smokestack industries of the Soviet period are being closed down, in many instances never to be replaced. Thus, issues such as economic restructuring and regional development are high on the policy agendas of many governments in central Europe and the former Soviet Union. It is now clear to all that the Soviet model imposed a strategy of economic development that was neither economically nor ecologically sustainable. However, there is no easy path to a fully functioning market economy; the political, economic and social costs of transition are proving to be high. The costs of transition are being inflated by a relative lack of cooperation and coordination between the transition economies.

The CMEA and socialist integration

Eastern Europe's economic dependence upon the Soviet Union was institutionalized within the Council for Mutual Economic Assistance (often referred to as CMEA or COMECON). Established in January 1949, the CMEA was Stalin's response to the United States' Marshall Plan to reconstruct post-war Europe. During the Cold War the CMEA, together with the Warsaw Pact, became the key institutions defining the 'Soviet bloc' (see Archer, 1994, pp. 252–264). While western Europe pursued closer economic integration through organizations like the European Free Trade Area (EFTA) and the European Economic Community (EEC), Moscow used the CMEA to promote 'socialist integration' and the creation of an 'International Socialist Division of Labour'. Without a market mechanism, socialist integration was based on plan coordination, specialization and the development of joint projects. The process of economic integration was therefore quite different from that operating within the EEC. Michalak (1994, p. 114) uses the term 'radial' to describe the fact that the core of the CMEA was a series of bilateral links between the Soviet Union and the other member states. Smith (1994, p. 35) describes the pattern of intra-CMEA trade as being like the spokes of a wheel radiating from the Soviet Union at its hub. As Table 13.4 illustrates, in every case the Soviet Union was the east European partners' most important export market.

Soviet subsidy of the CMEA

Although various attempts were made to enhance intra-CMEA cooperation and specialization, most notably the 1971 Comprehensive Programme for Socialist Integration, the organization was primarily a mechanism for managing trade between the Soviet Union and eastern Europe. As none of the trading partners had access to convertible currencies, they created an accounting unit known as the 'transferable rouble' to facilitate trade. The commodity structure of intra-CMEA trade shows that the Soviet Union exported energy and raw materials to eastern Europe and, in return, received manufactured goods. During the 1970s, the CMEA price of Soviet energy was considerably below the world price, while

Table 13.4 Geographical distribution of the exports of the Soviet Union and eastern Europe, 1988 (per cent of total exports)

Origin	Destination			
	Eastern Europe	Soviet Union	Developed countries	Rest of the world
Bulgaria	18	61	7	14
Czechoslovakia	30	43	19	8
German Dem. Rep.	24	42	27	7
Hungary	17	28	43	12
Poland	16	24	47	13
Romania	21	31	33	15
CMEA-6	22	40	27	11
Soviet Union	49	—	25	26

Source: adapted from Lawniczak (1992).

the price paid by the Soviet Union for imported east European manufactures was much closer to world price. Therefore for much of the 1970s and early 1980s the Soviet Union subsidized its trade with eastern Europe. Marrese and Vanous (1983) have calculated that this subsidy reached a maximum of US$18 600 million in 1981. While the precise figures are open to debate, what is not is that intra-CMEA trade imposed a significant 'opportunity cost' upon the Soviet Union. The oil and gas exported by the Soviet Union were 'hard' commodities in the sense that they could have been exported to Western markets to earn convertible currencies. The same was not true of the bulk of the manufactured goods exported to the Soviet Union from eastern Europe. These products were of inferior quality and could not compete on Western markets. Scott (1992, p. 45) reports that only 10–15 per cent of the industrial production of eastern Europe found an outlet on Western markets. Given that eastern Europe's energy dependence upon the Soviet Union was the direct consequence of the imposition of the Stalinist development strategy, this subsidy can be seen as the economic cost of ideological compliance, which brought with it the strategic benefits of a cordon of buffer states across Europe. Thus, to assess the CMEA on solely economic grounds is to underestimate its non-economic role in Soviet strategy.

The CMEA trading system functioned while the Soviet Union was willing to pay the price of subsidizing energy exports and while eastern Europe was prepared to accept the economic dominance of the Soviet Union. As Hungary and Czechoslovakia discovered to their cost, attempts to follow a different path from Moscow were met with force. The imposition of Soviet control and the creation of the CMEA severed eastern Europe's trading links with western and southern Europe, replacing them with trade with the Soviet Union. As a result of a reluctance to embrace socialist integration, and because Soviet development strategy reduced the level of complementarity between the east European economies, the countries of eastern Europe did not conduct that much trade between themselves (see the first column of Table 13.4). During the late 1970s, because of need to earn convertible currency to finance imports of Western technology and to service mounting foreign debts, individual east European countries sought to expand their trade links with the West.

The collapse of the CMEA

Because the whole CMEA trading system was dependent upon the Soviet Union's willingness and ability to supply cheap energy, the collapse of the oil price during 1986 undermined the basis of the CMEA. In the late 1980s the Soviet Union faced two problems with respect to energy exports: first, the decline in energy prices meant that to maintain convertible currency earnings it would have to increase the volume of oil exported to Western markets; second, the decline in world price coincided with a crisis in the domestic oil industry, when production stagnated and subsequently went into rapid decline. By the late 1980s the only solution was a reduction in the volume of oil exports to eastern Europe. Faced with domestic economic crisis, the Soviet Union could no longer afford the CMEA. At the same time, the countries of eastern Europe were trying to expand their trade with the West. Thus, the CMEA was falling apart. Figure 13.4 charts the changing geography of Soviet and east European exports during the 1980s (the ECE East comprises the Soviet Union and the six European members of the CMEA, the ECE West comprises western Europe and Japan). From the trade data, clearly 1986 represents a turning point in East–West economic relations. Following the collapse in the oil price and the reduction of

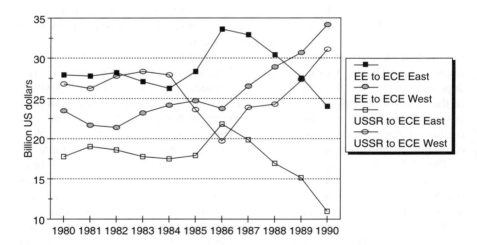

Figure 13.4   Value of Soviet and east European (EE) exports during the 1980s: ECE East comprises the USSR and the six European members of the CMEA; ECE West comprises western Europe and Japan (from UN ECE, 1993, p. 282

oil deliveries the value of intra-CMEA trade (east European trade with ECE East) started to decline, while east European exports to the ECE West started to increase rapidly. Meanwhile, Soviet exports to eastern Europe collapsed and trade with ECE West reversed a downward trend and started to increase. The oil shocks of the 1970s tied eastern Europe to the Soviet Union, the oil shock in the mid-1980s drove them apart.

By the late 1980s the Soviet leadership was making public its doubts about the future of the CMEA. Lawniczak (1992, p. 94) reports that at the 44th session of the Council of the CMEA the Soviet Prime Minister stated that: 'The model of the extensive division of labour among our countries which has developed historically has exhausted its potential.' Economic crisis in the Soviet Union, the political revolutions of 1989 and the subsequent reunification of Germany further undermined the future of socialist integration. In December 1989 the Soviet Prime Minister announced that as of January 1991 trade between the Soviet Union and eastern Europe would be conducted in convertible currency. The decision to trade in convertible currency simply compounded disintegrative tendencies that had been growing since the mid-1980s; thus it came as no surprise when the 46th session of the Council of the CMEA announced the formal dissolution of the CMEA in June 1991. For the second time in less than 50 years the states of eastern Europe and the Baltic states had to reorient themselves and establish a new set of trading relations. For the members of the CIS the challenge is to establish an independent identity in the world economy (Bradshaw, 1996). This (re)integration is a key dimension of economic transition.

THE CHALLENGES OF ECONOMIC TRANSITION

As Gregory and Stuart (1994, p. 306) note, 'transition implies the shift from one set of system arrangements to another (for example, the replacement of plan by market), while reform implies change in an existing system (for example, attempts to make the socialist system work better).' In such a context, *perestroika* represented a final attempt to reform the Soviet system (Aslund, 1991). Mikhail Gorbachev's initial intention was to restructure the Soviet system (*perestroika* literally means restructuring), not to replace it. We know that this attempt failed and it is now accepted that the only solution is to replace the entire system, hence the transition to the market.

Change in post-socialist states is often referred to as 'systemic transformation'. This term expresses the scale of the changes now underway. In the states of east/central Europe the entire political and economic system is being replaced. Economic transition is but a part, albeit a very important part, of this systemic transformation, which includes the transformation of the state and the development of a civil society. Economic transition is the focus of the following discussion, though it must be recognized that in the transition process politics and economics are inseparable.

The dimensions of economic transition

The dramatic changes taking place in the post-socialist states have spawned a large literature on 'transition economics'. There exists no blueprint for the transition from a planned to a market economy, thus for economists the process represents a unique opportunity to test their ideas. Many Western academic economists find themselves advising post-socialist states on their transition policies. Similarly, many home-grown economists now find themselves in positions of influence. Much of the writing published on transition economies is the work of international organizations, principally the World Bank (1992), the International Monetary Fund (see IMF *et al.*, 1991), the Organization for Economic Cooperation and Development (OECD, 1991) and the European Bank for Reconstruction and Development (EBRD, 1994). Unfortunately, due to the pace of change, many book-length studies are out of date before they are published. Therefore, the best places to find up-to-date analyses are the economic and area studies journals that deal with the post-socialist economies and the business media (see, for example, *Business Central Europe* and *Central European Economic Review*). A review of the literature in transition economics reveals a growing orthodoxy concerning the key dimensions of the transition process (Box 13.1 defines the key terms). Obviously, there are differences in terminology and this orthodoxy is not without its critiques; however, it is possible to identify four key processes: stabilization, liberalization, privatization and internationalization. The order in which these processes are dealt with below implies no ideal sequence of events; as we shall see, 'sequencing' has itself been the subject of debate.

BOX 13.1   Definitions

Macroeconomic stabilization means bringing severe repressed or open inflation and unsustainable deficits in the budget and/or in the balance of payments under control.

Structural–institutional economic reforms establish or strengthen market mechanisms and institutions, such as legal, accounting and tax systems, ownership, competition, financial institutions and instruments, and the like.

Economic liberalization is defined as moving towards a market-determined system of factor and product prices and opening up the economy by reducing barriers to international trade (**internationalization** is considered by some to be separate from **liberalization**) and factor movements. Introducing currency convertibility is a key element of domestic as well as foreign economic liberalization.

Enterprise restructuring refers to actions taken to bridge gaps between current performance and what is required to become internationally competitive.

Source: adapted from Marer (1991), p. 38.

Macroeconomic stabilization refers to the need to bring the economy into balance – balance in terms of the level of money incomes and the supply of goods, and in terms of the difference between government expenditures and revenues. During the late phase of the Soviet economic system a lack of consumer goods resulted in individuals amassing considerable personal savings. Table 13.5 provides a measure of the extent of this 'monetary overhang'. These savings represented 'repressed inflation' in that any improvement in the availability of goods would result in a sudden consumer expenditure boom that would fuel inflation. Thus, it was thought that measures such as wage controls should be introduced to dampen inflationary pressures. Following the initial increase in prices associated with liberalization, it is necessary to ensure a balance between money incomes and the supply of goods and services. If incomes race ahead of the supply of goods and services, the result is further inflation. Economists feared that the existence of a monetary overhang would be a major problem during transition. In the event, the scale of the inflationary shock caused by liberalization was sufficient to wipe out household savings. This loss of savings inflicted a high cost upon pensioners who lost their life's savings and now have no means of increasing their income beyond their state pensions. However, post-shock monetary stabilization has proved more elusive. Those

Table 13.5 The preconditions for transition in central Europe

Indicator	Hungary	Poland	Czechoslovakia	Bulgaria	Romania
Population (million, mid-1989)	10.6	37.9	15.6	9.0	23.2
GNP per capita (in 1989 $US)	2590	1790	3450	2320	2290
Administered prices (% of total)	15	100	100	100	100
State ownership (%)	90	70	100	100	100
Money[a] (M2)/GDP (1990)	0.4	0.9	0.7	1.3	0.6
External debt/GDP (1990, %)	65	80	19	50	3
External debt/service ratio	57	56	23	116	—
Exports to CMEA, 1990:					
% of total exports	43	41	60	69	—
% of GDP	16	14	25	34	—

[a]This measure, showing the relationship between the money supply and GDP, provides an indicator of the size of monetary overhang, money held by the population due to the shortage of consumer goods. A ratio of 0.4 would be normal, a value higher than that suggests an overhang.

Source: Bruno (1994), p. 23.

economies that have succeeded in controlling wage increases and the money supply have been able to get inflation under some degree of control.

The balance between state revenues and expenditure is the second component of stabilization. During transition the state, along with its traditional obligations, faces new and ever-increasing demands for expenditure. For example, there is a need to provide a social safety net. At the same time, the more 'privatized' the economy becomes the less successful the state is at capturing tax revenues. Add to this the cost of servicing pre-existing debts, the loss of tax revenue due to declining industrial production and the inability of the tax system to tax many of the new forms of economic activity, and it is easy to see why economic transition has resulted in increased state indebtedness. One solution is simply to print more money, but this only serves to fuel further inflation. A preferred solution is to seek outside help in the form of an IMF stabilization package. The intricacies of the various IMF stabilization policies are beyond the scope of this chapter; however, it is sufficient to note that external funding is necessary to support the state's transition policies. The policies recommended by the IMF include a reduction in state expenditure, to reduce indebtedness, and strict control over the money supply, to control inflation. In the short term, these policies result in a decline in living standards and an increase in unemployment. However, it is the view of the 'foreign advisers' that these short-term 'transition costs' are preferable to the long-term damage inflicted by a sustained period of hyperinflation. For the domestic politicians there is a clear desire to reduce the political and social costs of strict monetarist policies; thus, as in any market economy, there is a constant struggle between what is economically desirable and what is politically survivable. This conflict remains at the centre of the contemporary political arena in Moscow.

Economic liberalization refers, in general terms, to the removal of government restriction on economic activity. More specifically, it refers to the process of price formulation. As Table 13.5 shows, in most CPEs, including the Soviet Union, prices were controlled by the central authorities. Therefore, in the early stages of reform there is a need to free prices from state control and allow them to find their market level. Of course, this assumes the existence of market conditions. In many states the existence of monopoly producers has distorted the process of price liberalization. Because in most instances internal prices had been below world prices, liberalization resulted in an immediate and substantial price shock. However, as higher prices encouraged a better supply of goods, so behaviour of consumers changed. In the past consumers bought large quantities of goods whenever they became available, not knowing when they would become available again. Now, with goods in regular supply, they need only purchase goods when they are required. In theory, the same logic reduces the need for enterprises to carry large inventories. However, this all presupposes that inflation is under control. In a high-inflation environment there is a propensity to turn money into goods as soon as possible, or to avoid monetary transactions altogether and rely on barter. Thus, for money to retain its value and for the monetary economy to function, it is essential that price liberalization be supported by stabilization policies that can curb inflation. For the industrial economy this process of price liberalization produces a severe price shock. Suddenly the costs of inputs and services increase dramatically, and the natural response is to increase prices. Those producers that benefit from monopoly production can increase their prices beyond the 'market' price. Thus, initial liberalization sends further inflationary shock waves through the economy, dramatically changing the economy's cost surfaces. Rapid increases in transport costs mean that it is no longer profitable to produce certain products in the more peripheral locations. Thus, economic transition promotes spatial polarization and an increased level of spatial inequality between the core and the periphery.

In theory, a combination of price liberalization and macroeconomic stabilization should create conditions under which inefficient state-owned enterprises are no longer economically viable, a change from what Kornai (1980) called 'soft budget constraints' to 'hard budget constraints'. In reality, the insolvent state sector responds by making dramatic cutbacks in production and by demanding state subsidies and protection from import competition. While the state may feel that it has to respond to such political pressure, an alternative solution is to privatize the state sector, making the individual enterprises responsible for their own balance sheets.

Privatization is the third dimension of the transition process. In a CPE the state owns the vast majority of economic activity (see Table 13.5). Attempts to reform socialist economies often involved the creation of a limited 'private sector'. For example, in the Soviet Union during *perestroika* cooperatives were permitted as a form of private enterprise. Of course, private enterprise always existed in the socialist economy in the form of the black market or the second economy. Nonetheless, the creation of legal private independent economic actors is a key component of economic transition. One can identify two dimensions to the process of privatization: first, there is the privatization of previously state-owned enterprises; and second, and possibly of greater importance, there is the creation of new private economic activities. Given that many of the state-owned enterprises have little future, even when privatized, the growth of the private sector is essential to new job creation and the macroeconomic restructuring of the economy. The state has a key role to play in both dimensions of privatization. The state has been responsible for selling off state enterprises through various privatization schemes. This process of state privatization started with small- and medium-scale enterprises, initially in the retail and service sectors and later in manufacturing. The mechanics of the privatization process have differed from state to state, but almost everywhere it has been fraught with difficulty and progress has been slower than expected. In many states the largest state enterprises have yet to be privatized. Many of these huge organizations may have to stay in state ownership. For the second dimension of privatization, new enterprise creation, to be successful the state must create a stable economic and political and legal environment (see structural–institutional reform in Box 13.1). This has been a major problem in many of the post-socialist states. In some states the failure to introduce effective stabilization measures has resulted in high inflation, even hyperinflation, and a worthless domestic currency. In others, political instability, from separatism to civil war, has undermined normal economic life. In the majority of states the legal framework has constantly changed as legislation has been introduced on a trial-and-error basis with laws frequently revised and revoked, often for political purpose. Similarly, a lack of regulation has resulted in bad business practices and widespread corruption. All of these factors undermine the ability of individual entrepreneurs to prosper, and also deter potential foreign investors.

Internationalization is the fourth dimension of transition. Under the Soviet system the state exercised a monopoly over foreign economic relations. One the one hand, this state monopoly had the advantage of enabling foreign trade to be used to serve the needs of the political leadership. But, on the other hand, it had the major disadvantage of isolating domestic enterprises from the competitive pressures of the international economy. Furthermore, the confiscatory attitude of the state meant that few enterprises were interested in engaging in export activity. Consequently, the state-owned enterprises of the CPE are ill prepared for the opening up of their economies to import competition. In many states partial internationalization was an important component of their late-socialist reform programmes. *Perestroika*, for example, allowed the creation of joint ventures between Soviet enterprises and foreign companies (Geron, 1990). However, the domestic economy remained closed to import competition and the state still retained control over import and export activities. As the process of privatization gathers pace, the state is no longer an actor in foreign trade; instead its principal role is to regulate. Under the previous system the state often purchased goods and sold them on the domestic market at subsidized prices. Such import subsidies imposed considerable costs upon the state and the stabilization process has curtailed such practices. In the past the state obtained considerable revenue from its monopoly of foreign trade (the state purchased goods for export in depressed domestic prices and sold them at higher world prices), hence there remains a tendency to use regulation (duties, tariffs, etc.) as a means of revenue generation. At the same time, because of the uncompetitiveness of their domestic industries, most states wish to protect their economies from excessive import competition. In many countries industry is lobbying for protection against imports. Such protectionism, although criticized by Western governments, is understandable given the reluctance of Western economies to open their markets to exports from the post-socialist states (Gibb and Michalak 1993). In such a situation, the post-socialist states fear that foreign trade liberalization will result in an import boom that cannot be financed by exports. This would then create a balance of payments crisis. The foreign trade dimensions of economic transition remain the most uncertain. Data on foreign trade activity are unreliable, which makes effective policy formulation very difficult. In Russia, at present, no one has a clear idea of the real value of imports and exports and hence the balance of payments situation. One thing is clear: the processes of economic transition are changing the role played by the post-socialist states in the world economy. These emerging market economies represent new markets and investment opportunities and new sources of competition, thus economic transition in the post-socialist states is changing the economic conditions right across the globe.

Given the complexity of the transition process, it is not surprising that it has sparked controversy among economists. Two issues appear to have been the most contentious: the sequencing of the various dimensions of transition and the pace at which they are introduced. Fortunately, the pace of events has simply passed by the sequencing debate. The consensus seems to be that, because of the interrelated nature of the various dimensions of transition, as much as possible should be achieved at the same time. If nothing else, liberalization and stabilization should take place simultaneously. Where this has not been the case, as in Russia, inflation has remained a persistent problem. The debate over the pace of transition is usually described as a dichotomy between those advocating a 'big bang' or 'shock treatment' and those advocating a more gradual approach. There are examples of both: most central European states have opted for 'big bang', while Hungary opted for a more gradualist approach. This may be explained by the fact that Hungary had already introduced market-oriented reforms and thus did not need shock treatment. Again, this debate has been passed by events. The emerging pattern seems to be more of a compromise, an initial shock treatment related to price liberalization and some form of stabilization package, followed by a more gradualist approach towards privatization and internationalization. The key factor is that the initial shock treatment should render the reforms irreversible. Privatization then enhances the irreversibility of the reforms by removing the state from the everyday running of the economy. Obviously, it is too early to draw conclusions about the nature of the transition process. It is clear that while there are universal processes at work, there are unique preconditions and subsequent circumstances that shape the trajectories of individual states. They started from different starting points and therefore it is not surprising that they have had different rates of progress. Equally, it is unrealistic to assume that they will all seek the same solution or play a similar role in the global economy (Bradshaw and Lynn, 1994). So what is the economic situation in the post-socialist states in the mid-1990s?

The post-socialist economies in the 1990s

During 1990–92, the economies of Eastern Europe and Russia plunged into the second Great Depression of this century. In most countries, real per capita GDP plunged by 20–30% during this period, inflation surged to double- or even triple-digit levels, and unemployment rates surged from near zero to the mid-teen levels by end-1992.

PlanEcon (1994) p. 1

Unfortunately, the various dimensions of economic transition discussed above do not translate into a ready set of indicators to assess progress. Indicators such as inflation, unemployment and the size of the state deficit provide some idea of the progress of stabilization; but the scale of the structural changes underway defies simple quantification. Under the previous regimes, those studying the socialist economies faced the basic problem of a lack of information, and the fact that information was often distorted for political reasons. Now the situation is even more complex. Political liberalization and the involvement of international economic organizations have resulted in an expansion of the amount of information available. However, the reliability of this information is in serious doubt, not necessarily because it has been distorted for political gain, although it may have been, but because as the state has withdrawn from the economy its ability to monitor what is actually happening has diminished. The growing private sector is not adequately reported in official statistics. In fact the official statistics tend to concentrate on the decline of the state sector, rather than the growth of the private sector. As a consequence, official statistics actually exaggerate the scale of economic decline (for an alternative approach, see Dobozi and Pohl, 1995).

Accepting that one must treat the statistics with caution, how should one interpret them? It is dangerous to transfer Western market notions of economic progress to the transition economies. For example, is the decline of industrial production a bad thing? The evidence suggests that 'transformational recession' is inevitable. In other words, transition to the market must bring with it a substantial decline in economic activity (Winiecki, 1991). Therefore, is industrial decline a measure of the successful implementation of a transition programme? Unemployment poses a similar problem. If inefficient enterprises are to be forced out of business and if enterprise restructuring is taking place, then there must be a substantial amount of job loss. Again, an apparent problem, unemployment, is actually a measure of success. This discussion suggests that in the short term it may be a case of 'bad news is good news'. A key question is then: when should we expect signs of recovery from transformational recession?

In reviewing the economic performance of the states of east/central Europe we must remember that we are not comparing like with like. As Table 13.5 illustrated, these economies entered economic transition in different circumstances. For example, Hungary already had substantial experience of reform; Poland had created a sizeable private sector; Czechoslovakia and Romania had very little exposure to foreign debt; while Bulgaria had a large foreign debt and was particularly dependent upon intra-CMEA trade. All of these preconditions influence the progress of economic transition. A second factor is the amount of time that has elapsed since the initiation of the transition process. Poland was the first to go through 'shock therapy' in 1990. The other central European states started their transition programmes during 1991. The republics of the former Soviet Union did not embark upon the transition to the market until 1992. With these factors in mind, the following review divides the states of central Europe from those of the former Soviet Union. To provide a basis for comparison, Russia is considered in both analyses.

Following the introduction of radical economic programmes during 1990 and

1991, the economies of central Europe experienced a deep 'transformational recession'. Between 1989 and 1992 the cumulative contraction of the central European economies was about 30 per cent (UN ECE, 1993, p. 73). This recession turned out to be much deeper than expected. The UN ECE suggests three reasons for the depth of the recession: first, the distorted structure inherited from the past; second, the implementation of radical economic reforms; and third, the collapse of intra-CMEA trade in 1991. Of these factors, the implementation of economic reforms was the most significant. Within the region there are substantial variations in the depth of the recession. In Poland between 1989 and 1992 the cumulative fall in GDP was 18 per cent. In Hungary the equivalent decline was 19 per cent. By comparison, in Bulgaria and Romania the cumulative falls were 50 and 30 per cent. According to the UN ECE (1993, p. 75) these variations are the result of a combination of internal preconditions and external shocks. For example, Poland introduced reform in 1990, ahead of the collapse of the CMEA. In Czechoslovakia the deep industrial slump (16 per cent) in 1991 was due to a coincidence of the introduction of reform with the collapse of CMEA trade. If 1990–92 are the years of recession, then 1993 is the year that brought the first signs of recovery.

Economic indicators for 1993 and early 1994 show clear signs of recovery (Table 13.6). In some cases, principally Poland, there is economic growth; in others economic decline has slowed and there is hope that by the end of 1994 there will be growth. The economic performance of central Europe also shows increasing signs of divergence, the emergence of 'winners' and 'losers'. The fast-reforming economies are Poland, Hungary and the Czech and Slovak Republics, while the laggards are Romania (there is widespread disbelief of the official statistics) and Bulgaria. On 1 March 1993, Poland, Hungary and the Czech and Slovak Republics established the Central European Free Trade Area (CEFTA) (see Michalak, 1994). These countries, known as the 'Visegrad Four', hope to use this agreement to halt the collapse in intraregional trade. It is early days, but it is already clear that for most of the members CEFTA is only a stepping stone to full membership of the European Union. A lasting legacy of the CMEA is the fact that these countries do not conduct much trade among themselves. During 1993 intraregional trade within CEFTA was about $US7 billion, but 70 per cent of that was trade between the Czech and Slovak Republics. As we know, these countries have reoriented their trade away from the CIS and eastern Europe towards the Western developed market economies, principally western Europe. For example, in 1989 the developed market economies accounted for 37.6 per cent of Czechoslovakian exports; by 1992 their share had increased to 63.7 per cent. This leaves Romania and Bulgaria as the losers in relative isolation. However, when compared with Russia these economies are clearly on the road to renewal.

The level of foreign direct investment (FDI) offers a further indicator of relative economic performance. Overall, the level of FDI in the region has been disappointing (see Dunning, 1994). According to the UN ECE (1994), by the end of 1993 the cumulative value of FDI was $US11.5 billion. Alternative figures

Table 13.6 Economic situation in central Europe and Russia, 1993–94

Indicator	Bulgaria	Czech Republic	Hungary	Poland	Romania	Russia	Slovak Republic
Nominal GDP ($bn)[a]	11.9 (1993)	29.3 (1993)	35.2 (1993)	85.2 (1993)	24.6 (1993)	164.8 (1993)	11.0 (1993)
GDP (% real growth)[a]	-4.0 (1993)	-0.3 (1993)	-1.6 (1993)	3.9 (1993)	1.0 (1993)	-12.0 (1993)	-4.1 (1993)
Industrial output (%)[a]	-8.0 (1993)	3.0 (1993)	-0.9 (3-94)	-8.0 (3-94)	-1.0 (3-94)	-0.4 (4-94)	-12.4 (4-94)
Budget balance (% of GDP)[a]	-11.4 (1993)	0.4 (11-93)	-6.6 (1993)	-3.5 (1993)	-12.0 (1993)	-16.0 (1993)	-6.8 (1993)
Unemployment (%)[a]	16.5 (1-94)	3.1 (5-94)	11.4 (5-94)	15.7 (4-94)	11.3 (3-94)	1.6 (4-94)	14.2 (4-94)
Average monthly wage ($US)[a]	135.0 (9-93)	232.0 (4-94)	298.9 (3-94)	193.3 (4-94)	70.3 (3-94)	97.8 (4-94)	184.8 (4-94)
Monthly inflation (%)[a]	21.7 (4-94)	0.4 (4-94)	1.2 (4-94)	2.9 (4-94)	8.3 (3-94)	9.7 (4-94)	0.4 (4-94)
One-year inflation (%)[a]	75.0 (12-93)	9.1 (4-94)	17.6 (3-94)	32.3 (4-94)	261.2 (3-94)	574.0 (4-94)	13.7 (4-94)
Trade balance ($USm)[a]	-53.0 (1993)	57.0 (3-94)	-1112.0 (4-94)	-268.0 (3-94)	60.0 (3-94)	7800.0 (4-94)	-101 (4-94)
Gross debt ($USbn)[a]	13.0 (1993)	8.7 (1993)	26.1 (2-94)	47.1 (2-94)	3.3 (1993)	82.7 (1993)	3.1 (1993)
FIEs (number)[b]	2300 (1993)	5000 (1993)	21468 (1993)	2100 (1993)	29115 (1993)	7989 (1993)	4350 (1993)
FDI per capita ($)[b]	23.5 (1993)	199.3 (1993)	583.1 (1993)	54.7 (1993)	22.7 (1993)	21.2 (1993)	71.70 (1993)

Sources: [a]*Business Eastern Europe*, 1994, **2** (13): 73; [b]UN ECE (1994), pp. 12–13.

from the *Central European Economic Review* suggest a total of $US14.5 billion (Roth, 1994, p. 6). Accepting the UN ECE figures, when one adds investment in the CIS (a total of $US6.3 billion), the cumulative total of FDI in the post-socialist economies is $US17.79 billion. This figure is very modest when one considers that in 1993 total global investment flows amounted to $US200 billion and that $US26 billion went to China alone (*Business Central Europe*, April 1994, p. 35). Table 13.6 presents the regional distribution of foreign investment. Two types of information are included: the number of foreign investment enterprises (FIEs) and the per capita value of FDI. The number of FIEs is very misleading as the bulk of these enterprises are not actually operational. On the basis of per capita FDI, Hungary is the clear favourite (total FDI $US6 billion), followed by the Czech Republic (total FDI $US2 billion). The vast majority of foreign investment has come from the developed market economies, with western Europe accounting for 77 per cent of investment in Hungary, 72 per cent in Romania, 67 per cent in the Slovak Republic and 57 per cent in Poland. Data on the sectoral distribution of FDI are not particularly reliable; however, they suggest that over 50 per cent of investment is in manufacturing (for a general survey see Murphy (1992); for a sectoral case study see Sadler *et al.* (1993)). Given that such investment as there has been has taken place during a period of severe economic recession, there is every reason to hope that economic recovery in central Europe will encourage a more substantial flow of FDI. Because of the impoverished state of their domestic economies, external sources of capital are a crucial source of financing for economic restructuring.

While it would seem that the economies of central Europe are emerging from 'transformational recession', the same cannot be said of the states of the former Soviet Union. Table 13.6 places Russia in the context of the economies of central Europe. Table 13.7 presents the economic situation in the Baltic states and the CIS. The two sets of data are not directly comparable. Nevertheless, it is clear that while Russia is a distinct 'laggard' within the context of central Europe, it is leading the way among the CIS states. There are, of course, very good reasons why there has been less progress in the CIS. First, these states have only recently embarked upon economic transition. Second, their economies have felt the imprint of over 60 years of Soviet socialism and therefore have further to go. Third, besides the trade shock induced by the collapse of the CMEA, these states (and the Baltic states) have had to deal with the collapse of intra-republican trade and the rouble zone. The relative progress of the Baltic states can be ascribed to their relatively recent inclusion in the Soviet Union, the small size of their economies and their proximity to north-west Europe.

Clearly, there is insufficient space to engage in a thorough examination of all the CIS states. Nevertheless, it is possible to discern groups of states (see Schroeder, 1993, 1994; Reddaway *et al.*, 1993). At present, Russia and the Baltic states are leading the way; however, the success of Russia's reforms remains tempered by the problem of economic stabilization. The states of Ukraine, Belarus, and Moldova resisted shock treatment, but their more gradualist

Table 13.7   Economic situation in the Baltic states and the CIS, 1993

	Real GDP % growth[a]	Industrial production (%)[a]	Unemployment (%)[b]	Consumer price % (yearly)[a]	Trade balance ($m)[b]
CIS:					
Azerbaijan	−14.4	−6.8	0.72	981	115.6
Armenia	−28.0	−11.1	6.28	1823	−56.0
Belarus	−11.7	−10.9	1.39	1577	−32.9
Georgia	−30.0	−26.6	NA[c]	2000	NA
Kazakhstan	−12.9	−16.1	0.54	1516.1	912.3
Kyrgyzstan	−17.0	−24.2	0.16	2726	−5.4
Moldova	−15.0	4.2	0.69	1184	−17.8
Russia	−12.0	−16.2	1.16	940	13738.8
Tajikistan	−30.0	−19.5	1.15	1484	−107.4
Turkmenistan	−8.5	5.3	NA	3146	667.0
Uzbekistan	−10.0	4.1	0.16	550	−240.8
Ukraine	−17.0	−12.5	0.35	3309.7	820.0
Baltic states:					
Estonia	−2.3	NA	NA	90	−128[d]
Latvia	−10.0	NA	NA	110	81[d]
Lithuania	−9.4	NA	NA	410	32[d]

[c]NA = not available.
[d]Includes trade with CIS and Baltic states.
Sources: [a]Economic Intelligence Unit, 1994, *Country Reports, 2nd Quarter*; [b]PlanEcon (1994), Russian Economic Monitor, *PlanEcon Report*, 8–9.

approach seems to have failed. Belarus has sought a solution in economic union with Russia. In the Trans-Caucasus, Georgia has suffered from a civil war and Armenia and Azerbaijan have been embroiled in armed conflict and have, therefore, made limited economic progress. In central Asia, Kazakhstan and Kyrgyzstan have followed the path of Russia's reform; while Uzbekistan, Turkmenistan and Tajikistan have favoured state-managed gradualism and the creation of 'socially oriented market economies' (Schroeder, 1993, p. 9). From the information presented in Table 13.7, it is clear that all the CIS economies are still in a deep 'transformational recession', exhibiting continuing economic decline and persistently high inflation rates. At the same time, the unbelievably low levels of unemployment suggest continued state subsidies and a lack of enterprise restructuring. In Russia, successful privatization will bring an end to such subsidies and may herald an increase in unemployment. The economic performance of Russia is the key to economic recovery in the CIS. It remains to be seen if 1995 will mark the beginning of economic recovery in Russia; much depends upon the ability of the government to enforce its stabilization policies. The prospects for the rest of the CIS do not look so good. The 'transformational recession' may bottom out, but it is difficult to see sustained economic renewal without substantial outside support, from Russia and the international community.

CONCLUSIONS: THE POST-SOCIALIST STATES IN THE WORLD ECONOMY

It is already apparent that the 21 post-socialist states will occupy quite different roles in the global economy from the previous seven socialist states of the 'Soviet bloc'. In assessing their progress to date, it is clear that those that started first have come the furthest. There is already a clear distinction between the states of central Europe and those of the former Soviet Union. How much their relative success can be attributed to better preconditions, and how much is due to the formulation and implementation of transition programmes, it is difficult to say. It is also the case that most of the central European states do not face the problems of state formation and internal instability that confront the former Soviet republics.

Within central Europe a distinction can be made between the fast-reforming economies of the Visegrad four (with the Slovak Republic trailing the other three) and the relative laggards of Romania and Bulgaria. The Visegrad four clearly see their future tied to full membership of the European Union. For these countries it is no longer a matter of 'if', but 'when' they become members. Thus, CEFTA may have a very short existence. This will leave Romania and Bulgaria economically isolated. If peace were to come to the former Yugoslavia, it may be that some form of Balkan trade area would emerge.

The Baltic states have succeeded in removing themselves from 'post-Soviet economic space'. But their future role in Europe remains uncertain. A strategic location between north-west Europe and Russia may provide for an outwardly oriented development strategy. However, such a strategy is dependent upon continued access to Russia's market of 150 million people. Elsewhere, there are already signs of increasing 'differentiation' among the member states of the CIS. Russia and Kazakhstan are perceived as the most progressive economies. Both are backed by considerable mineral wealth. Belarus has sought economic union with Russia as a means of ensuring access to energy and raw materials and a stable currency. The status of Ukraine remains unclear. The new pro-Russian president may seek some form of economic union with Russia. Thus, there is a possibility of some form of Slavic economic union – comprised of Russia, Belarus and Ukraine – emerging in the near future. It is unclear how the other CIS states would respond to such a development. The Slavic states, perhaps together with Kazakhstan, might form the economic core of the CIS, surrounded by a less developed periphery comprised of Moldova, the Trans-Caucasus and central Asia.

At present, the post-socialist economies are still in the throes of economic transition. There are clear signs that the states of central Europe are on the road to recovery. It is to be hoped that they will soon be followed by the Baltic states and Russia. However, the emergence of new market economies is bringing increased polarization. This chapter has shown how transition is leading to increased disparities between the individual post-socialist states. At the same time, one can speculate that economic transition is also leading to polarization and increased spatial inequality within the individual states. This would be no surprise; if capitalism generates uneven development, then successful transition to the market brings with it increased inequality. If one combines the increased polarization associated with the emergence of a market economy with the economic hardships associated with the collapse of the Soviet system, it is likely that issues of spatial inequality will soon dominate the political agenda in many of the post-socialist states.

FURTHER READING

EBRD 1995 *The EBRD transition report*. EBRD, London.

Gregory, P.R., Stuart, R.C. 1994 *Soviet and post-Soviet economic structure and performance*. Harper Collins, New York.

Jefferies, I. 1993 *Socialist economies and transition to the market: a guide*. Routledge, London.

Shaw, D.J.B. 1995 *The post-Soviet republics: a systematic geography*. Longman, Harlow.

PART 4

GLOBALIZATION OF PRODUCTION SYSTEMS: SPACE

CHAPTER 14

MARKET ENLARGEMENT: THE SINGLE EUROPEAN MARKET

William Lever

INTRODUCTION

With the globalization of the world economy, it has been argued, nation-states and national governments have diminished in importance. In part this is because multinational enterprises have become much more powerful and able, both managerially and technically, to move large amounts of resources and invest-ment around the globe, thus undermining the concept of a national economy managed by a government capable of, for example, defending the exchange value of its currency or restricting outward investment. One solution to this weakening of national power has been for several governments to form a multinational bloc with common interests within the set of world trade flows. The creation of such blocs has several advantages. Firstly, the large markets which they provide offer scope for considerable economies of scale, especially where internal barriers to trade such as customs duties, differential levels and forms of taxation and differences in quality and environmental standards are abolished or harmonized. The creation of such blocs also offers the possibility of erecting tariff barriers around them to exclude foreign imported goods whilst securing an internal market of adequate size. Lastly, where such blocs permit, or encourage, the freer internal movement of capital or labour, greater efficiency is likely to result. These advantages all facilitate greater competition for such blocs within world trade and especially between the blocs themselves.

It is possible to identify three such blocs in the advanced market economies of the world: these are the European Union, which comprises the group of nations which signed the Treaty of Rome, plus the subsequent additions; the North American Free Trade Association comprising the United States, Canada and Mexico; and the bloc of south-east Asian countries comprising Japan and a number of the Newly Industrializing Countries. Three further blocs outside the advanced market economies can be identified. These are the member states within the Organization of Petroleum Exporting Countries (OPEC), the centrally planned economies which formerly comprised the members of COMECON, and the members of the Latin American Free Trade Association (LAFTA). The first three blocs, however, are the real powerhouses of world trade. By the late 1980s some 85 per cent of world trade involved these three blocs; 46 per cent of world trade flowed between the blocs and 39 per cent flowed between them and the rest of the world. Of this, 15 per cent is represented by flows between them and OPEC, 6 per cent is represented by flows to and from the centrally planned economies, and 18 per cent is represented by flows to and from the Third World. By contrast flows outside the three main advanced market economy blocs represent only 15 per cent of all world trade (Waugh, 1990, p. 478; Dicken, 1986; see also Chapter 10).

There is now concern that the crystallization and reinforcement of these three blocs will exacerbate the problem of 'fortress' economies in which internal flows are improved but higher barriers are erected against goods and services produced in other trade blocs. Such barriers may take the form of customs levies in an overt way, or more covertly may rely upon high product and environmental standards for imported goods, such as those imposed by Japan upon American and European-produced cars, upon sourcing conditions which enforce rules on the minimum share of components which a producer must purchase from within the bloc in which he is located, and upon the jealous guarding of trade names and trademarks such as French objections to the use of the term 'champagne' by American wine producers.

This chapter will focus on the effects of the creation and expansion of the European Union. The first section will trace the origins and progress of the Single European Market. The second section will look specifically at the impact of the recent additions to the economic community of both Scandinavian and Alpine countries and the prospective inclusion of some of the countries of east-central Europe. The third section will examine the role of the regions, both national and transnational, in the context of the diminishing power of the nation-states within the community. The fourth section will examine how cities are now competing and collaborating within the community. The final section will look at the spatial patterns of economic growth and decline within the community in order to examine whether, over time, areas become more or less alike within Europe and what economic mechanisms are involved.

THE DEVELOPMENT OF THE SINGLE EUROPEAN MARKET

The processes of integration within western Europe can be seen as having three elements. The first, naturally enough in the wake of the Second World War, was concerned with creating rules and institutions which would lessen the likelihood of European war at a time when Europe was divided between the democratic West and the communist East. The second was concerned with economic well-being and growth through the creation, eventually, of a fully integrated single economy. The third was concerned with social welfare through the standardization of welfare incomes, working conditions and overall quality of life (Wise and Gibb, 1993).

Immediately after the Second World War the economic and political problems were tackled by the creation of the Marshall Plan and the Organization for European Economic Cooperation (OEEC) to assist economic recovery and by the formation of the North Atlantic Treaty Organization (NATO) to provide American guarantees against the threat of Soviet attack. A key issue was the problem of the division of Germany and French concern that the German industrial base should not be used for military purposes. The International Ruhr Authority was set up in 1949 to manage the coal and steel complex transnationally. By 1950, at the prompting of the Director of the Marshall Fund, it was suggested that a similar arrangement might be extended to cover Lorraine, the Saar, Belgium and Luxembourg. Coal and steel thus presented an ideal sector for an experiment in European economic integration. The Schuman Plan thus led to the creation of the European Coal and Steel Community signed at the Treaty of Paris in April 1951 and ratified by the governments of France, West Germany, Italy, Belgium, the Netherlands and Luxembourg by June 1952 (Archer, 1994, p. 75). The British government felt itself unable to join an association based on Franco-German agreement (Vaughan, 1976). Alongside the economic and defence concerns there were proposals even as early as 1949 for an elective European parliament but a British counterproposal led to the creation of the Council of Europe with its Committee of Ministers, whose objectives are largely social and democratic (Archer, 1994, p. 59).

During the 1950s further steps towards European integration were taken. In 1952, the six members of the ECSC signed the European Defence Community treaty but it was not ratified by France and thus failed to come into effect. A proposal for a European Political Community was rejected by France in 1953 but the Beyen Report, which demonstrated the potential of a common market in western Europe, was favourably received by the foreign ministers of the ECSC group of countries. In 1954 the Western European Union was signed adding Italy and West Germany to the group of France and the Benelux countries, which had earlier signed the Brussels Treaty for neutral defence (Williams, 1991, p. 22). The next major step in economic union, however, was the 1955 Messina Conference, which prepared the way for the creation of two new institutions. Representatives of the six ECSC nations, under the Belgian foreign minister, Paul-Henri Spaak, determined to create a body to manage European atomic energy generation and more significantly to create, by stages, a 'European market' without customs duties or quantitative restrictions to trade (quotas) between member states. Consideration was given to other components of a treaty such as the harmonization of economic, financial and social policies. The Italians offered strong support for some form of regional policy and it was agreed that Britain should be invited to join the discussions. Britain, however, although now associated with the ECSC and with the Atomic Energy Commission, had a different view of western Europe's economic development, preferring a free trade agreement rather than a customs union, because of its links with the Commonwealth (Camps, 1964, p. 28).

The six members of the ECSC rapidly moved towards the signing of the Treaty of Rome, which was mainly concerned with the economic framework of integration, establishing a customs union, and common markets in labour and capital. There was also a commitment to develop common policies in agriculture and transport, and to create a European Investment Bank. The Treaty itself was quite general and unspecific but it did commit the six signatories to six objectives. There would be a customs union which would eliminate all tariff and other barriers to trade between the member states. There would be a common external tariff between the Six and all other external states generating beneficial trade diversion effects. There would be a free market in labour guaranteeing freedom of movement of workers and equality of treatment in terms of wages, conditions and entitlement to welfare benefits. There would be a free market in capital including the transnational sale of financial services. Common policies would be established including a Common Agricultural Policy (CAP), a Social Fund and a Common Transport Policy. Lastly, there would be a European Investment Bank financed by member states and empowered to provide loans for economic restructuring within the Community.

The customs union was established earlier than required by the Treaty of Rome. By July 1968 all customs duties between the Six were removed and the Common External Tariff was established. However, non-tariff barriers to trade such as customs formalities and differing rules on safety, packaging and contents often proved a severe impediment to the free movement of goods. The Commission sought to harmonize industrial standards (for example, in the electronics and automobile industries) and by 1983 national standards would be checked by the Community, although excessive uniformity was avoided. Since 1985 a more flexible system has been introduced to lessen the bureaucracy associated with creating new technical barriers to the movement of goods whilst promoting health, safety, welfare and environmental standards (Pelkmans, 1987). The European Community has also tried to limit state subsidies, tax breaks and other help which would unfairly advantage an industry in one member state at the expense of the others. Where there has been state intervention to help structural change, as for example in former shipbuilding or steel-producing areas, then the Community has sought to harmonize the rules governing this assistance. These policies against 'unfair competition' have as their intent the creation of a more perfect and hence more efficiently competitive economy within the Community. The Community has sought to develop an overall commercial policy to govern its trade dealings with other areas of the globe such as the remainder of western Europe, formerly comprising the members of the European Free Trade Area (EFTA), eastern Europe, and the Soviet Union.

The transition from a customs union to a common market involved a number of policies to cover additional areas, the most notable of which have been the Common Agricultural Policy and the Common Fisheries Policy (CFP). The CAP dominated the early years of the Community and still takes up about two-thirds of the Community's budget. The CAP, initiated in 1964, has two main aspects – price support and structural change policy. Price support takes the form of an intervention price which guarantees to the farmer a minimum price for basic foodstuffs. If market prices fall below that price the Community will buy in the excess quantity to sustain prices, hence descriptions of butter mountains and wine lakes. In order to prevent farmers capitalizing on this system by overproducing foodstuffs whose prices are guaranteed, quotas have been introduced for milk and meat products, for example, hence the policy of 'set aside' by which land is taken out of production (Lintner and Mazey, 1991, pp. 108–109). The CAP has undoubtedly stabilized food production but at the cost of higher prices and an enormous drain on the Community's budget. The Common Fisheries Policy has largely been concerned with the management of fish stocks off the Community's coasts, particularly by dealing with overfishing.

The free movement of labour was allowed by the EEC's treaty and workers should be able to move from one country to another. In practice there were bureaucratic difficulties concerning pensions, differing wage rates and welfare entitlements and, for most jobs, employment agencies limit their scope to single countries, not least because of linguistic differences. It should be noted that the largest numbers of workers migrating transnationally took place before free movement was introduced (Straubhaar, 1988, pp. 59–60). In fact the lifting of legal barriers to migration within the Community has not produced a significant rise in migratory flows (Molle and van Mourik, 1988). Free movement in the service industry and in the professions was low on the Community's list of priorities until the mid-1980s. Different professional qualifications, barriers to entry to the professions, and linguistic barriers made it difficult to achieve the free movement of labour in the white-collar sectors. The free movement of capital has also proved difficult within the Community. The existence of different fiscal and economic policies devised by the national governments restricted capital movements, and the absence of a single European currency inevitably raised difficulties of exchange rate calculation, even once the European 'snake', which theoretically constrained the relative movements of European currencies, was developed. The Treaty of Rome did foreshadow the progressive coordination of the exchange rate policies of member states, but severe disruption of the European monetary markets between 1967 and 1969 led to the formation of the Werner Committee to consider monetary unification. This led to the creation of the 'snake', which permitted a difference between the highest and lowest currency values of no more than 2.25 per cent. The economic problems of the 1970s made it difficult to sustain this narrow banding of currencies and by 1979 the European Community began to operate the European Monetary System (EMS) based on the relativities between the individual currencies and the European Currency Unit (ECU). The Exchange Rate Mechanism (ERM) was devised to engineer joint interventions to support currencies in danger of falling through their floor value, or to offload currencies in danger of bursting through their ceiling values. The concept of a single European currency has come to play an increasingly significant role in the development of the Single European Market.

How successful was the European Community in fostering and managing economic growth between 1960 and the late 1980s? Table 14.1 compares several indices of economic change for the EEC, the United States and Japan, the cores of the three major trade blocs. The period of rapid global economic growth to the early 1970s shows Europe enjoying a marginally higher rate of growth than the United States but a rate significantly below that of Japan. Capital formation shows a similar pattern but trade balances generally were poorer in Europe than in the United States. The slump of the world economies in the mid- and late 1970s, largely created by major energy price rises, created much more uniform growth rates between the three blocs in 1974–79 and sharp deteriorations in the balances of trade.

By the 1980s Europe's rate of growth of GDP had fallen behind that of the United States and was only a little more than half the rate of Japan's growth; investment, however, was still higher than that of the United States and the balance of payments was better. How much of the better performance of the west European economy over the United States' economy is due to the creation of the Common Market is debatable. Some, such as Matthews (1968), have argued that the 'long boom' in the European economy in the 1950s and 1960s was due more to the private sector's increase in investment and trade than to public sector intervention by agencies such as the Common Market. It can also be argued that the relative success of the European economy, up to 1973 at least, reflects the greater disturbance to the European economy by the Second World War compared with that experienced by the United States (the even better performance by Japan would also support this view) and thus represents a catching up from a lower base in the 1950s.

Table 14.1   Comparative European growth, investment and trade, 1960–88

	1960–67	1968–73	1974–79	1980–88	1960–88
Real GDP growth p.a.:					
European Community	4.7	4.9	2.6	2.2	3.5
United States	4.5	3.2	2.4	2.8	3.3
Japan	10.2	8.7	3.6	4.1	6.5
Gross capital formation (as % of GDP):					
European Community	22.9	23.5	22.4	20.3	22.1
United States	18.0	18.4	18.7	17.8	18.2
Japan	31.0	34.6	31.8	29.1	31.4
Trade balance (as % of GDP):					
European Community	–0.1	0.3	–0.5	0.4	0.0
United States	0.7	0.1	–0.4	–2.0	–0.5
Japan	0.2	1.5	0.4	2.0	1.1

Source: OECD Historical Statistics, 1960–88. 1990, OECD, Paris.

By the mid-1980s, Europe was ready for the next stage in economic and political integration after the shock of the recession of the early 1980s. The European Unity Treaty was adopted in 1984 as a commitment to European unity and two committees were set up to examine the development of the new institutions and the foundation of a 'people's Europe' (coinage, stamps, etc.). There was agreement to complete a programme to establish the Single European Market (SEM) by 1 January 1993 and the member states agreed to sign the Single European Act to amend the Treaty of Rome. The economic arguments for the creation of the Single European Market were summarized in the Cecchini report in 1988, which sought to estimate the costs of the 'non-single market' or the continuation of national market fragmentation. Cecchini (1988) estimated that the benefits of a total removal of all market barriers would amount to an economic stimulus of 200 billion ECUs and that thereafter there would be a 'self-sustaining virtuous circle' of competitive advantage, scale economies and multiplier effects. Prices would fall, demand and output would increase as would productivity and investment in research and development. This would produce a supply-side shock of 4.5 per cent of GDP for the European Community. Table 14.2 details the individual effects of the abolition of customs duties, the elimination of public procurement national favouritism, the deregulation of financial services and general supply-side effects. There would also be a price deflation equivalent to 6.1 per cent, substantial savings on public sector expenditure and an improvement in the European Community's external balance of trade. The result of these anticipated effects was a net gain of 1.8 million jobs in Europe at a time when unemployment was higher than in the United States or Japan. If the resources saved by the implementation of the single market were then used to fund additional expansionary measures, rather than merely to fund tax cuts, then additional employment might be found for between 5 and 6 million workers (see Figure 14.1).

The realization of the Single European Market was described in the 1985

Table 14.2 Macroeconomic consequences of EC market integration for the Community in the medium term

	Abolition of customs	Open public procurement	Liberalization of finance	Supply side[a]	Total
GDP (%)	0.4	0.5	1.5	2.1	4.5
Consumer prices (%)	−1.0	−1.4	−1.4	−2.3	−6.1
Employment (1000s)	200	350	400	850	1800
Budgetary balance (% of GDP)	0.2	0.3	1.1	0.6	2.2
External balance (% of GDP)	0.2	0.1	0.3	0.4	1.0

[a]Economies of scale, increased competition, etc.

Source: The economics of 1992, in *European Economy*, No. 35, March 1988 (Cecchini Report).

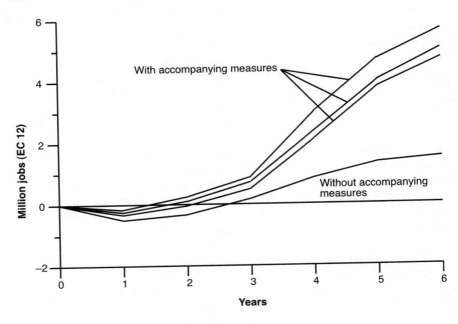

Figure 14.1 Employment prospects in the EC single market

White Paper, which identified 279 measures which would be necessary to eliminate all barriers. These can be classified as physical, fiscal and technical barriers. The physical barriers were the frontier controls on the movement of goods, people and capital. The fiscal barriers were the differentials in value added taxes and other purchase taxes and in the goods to which these applied. The technical barriers were the diverse set of regulations which applied to standards, codes of practice and subsidies. By the beginning of 1993, 95 per cent of the measures set out in the White Paper had been agreed. Of the 279 measures, 261 had been definitely adopted and three adopted by European ministers had still to come before the European Parliament. However, only 95 had been accepted by all 12 member state governments. Denmark has adopted the largest percentage of the European 'laws' (92 per cent) whilst Greece has adopted the smallest proportion (72 per cent). Of the 'four freedoms of movement' promised by the Single Market, three – goods, services and capital – are virtually complete, although by 1996 there still remains a number of concerns over the fourth – the movement of people, where, although some nations have adopted movement without passports, concerns over terrorism and the movement of economic refugees from eastern Europe and north Africa have led other nations to retain controls on migration (Nicoll and Salmon, 1994, p. 147).

The Single European Act also contains reference to Economic and Monetary Union (EMU). The timing is a matter of some uncertainty but initially moves were programmed to commence in 1997 and to be complete by 1999. Membership of the EMU would be conditional upon national economies converging on a set of desirable criteria. The most important criterion was inflation, where member states would require an inflation rate equal to the average of the three lowest national rates of inflation plus 1.5 per cent. The second criterion was that government spending deficits should be no more than 3 per cent of GDP. The third criterion was that interest rates should not exceed the average of the three lowest national interest rates plus 2 per cent. The fourth criterion covered international currency exchange rates, stating that currencies should have been trading within the ERM 2.25 per cent narrow band for at least two years. At the time of the Maastricht Agreement, which defined these criteria, only three of the 12 member nations would have met the EMU criteria – Denmark, Ireland and the Netherlands. France and Germany would have been excluded on their levels of government spending and Britain on its inflation rate. Italy would have been excluded on all the criteria.

It is difficult to measure whether the Single European Market as instituted between 1988 and 1993 has been a success. The difficulty lies largely in the fact that the period 1990–93 has seen a global recession with depressed levels of output and trade, which makes temporal comparison awkward. In addition, there have been special factors in Europe, such as the need for Germany to cover the costs of reunification, which have had a more serious effect on Europe than on the United States or east Asia, thus making cross-sectional comparisons difficult. In particular the decision by the West German government to keep interest rates high to attract foreign money to cover reunification costs rather than raising taxes, has had the effect of keeping all West European interest rates high to protect currencies, thus suppressing both capital investment and disposable income spending (Schatzl, 1995). By 1992, these difficulties were destabilizing the ERM and damaging economic growth in the Single European Market. Britain had refused to ratify all the elements of the Maastricht Treaty. In June 1992 the Danes voted against the treaty and in September the French vote was only narrowly in favour. The currency markets came under pressure as the Italian lira was devalued and the Germans increased their interest rates. On Wednesday, 16 September 1992, after massive intervention, Britain substantially raised interest rates and shortly thereafter Britain and Italy left the ERM as their currencies floated freely, and then devalued effectively by about 15 per cent. Attention switched to the French franc, which was saved only by the intervention of the German Bundesbank.

The conclusions, by 1996, appear to be that the ending of the global recession in 1993–94 will provide an opportunity for the Single European Market to begin delivering the advantages predicted in the Cecchini Report. However, by 1994 critics of the SEM had begun to argue that any economic gains achieved would have occurred anyway as consequences of changes in the global economy. European integration would have come about in any case, Minc (1994) argues, because of the growing detachment of the United States from Europe, because of the marketization of the eastern European and former Soviet economies, and because of continuing pressure from the growth of the south-east Asian economies. In monetary terms, whilst the commitment to a single European currency and a development of a central European bank based on the European System of Central Banks (ESCB) remains, the date for the completion of monetary union would appear to be receding (Thompson, 1993).

COMMUNITY ENLARGEMENT

Whilst we have traced the growing institutional complexity of the Common Market, it has also grown geographically. For more than 20 years from 1952 to 1973 there were only the six members – Belgium, France, Germany, Italy, Luxembourg and the Netherlands – all states with a well-developed industrial base at the centre of western Europe. Only southern Italy, the Mezzogiorno, could be considered lacking in industrial development and slightly peripherally located (Blacksell and Williams, 1995, p. 89; Garofoli, 1992). The first enlargement added three more nations – Denmark, Ireland and the United Kingdom – all of which were north European and closely linked economically with one another and to the founding member states. Their admission did change the nature of the Community. They had regional problems associated with their peripheral location and for the first time the idea of a geographical core and a geographical periphery began to affect the Community. In addition, two of the three were geographical islands which had implications for policies relating to transportation and the movement of people.

The 1980s saw three further additions to the Community, Greece in 1981 and Spain and Portugal in 1986. These three additions radically changed the nature of the Community, for all three had much less well developed industrial economies, were less urbanized in the 1960s and early 1970s and had served as sources of cheap immigrant labour. In 1986, their GDP per head was only between 53 and 72 per cent of the average for the Community as a whole (Table 14.3). In the period 1982–85 their growth rates were all below those of the Community but membership, with the exception of Greece, caused their growth rates to rise above that of the Community by the period 1986–90. However, as Perrons (1992) points out, at the regional scale the poorest regions were all to be found in Greece, Spain and Portugal in 1988 (except for the French Départements d'Outremer, which are scarcely comparable). By 1988 the weakest ten regions, out of 171, had GDP per head figures only 45 per cent of the EC average, and the weakest 25 regions only had 56 per cent of the EC average. By comparison the top ten and the top 25 regions, largely German, Dutch and French, had figures 51 per cent and 37 per cent above the EC average respectively. The admission of Spain, Portugal and Greece, and Ireland earlier, not only reduced the average GDP per head of the European Community and increased the inequality between regions but forced a reconsideration of regional policy within Europe by introducing underdevelopment (i.e. areas over-dependent on subsistence or near-subsistence agriculture) as a regional concern

Table 14.3 Trends in inequalities, 1982–90

	Change in GDP p.a.		GDP per head (EC12 = 100)	
	1982–85	1986–90	1986	1990
Greece	1.6	1.8	56	53
Spain	1.8	4.5	72	77
Ireland	1.5	3.7	63	65
Portugal	0.9	4.5	53	56
EC4	1.9	4.5	66	69
EC8	1.8	3.0	108	107
EC12	1.8	3.1	100	100

Source: Commission of the European Community (1991).

alongside the previous problem areas, which had generally been post-industrial dependences on coal, steelmaking, shipbuilding and metalworking (Cappellin and Molle, 1988, pp. 11–12). In consequence regions eligible for structural funds are now divided into three types: Objective 1, 'lagging behind', comprising Ireland, most of Spain, Portugal, Mezzogiorno Italy and Greece; Objective 2, declining industrial, typically British, north French, Belgian and north-eastern Spain; and Objective 5(b), rural.

The most recent group of countries to seek economic association or full membership of the European Community are somewhat different – Austria, Finland, Sweden, Iceland and Switzerland have all been brought into the customs union although Switzerland, because of its political neutrality, has not sought full membership of all the political institutions. Unlike the new members of the 1980s these are all high-income, industrialized economies with strong social welfare traditions. They are therefore likely to be net contributors to the Community's budget rather than net recipients. Their desire for membership, at least of the customs union termed the European Economic Area, if not of the full Community, is based on a concern not to be excluded from European markets if exclusionary tariffs are raised further. There is concern that without increasing the linkages to western Europe capital investment will be deflected away from Scandinavia with its high labour costs and that membership of the Single European Market is the only way to avoid the area's peripherality, much as Scotland and Ireland have been able to do (Bachtler *et al.*, 1993, pp. 92–93).

Whilst in the more distant future countries such as Turkey, Malta and Cyprus may wish to join the European Community at least as economic partners, if not as political partners, the next cohort to seek admission will be the newly marketized economies of Hungary, Poland, the Czech and Slovak Republics (see Chapter 13). De Benedictis and Padoan (1995) argue that the inclusion of the CMEA countries will radically change the European Community again. The CMEA countries will have a comparative advantage in energy and in agricultural products, thus having a negative effect on the western European countries which have a relative specialization in these sectors. The CAP and the ECSC will have to adjust to cheaper imports of food and coal. Conversely the CMEA countries will be markets for finished goods and for services, thus advantaging Western countries such as Germany which are well placed technically and geographically to supply these.

The period from 1952 to 2000 will have seen the European Community grow almost threefold. More important than the absolute growth in size is the much greater heterogeneity in terms of wealth and economic structure which the Community now exhibits. This in its turn has caused the Commission to extend its range of policies designed to achieve greater uniformity both by permitting the freer movement of people and resources and by offering financial help and advice to disadvantaged areas. The geography of Europe is not only changing administratively but also in terms of the units of which it is comprised. It is to the regional and urban levels that we now turn.

A EUROPE OF THE REGIONS

The reduction of powers of the nation-state within the European Community together with the doctrine of subsidiarity, which states that decisions should be made at the lowest, or most local, level practicable, have offered more powers to the 'regions' (see also Chapter 15). Regionalism is a complex phenomenon which has both economic and political origins. Some regions were imposed 'top down' by national governments either as regional physical planning or as regional economic policy; other regions were generated 'bottom up' by popular movements often with a historical basis. The movement towards greater uniformity and fewer barriers to movement should have reduced regional identities and inequalities, but the admission of the Mediterranean countries has sustained regional differentials by feeding in successively poorer regions to the European ranking. The persistence and indeed the exacerbation of regional differentials has provoked two responses within the Community. The first is a set of oppositions to the project and defence of the nation-state – the so-called Eurosceptic viewpoint in which national governments are thought to be the most appropriate agency for the delivery of equity policies (Keating, 1995, pp. 5–6). The second is to use the institutions of the Community to redistribute income and investment more evenly, especially to regions in the last round of enlargement. Peripheral regions with low income and low output such as those of Iberia and Greece can claim to be in need of substantial long-term development assistance and use this as the price of acquiescence in further integration (Keeble *et al.*, 1988). Spain has emerged as the leader of the poorer states pressing for a Community anti-disparity programme. Whilst Spain and member states would generally prefer simple intergovernmental transfers, the Commission has argued that this would not be in the spirit of European unification and that transfers must take the form of Community policy measures, of which structural funds are the most important.

The most important of the structural funds is the European Regional Development Fund, founded in 1975. Initially each country had a quota of ERDF which must be allocated to regions defined by national governments as needing assistance. The two largest users were Italy (40 per cent) and the United Kingdom (28 per cent). Such areas must have GDP per head rates below the EEC average and either be dependent upon agriculture, or have declining industries, or suffer structural unemployment. Investment must be in industrial or service activities and must involve the creation or maintenance of jobs, or must cover infrastructure deemed necessary for industrial or service projects. In addition ERDF money could be combined with other structural funds such as the Guidance Section of the Agriculture Fund (EAGGF), the European Social Fund (ESF), the European Coal and Steel Community (ECSC) and the European Investment Bank (EIB). The creation of the Single European Market in 1988 required a reform of the structural funds. This reform identified three types of region eligible for assistance – structurally backward regions, regions in industrial decline, and rural areas. The major change in 1988, however, was the introduction of the Community's right to select the areas in receipt of assistance rather than be dependent on national governmental definition. This it was hoped would facilitate the concentration of assistance in the most needy regions. By 1993 the system of structural funds was in need of further change to accommodate changes caused by the Maastricht Treaty. These changes led to a further redefinition of areas to receive assistance to include the former East Germany, an increase in the budget of the structural funds, the creation of a new fund, the Cohesion Fund, to finance environmental and transport investment in areas where GDP per head is less than 90 per cent of the EC average, and the introduction of faster administrative procedures (Armstrong, 1995).

The distribution of structural funds for 1989–93 is shown in Table 14.4. The major beneficiaries are Spain, Italy, Portugal and Greece because of their Objective 1 status and to a lesser extent Britain, France and Spain because of their declining industrial regions. The countries which fare poorly within the structural funds are Denmark, Germany, the Netherlands and Belgium, but the system is carefully calibrated so that every one of the twelve member states in 1989–93 received some assistance, even Luxembourg. Over that period the EC took a much firmer grip on regional policy, selecting areas to benefit and targeting more precise objectives. The admission of the Scandinavian–Alpine states is unlikely to necessitate further changes but the prospective admission of CMEA countries would inevitably cause a major recasting of policy.

Outside formal regional policy through structural funds there is another sense in which regions have grown in importance in the EC. In thinking of the regional implications of a Europe without national frontiers the EC has drawn up a map of Europe with transnational regions defined largely in terms of external impacts. Thus the Arc Atlantique stretching from southern Portugal to the Shetlands, the west Mediterranean arc, the central Mediterranean, the northern arc (around the North Sea) and Scandinavia are all seen as transnational regions defined by linkages external to Europe, whilst the capitals centre (London–Paris–

Table 14.4   ERDF allocation, 1989–93 (million ECUs)

	Objective 1 Structurally backward	Objective 2 Industrial decline	Objective 5(b)	Total
Belgium	0	0.3	0.03	0.33
Denmark	0	0.03	0.01	0.04
Germany	0	0.6	0.77	1.37
Greece	6.2	0	0	6.20
Spain	12.5	1.5	0.20	14.20
France	0.8	1.3	1.04	3.14
Republic of Ireland	2.1	0	0	2.10
Italy	9.4	0.5	0.46	10.36
Luxembourg	0	0.01	0.01	0.02
Netherlands	0	0.2	0.06	0.26
Portugal	6.7	0	0	6.70
United Kingdom	0.6	2.8	0.21	3.61
Total	38.3	7.24	2.79	48.33

Amsterdam–Bonn), the Alpine zone, and the diagonal continental (Madrid–Paris) are defined by their internal perspective at the core of Europe.

CITIES AS ECONOMIES IN EUROPE

Just as regions have sought more autonomy within Europe as national governments have been weakened within the Single European Market, city governments also have sought to manage their economies more effectively using European assistance under the concept of subsidiarity. European assistance has taken the form of either structural funds such as the European Social Fund to assist towns and cities with high rates of unemployment, or demonstration projects through urban networks such as Quartiers en Crises. The perception of cities in Europe being in competition one with another, competing for mobile investment within the Single European Market, has been fostered by the publication of league tables which have sought to rank cities, consistently defined, in terms of their problems, their suitability for commercial investment, or their quality of life. In the case of investment the ranking tends to be made on the basis of economic variables such as GDP per head, the unemployment rate, some measure of pressure of demand for space (rents, new floorspace completions, etc.) or the proportion of the workforce employed in higher-order occupations. In the case of quality-of-life rankings, studies include not only economic variables but the presence of cultural or leisure facilities, environmental variables (air pollution, age and quality of housing) and the quality of local services such as education, health and policing.

One of the best-known such rankings is that prepared by DATAR (Délégation à l'Aménagement du Territoire et à l'Action Régionale, 1989). Whilst some of the variables included in the analysis were specifically economic, such as the presence of multinational companies, the DATAR report placed a great deal more emphasis on infrastructure, on the quality of the labour force and on socio-cultural variables such as cultural facilities, major fairs and exhibitions, and the scale of the local publishing industry. The final ranking of European cities was heavily influenced by outright size as measured by resident population. Thus the two largest cities, Paris and London, comprise the sole members of Class 1, and the next largest cities, Milan, Munich, Madrid, Frankfurt and Barcelona, comprise the next two classes.

Amongst the other studies of European city rankings probably the best known is the work of Cheshire for the EC (Cheshire *et al.*, 1986; Cheshire and Hay, 1989; Cheshire, 1990). This work concentrates upon a smaller number of economic variables including unemployment, GDP per head, migration and an index of commercial development pressure to rank 117 European cities over the period 1971–88. Although the ranking is transnational it is clear that there are national clusterings on the 'problem' score. Almost half of the top 30 cities are German whilst most of the others are concentrated in the 'golden triangle' – Brussels, Amsterdam, Paris and Antwerp – or in northern Italy – Venice, Florence, Bologna and Milan. Only two British cities, neither of them heavily industrialized (Brighton and Norwich), find a place in the top 30, and only one Spanish city (the highly atypical Palma de Majorca). The bottom 30 cities comprise mainly old British industrial cities and the relatively undeveloped towns of Spain and southern Italy, with an outlier in the depressed coalfield areas of northern France and southern Belgium (Liège, Valenciennes, Charleroi). The bottom 30 cities therefore clearly represent the urban expression of the EC's distinction between Objective 1 and Objective 2 regions. Other general conclusions are that national capitals tend to lie in the second quartile of the ranking (Berlin 34, London 35, Rome 50, Madrid 54) and cities with an explicit European administrative role such as Brussels and Strasbourg also do well. Overall, manufacturing cities do less well in Cheshire's ranking than those with a high proportion of employment in services, and ports and coalfield towns do poorly.

Cheshire subsequently goes on to compare cities' problem scores with population change. In this he recognizes that in some cases population loss, via emigration, may reflect poor economic performance but in other cases population change may reflect relative birth and death rates, which have nothing to do with economic performance. By graphing the two variables the cities of Europe are allocated to four quadrants. There are cities which have few problems and experience population growth typified by French cities such as Strasbourg, Dijon, Orléans and Montpellier. There are cities which have few problems but experience population decline typified by German cities such as Frankfurt, Düsseldorf, Stuttgart, Nuremberg and Dortmund. There are cities which have serious problems but whose population is still growing, largely through an excess of births over deaths, typified by Italian cities such as Rome, Palermo,

Naples and Cagliari (significantly, northern Italian cities such as Milan, Turin, Genoa and Venice have population *loss* and behave more like British or German cities). Finally, there are cities with problems which are experiencing population decline typified by British cities such as Glasgow, Manchester, Newcastle and Birmingham.

CONVERGENCE OR DIVERGENCE

The last two sections have indicated that whilst there has been economic growth in western Europe since 1952, that growth has not been uniform. At the level of nations, regions and cities there have been marked differentials. Where these differentials are identified politicians and government officials have been quick to ask how policies have been developed to help laggard regions to catch up, and for regional economic standards to converge. On the theoretical level, models that predict convergence, like neoclassical economic growth models, coexist with models that imply a progressive increase in disparities between rich and poor areas, like the cumulative causation models (Dixon and Thirlwall, 1975) and, more recently, the 'new growth theories' (Lucas, 1988) whilst a third stream, the 'filter down theories' (Aydalot, 1992), forecasts that regions will grow at the same rate, keeping the relative income differences (Pettenati and Camillo, 1994, p. 37). Cumulative causation models argue that successful regions or cities are able to build on that success using income as investment in research and development, labour training and infrastructural development to sustain and enhance their competitive and comparative advantage. The opposite view is that successful regions and cities develop economies which 'overheat', pushing up the price of factors of production – labour, capital and land – and incurring agglomerative diseconomies such as congestion to a point where the initial comparative advantage is nullified and new investment looks to other areas where costs are lower, thus causing convergence.

Table 14.5 compares the income per head, standardized by purchasing power (PPS = purchasing parity standard), for the 12 member nations of the EC in 1980 and 1990. Of the 12, only three show a trend towards greater divergence, Greece because it is falling further behind the Community average, and Luxembourg and Denmark because they have seen their average incomes move further above the Community average. All the rest, except Italy, which has seen incomes remain constantly just 2 per cent above average, have moved closer to the Community average.

Table 14.6 shows the income figures for the poorest and richest regions in nine of the member states. The figures show the diversity of regional incomes within each state. In every country in both 1980 and 1990 there is at least one region with an income significantly below the EC average. In both years Greece's, Spain's and Portugal's respective richest regions have incomes below the EC average. Even in 1990, almost without exception, each country's richest region has incomes twice the level of those in that country's poorest region (Collier,

Table 14.5   Country level per capita PPS, 1980–90 (EUR = 100)

	1980	1990	Convergence/Divergence
Greece	52	47	D
Spain	72	75	C
France	114	112	C
Portugal	53	56	C
UK	97	101	C
Ireland	61	68	C
Italy	102	102	—
Luxembourg	115	124	D
Denmark	106	107	D
Germany[a]	119	117	C
Belgium	106	105	C
Netherlands	108	101	C

[a]German figures exclude the former German Democratic Republic (East Germany).
Source: Eurostat.

Table 14.6   Regional per capita PPS, 1980–90 (EUR = 100)

	1980		1990	
	Lowest	Highest	Lowest	Highest
Greece	35	71	34	58
Spain	45	91	49	98
France	87	182	79	166
Portugal	44	69	35	76
UK	74	114	74	154 (121)[a]
Italy	58	135	61	135
Germany	85	187	81	183
Belgium	83	166	78	166
Netherlands	87	208	61 (82)[a]	135

[a]Because figures for 1990 are incomplete comparable figures are given in brackets.
Note that Ireland, Luxembourg and Denmark, treated as single regions by Eurostat, are omitted from the table.
Source: Eurostat.

1994). Perrons (1992), in examining changes in regional income over time, concludes that there is not a single unambiguous trend towards either convergence or divergence, but that there is a pattern of diminishing inequalities between regions during periods of general economic expansion and widening inequalities during periods of economic recession. Thus there was a period of convergence between member states and regions from the early years of the Community to the mid-1970s coinciding with the period of 'the long boom'. This was followed by a phase of recession and stagnation (the crisis of Fordism) in which regional inequalities widened in the late 1970s and the early 1980s. In the late 1980s overall growth rates improved and again differentials between regions diminished. This finding agrees with both major theories in that at times of economic growth pressures force investment out of the most rapidly growing regions and cities through high rents, high labour costs and congestion, thus spreading the growth to other regions, but in times of recession these marginal plants tend to be the first to be closed as companies retreat towards their more secure heartlands (Lever, 1993).

In seeking to explain the distribution of successful cities, Lever (1993) examines the core–periphery argument, which states that cities and regions located along the major growth axis of Europe extending from London to Milan have incontrovertible advantages which will secure their position as the most rapidly growing areas. Figures of GDP per head for 1975–95 show that the cities of the core axis did grow more quickly in 1975–85, but in the period 1985–95 the more peripheral cities grew more quickly, and this could be interpreted as a 'crowding out' of growth from the axis to the periphery aided by improved transportation such as the Train à Grande Vitesse (TGV), improved airport links in the periphery and the switch from manufacturing to services. Lever also tested the north–south divide hypothesis in Europe, which argues that historically the cities of the north have grown much more rapidly than those of the south. Data for the period 1975–95 show that the cities of the south have now begun to catch up, with growth rates typically 30 per cent higher than the cities of the north – this in part gives rise to the identification of Europe's recent growth axis extending from Valencia to central Italy (Hebbert and Hansen, 1990).

CONCLUSION

This chapter has traced the development of the integrated European market. The initial moves owed much to concerns that another war should not break out in Europe. These were succeeded by early attempts at economic integration such as the European Coal and Steel Community. The early 1950s saw the Treaty of Rome creating the European Common Market from the committed Europeans and the creation of the European Free Trade Association. Evidence suggests that west European economic growth was faster than would have occurred in the absence of the Common Market through the 'long boom' of the 1960s and early 1970s, but growth was still restricted by western Europe's multiplicity of languages, currencies and national laws. The economic recession of the late 1970s and early 1980s with its slow growth led to a rethink of the integrated Europe model. At the same time the admission of Greece, Spain and Portugal changed perceptions of economic problems by raising the profile of the underdeveloped regions and exacerbated the problems of peripherality. By the late 1980s most of western Europe was committed to the idea of a Single Market with the abolition of national economic frontiers and the four freedoms of movement – capital, labour, goods and services. By 1993 most of this had been implemented but the recession of 1990–93 made it difficult to assess whether the benefits were as great as Cecchini had predicted. Whilst there remain substantial differentials in income, output and quality of life between the cities and regions of the now further enlarged Community, there is evidence of convergence, although this seems easier to achieve at times of economic boom and less easy to achieve in recession. Whilst economic union has progressed steadily there is evidence that social and monetary union have had, and will continue to have, a less smooth ride. The social proposals of Maastricht covering working conditions, health and welfare, and quality of life have not been welcomed by everyone, as witnessed by Britain's concern that such proposals would raise non-wage labour costs and thus reduce Europe's competitiveness in a world of trade blocs. The proposals for monetary union, whilst ultimately critical for Europe's economic integration, appear to be less likely to be achieved by 1999 than when they were first proposed as national governments find it increasingly difficult to manage their economies in the context of increasing globalization.

FURTHER READING

Blacksell, M., Williams, A.M. (eds) 1995 *The European challenge: geography and development in the European Community.* Oxford University Press, Oxford.

Dunford, M., Kafkalas, G. 1992 *Cities and regions in the new Europe.* Belhaven, London.

Lever, W.F., Bailly, A. 1996 *The spatial impact of economic changes in Europe.* Avebury, Aldershot.

Nicoll, W., Salmon, T.C. 1994 *Understanding the new European Community.* Harvester Wheatsheaf, Hemel Hempstead.

Vickerman, R.W. 1992 *The Single European Market.* Harvester Wheatsheaf, Hemel Hempstead.

Wise, M., Gibb, R. 1993 *Single market to social Europe: the European Community in the 1990s.* Longman, Harlow.

In addition, the *Journal of Common Market Studies* (from 1962) and *European Urban and Regional Studies* (from 1994) offer many papers of interest.

For insights into the European Commission's thinking reference could be made to the Europe 2000+ series on regional policies, the European Commission, Luxembourg.

CHAPTER 15

REINVENTING THE REGION:
Firms, clusters and networks in economic development
Philip Cooke

INTRODUCTION

Increased global economic turbulence is causing a re-evaluation of the appropriateness of nation-state responses to regional problems. Thus, interest in the regional and local levels of economic activity has both changed and grown significantly since the early 1980s (see, for example, Boddy and Fudge, 1984; Henderson and Castells, 1987; Scott, 1988a; Cooke, 1989; Campbell, 1990; Pyke *et al.*, 1990; Bennett and Krebs, 1991; Pyke and Sengenberger, 1992; Geddes and Benington, 1992; Harrison, 1994a). It has changed because of a major decline in confidence in traditional recipes for regional assistance. In response to rising unemployment, with a perceived inadequacy in the quality of jobs on offer and as a consequence of more general dissatisfaction with centralist administration, regions began to emerge in the 1970s as administrative units and policy actors in their own right, albeit with very limited powers at the outset.

In nearly every case, and for understandable reasons, the activities of such authorities have focused particularly on developing industrial policies in support of small and medium enterprises (SMEs). In this respect, interest in economic activity at the regional level has grown as well as changed. The reason for this is simple. By the early 1990s SMEs were the only source of employment growth in the OECD area (OECD, 1994). Large, privately owned firms were everywhere to be seen 'downsizing' and 'rightsizing', to use the corporate graffiti of management jargon. Moreover, the public sector, which until the early 1980s had been a source of employment growth, also began to contract from the mid-1980s. In the European Union (EU), policies in support of small business growth and entrepreneurship assisted regional administrations to develop coherent support policies especially in the areas of training, information and innovation.

By the early 1990s, the OECD, and within it the European Union, authorities had considerable experience, over a period of more than ten years, of different SME support systems, policies and instruments. The stage had been reached where inter-firm business networking (for discussion, see Cooke and Morgan, 1993) initiatives had become *de rigueur*. Networking policies emanating from the EU often supported collaborative business activities in the field of Regional

Technology Development. The Science and Technology Directorate (DG12) had lengthy experience of inter-firm collaboration in research and development (R&D) between large enterprises, sometimes with SMEs also involved. This experience was gradually applied to inter-firm collaborative activity between SMEs, as with initiatives such as Cooperative Research Action for Technology (CRAFT) and Strategic Programme for Innovation and Technology Transfer (SPRINT).

As will be shown in outline in the next section, many regions (and smaller countries such as Denmark and Portugal) have adopted network models of SME-oriented industrial policy in the hope and expectation of improving business competitiveness. This approach gains increasing support from writers such as Porter (1990) who bases his recipe for business success, to a considerable extent, on the clustering configurations of SMEs and large enterprises in successful regional economies. The Porter 'diamond' of success factors effectively represents a conceptual model of the networked regional growth economy (Figure 15.1).

The question this chapter poses in sections 3 and 4 is in what ways and to what extent can such infrastructures really assist business, both large and small, but especially the latter, during a period of history which, unlike the 40 or so years after 1945, is extraordinarily turbulent economically and politically? The question is posed in this way not because of a sense of the worthlessness of public action, but rather a genuine interest in how intelligent regional and local economic development personnel and their institutions themselves seek to deal

Figure 15.1 Factors in competitive advantage (from Porter, 1990, and Boekholt, 1994)

with turbulence and uncertainty. In such a context, which shows little sign of stabilizing significantly in the foreseeable future, how do firms and their managements deal with the need to be more and more competitive when the rules may be changing unpredictably? To what extent and in what ways, if any, do they comply with a Porterian model of competitive advantage, and do they seek network-type support arrangements from either the governmental agencies to which they may relate or their closest competitive rivals? In a globalizing economic context how local do firms go?

ADVANCED REGIONAL AUTHORITIES AND A NEW APPROACH TO REGIONAL DEVELOPMENT

An interesting conclusion drawn from the findings of research into the impact of the Single European Market upon economic development (Begg and Mayes, 1993) is that the future of industrial policy throughout the European Union lies at the *regional* level (see also Chapter 14). The argument developed shows that central government fears, throughout the Union, of transgressing the convergence criteria for monetary targets in connection with economic and monetary union, mean they are reluctant to pursue national industrial policies. Moreover, the general economic uncertainty, alluded to earlier, combined with a sense of failure by some – notably Mitterand's France after 1981 – in the efficacy of the nation-state as a vehicle, add to the sense of paralysis. *Global monetarism* has, for the time being, triumphed.

However, Begg and Mayes (1993) found instances of judicious sub-central industrial policy operating in support of regional economies within the interstices of global monetarism and see a future for such interventions. This links with a very different kind of analysis reported recently by Ohmae (1993) and furthered with great insight by de Vet (1993). Ohmae's case is simply stated in the subtitle of his opening section: *The Nation State is Dysfunctional*. He continues:

> On the global economic map the lines that now matter are those defining what may be called 'region states'. The boundaries of the region state are not imposed by political fiat. They are drawn by the deft but invisible hand of the global market for goods and services (Ohmae, 1993, p. 78)

Ohmae's argument is that in what he referred to elsewhere as an increasingly 'borderless world' (Ohmae, 1990) region states are the natural economic zones. Citing examples, some of which will be discussed in more detail below, such as northern Italy, Wales, Catalonia, Alsace-Lorraine and Baden-Württemberg, he avers that they and border regions such as San Diego–Tijuana or the Hong Kong and Singapore hinterlands hold the key ingredients for economic success. The historic nation-states, by contrast, represent no genuine community of economic interests, define no meaningful flows of economic activity and neglect true linkages and synergies among economic actors.

We may find some of Ohmae's rhetoric and even analysis somewhat overdrawn and prone to the fallacy of composition, but of the verisimilitude of his basic insight and the general processes being referred to in this chapter there can be relatively little to query. The fallacy of composition occurs, as with much higher journalism, when to prove a case an extreme instance is presented as if it were universal. Thus, Ohmae cites Italy as an obvious case of a meaningless *economic* entity because of the huge differences between north and south. However, other nation-states (e.g. West Germany before unification, but not Germany afterwards) exist in which disparities are relatively insignificant and much trade occurs within domestic boundaries. Nevertheless, Ohmae's notion of the *region state*, though rather overstated, has something to commend it concerning the unquestionable decline in the sovereign economic powers of states that become members of free trade areas (Held, 1991) and the self-evident emergence, in some of the stronger sub-central economic regions of such states, of greater policy proactivity to further the interests of those economies.

This dimension of the argument is explored more fully and quite objectively by de Vet (1993). His argument is that despite the development of global networks of interlinked firms and the globalization of factors of production, the region will become stronger as an economic entity. This is because globalization will reinforce geographic clusters of production. This occurs as an effect of increased international competition, which induces regional economies to seek competitive advantage from mobilizing all their assets, including institutional and governmental ones where these exist, or demanding them where they do not. This process leads to regional economic specialization tendencies, a feature reinforced by globalization. As regional economies become more specialized and pull the institutional support structure along, so foreign direct investment seeks out such centres of expertise by following domestic investment as part of a global locational strategy. In an empirical study of foreign direct investment in seven OECD countries de Vet demonstrates that globalization indeed reinforces regional specialization in the anticipated manner. The key policy recommendation is that regional and local competitiveness in the 1990s rests on a successful interlinking of local and regional networks with global networks of innovation and production.

Hence, the region, as the optimal level of industrial, governmental and technological support, especially for SMEs in association with large enterprises, becomes the spatial correlate of the *cluster*, Porter's (1990) definitive industrial organizational form of the competitively advantaged economy. Advanced regional administrations of the kind alluded to by Ohmae (1993) are fashioning a new approach to regional development based on the central idea of the *networked regional innovation architecture*. It involves, *inter alia*, regionally based science and technology foresight, networked information services, advanced telecommunications hardware, technological centres, gateway services to international markets and expert governance systems. This takes established structures such as development agencies, universities and research institutes, vocational training bodies, chambers of commerce and local economic development bodies a step forward. Instead of relatively static and task-specific competences, network forms of innovation architecture are based on flow processes aimed at maximizing innovation capacity of firms in the system, whether as active or passive users and beneficiaries of system provision.

Networking is the key to this kind of support infrastructure. As noted in Cooke and Morgan (1993) this involves reciprocity (an initial predisposition to exchange information, know-how etc.), trust (faith in the reliability of other firms or bodies), learning (a recognition that practice is transferable and good or best practice can be assimilated from others), partnership (realization that key reciprocal relationships are preferable), and, finally the recognition that empowerment (inclusion and self-responsibility) is an essential element of successful institutional organization and inter-institutional interaction. The five following sketches give examples of the approach.

Denmark

With a population of 5.1 million Denmark has a relative lack of both large, research-based firms and a government technology policy. Research by the European Commission shows, for example, that Denmark was slow to introduce microelectronics equipment and that when efforts were made to catch up in the 1980s there were organizational inadequacies and skills shortages. However, Denmark is the EU's second most prosperous country in terms of GDP per head. Being small, it can generate communication and interaction economies, especially in its system of SMEs.

Of key importance to this system are the support infrastructures for small business, the most important being chambers of commerce and industry, local and regional technical and special technical schools, local and regional banks providing long-term loans for local SMEs, and the Danish Technological Institute (DTI) and its 15 technology centres. The DTI is a privatized branch of the Ministry of Industry. It employs 1200 technologists and others in developing, identifying and transferring generic technologies, largely to SMEs. Some 55 per cent of the DTI's contract income is from firms employing less than 50 people.

Recognizing that isolation from information and know-how was a handicap to SMEs, the DTI in 1989 established a 'Network Programme' which channelled government support to firms willing to cooperate in certain business activities. In one small town in Jutland, the following case history is instructive: seven small furniture makers found local markets shrinking, so they took advantage of the Network Programme and created a trading company. They divided up key tasks, so that, for example, design for all firms is done by two designers and each firm specializes in a particular production phase. The company now exports high-quality furniture to the EU and beyond.

By 1992, 175 networks existed, in which 42 per cent of firms had increased turnover per year by 4 per cent or more, and one in five by 10 per cent or more since joining. Of key importance to the success of this programme was the appointment by the DTI of 'network brokers'. These are local professionals, lawyers, consultants or engineers whose job it is to create networks of firms, colleges, local authorities, enterprise agencies and so on. These networks then bid for grants from technology programmes aimed at product and process innovation, quality improvement, product differentiation, and, very importantly, design, which is seen as a key selling point. The philosophy is that 'the competitive advantage of regions is achieved through the competitive advantage of firms' (Gelsing and Knop, 1991).

Pennsylvania

This state lost large numbers of jobs in the 1980s; 50000 disappeared from the clothing industry and 15000 from the foundry industry, for example, adding to the strife caused by the closure of Pittsburgh's steel mills in the 1970s and 1980s, which cost 100000 jobs. Typically, in such a context, state and local governments took the lead in seeking economic regeneration, including trying to stimulate innovation in the regional economy.

Pennsylvania's economic strategy moved through three phases during this period of extended industrial and employment crisis:

- *Phase 1.* Up to 1975 economic development policy was aimed at providing traditional services (information, business advice, 'signposting') to help individual firms innovate. This was a clear failure.

- *Phase 2.* Policy changed as the crisis deepened. The strategy became one of helping firms and institutions (trade associations, colleges, unions, local government) in localities to define collectively the services they need. To manage this the state set up the Ben Franklin Partnership (BFP), a development bank to fund joint R&D projects between firms and universities. The assumption was that innovation required finance and technology so the state provided the means to access both. Key to this was BFP's extension service of nine industrial resource centres. These were needed because it quickly became clear that bank finance and technology were not enough. Firms (mostly SMEs) needed management, marketing, technical and worker training services as well. Above all, SMEs were discovering that innovating in mature industries was more successful than aiming for breakthrough technologies.

- *Phase 3.* This was the new phase built on this experience. BFP concluded that the most successful element of its work was helping networks of local firms and institutions to help themselves. To support this the Manufacturing Innovation Networks (MAIN) project was set up in 1989. MAIN was learnt from Europe, Denmark in particular. It works by inviting bids for strategic regeneration projects up to a maximum of $100000 for one year. Only networks need apply and only four are selected. The first winners were Pittsburgh foundries, Lehigh Valley clothing, Lake Erie plastic and

Philadelphia/Pittsburgh tool-and-die networks. The networks cooperate around any one of four special technology centres which protect network members' know-how; they also have access to specially skilled workers from any of 45 educational centres of excellence.

Although it is early to judge the significance of these efforts, it is worth noting the move up-market by the Pittsburgh foundries. Of 45 in the locality, between a third and a half were selling design, engineering, drafting, welding and machining services as well as, in many cases, just-in-time delivery. Moreover, some were engaging in successful joint-bidding for contracts and cooperating in provision of complementary services. The region was being advertised as a 'Foundry Centre', something that had not happened before (Coy, 1992).

The Basque and Valencia regions

These two represent an interesting contrast because, although they started out with similar kinds of innovation institution, local divergences have resulted in different policy avenues being pursued. The Basque country has a better GDP per capita but a worse unemployment index than Valencia because it is an older industrial region (steel and shipbuilding) in decline, while Valencia is an up-and-coming consumer industry economy.

In response to its problems of industrial crisis, the Basque regional government devised a technology strategy which established R&D support funding to firms and to five technology centres; SPRI, a regional technology transfer agency; and a technology park in a rural campus setting near Bilbao. While the technology park (£100 million of public investment) has begun attracting innovative firms, mostly from the region, it is the R&D support, managed by SPRI (Sociedad para la Promoción y la Reconversión Industrial), that has yielded the most impressive results. In ten years, Basque R&D expenditure moved from 0.1 per cent of GDP to 1.4 per cent, equivalent to Italy by 1989 (see also Chapters 6 and 9). Five key technology centres, employing between 100 and 200 scientists and support staff, are responsible for this. They specialize in new materials, factory automation, information technology, machine tools and energy technologies. Each works with a 'club' of associate SMEs to transfer technology on a contract basis. Subsidy to client and supplier is about 30 per cent of the market rate. The centres are well networked into EU science and technology programmes so that best practice is quickly diffused into local firms. Special attention has been devoted to automotive components firms and machine tool manufacturers. Some of the latter have grown into major competitors to German companies at the cheaper end of the market and, overall, while there are still problems of receptivity towards innovation by many SMEs, leading firms have been able to survive and some to do well in increasingly difficult and competitive international markets.

Like the Basque government, that of the Valencia region has also adopted a technology centres approach to its innovation strategy and an agency, IMPIVA, to manage them. Moreover a science and technology park has been built. Industries in Valencia receiving special support are ceramics, footwear, textiles and science-based activities. Each of these is located, as in northern Italy, in industrial districts. Because of this, Valencia formed a partnership with Emilia-Romagna to model its strategy on theirs. But more importantly, the Valencians visited Denmark and purchased the Danish idea of network brokerage.

The network brokerage idea builds on the other elements of the innovation strategy. There are several networks: an inner network composed of IMPIVA, the technology centres, five business innovation centres and the technology park; an outer network composed of four regional universities, chambers of commerce, trades unions, and design and training agencies; and Spanish and EU networks. Network brokers are drawn from the professions (consultants, engineers, etc.) and link networks of firms in particular industries to any or all of these network players. Firms can thus cooperate, as in Denmark, on distribution, sales and promotion, exports, joint purchasing and product and process innovations. Valencian SMEs are, however, overdependent on support from what is, nevertheless, an expanding public support infrastructure. Even the Emilians are impressed by the excellence of Valencian ceramics but the shoe industry is surviving rather than booming.

North-Rhine Westphalia

This is Germany's largest *länd* with 17 million people, thus hardly a region. It is often associated with the Ruhrgebiet but covers a much wider set of economies than that older, heavy industry area. South of the Ruhr are old industrial districts such as Remscheid and Solingen, centres still of high-quality tools and cutlery production. In the Bergischland and Siegerland are numerous mechanical engineering, machine tool and automotive components clusters and in Aachen, Cologne and Düsseldorf centres of advanced machinery, media and commerce respectively.

Nevertheless, dealing with the inevitable restructuring of an old-established industrial economy has meant that a considerable amount of future-oriented thinking and policy formation has been necessary. ZIM and ZIN are acronyms for two of these; the 'Z' stands for *zukunft* or 'future' and the future is seen firmly as technological innovation. Key elements of these policies have included the establishment of 51 higher education institutions and five new Fraunhofer Institutes in the 1980s; the establishment of 11 new Max Planck Institutes since 1984; a TPZ (future technologies programme) for SMEs in eight industry sectors; the ZENIT (innovation centre) set up by partnership of *land*, bank and firms; a network centre; the establishment of the Ruhr Environment Agency, possessing five centres with DM79 million turnover; a further network of technology centres (58 either built or planned); and the TZ (tech-centre) Dortmund, which now has 120 firms employing 5500 persons. Altogether, the technology centres alone have created some 15000 new, high-skilled jobs in over 1000 new firms. Of great interest and importance too is the fact that, in combination with older, large firms which are diversifying out of coal and steel, new start-up firms have created some 60000–100000 new jobs in environmental technologies in North-Rhine Westphalia from 1983 to 1993. These assist in cleaning up the Ruhrgebiet while exporting technology and services to central and eastern Europe (Hassink, 1992; Rehfeld, 1993; Davies, 1994b).

Wales

Building on traditional regional development institutions and programmes such as selective regional grants and tax reliefs, with an aggressive programme from the Welsh Development Agency (WDA) to attract innovative foreign direct investment, Wales has now built a new industrial platform. On this platform are being constructed several innovative regional technological programmes. Amongst the most important of these are RTP – the Regional Technology Plan; a Technology Strategy for Wales; the South Wales Regional Technopole; an innovation network; relocation to Wales of the UK National Patent Office, established in 1991; the establishment of an EC relay centre; a technology exploitation network; the opening of an engineering centre for the promotion of advanced engineering and of two mechatronics training centres; the establishment of Imperial College Science Park at Cardiff and the consolidation of six sub-regional technology and innovation centres. In numerous ways these initiatives interact with and build upon or replace existing programmes, many of which are aimed at supporting SME development (Price *et al.*, 1994).

One indicator of the relative success of creating an innovative milieu consisting of innovative foreign firms, especially Japanese and German, and an innovation architecture of business support is that the success of Welsh SME performance in winning both UK government and EU innovation grants is higher than its GDP, population or manufacturing share of the UK total. The latter are all approximately 5 per cent whereas the Welsh shares of UK SMART (SME Merit Awards in Research and Technology) ranged between 9 and 14 per cent from 1989 to 1993, while Welsh SMEs secured 7 per cent of the UK shares of EU Third Framework (Science and Technology) funding between 1987 and 1991. Since 1990 Wales has been a partner of Baden-Württemberg, Lombardy, Rhône-Alps, Catalonia (and now Ontario) in what was the *Four Motors of Europe* partnership, but has now grown to *Six Motors of the Transatlantic*.

In response to this situation further initiatives have been taken by the WDA in partnership with firms and institutions to assist innovation. These include first, a redoubling of the WDA and Welsh Office foreign direct investment programme, which has attracted up to 15 per cent of UK inward investment since 1980. The total amount of inward investment and reinvestment in 1992 was over £1 billion. Many of these firms are themselves innovative. Second, in order to balance this success a supplier development programme, which links 'clubs' of medium-sized firms vertically to large firms in a supply chain, has been established. Twenty supplier clubs now exist in Wales. Third, to help to improve the skills of workers and management in supplier firms, innovative training initiatives, aimed at improving the quality of products and processes, are in place. These are managed in partnership between the WDA, Training and Enterprise Councils, enterprise agencies and higher education institutes. Fourth, technology and innovation centres where new start-up firms are housed or applied technology services are supplied to firms have been set up in six locations. An EC relay centre, enabling firms to exploit EC science and technology programme results, links to these centres. Fifth, the WDA manages Eurolink, a programme linking innovative small firms in Wales to firms in partner regions such as Baden-Württemberg, Lombardy, Catalonia, and Rhône-Alps. These firms exchange technologies and marketing networks. Sixth, the Danish network scheme has been adopted for SME networking at TEC and enterprise agency levels in south, north and west Wales.

The next step, soon to be taken, is to develop a network of networks in an innovation network, which will enable firms in any location or industry to be put in immediate contact with the precise business support service they require. This is the next stage of development beyond the localized 'Business Link' initiative which was recently established in England.

REGIONAL NETWORK INFRASTRUCTURES AND BUSINESS NEEDS

It is clear from the examples quoted that older industrial regions, in particular, are making great efforts to reconvert using network models of economic development. Based to some extent on the apparently successful Danish method of network brokerage, they are seeking to fashion an innovative infrastructure of vertical and lateral network linkages between large and small firms, research institutions and public technology and information transfer agencies. There is a belief – it cannot be stated as more than that – that small businesses are worth supporting and that because they are small they can be supplied with some of the advantages of economies of scale, without losing those of scope, if they are willing and able to operate in networks. This comes from observations and reports about what seemed to be generic features of successful small-firm based regional economies in the 1980s, notably the Italian example of Emilia-Romagna (the template for the Danish model) and the German one of Baden-Württemberg.

Now, officially, small firms are seen as the main source of new employment opportunities in Western countries (OECD, 1994). However, just as this straw of hope is being grasped the exemplar regional economies have been confronted with contextual problems that make the prospects for small firm success – especially in manufacturing industries, but with implications for service businesses also – problematic. During the 1990s in both Germany and Italy changes in the economic context have been dramatic. There have been significant changes in trading, competitiveness and financial conditions which have brought crisis conditions to the fore.

The three contextual changes are as follows. First, there has been a considerable lessening of trade barriers within the European Union consequent upon the Single Market, which took effect at the end of 1992 (see also Chapter 4). Second, there has been a wider globalization of trade which, for European firms of all sizes and most sectors of industry, has meant an increased level of market penetration from, especially, Asian countries. Finally, in Germany and Italy there have been recessions, in part a consequence of high interest rates caused by German reunification. This led to the high exchange rate from which Italy exited when it left the Exchange Rate Mechanism in 1993 and to which the Bundesbank has wedded Germany up to the time of writing. These latter conditions made German and, for a time, Italian firms even more uncompetitive than they had, in any case, become. Problems of this kind are taken extremely seriously in both countries, especially in the regional economies most affected. The small-firm sector is subject to special legislation and has a considerable array of both public and private sector support mechanisms. But an important part of the problem posed for leading small-firm dominated regional economies such as Emilia-Romagna and Baden-Württemberg is that the institutional infrastructure of business support mechanisms has itself become ill attuned to the needs of business. This has caused small businesses to look inward and, in the most advanced cases, seek to 'reinvent' themselves. The key driver of this process is the need to innovate in order to survive competitively.

Two examples from Baden-Württemberg may be taken as emblematic of this process. In the heart of the Black Forest, at Albstadt, Mettler-Toledo, a weighing-machine company, found itself in difficulties which only came to light when it became aware of the management toolkit known as lean production (Womack and Jones, 1994). Until 1989 it had operated on what were highly Taylorized principles with a complex management hierarchy and workshop division of labour. Mettler-Toledo has now dispensed with accountant-led purchasing which bloated in-house stock value to 50 per cent of turnover and led to unsatisfied customers and half-processed products being scrapped. It involved the work-force in designing new cost-control, inventory and marketing methods. Productivity and competitiveness have risen considerably. This is seen as a result of cost-targeting, project-based management, worker participation and a market rather than a production focus. As a result, turnover is now DM100 million (*cf.* DM40 million) and stocks are DM4–5 million, or 4–5 per cent of turnover (*cf.* DM20 million, or 50 per cent of turnover). Average product development time is now less than six months, whereas it was over two years. Some 30 per cent of turnover goes towards developing new products; 15–18 are in development. Manufacturing depth (in-house production) has been reduced to 40 per cent, below the industry average of 42 per cent. The firm is in credit, and has been profit making since 1989, and productivity has increased greatly (Gassmann *et al.*, 1993). The twelve-member management group, which replaced a five-level management hierarchy, meets weekly and discusses everything with no minutes, no flip charts and no overhead projector. Above all, the managing director prides himself on not having sent a memo for five years. This is what Professor Warnecke, formerly of Fraunhofer-IPA in Stuttgart, calls the 'fractal factory', a concept taken from chaos theory. One key feature of the fractal nature of the new Mettler-Toledo is that it produces less and less in-house and assembles more and more bought-in componentry. It has thus become an SME leader of a flotilla of component and service suppliers with whom network relationships have had to become much stronger then before.

If lean production reduces production costs, what about the impact upon skills, work organization and worker participation? Too many *mittelstand* (medium-sized) firms are, despite the mythology, more hierarchical, less open or transparent, have less frequent consultation and a weaker information flow than their Japanese competitors. The skill division of labour and power of the *meister* (foremen) reinforce the hierarchical tendency and undermine the requirement for meeting new demands of flexibility and multi-skilling. Once again, the Mettler-Toledo example points the way forward. The cornerstones of the new policy towards the production process are self-management, individual responsibility based on information, integrated functions (no more Taylorism), open communication, and organization based on trust (see also Chapter 3).

Each worker would be able to conduct many more work tasks. Teams of workers should work on simultaneous product development instead of being compartmentalized. Employee desire to work well should be capitalized upon by recognition of the fact that people are the only source of creativity. In return flexi-time and working elasticity can be achieved.

The concept of the fractal factory can also be applied to Getrag, a leading German firm of automotive gearbox manufacturers based in Rosenberg, Ludwigsburg and Oberstenfeld. It is a key supplier to BMW and does development work for Audi, Opel, GM and Mitsubishi. In 1991 turnover was DM1 billion but by 1993 it was down to DM700 million – Rosenberg employs 320 people, 80–85 per cent of them skilled workers. It too has recently 'reinvented' itself, in the following ways:

- Extending capacity.   To raise productivity at a time when demand was high the Rosenberg plant's size was doubled and the firm moved from two to three shifts. Accordingly production is now 24 hours a day, five days a week (relatively high for Germany). Machine use is 85 per cent, the residue being setting-up and downtime.
- New philosophy.   Since 1991, under pressure from BMW, the POTZ system of production optimization was transferred from BMW to Getrag. Under the slogan 'we do it better' the financial results of the optimized production are split 50:50 between customer and supplier.
- New company hierarchy.   Based on the concept of 'people at the centre' the influence of skilled workers has increased. In this flattened organization where work-teams have greater responsibility the following happens:
  (a) team spokesperson is elected every six months and receives a higher wage

(b) team discussions occur monthly for up to one and a half hours, outside shift-time but inside working hours

(c) team members increasingly influence equipment-purchasing decisions.

■   Skills.   Internal and external training in the new system was provided and teams have begun demanding more. Difficulties are experienced, especially at Ludwigsburg where 60 per cent of the workforce are foreign and language problems exist. The new system demands highly skilled, highly articulate employees.

Amongst the observed results of these changes are the following. Wage levels have, on balance, improved but at some cost to Swabian lifestyles due to the introduction of the night shift. In economic terms the doubling of capacity and flat-out working has reduced plant flexibility. In an upturn production levels could only increase by further expansion or subcontracting. But there have been enormous increases in efficiency and productivity due to the greater motivation of skilled workers consequent upon their greater responsibility and reductions in lost time (sickness, etc.), which has been reduced by half to only 4 per cent. Manufacturing time has been reduced from five weeks to ten days, a huge productivity gain. Employment has increased by 150 since 1990 to the present 320 employees, many of whom are below 30 years of age.

This is a good example of the fractal factory in the following senses: first, it is a response to turbulence, increased uncertainty and a decline in performance experienced both generically in the industrial sector, and by the individual firm. Second, it is not an isolated or lone response, but one which is universal to the Getrag group's three plants. Third, it is integrated with the changing requirements of a key customer (BMW) but consistent with changing demands for lean production from other automotive customers. Fourth, it is inclusive and empowering with regard to the workforce yet clearly successful in terms of enhancing economic efficiency. Fifth, it enables a small-medium or *mittelstand* firm to remain small, rather than being merged or acquired or in some way concentrated.

REGIONAL NETWORK INFRASTRUCTURE AND DISTRICT NEEDS

The pressures in Italy, and particularly its leading small-firm region of Emilia-Romagna, are comparable in respect of heightened competitiveness within the European Single Market, global competition from Asian newly industrializing economies and recession. But Italy's government machinery has had to change more than that of Germany. With the ending of the Cold War Italy's bulwark role against the Soviet bloc countries has evaporated and with it the effectively 'single party state' which had governed the country since 1945. In the 1994 general election two contradictory political events have posed problems for regional industrial policy. On the one hand a far-right government led by Forza Italia and its prime minister Berlusconi gained power in Rome, supported by neo-fascists. Emilia-Romagna is a stronghold of PDS (formerly the Italian Communist Party: PCI). But the Northern League is a coalition partner of Berlusconi, right-wing too, but regionalist. Emilia-Romagna has traditionally been left-wing, moderately regionalist but seeking to pursue a distinctive regional industrial policy within a unified state.

At present, therefore, it seems highly likely that the Italian regions will be given greater responsibilities by Rome than they have hitherto enjoyed. But these will have to be tempered by the requirements that budgets will have to be spent parsimoniously and that business should manage business affairs. The Emilia-Romagna government thus has to walk a narrow line most carefully. Even before the advent of the Berlusconi government, regional industrial pressures were building up, in Emilia-Romagna, against the judicious interventionary posture of support that the regional government, through its development agency, ERVET, had taken. Innovative business services centres had been established and these were argued by the industrial association Confindustria and the chambers of commerce in Emilia-Romagna to constitute unfair competition to their services and those of private consultants. The fact that such services were not being provided before the regional government set them up is, argues ERVET, conveniently overlooked in this analysis.

In any case, for a four-year period up to spring 1994 the regional government had wrestled with the question of how to reform its regional industrial policy in ways which satisfied business interests, but crucially without undermining the effective, collaborative basis upon which much of the small-firm business sector had successfully developed its capacity for competitiveness over the preceding three decades.

In addition there was the question of how to maintain a policy, hence a political role, during a period when the siren-call was one which forecast the demise of the districts, the concentration of small firms and the acquisition of leading firms by outside capital as the only means of survival for business in the barrier-free EU.

The approach that has now been adopted by ERVET is that funding for business support must be conducted as a project-based competitive tendering process. In this way excellent business support service centres will be likely to retain their funding while those that have performed suboptimally are more likely to lose it. Cash saved in the latter exercise is then conceivably available to fund further innovative projects.

Amongst the latter could be projects which meet the widely perceived and agreed need for Emilian small firms, like those in Baden-Württemberg, *themselves* to become more innovative. Not least, this is expected to require that ways be found for small firms to engage in collaborative research projects with universities or research institutes. There is little experience of direct university–industry research collaboration in Italy generally, because until 1992 it was constitutionally unacceptable. A change of law has since made it possible, but the learning curve even for large, let alone small, enterprises is a steep one. Links with research institutes are stronger, even for Emilian small business. A successful collaboration between CITER, the textiles innovation centre at Carpi, near Bologna, and ENEA, the energy research institute, resulted in an innovative CAD-CAM system for knitwear firms, now widely marketed both inside and outside Italy.

Of great interest to the project of assisting small-firm competitiveness without losing the collaborative or networking philosophy that underpins the industrial district model of flexible specialization through clever niche-marketing is the recent research reported by the Emilia-Romagna regional Department of Industry (Franchi, 1994). The Department of Industry asked the question: what has been going on in the industrial districts during the past three or four years, especially the recent years of economic recession? For example had there been, as the soothsayers had been foretelling, an increase in the hierarchization of firms in the districts? Were there strong signs of concentration of ownership? Had relationships with the economic world outside the localized districts changed? Were recent developments still compatible with the policy and political goal of social integration rather than social polarization?

The main conclusions of the research are as follows. First, firms in industrial districts performed better in terms of employment and wages than firms in the same sector not located in districts. Although it is not stated, it can be assumed that turnover performance was also better. Second, all districts increased the volume of their operations occurring outside the district, even outside the region, seeking lower labour costs. In Carpi, 1988–92 offshore production (i.e. outside Italy) increased from 7 to 9 per cent of total turnover. Third, upstream and downstream diversification by district firms was only marginal, and innovation was limited. Fourth, vertical integration occurred to a limited extent as some, but relatively few, multinationals acquired district-based firms. Fifth, formation of groups of independent small firms was much the most common form of integration (or quasi-integration) between firms within the districts. Sixth, companies employing around 20 people grew strongly while those employing five or less showed a higher death rate than birth rate. Seventh, there was a radical change in the management of the small firms employing up to 20 or so persons. A minimum efficient size seems to have emerged below which organizational demands upon the contemporary firms cannot be adequately satisfied.

In conclusion, small firms in industrial districts gain substantially from operating in a collaborative, networked business milieu. They have been able to offer better levels of employment, better wage levels and, for the larger small enterprises, higher rates of growth than firms in the same industry not operating in a district-type setting. Firms in districts have, like large companies, sought and found suppliers elsewhere in Italy and overseas. Lower labour costs have been the main incentive for doing this. Small firms in districts have been able to acquire some of the advantages of scale without losing the benefits of scope, by forming groups of different size and type.

Thus, in both regions there is evidence of competitiveness problems which are, nevertheless, being confronted in new, often increasingly collaborative ways. The imperative of enhancing competitiveness is not producing the response of greater and greater isolationism or 'rugged individualism' but a reasoned and sensible approach in which, where a problem shared means a problem halved, that option is taken. In the process the small firm survives and gains in efficiency and effectiveness.

CONCLUSIONS

There are three interlinked conclusions to be drawn from this limited account of recent developments in regional industrial practice. Before summarizing these it is important to restate two key factors which set the parameters within which these changes operate and to remind ourselves of a third unfolding, generic element which constitutes a key response. First, *globalization*, particularly in the sense of a heightened capacity for the interpenetration of domestic markets by foreign producers, is a key, even defining parameter of the present economic conjuncture. In tandem with deregulation it creates enormous uncertainty of the kind that leaves firms in a situation where, because they do not know what to do, doing anything is better than doing nothing. This creates a mentality which Sabel (1994) has referred to as 'bootstrapping reform' among firms, unions and regional governments.

A second key parameter of the present turbulent context is the sense, amongst the alert firms and institutions, that somehow *innovation* is the key to survival. By innovation is meant not only product or process innovation but managerial, organizational and cultural innovation. This is why the two German examples were characterized as seeking to reinvent themselves. This follows the theme developed by Goss *et al.* (1993) that 'change is not enough' and firms must engage in 'heroic acts' to reinvent products, processes and culture not once but permanently to maintain competitive advantage. Some contexts are better than others in which to achieve this. The innovative firm must constantly interact with its environment to function successfully, but so must the innovative region.

Networking is one name given to such a form of interactive exchange, learning, trust-building, partnering and empowering practice. If Baden-Württemberg and Emilia-Romagna have a comparative (competitive) advantage, it lies precisely in the rich milieu of other firms, institutions and informed personnel which constitutes their regional economies. Through the information flows made possible by the innovative regional business infrastructure found in the regions, firms are able to engage in rapid response to turbulent conditions. Even when the 'institutional reflexivity' (Cooke, 1995), in which the public and private elements of the network architecture are engaged, is out of synchronization with business needs, there is enough useful information flowing informally for firms to be able to experiment with their own *bootstrapping* solutions. These then become demonstration models for the rest.

So, the three key findings of this study are, first, that there is quite strong support for the ideas of Ohmae (1993), de Vet (1993) and others that globalization weakens the economic sovereignty of the traditional nation-state (see also Held, 1991, on the 'hollowing out' of the nation-state) and raises the salience of the *region state* in economic terms. As the region state interacts increasingly with its economic base, it helps it seek competitive advantage through policy support instruments, institution building and information supply, which contribute to its innovation capacity. There is an inevitable tendency towards regional economic specialization built into this process which can logically be expected to be reinforced by locational decisions of globalizing firms, too.

Then, second, the region state operates most effectively where there is a *cluster* or clusters (Porter, 1990) of firms in dynamic interaction with each other present in the regional economy. These clusters can be predominantly laterally organized as in the case of Italian industrial districts, or they can be vertically structured as in the case of supplier clubs or informal groupings of subcontractors seeking to improve their capacity to meet the requirements of a large customer firm as happens in Baden-Württemberg or Wales. Networks of firms operating in relatively open environments can be inclusive towards public or quasi-public agencies that have a useful function to contribute to their innovative and competitive imperatives.

Last, and this is very clear in the case of the German exemplar firms, less transparently so in the case of Emilian industrial districts, but consistent with their recent experience of recession, at the *firm* level the behaviour most appropriate to the contemporary context is that described above as emulating the *fractal factory*. Chaos theory tells us that, amongst other things, small events can have large-scale and unpredictable effects. The present economic environment is turbulent, uncertain and unpredictable. Global firms are not necessarily clearer about how and in which direction to proceed than smaller ones. The desired response is non-isolationist, interactive, participatory, non-hierarchical, flexible, inclusive and empowering. In other words, both small and larger firms are confronted with the requirement to show they are capable of 'thriving on chaos'.

FURTHER READING

Amin, A., Thrift, N. (eds) 1994 *Globalization, institutions and regional development*. Oxford University Press, Oxford.

Bergman, E., Mair, F., Tödtling, F. (eds) 1992 *Regions reconsidered*. Mansell, London.

Cooke, P., Morgan, K. 1996 *The collective entrepreneur: strategies for corporate and regional renewal*. Oxford University Press, Oxford.

Getimis, P., Kafkalas, G. (eds) 1993 *Urban and regional development in the new Europe*. Topos, Athens.

Harrison, B. 1994 *Lean and mean: the changing landscape of corporate power in the age of flexibility*. Basic Books, New York.

Leonardi, R. (ed.) 1993 *The regions and the European Community*. Frank Cass, London.

Leonardi, R., Nanetti, R. (eds) 1990 *The regions and European integration: the case of Emilia-Romagna*. Francis Pinter, London.

Leonardi, R., Nanetti, R. (eds) 1994 *Regional development in a modern European economy: the case of Tuscany*. Francis Pinter, London.

Putnam, R. 1993 *Making democracy work*. Princeton University Press, Princeton, NJ.

CHAPTER 16

PRODUCER SERVICES AND COMPETITION FROM OFFSHORE:
US data entry and banking

Marie Howland

One component of the emerging global economy is the offshore movement of services jobs from North America, mainland Europe, the UK, and the wealthy Asian countries to the Third World. While the shift is small relative to service trade flows between the developed countries and the offshore movement of manufacturing, the phenomenon is of growing importance in the global economy and worth examining for several reasons. First, the offshore flow of jobs can have discernible and adverse ramifications for competing regions and labour pools in the core countries. The regions that compete most directly with offshore sites will be near-term losers in the international competition for jobs. Second, the shift of services is an important source of job creation for some Third World countries. For example, attraction of offshore services is the cornerstone of development policy in Jamaica, Barbados and the Cayman Islands, and an important development strategy for Ireland, the Philippines and Thailand as well. Finally, the emergent offshore movement of back-office and now software development jobs is reminiscent of the movement of manufacturing employment in earlier decades. Does the offshore movement of services signal a looming lack of national competitiveness in services in the core countries?

The purpose of this chapter is to examine the global locational tendencies of two producer services, computer services and banking. The chapter addresses the magnitude and reasons for the offshore movement of computer and banking services, and identifies which regions in the core countries, central cities, suburbs or rural areas compete most directly with offshore sites. Finally, based on an analysis of industry and technological change, the chapter identifies which regions within core countries will be net winners and losers in the emerging global economy.

The emphasis is on the United States, and the offshore movement of service jobs to the Caribbean, the major recipient of data entry and banking services from the US. However, with the worldwide spread of technology and management strategies, the patterns described are also applicable to the relationships between the industrialized countries of Great Britain, Europe and Asia, and the less developed economies of Asia, Africa, Latin America and Europe.

Computer services and banking were selected because of their high-profile globalization. The potential for the offshore movement of data entry tasks captured national attention in the US when American Airlines closed its data processing facility in Tulsa, Oklahoma, in 1984 and moved 500 jobs to Barbados. Ireland, China and the Philippines, as well as the Caribbean, are major centres of offshore data entry. In the case of banking, more than 27 per cent of cross-border bank and non-bank loans now pass through offshore banks (*International Financial Statistics Yearbook*, 1990).

Computer services and banking are sophisticated, non-routine services that, for the most part, require face-to-face communication to transfer non-tangible products. They require access to specialized, knowledge-intensive inputs, and proximity to a diverse labour pool. These so-called advanced services are, therefore, tightly anchored to the urban centres of the developed world. When pulled across international borders, it is generally to gain access to markets, not to reduce production costs. Even offshore banking is a highly market-oriented activity, as demonstrated by its evolution in countries, such as the Cayman Islands, close to the industrialized economies, within the same time zone as the world's financial centres. Further, a large share of 'offshore' banking transactions are conducted face-to-face in the core country, while fund transfers are merely 'booked' offshore.

In contrast, the output of the data entry industry, a subset of computer services, is a tangible, permanent product that can be shipped across space. This allows the separation of consumption from production, frees data entry activities from the tight spatial attachment to customers, and permits the minimization of production costs in the location decision.

Computer services and banking are alike in their continued concentration in the urban centres of the developed world and their market-driven location decisions. However, their reasons for moving offshore differ. Data entry is moved offshore to cut production costs; banking services are conducted offshore to avoid the regulatory constraints and taxes of the core countries. The regions that will be net losers in the core countries also differ for the two industries. Offshore data entry competes directly with rural-based operations in the US and Great Britain, and offshore banking competes with central city banking.

The spatial division of labour model (SDL) is a widely adopted framework for analysing the global shift of manufacturing. This model is used as a starting point for analysing the intra- and international movement of computer services and banking. In the SDL model, production costs, especially international labour costs, drive location decisions. A firm's ability to manage far-flung operations, telecommunications capabilities and transportation costs influence the range of locations a firm will consider for production. Complex, non-routine tasks are conducted in the urban core of the developed world, to be near educated and skilled labour, specialized inputs and customers. Products or production processes that are standardized and require little labour skill, that have high elasticities of demand so that lower prices result in larger markets, and that are relatively inexpensive to transport are likely candidates for assembly offshore (Lipietz, 1982; Storper and Walker, 1984; Sayers, 1986; Scott, 1988b). The SDL model has been applied to services by Castells (1993) who argues that modern telecommunications and computers allow the back rooms of offices to move to remote geographical locations in pursuit of low labour costs (Willmore, 1995). The following cases are considered in the context of the SDL model.

COMPUTER SERVICES

National locational trends

United States computer services employment grew nearly 25 per cent between 1986 and 1990. Computer services are highly and increasingly concentrated in the largest cities, of 1 million population and above (see Figure 16.1). The following section combines business interviews and national-level data to describe why.

Industry interviews indicate that evolving computer services 'products' increasingly require greater rather than less intense client contacts. With the

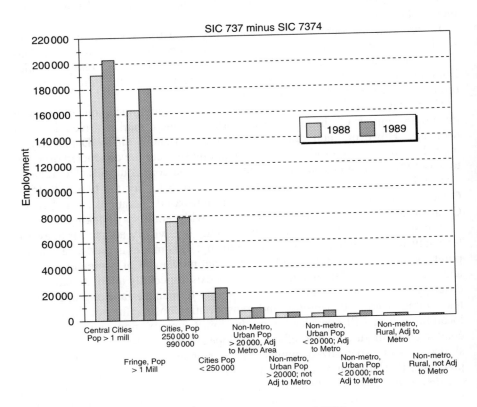

Figure 16.1   Advanced computer services, US, 1988 and 1989

exception of data entry, computer services firms are moving towards vertical specialization, or the offering of a wider range of specialized services to existing and new customers; increased provision of sophisticated client-specific computer solutions to issues of company management, inventory control, and product delivery; and rapid development and marketing of software products. All are activities that require intensive company–client interaction. Many of the more routine tasks in this sector have been made obsolete by the general availability of personal computers and compatible software, widely available databases, and optical scanners.

Speculation that the revolution in communications technologies will make cities obsolete (Stanback and Noyelle, 1982; Drucker, 1989) has turned out to be inaccurate or, at least, premature. Across the board, the trend is towards more specialized services, increasing skill requirements, and firm diversification, which anchor computer services firms to markets and large urban areas even more than in the past.

Several concrete examples are illustrative. Automated Data Processing (ADP), the US's largest data processing company, receives client time sheets by courier or via telephone lines into the ADP computers. ADP processes the information and prints employee pay cheques, which are then delivered by courier to large and small customers. Since products are delivered in hard copy, proximity to markets is still a critical determinant of location. On-site equipment for printing cheques is too expensive for individual employers to purchase. However, as the price of this technology drops, printing could eventually be done at the customer's location, reducing the pull between ADP and its customers. Although a reduction in the cost of cheque printing technologies would free ADP from its tight attachment to the urban market, firm diversification offsets any such tendency.

ADP is moving away from simple data processing and towards developing solutions to tax and employment planning. Developing client-specific products requires intense face-to-face contacts to identify the client issues, design the products, and assist with implementation. Proximity to clients is becoming increasingly important for ADP branches. Although providing different products, the stories for CSC and General Electric's computer services branch were similar. CSC is a major computer services software designer conducting work for the US Department of Defense, among other clients. For large contracts, CSC will open a new branch and pay to move highly skilled employees near a prominent customer. General Electric (GE) of Rockville, Maryland, began as a computer time-sharing company. With the introduction of personal computers in the early 1980s, GE and other time-sharing companies have diversified into specialized software and computer systems development. The trade journals confirm that these patterns are typical across the industry (Fersko-Weiss, 1987; United States Congress, 1987). The implication for the near-term location of computer services activities is clear. This is an industry with a tight attachment to urban areas, and not one that is sending large amounts of work to either rural America or offshore.

Data entry and processing services, Standard Industrial Code (SIC) 7374, are the least knowledge-intensive activities within the computer services industry (SIC 737). Yet even with their low skill level, data entry and processing turn out to be highly concentrated in the large central cities (Figure 16.2 and Table 16.1).[1]

Offshore movement of computer services

With few exceptions, offshore computer services operations are the most repetitious aspect of computer services work – data entry. Barbados, Jamaica, St Lucia, Ireland, the Philippines, Taiwan, Sri Lanka and China are all now attracting data entry jobs from the US and mainland Europe.

Barbados attracted eleven data entry operations in the last decade. Saztec, a

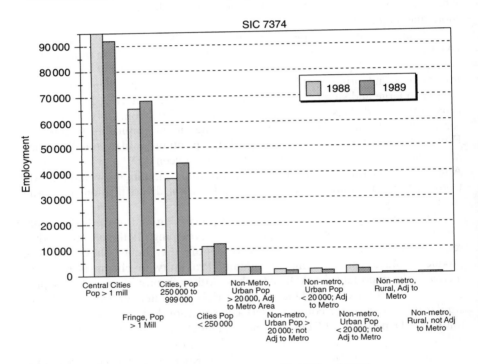

Figure 16.2   Data entry and processing services, US, 1988 and 1989

[1] The analysis is limited to the two years for which Enhanced County Business Patterns data are available (1989 and earlier) and for which the four-digit industry data are consistent (1988 and later). The Enhanced County Business Patterns use an algorithm to assign missing data to industry and county categories. Missing data are a problem for many rural counties where enterprise populations are low, and therefore information is suppressed to keep confidentiality. For a more detailed description, see Glasmeier and Howland (1995).

Table 16.1 Employment in computer services and data entry services, 1988 and 1989, and per cent change, 1988 to 1989

	Computer services (737)			Data entry and processing services (7374)			All other computer services (737–7374)		
	1988	1989	Per cent change 1988–89	1988	1989	Per cent change 1988–89	1988	1989	Per cent change 1988–89
Central cities, pop. > 1 million	285025	294230	3.2	94885	91452	−3.7	190140	202778	6.4
Fringe counties, pop. > 1 million	227267	248899	9.1	64966	68602	5.4	162301	180297	10.5
Cities, pop. 250000 to 999000	114353	121627	6.2	38994	43310	10.6	75409	78317	3.8
Cities, pop. < 250000	30427	34886	13.7	10371	11344	9.0	20056	23542	16.0
Non-metro counties, urban pop. > 20000, adj. to metro county	6839	8020	15.9	2336	2400	2.6	4501	5620	22.1
Non-metro counties, urban pop. > 20000, not adj. to metro county	4005	3839	−4.2	1677	1379	−19.5	2238	2460	5.5
Non-metro counties, urban pop. < 20000, adj. to metro county	3486	3741	7.1	1544	1400	−9.8	1942	2341	18.6

Table 16.1 (cont.)

	Computer services (737)			Data entry and processing services (7374)			All other computer services (737–7374)		
	1988	1989	Per cent change 1988–89	1988	1989	Per cent change 1988–89	1988	1989	Per cent change 1988–89
Non-metro counties, urban pop. <20000, not adj. to metro county	4395	4248	–3.4	2554	2056	–21.6	1841	2192	17.4
Non-metro counties, completely rural, adj. to metro county	117	1187	6.1	233	246	5.4	884	941	6.3
Non-metro counties, completely rural, not adj. to metro county	673	798	17.0	301	344	13.3	372	454	19.9
Total	677587	721475	6.3	217813	222533	2.1	498942	459774	8.2

Notes: Computer services = SIC 737, Data entry and processing services = SIC 7374. 1989 is the last year for which enhanced data are available. The enhanced data are required to analyse data at the 3-digit and 4-digit level of industry detail, otherwise data suppression in the rural counties is too great to analyse geographical trends. Per cent change is calculated as 100 (year 2 – year 1)½ (year 2 + year 1).

Source: Enhanced County Business Patterns, 1988 and 1989, using the 1988 Beale Codes.

Kansas-based data entry company, has a labour force of 900 in the Philippines (Skinner, 1994). Between 1980 and 1985, 40 companies in the US, Japan and the UK sent their data entry work overseas (Beers, 1987). Table 16.2 reports data entry and processing employment totals for the largest Caribbean centres of offshore data entry and processing, and compares the totals with US employment.

While there is variation across firms, most information to be translated into machine-readable form is delivered offshore in hard copy by air. The mostly female labour force manually keys in and verifies information at computer workstations. The completed jobs are then returned by telephone line or satellite to the client or on magnetic tape or disk via private courier, US Mail or Federal Express. Some examples of work carried out at both offshore operations of American firms and foreign-owned data entry firms include the keying in of publishers' mailing lists, doctors' patient records, appliance warranty information, medical claim forms, credit card receipts, databases, book manuscripts, coding abstracting and indexing, database creation and management, and legal depositions.

Reason for offshore work

Labour availability and low wages are the primary reasons for data entry to move offshore. The Office of Technology Assessment estimates that offshore wages range from one-fourth to one-fifth of US wages, with the lowest wages found in Asia (Ludlum, 1986). This ratio holds true when comparing foreign wages with rural US labour as well. Data entry operators in Barbados, for example, earn an average of $US2.55 an hour, compared with a current minimum of $US4.25 in rural areas of the United States. In the case of American Airlines, approximately 900 pounds of used airline tickets are delivered daily by air to Caribbean Data Services, an American Airlines subsidiary in Barbados. Employees sort the tickets and enter information into computer terminals. American Airlines estimates that, with all costs included, salaries are about $US6.00 an hour less in Barbados than in the US. The company estimated a $US3.5 million saving per year due to the move (Beers, 1987).

Table 16.2   Offshore data entry and processing employment in the Caribbean

	Number of firms, 1993	Number of employees, 1993
Barbados[a]	11	2200
Jamaica	29	3299
St Lucia	3	88
United States[b]		217813

[a]Data from Barbados Industrial Development Corporation for March 1995.
[b]US data for 1989.

Source: Willmore (1993).

Another equally important advantage of offshore operations over a competing rural American location is the availability of labour. Barbados contains large pools of unemployed, underemployed and literate labour. Therefore, a single plant is not constrained from achieving technological economies of scale. One American firm operating in Barbados operates in several rural communities in the United States as well. In recent years, attempts to expand in those rural locations resulted in the tapping of a poorly educated, less reliable labour pool. Even allowing for the relatively wider commuting ranges for rural workers, managers of data entry facilities in rural areas of the US find that the labour pool is exhausted relatively quickly. Expansions then require a new facility in another town, with all the inherent expenses of duplicating infrastructure.

Verdicts on the quality of labour are mixed. All offshore managers of US-headquartered firms in Barbados concurred that their foreign workers are as reliable and accurate as the best rural workers in the US. In contrast, an assessment of Jamaica and St Lucia found that expansion of the data processing and entry industry was supply-constrained (Skinner, 1994). Both Barbados and Jamaica have high literacy rates. The illiteracy rate in Barbados is only 0.7 per cent, lower than that of the US.[2] The illiteracy rate in Jamaica is 3.9 percent (Pelzman and Schoepfle, 1988).

Although English-speaking countries have an advantage, China is also providing data entry services. The lack of minimum wage laws and less stringent worker safety restrictions are attractions for firms moving operations overseas. The more lenient environmental regulations are not as much an issue for the 'cleaner' service industries as for manufacturing, but socialized health benefits further reduce offshore costs to business.

Investments in telecommunications

Attracting back-office jobs from the US is part of a conscious development programme in Barbados, Jamaica and St Lucia. Advanced telecommunications technologies are critical for attracting routine services such as data entry and telemarketing. In 1988, a joint venture between ATT, Cable and Wireless plc of the United Kingdom, and Telecommunications of Jamaica invested $8 million to install image transmitters and satellite transmission at Montego Bay, Jamaica (Kuzela, 1987; Thurston, 1990). The station now offers digital international long-distance, 0800 number services, and switched and dedicated high-speed data circuits up to 1.5 megabytes. Barbados External Telecommunications (BET) provides direct access to the global space communications system via earth station to satellite, and a microwave link to communications networks to the US and the Atlantic underwater cables. BET also leases fibre optic dedicated lines with digital switching to companies that require continuously available circuits,

---

[2] Literacy rates are not collected in the US. One measure is the percentage of the population with less than five years of schooling; in 1987, for rural areas this was 2.6 per cent (United States Department of Commerce, 1988).

such as data entry companies. While only a few of the local companies currently take advantage of returning data by telecommunications channels, lack of telecommunications access is not a barrier to further growth. These communications links are quickly surpassing the links available between urban and rural regions of the United States and further threaten the ability of rural areas to hold on to data entry jobs. In 1989, the Jamaica Digiport International (JDI) opened to provide low-cost satellite communications for data processing and telemarketing. JDI offers residents speeds of 9600 bits per second and rates as low as $US0.24 per minute for calls to the US (Willmore, 1993).

Although the offshore movement of data entry threatens domestic, particularly rural, US data entry jobs, it is only one threat. Optical scanning and point of transaction data entry are also eroding domestic job opportunities in data entry.

Barcoding and optical scanning

Optical scanning permits the sidestepping of manual data entry entirely. Innovation in barcoding technology has already eliminated the need for vast numbers of manual data entry workers. Nonetheless, there are still tasks that do not lend themselves to barcode scanning.

Optical Character Recognition (OCR) technologies permit the mechanical translation of documents into machine-readable form. However, the technology, in its current configuration, has limitations. Scanning documents with numerous font changes, small or decorative typefaces, dirty images and misaligned pages results in high error rates. Further, scanning technologies are limited in their ability to read handwritten entries. Machines with Intelligent Character Recognition (ICR) are designed to read handwritten documents, but error rates currently run at about 50%. This error rate is too high to make ICR use economically feasible. Experts suggest, barring an unforeseen technological breakthrough, that accurate machine scanning of handwritten documents will not be available until the end of the decade. Third, scanning technology is expensive and in many cases must be designed specifically to read the document being entered. Because most data entry jobs are short-term contracts, rarely does one job justify the cost of a specially designed scanner. Commercial scanning equipment costs in excess of $US25000 for both hardware and software.[3] Appalachian Computer Services (ACS) has a long-running contract with a number of banks to translate credit card receipts into machine-readable form. The scanner reads customers' credit card numbers, but the amount purchased and the date, which are handwritten, are keypunched manually. As long as optical character recognition technologies are limited to typeset documents, and even then not all typed documents, there will continue to be a market niche, albeit a smaller one, for manual data entry.

---

[3] Telephone interview with Haley Collins, Xerox Imaging Systems.

Point-of-transaction data entry

Increasingly, information is entered into machine-readable form at the point of transaction, displacing the demand for specialized key-entry workers altogether. For example, merchants and service providers are moving towards credit card transactions where the information is entered into the computer at the point of sale. Insurance underwriters now write and sell policies and enter information directly into the computer, eliminating data entry worker positions (Baran, 1985). Doctors are submitting medical insurance claims on computer disks, many courts have switched to recording legal cases directly into computer-decipherable form, and book manuscripts are received from authors in machine-readable form.

While these changes reduce the demand for manual key entry, the demand for computer-readable data is growing as information flows and computer use expand into new frontiers. The current net impact is slower employment growth in data entry and processing than in the rest of the computer services industry (see Table 16.1). Therefore, in the long run, the need for data entry workers will most likely decline. As one industry official put it, data entry is an industry 'dying on the increase' (Skinner, 1994).

Implications for the domestic economy

While not responsible for a dramatic loss of US jobs, the offshore movement of data entry work threatens the well-being of selected rural communities and low-wage workers. Rural data entry firms are often located in remote locations. Among the rural businesses interviewed for this study, ACS is a two-hour drive out of Lexington, Kentucky; TDEC is situated in Oakland, Maryland, approximately $3\frac{1}{2}$ hours from Washington, DC; and Highland Data is in Blue Grass, Virginia, approximately $2\frac{1}{2}$ hours from Roanoke in the Allegheny Mountains. These are not small operations. ACS is the largest domestic data entry firm, with 1800 employees in 1991 and steady subsequent growth. All of the above firms employ more than 50 workers in each of their rural facilities.

While labour costs in Third World countries are substantially lower than rural wages in the US, at this point rural data entry firms still hold a competitive market niche for quick turnaround jobs. The quickest turnaround currently possible from the Caribbean is 48 hours. Rural US sites can return data in 12 hours.

A second market niche for rural operations in the more developed countries combines some intellectual processing and knowledge of Western cultures combined with data entry. For example, a job for the British Broadcasting Corporation cataloguing its music library was allocated to the Philippines. The result was unsatisfactory, as workers in the Philippines were unable to distinguish between song titles and authors. The work was shifted back onshore to a branch of Saztec in Ardrossan, Scotland. This rural onshore branch justifies the higher salaries by combining indexing and bibliographic reference tasks with data entry. The fact remains, however, that while overall growth is positive, offshore data entry operations pose a serious threat to rural operations in the industrialized countries. These interview findings are confirmed by the data, which show declines in data entry and processing services in three categories of rural county (see Table 16.1).

In the long run, innovations in imaging technology and massive investments in state-of-the-art telecommunications technologies threaten even the secure data capture market niches. At present, the delays and costs of transferring hard-copy information to overseas data entry sites curb the offshore movement of data entry work. Imaging technology that enables the quick, accurate and inexpensive transmission of pictures will shrink delays to the hours required to send an image, keypunch the data, and return the data on-line. High-speed imaging would also dramatically reduce document transport costs.

Currently, high-speed imaging technology is too costly for all but the larger data entry firms.[4] However, imaging equipment will follow the path of all other computer technologies: enhanced speed and quality accompanied by falling prices. Projections are that within the decade, high-speed document imaging will be feasible on a large scale. Once this occurs, one competitive advantage for rural firms – quick turnaround – will disappear.

Several of these firms are adjusting to the competitive challenge by purchasing branch operations in the Caribbean. In one case, documents are imaged to computer tape at the domestic rural site and the tapes are mailed offshore for keypunching. A second firm is purchasing imaging technology that will transmit 18000 pages every 24 hours to a branch in Jamaica. According to the vice president of this firm, the domestic operation could eventually become a document receiving and transmitting centre, with the major share of keypunching carried out in Jamaica. For firms adjusting to offshore competition by moving offshore themselves, the business may thrive, but the workers and communities left behind most likely will not.

BANKING

Banking is an industry that has experienced growth during the 1986 to 1990 period[5] (see Table 16.3), followed by large-scale employment declines since 1990. Retrenchment due to massive defaults on Third World loans, low-grade corporate or junk bonds, and bad real estate loans are, in part, responsible for the post-1990 employment losses. Intense competition for funds and markets from non-bank financial institutions and an often unpredictable regulatory environment have all contributed to the changing dynamics of banking practice, location

---

[4] Data entry is a competitive industry made up of many small firms. Owners of small firms view this cost as a barrier to technology adoption.
[5] 1990 is the last year for which employment data in banking by US county are available.

Table 16.3   Bank employment, 1986 to 1990

	Total employment		
	1986	1990	Per cent change[a]
Central cities, pop. > 1 million	911781	1149549	23.07
Fringe counties, pop. > 1 million	30535	44132	36.42
Cities, pop. 250000 to 999000	313406	403818	25.21
Cities, pop. < 250000	107548	135026	22.66
Non-metro counties, urban pop. > 20000, adj. to metro county	44324	54697	20.95
Non-metro counties, urban pop. > 20000, not adj. to metro county	33480	39276	15.93
Non-metro counties, urban pop. < 20000, adj. to metro county	67566	81429	18.61
Non-metro counties, urban pop. < 20000, not adj. to metro county	60043	79003	15.32
Non-metro counties, completely rural, adj. to metro county	6001	6257	4.18
Non-metro counties, completely rural, not adj. to metro county	10395	9342	−10.67
Total	1585079	1993529	22.83

[a]Calculated as in Table 16.1.

Source: County Business Patterns, 1986 and 1990. Rural–urban continuum codes for metropolitan and non-metropolitan counties, as of June 1993.

and overall employment. Banks are no longer sleepy gatherers of local deposits and dispensers of loans to local business. They now compete for funds in world markets and provide a wide range of financial services to households and businesses around the globe (see also Chapters 8 and 17).

Domestic banking: the national picture

In spite of prognostications to the contrary, there is every sign that even the most troubled of the large banks are recovering (*Economist*, 30 April 1994; *Wall Street Journal*, 31 January 1994, p. 1).[6] Faced with intense competitive challenges banks have cut costs, expanded markets and increased productivity. From 1990 to 1992, US domestic employment in banking fell by 46000 jobs. Full-time employment fell from 1.8 million in 1984 to 1.4 million in 1992, and more employees are engaged part-time. At the same time, information technology

[6] BancOne of Ohio reported profits of $US1.1 billion; NationsBank reported profits of $US1.5 billion, and Citibank reported profits of $US2.2 billion in 1993 (*Economist*, 30 April 1994).

spending rose from less than \$10 billion in 1984 to more than \$20 billion in 1993, and productivity increased from \$US7500 in revenues per employee to \$30000 in revenues per employee (*Economist* 30 April 1994, p. 25; NationsBank Annual Report, 1993, p. 9).

Functions we traditionally think of as banking are increasingly conducted outside the banking sector. Competition from non-bank financial institutions has eroded the once traditional monopoly position of banks in corporate and consumer lending and household and business savings. Corporate borrowers are bypassing banks and turning directly to capital markets. In 1981, approximately 40 per cent of corporate debt was in the form of bank loans. By 1992, corporations obtained only 30 per cent of their capital from banks (*Economist*, 30 April 1994). Consumers have also shifted away from bank debt.[7]

Moreover, activities taking place inside banks look less and less like traditional banking and include services that were once forbidden bank activities. In response to the loss of corporate and household customers, banks have expanded into other sources of revenue. In 1981, 76 per cent of American bank revenues came from lending. By 1992, only 58 per cent of bank revenues were from lending, with the remaining 42 per cent from less traditional sources such as securities trading, foreign exchange dealing and financial services. Banks now underwrite commercial paper, mortgage-backed securities, municipal revenue bonds, consumer instalment debt, securities, and insurance. Nearly 2000 banks operate discount stockbrokers and a handful run property brokers. Major banks are providing computer-based services that manage corporate risk, conduct corporate business overseas, and cut client payrolls by taking over financial functions (*Wall Street Journal*, 31 January 1994, p. 1). The exodus of major businesses from banks as a source of credit induced banks to seek out other customers such as smaller domestic companies, Third World countries and investment banking overseas, as well as to branch out into new product lines.

The banking picture is changing on the liability side of the balance sheet as well. Households and businesses, once dependent on banks as depositories for savings, now have a range of other options, such as mutual and money market funds. Large banks' funds that, in the past, came from the savings of local households, businesses and government have been superseded by the hundreds of billions of dollars banks now raise each year in domestic and international financial markets. Large banks raise funds through short-term highly liquid money market debt in world markets, directly competing with the short-term debt issued by governments and multinational firms. This expansion is an inevitable consequence of desire by the banks to have more funds than their local depositor base can provide.

---

[7] For example, a number of manufacturing and retail companies now operate consumer credit finance arms. Examples include General Electric's GE Capital Services, General Motors' GMAC, Westinghouse's Westinghouse Credit, Ford's Financial Services, Sears, and Marks and Spencer in Britain. These financial service activities compete with banks for consumer lending and personal investment planning.

Regulatory reform is also causing sweeping change and spatial restructuring in the banking industry. In the early 1980s, most states followed the lead of Maine and Alaska and permitted out-of-state banks. The growth of 'super regionals' such as BancOne and NationsBank is one result, followed by bank consolidations and the closing of smaller and more remote banks. The resulting losses of banking employment were already evident in the last years of the 1980s in the most remote US locations (see Table 16.3). These rural losses are the result of changes in telecommunications which permit rural residents access to urban banks through ATM and telephone lines, bank cost-cutting measures which led to closure of the smallest and often most remote facilities, a scaling back of functions carried out in the branches (Glasmeier and Howland, 1995), and the aforementioned changes which require location in higher-order cities. During the last period for which geographically detailed industry data are available (1990) banking employment showed its strongest growth in the metropolitan core. There were signs of regional weakness, in the central cities of the north-east where the economy was hard hit by cutbacks in defence, and in the state of Texas, hard hit by declining oil prices and widespread real estate bankruptcies (see Table 16.4). But, in general, banking continues its tight attachment to the largest cities with strong growth in the central cities but the strongest growth in the suburbs of the largest metropolitan regions (see also Chapter 17).

Strong metropolitan growth reflects banking's increased need for access to specialized services, face-to-face contacts with clients to negotiate individual contracts and agreements, and the need for a highly trained, flexible workforce. As banks expand into new activities, such as underwriting and trading in corporate debt, financial advice to clients, debt syndication, etc., bankers' tasks become more sophisticated, more knowledge-based and less routine.

Even in branches, employees are now more focused on the sales of financial products and the provision of non-routine transactions. For example, branches used to take loans from beginning to end, including filling in applications, calling the credit bureau, checking references, verifying employment and confirming income, calling back with a credit decision, and filling out the documents. Now centralized administrative centres prepare documents, and computers provide detailed information about a borrower's creditworthiness. Branch employees spend more time selling financial products and less time processing papers.

Previous observers of the spatial pattern of producer services employment hypothesized the concentration of headquarters in city centres, consumer and business banking in both centres and suburbs, and back-office functions in suburbs and rural areas (Stanback and Noyelle, 1982). Recent evidence does not support this theoretical model. There are no clear distinctions between the banking functions carried out in central city and suburban locations. For example, offices conducting complex, corporate strategic planning can be found in both city centres and suburbs.

Although there have been several high-profile moves, for example to South Dakota and to Frederick, Maryland, the evidence does not bear out the wholesale decentralization of back-office functions. Back-office functions are growing in

Table 16.4 Banking employment and employment change in the largest metropolitan areas, 1986 to 1990

| | Total employment | | |
	1986	1990	Per cent change[a]
New York, PMSA			
Central county	145560	126761	−13.77
Fringe counties	24089	27385	12.81
Los Angeles, CMSA			
Central county	64517	88402	31.24
Fringe counties	24863	39518	45.53
Chicago, PMSA			
Central county	56367	69580	20.98
Fringe counties	4808	6931	36.17
San Francisco, PMSA			
Central county	44568	30273	−38.19
Fringe counties	1286	6481	133.77
Philadelphia, PMSA			
Central county	16553	20450	21.06
Fringe counties	13616	22792	50.41
Detroit, PMSA			
Central county	15628	18608	14.41
Fringe counties	10695	14941	33.13
Boston, PMSA			
Central county	20498	19463	−5.18
Fringe counties	26851	37420	32.89
Washington, DC, PMSA			
Central county	6788	9723	35.55
Fringe counties	12117	25433	70.92
Dallas/Fort Worth, PMSA			
Central county	18141	21664	17.70
Fringe counties	2760	2476	−10.85
Houston, PMSA			
Central county	21322	22681	6.18
Fringe counties	1552	1415	−9.23

[a]Calculated as in Table 16.1.

Source: County Business Patterns, 1986 and 1990. PMSA = Primary Metropolitan Statistical Area. CMSA = Consolidated Metropolitan Statistical Area.

cities, as scanning technologies have reduced the labour involved in routine back-office credit card and data entry functions (see Table 16.1). The one-time search for the lowest cost labour no longer drives the location of many back-office functions. For example, after NationsBank acquired Maryland National Bank, it closed the cheque clearing, data entry facility in the Washington, DC, suburbs and relocated those activities to a lower cost, more mechanized facility in downtown Baltimore.[8]

The emergence of offshore banking

Like the growth in data processing and entry, the expansion in offshore banking in the Caribbean is the result of conscious economic development strategies. The Bahamas, Cayman Islands, Barbados and Bermuda, along with other European and Asian-oriented banking havens around the world, including Switzerland, Luxembourg, Gibraltar, Jersey, Madeira, and increasingly Ireland and Thailand, have adopted favourable tax laws and lax regulatory restrictions as part of a calculated strategy to attract banking activity. In general, offshore banking havens provide (1) freedom from regulation, (2) freedom from reserve requirements, (3) freedom from controls on interest rates, (4) freedom from or reductions in taxes on profits and interest income, (5) freedom from insurance fees, and (6) freedom from exchange controls. Numbered accounts provide a confidentiality that attracts deposits from politically unstable countries and illegally gained money, such as that earned in drug trafficking. Licence fees, legal costs and asset requirements are inconsequential when compared with branch start-ups in the core countries. Whereas a London establishment may cost as much as $1 million, exclusive of daily operations and overheads, one can set up in Montserrat or Antigua in a few days for a few thousand dollars (Blum, 1984). Finally, immigration laws encourage the hiring of middle and upper management from abroad.

Table 16.5 summarizes the share of non-bank and inter-bank loans that originate in offshore banking centres. Next to Switzerland,[9] the Cayman Islands is the largest offshore banking centre, with 5.4 per cent of all cross-border inter-bank and non-bank loans. While some banking in the Caribbean represents services to local residents and tourists, banking in these countries is primarily an export industry representing offshore branches of US and foreign banks serving US customers.

Implications for core countries

Although large in terms of cross-border activities and number of banks, offshore banking centres displace little core country employment. Many banks do not bother to set up an active offshore office; the operations are frequently little more than a brass plate and an address. Moreover, the actual financial negotiations and

---

[8] Interview with Rick Holmes, NationsBank, Bethesda, Maryland, May 1994.

[9] Switzerland can be considered a 'financial centre' rather than a tax haven. Fully 3 per cent of its labour force is in banking. Swiss-registered companies pay taxes, taxes are withheld on dividends and interest, and licensing procedures are strict. However, secrecy laws make Switzerland a sanctuary for tax evaders and capital flight (Blum, 1984). Data for Luxembourg were not reported separately from Belgium.

Table 16.5   Share of cross-border inter-bank and non-bank loans by residence of lending bank, and world total ($US billion)

	1980	1991
United States	11.0	9.2
Offshore market share	22.0	27.4
Switzerland	7.5	6.0
Bahamas	0	2.5
Cayman Islands[a]	4.6	5.4
Netherlands Antilles[a]	0.2	0.2
Panama	1.9	0
Others (Hong Kong, Kuwait, Philippines, Singapore, UAE, Bahrain)	7.6	13.3
Total for all countries ($US billion)	1855.5	7158.6

[a]Data for 1990; 1991 data not available.

Source: *International Financial Statistics Yearbook*, International Monetary Fund, vol. XLV, 1992, pp. 63, 65, 67, 69.

decisions often take place in the core country, with the loan merely booked offshore.

For example, the Cayman Islands has more telex machines per capita than any country in the world (Blum, 1984), and is the fourth largest banking centre in terms of the number of banks, with over 500 (Myers and Alberga, 1992). But only about 50 banks have an actual physical presence. In 1991, non-banks in the US borrowed $US278 billion from abroad, and about 45 per cent of these loans were booked through the Cayman Islands (McCauley and Seth, 1992). Yet, in 1993, banking employment totalled only 1272 employees (Cayman Islands, Department of Economic Development, personal correspondence, 1994). With approximately 330 banks and more than $US100 billion in Eurodollar assets (Blum, 1984), the Bahamas has only 1200 workers employed in banking (Bahamas, Department of Economic Development, personal correspondence, 1994).

In addition, unlike data entry, losses in US banking employment due to offshore competition do not affect the most disadvantaged US workers. Supplanted jobs are primarily middle and upper level professional tasks, which would be located in the urban centres. The more serious losses to the US are lost tax revenues, concealed profits, forgone community investments, and sheltered illegally gained funds. Estimates of these losses range from $US9 billion to $US40 billion annually (Blum, 1984, p. xv).

Future of offshore banking

Banking, like data entry, provides a tenuous base of employment for Third World countries. Offshore banking involves inconsequential investments in fixed capital stock, buildings and equipment, and with current communications technologies, bookings can be relocated to other countries instantaneously. Thus, when demand for offshore banking declines, due for example to regulatory reform in the core countries, the fall in offshore revenues and employment is rapid and precipitous. For example, in response to regulatory reform in the early 1980s, Bahamian banking assets declined from $US43 billion in 1981 to $US30 billion in 1985 (Khambata, 1986).

For a more recent example, prior to December 1990 Regulation D required 'a depository institution, a U.S. branch or agency of a foreign bank and an edge agreement corporation [to] maintain reserves [of 3 per cent] against its deposits and Eurocurrency liabilities.'[10] Loans booked through offshore branches could avoid meeting these requirements, and therefore lenders could avoid maintaining substantial funds in non-interest-bearing accounts. From 1983 to the end of 1990, loans booked offshore increased from $US37 billion to $US174 billion.[11] Once the Eurodollar reserve requirement was reduced to zero, the growth of offshore loans slowed to a crawl. Loans booked at shell branches in the Cayman Islands actually fell for the first time in 1991 (McCauley and Seth, 1992).

Because of secrecy provisions offshore banks are depots for illegally obtained money. The US and European countries exert continuous pressure on the Caribbean banking centres to verify and ensure the legality of their banking practices. In 1984, the US, the UK, and the Cayman Islands signed a treaty allowing the US access to financial information when there is proof of drug-related activities by customers (Khambata, 1986). Increasing pressure by the US to reduce the protection of drug money laundering and the relaxation of regulations in the US limit the attractiveness of the Caribbean as an offshore banking haven.

IMPLICATIONS FOR MODELS OF THE SPATIAL DIVISION OF LABOUR

The spatial division of labour (SDL) model is a common framework for analysing the offshore movement of manufacturing. These cases highlight the model's applicability and shortcomings for the analysis of advanced services.

The SDL model is most applicable to firms whose location decision is driven by the minimization of production costs. The location of most computer and banking service activities is driven by revenue maximization. Because of the non-tangible nature of the product and the unique and complex nature of the service transaction, access to markets in the US or abroad is the driving force in the location decisions of these firms (Thomas, 1994).

---

[10] Board of Directors of the Federal Reserve System, 'Regulation D, Reserve Requirements of Depository Institutions', 12 C.F.R. 204, and Federal Reserve Bank of New York, 'Reserve Requirements', Circular No. 10406, 4 December, 1990.
    [11] Although the actual origins of these loans were primarily Europe, Japan and Canada (McCauley and Seth, 1992).

Second, the SDL model hypothesizes a temporal pattern whereby products and production processes move from an innovation stage to a highly routinized and standardized phase. It is at this later phase that proximity to skilled labour is no longer a prerequisite and firms are free to spin off branches to low-wage regions. While this model provided great insights into the locational tendencies of textiles, electronics, apparel and other manufacturing, there is no indication that producer services will follow the same path. Rather, even in the instances where a tangible product, such as a software program, is produced, the industry shows every signs of becoming less routine and more specialized over time.

A third area where the SDL model falls short for understanding computer services and banking is that because service products are often unique, being individually tailored for a client, they are not price elastic. Without a market full of perfect substitutes, service firms do not feel the relentless pressure to minimize costs. Small reductions in production costs will not result in substantially larger markets.

Fourth, we find that with services, technology plays a more central role than the SDL model suggests. According to the SDL model communications technologies are critical in determining how far afield domestic production can spread. This applies best to our case of data entry and other back-office banking functions, where limits in technology constrain distance from the market. As long as work has to be shipped in hard copy, there is a limit to the speed with which offshore work can be sent and returned, and therefore a constraint on the type of work going overseas. However, contrary to the model, we find other instances where technology renders labour costs nearly irrelevant. When technology replaces labour, the spatial division of labour model becomes less applicable as labour costs are reduced to a small proportion of total firm costs.

The SDL model was developed with manufacturing industries in mind, and there are essential differences between the services and manufacturing sectors. Even where there are pockets of service activities, like data entry and back-office functions, that produce permanent, tangible products, services are inevitably more sensitive to technological change in telecommunications than are manufacturing firms. As long as raw materials have to be shipped to the production site, manufactured goods moved to markets, and goods transferred across international barriers, with all the attendant taxes, tariffs and red tape, the dispersal of manufacturing is constrained. Most services, in contrast, can be transmitted at very low cost across telephone lines, by satellite or microwave. Moreover, services do not face the same array of tax, surcharge and tariff barriers confronted by manufactured goods. For example, a computer disk carrying hours worth of data entry work is taxed at the US border at the same value as an empty disk. Software programs transmitted across international borders by facsimile machine, over the Internet or via satellite are not taxed at all. Therefore, when service products are not market oriented, are price elastic, and can be produced by lower cost labour abroad, the potential is for even more rapid and widespread decentralization than is the case for manufacturing.[12]

Finally, service activities require less capital investment than offshore manufacturing. From data entry to computer programming to banking, offshore capital investments are relatively small. Thus when the calculations of an optimal location changes, disinvestment in the offshore location has the potential to be more rapid than that of offshore manufacturing.

CONCLUSIONS

Recent data and interviews suggest five findings about the spatial tendencies of computer services and banking and their offshore movement. The offshore movement of banking, data entry, and to a limited extent software development has further integrated the Third World into the international economy. While the number of jobs lost from the core countries is small, the contributions to communities in the Third World and losses for rural communities dependent on data entry work are often significant.

However, the offshore movement of computer services and banking is not the only, or even the major, factor affecting the spatial reallocation of producer services. Both computer services and banking are increasingly concentrated in the largest metropolitan areas of the US, due to the expansion of unique, client-specific service 'products' requiring more intense face-to-face contacts with clients. The increasing skill level required of the labour force and use of specialized inputs make an urban location more important than ever. Furthermore, the elimination of many routine tasks because of scanning, barcoding, point-of-transaction data entry, widely available databases, and regulatory changes affecting the industry are reducing the use of lower-skilled labour. As a consequence, rural and offshore back-office locations will be less attractive. When these advanced services move offshore, it will increasingly be for reasons of access and proximity to markets, not to cut production costs. In spite of predictions that technological change in telecommunications is rendering urban areas obsolete, spatial propinquity continues to be the driving force in the location of most computer services and banking activities.

Finally, the tendencies for decentralization are limited to the borders of the metropolitan region, where employment continues to suburbanize. The distinction between the urban core and suburban nodes is disappearing. In a suburban location, firms are linked to clients and specialized service inputs through facsimile machines and teleconference calls, and still have the option of frequent face-to-face meetings when necessary.

---

[12] A contrary argument is made by Willmore, who claims firms are less likely to send their data entry and processing tasks offshore than their manufacturing because of the risk of lost records or data. 'A lost shirt or toy is not the same as a lost client ledger, medical claim, banking or insurance account' (Willmore, 1995, p. 3).

ACKNOWLEDGEMENTS

I am grateful to Kui Zhou for compiling the industry statistics, to Jessica Hanson and Angela Stewart for their research assistance, and to Melvin R. Levin and Peter Daniels for their comments on an earlier draft.

FURTHER READING

In addition to Peter Daniels' many books:

Glasmeier, K.A., Howland, M. 1995 *From combines to computers: rural development in the age of information technology*. State University of New York Press, New York.

Hamilton, J.M. 1990 *Entangling alliances: how the Third World shapes our lives*. Seven Locks Press, Cabin John, MD.

Henderson, J. 1990 *The globalization of high technology production*. Routledge, New York.

Hepworth, M. 1990 *Geography of the information economy*. Guilford Press, New York.

Hudson, H., Parker, E.B. 1990 Information gaps in rural America. *Telecommunications Policy* (June): 193–205.

Johns, R.A. 1983 *Tax havens and offshore finance: a study of transnational economic development*. St Martins Press, New York.

Pierce, J.L. 1991 *The future of banking*. Twentieth Century Fund report, Yale University Press, New Haven, CT.

Terrell, H. 1993 U.S. branches and agencies of foreign banks: a new look. *Federal Reserve Bulletin* (October): 913–25.

United States Department of Commerce 1987 *U.S. Census of Service Industries, Geographic Area Series*.

APPENDIX. FIRMS INTERVIEWED FOR DATA ENTRY AND PROCESSING

Domestic on-site interviews

TDEC, headquartered in Washington, DC, with plants in rural Maryland and West Virginia. Interviews held with J. Timothy Mann, Director, in Washington, DC headquarters, October 1990, and with Wanda Dawson, Vice President, in Oakland, Maryland, November 1990, and telephone interview, March 1995.

Highland Data, headquartered in Blue Grass, Virginia, and a branch office in West Virginia. Interview held with Edward Hevener, Manager, in Blue Grass, October 1990, and telephone interview, March 1995.

Appalachian Computer Services (ACS) headquartered in New London, Kentucky, with branches in Berea, Bateyville and Montecello, Kentucky, and Mount Vernon, Illinois. Interview held in London, Kentucky with Ed Miller, Vice President, November 1990, and telephone interview with Andrea Lyles, March 1995.

Computer Science Corporation (CSC), headquartered in El Segundo,

California, offices in a number of cities in the US. Interviews held in Falls Church, Virginia, with Howard Chambers, Vice President, and Floyd H. Jean, Vice President, November 1990.

C C and H, headquartered in Los Angeles, branch offices throughout cities in the US. Interview held in Walnut Creek, California, with Hank Klor, Assistant Director, March 1991.

Automated Data Processing, headquartered in Roseland, New Jersey, with offices in urban centres across the US. Interview with Tom Ryan, Operations Manager, in Towson, Maryland, November 1990.

General Electric in Rockville, Maryland. Interview with William McGowen, Manager, November 1990.

Automated Business Systems and Services, offices in Washington, DC, and Riverdale, Maryland. Interview with James T. Young, Program Manager in Riverdale, January 1991.

Domestic telephone interviews

Mead Data Central, a large data entry user, based in Dayton, Ohio. Interview with Michelle Love, Public Relations, April 1991.

ILM, headquartered in Fredricksburg, Virginia, an independent firm with a sister operation in Jamaica. Interviews with James Griggs, Vice President, in Fredricksburg, January 1991, and Jason Cohen, March 1995.

Saztec, headquartered in Kansas City, with branches in the Philippines and Ardrossan, Scotland. Interview with Scott Fancher, Vice President, in Kansas City, 21 June, 1991.

Offshore on-site interviews

Donnelly & Sons, headquartered in Chicago, interview held in Barbados branch with Ronald Wolfe, Senior Vice President, March 1991.

American Demographics, headquartered in Denver, Colorado, interview held in Barbados branch with Enid Blackman, Division Manager, March 1991.

Southwest, headquartered in Dallas, Texas, interview held in Barbados branch with Cynthia Chandler, Manager, March 1991.

Data Research Ltd, a Barbadian-owned firm, interview with Ms Sharpe, owner, March 1991.

Compudata Business Bureau, a Barbadian-owned firm, interview with Jean Alleyne, branch manager, March 1991.

The Barbados External Telecommunications (BET) Agency, interview with Keith Seale, Manager of Telecommunications Services, March 1991.

The Barbados Industrial Development Corporation, the agency responsible for economic development. Interviews held with Reginald Farley, Business Development Officer, in Barbados, March 1991, and John Mills, Business Development Officer, in New York, April 1991, and Henderson Holmes, in New York, March 1995.

Saztec Europe, Ardrossan, Scotland, interview with Ralph Wassell, Operations Manager, July 1991.

Producers of telecommunications, optical scanning, and imaging technologies

International Business Machines, interviews with Mark House, Senior Engineer, and Jeff Hamilton, Advisory Programmer, Arlington, Virginia, August 1991.

Xerox Imaging Systems, interview with Haley Collins, Account Representative, Southeastern Region, August 1991.

CHAPTER 17

THE DOMINANCE OF INTERNATIONAL FINANCE BY LONDON, NEW YORK AND TOKYO

Matthew P. Drennan

INTRODUCTION

In the final quarter of this century a truly global economy has emerged. That is, the international volume of trade in goods and services, of bank lending, of direct investment, of cross-border purchases of financial assets, and of currency exchange have all increased enormously. Financial institutions and financial markets are central to those international flows of trade and capital. The financial institutions and financial markets specialized in international transactions are not ubiquitous. Agglomeration economies, i.e. the gains to firms from locating near similar firms, suppliers and customers, argue for concentration in space. Large business firms and governments around the world that require international bank loans, wish to buy a foreign firm or float a large bond issue or a new stock offering turn to financial institutions and markets in centres of international finance.

There are three major centres of international finance: London, New York and Tokyo. To understand why those three have emerged as the dominant centres requires understanding the economic, the historical and the institutional dimension of that development. Large as those cities are, the size and economic power of their financial and related sectors (accounting, law, management consulting, computer software, advertising) strongly colour the cities' economies. That was not always the case. Extraordinary growth in the last twenty years of those economic sectors in those cities has made them more dominant economic sectors, greatly affecting the economic fortunes, and misfortunes, of their urban economies.

The financial sector and related sectors together have been called 'producer services' or 'business services'. The common characteristics of producer services industries are that much or most of their service output is intermediate input for other businesses (Beyers, 1992; Bonamy and Daniels, 1993; Drennan, 1992); the output is often customized, non-routine and information intensive; and finally the critical inputs for production of producer services are information and highly skilled professional workers whose raw material is information and whose output is information (brokers, financial analysts, investment bankers, attorneys, accountants, portfolio managers, computer analysts) (see also Chapter 4).

The professional workforce of producer services spends much of its time assembling and exchanging information, both within and outside the firm. Spatial concentration in some major urban centres is an enduring characteristic for the professional workforce even as telecommunication and computer technology disperses the routine information work to lower cost minor urban or suburban areas. Being professional, the producer services urban workforce earns well above average compensation, so its support of the local consumer economy is far greater than their employment numbers would suggest. As illustration, in the third quarter of 1993, securities industry (stock and commodity brokerages and investment banks) employment in New York city was 5 per cent of all private employment but provided 13 per cent of all private earnings (New York State Department of Labor, 1994).

An obvious characteristic of the three major financial centres is that the very largest producer services firms – the commercial banks, investment banks, brokerages, accounting firms, law firms, management consulting firms, and advertising agencies – tend to have their head offices and major activities there. Thus each city is a huge labour market for professionals in producer services. Producer services firms critically depend upon the quality of their professional labour force. For industrial corporations, profitability is often linked to production processes, patents and brand names, but for producer services firms, profitability is more linked to the quality of the professional workers.

The professional workforce has requirements beyond competitive pay. If the urban ambience – public safety, education for children, housing, leisure activities, public infrastructure – erodes, the supply of such labour will fall in that place, pushing up wages and thus reducing the competitive advantage of producer services firms there. As some producer services firms shift some or all of their operations to competing centres, the agglomeration economies which arise from the critical mass of producer services firms in one dense urban space will begin to erode. The public sector then has a critical role in maintaining or improving that urban ambience or it risks the unravelling of the agglomeration economies. The consequences would be declining producer services employment, rising office vacancies, falling land and property values, declining employment in dependent sectors, and declining local public sector revenues. Protection and improvement of the urban ambience by the public sector is not a narrow policy of making the world, the city, safe for yuppies. Rather it is a policy for preserving and protecting the only successful, economically viable huge urban concentrations of the late twentieth century in advanced capitalist nations, the centres of producer services. The large industrial cities – Liverpool, Detroit – are anachronisms of urban form, the imperative of goods production concentration in space having been wiped away by technology. Modern one-storey manufacturing plants with loading docks for lorries and car parks for employees and easy access to major highways are not built in old industrial cities. Cheap open land in low-density areas is more cost effective.

The first part of this chapter documents the vast expansion in international economic activity over the past two decades and the importance of transnational corporations (TNCs) in that expansion. The evidence for the dominance of London, New York and Tokyo in international finance is presented in the second part. The next part presents the elements of a theory for explaining the present dominance of those three places as the major centres of international finance (see also Chapters 5 and 8). The theory is, with qualifications, within the neoclassical economic paradigm. It yields testable hypotheses and conditions for decline. The theory fails to explain the rise of those particular places. That rise is the topic of part four. As Krugman (1991) has argued, some international trade can only be explained by history. Similarly, the rise to dominance of international finance by London, New York and Tokyo is a narrative about institutions, regulations and historical accidents rather than a unique solution to a set of equations. The impact on the local urban economies of the concentration of producer services is then explained in the following section, and finally, guided by the rough theory of part three, the concluding part of the chapter addresses the threats or challenges to dominance faced by those three cities.

RISE OF THE GLOBAL ECONOMY: TRADE, INVESTMENT, AND TRANSNATIONAL CORPORATIONS (TNCs)

What is meant by the rise of the global economy is very concrete. International transactions – trade in goods, trade in services, cross-border capital flows for direct investment or for the purchase of financial assets – have become a larger component of all the advanced capitalist economies in the past two decades. The rise of the global economy is caused by changes in technology, the increasing relative importance of TNCs in advanced economies, financial market deregulation, and long-term growth in real per capita income in developed nations (see also Chapter 7).

The evidence is not in dispute. From 1975 to 1991, the growth in real GDP of OECD countries collectively was 2.8 per cent annually while growth in OECD exports was 5.4 per cent annually. So exports as a share of GDP rose from 15 per cent in 1975 to 23 per cent in 1991 (OECD, 1993). The pattern was similar for the United States, Japan and the EEC countries over that period: export growth was about double the rate of GDP growth (Table 17.1). The increased importance of international trade makes each economy more susceptible to foreign exchange induced inflation.

Expansion of foreign direct investment (FDI) has been greater than the expansion of trade. FDI is defined as the purchase or start-up of a business in a foreign country in which the parent firm has a majority interest. Most FDI originates in developed nations and is directed to other developed nations. Outflows of FDI from developed countries in the mid-1970s were $US28 billion annually. By the late 1980s such outflows were $US181 billion. Inflows of FDI into developed countries were $US16 billion in the mid-1970s and $US143 billion in the late 1980s. The difference between outflows and inflows is roughly

Table 17.1   GDP and exports, OECD nations, 1975 and 1991 (billion 1985 $US)

		GDP	Exports	Exports/GDP
US	1975	3044	219	7.2%
	1991	4496	587	13.1%
Avg. Ann.	% Gr.	2.5%	6.4%	
EEC	1975	2914	706	24.2%
	1991	4327	1508	34.9%
Avg. Ann.	% Gr.	2.5%	4.9%	
Japan	1975	718	68	9.5%
	1991	1410	195	13.8%
Avg. Ann.	% Gr.	4.3%	6.8%	
Other	1975	1105	208	18.8%
	1991	1798	509	28.3%
Avg. Ann.	% Gr.	3.1%	5.8%	
OECD	1975	7781	1201	15.4%
	1991	12031	2799	23.3%
Avg. Ann.	% Gr.	2.8%	5.4%	

Source: National Accounts, 1960–91, OECD, Paris, 1993.

the FDI from developed to developing nations. So it appears that FDI in developing countries was 40 per cent of outflows in the mid-1970s but only 20 per cent in the late 1980s. There has been a marked shift in FDI flows among developed nations (Table 17.2). The United States is no longer the major source of FDI outflows as it was in the 1970s. But it has become far and away the largest receiver of FDI: $US57.6 billion annually in the late 1980s or 40 per cent of all FDI inflows into developed nations. That reflects the chronic and large trade deficit of the United States and the weak dollar post-1985. Foreign firms with surplus dollars see US assets as bargains. The UK ranks second after Japan and well above the US in outflows of FDI. It also ranks second in inflows of FDI and is well above France and Germany in both outflows and inflows. The major position of the UK as a source of FDI is in part explained by the large number and decidedly international orientation of British TNCs, not by the size of the UK economy. Also, a low rate of return on domestic investment, as in the UK in the early 1980s, can prompt TNCs to increase their FDI.

There is a striking asymmetry with respect to FDI flows of Japan. Japan ranked first in the late 1980s with $US36.5 billion of FDI outflows, which is understandable given that nation's huge and chronic trade surplus, high savings rate, and rising value of the yen. But inflows of FDI were a slight $US0.3 billion, a little lower than Turkey's. While major developed nations are open to Japanese FDI, Japan is much less open to receive FDI. If that asymmetry persists, Tokyo will never equal New York or London as a centre of international finance.

As a consequence of the huge growth in FDI, the stock of non-financial assets

Table 17.2   Flow of foreign direct investment, developed nations (annual average for years shown, $US billion)

	1975–77	1987–90
Outflows of FDI		
Japan	1.8	36.5
UK	3.8	30.5
US	12.8	23.9
France	1.3	19.5
Germany	2.5	17.1
Other OECD	6.1	53.5
Total	28.3	181.0
Inflows of FDI		
US	3.6	57.6
UK	3.6	23.3
France	1.5	9.3
Spain	0.6	8.5
Japan	0.1	0.3
Other OECD	6.7	44.4
Total	16.1	143.4

Source: World Investment Report 1993: Developed Countries, Table 6, p. 18, and Table 14, p. 42, United Nations, New York City, 1993.

held in foreign nations has risen among the developed countries. And there have been some marked shifts. Assets owned by Japanese firms outside Japan increased nine-fold from 1980 to 1990, British assets owned abroad increased four-fold, while US assets owned abroad doubled (Table 17.3). Assets owned by Japanese in the US are 40 per cent of all Japanese foreign assets. Assets owned by the British in the US are also 40 per cent of all British foreign assets. US foreign assets are more dispersed but Canada and the UK rank first and second with 15 per cent each. Again there is asymmetry in the case of Japan. US assets in Japan are only 5 per cent of all US-owned foreign assets, and British assets in Japan are only 1 per cent of all UK-owned foreign assets, but Japanese owned-assets in the US and UK combined are one-half of all Japanese-owned foreign assets. This reflects the fact that Japanese government policies discourage foreign ownership of businesses in Japan but at the same time encourage Japanese corporations to own businesses outside Japan.

Most of the FDI originates from TNCs (United Nations, 1993). The definition of a TNC is a non-financial corporation with a significant share of its assets or sales originating from its foreign subsidiaries. The largest TNCs have been growing much faster than the developed economies. In real terms, sales of the 50 largest TNCs rose 3.5 per cent annually between 1975 and 1990 while real OECD GDP rose 2.9 per cent annually. Sales of the 50 largest TNCs were 28 per cent of US GDP in 1975 and were 39 per cent of US GDP in 1989 (Carnoy, 1993).

Table 17.3 Stock of foreign direct investment of Japan, UK, and US by location, 1980 and 1990 ($US billion)

	1980	1990
Stock of FDI of Japan in:		
US	8.9	130.5
UK	2.0	22.6
Australia	2.2	16.1
Other developed	3.3	42.9
Less developed	19.9	98.4
Total	36.3	310.5
Stock of FDI of UK in:		
US	8.0	53.0
Australia	3.5	10.2
Netherlands	1.1	9.0
Japan	0.2	1.4
Other developed	9.5	35.1
Less developed	6.2	17.9
Total	28.5	126.6
Stock of FDI of US in:		
Canada	45.1	68.4
UK	28.5	65.0
Switzerland	11.3	23.7
Japan	6.2	21.0
Other developed	71.4	138.4
Less developed	57.6	106.7
Total	220.1	423.2

Source: World Investment Report 1993: Developed Countries, and Table 6, p. 18, Table 14, p. 42, United Nations, New York City, 1993.

The central roles of London, New York and Tokyo in international finance in large part reflect the central importance of the TNCs of their respective nations (see also Chapter 10). Of the world's 100 largest TNCs in 1990, 51 of them were either US (27), British (12) or Japanese (12) corporations. The count is not as important as the assets and foreign assets controlled by those corporations. Those 51 corporations owned 60 per cent of the foreign assets of the 100 largest TNCs and 67 per cent of the total assets. Although France has more (14) of the 100 largest TNCs than the UK (12), the foreign assets and total assets of the British TNCs are much larger. The British TNCs are relatively more international than their US or Japanese counterparts. Foreign assets of British TNCs are 57 per cent of their total assets compared with 31 per cent for US TNCs and 25 per cent for Japanese TNCs (United Nations, 1993). Among the 500 largest industrial corporations in the world in 1991, transnational or not, the US ranked first with 157, Japan second with 119, and the UK third with 45. Germany ranked fourth

(33) and France fifth (32) (United States Census Bureau, 1993).

A central feature of the new global economy is the great expansion in merchandise trade. Evidence for the United States, the largest trading nation, establishes that TNCs are also the dominant actors in international trade (Table 17.4). TNCs accounted for 80 per cent of US exports and 73 per cent of US imports in 1992.

Given that TNCs dominate international trade and FDI and given that the foreign asset ownership of TNCs is concentrated in the US, UK and Japan, then aside from any regulatory considerations, it is not surprising that international financial transactions are concentrated in the financial centres of those three nations. This is critical to understanding the dominance of London, New York and Tokyo in international finance. In a recent book, Sassen (1994) presents data showing the importance of TNCs in the global economy but does not place them at the centre of her argument that a more international economy is transforming major cities. However, she does clearly state the link between the expanding international economy and global cities such as London, New York and Tokyo:

> Global cities are key sites for the advanced services and telecommunications facilities necessary for the implementation and management of global economic operations. They also tend to concentrate the headquarters of firms, especially firms that operate in more than one country. The growth of international investment and trade and the need to finance and service such activities have fed the growth of these functions in major cities. (Sassen, 1994, p. 19)

Trade in goods, in services, FDI, repatriation of TNC's subsidiaries' income to the parent corporations, and international exchange of financial instruments all involve financial transactions. Because of the enormous growth over the past two decades in those international activities, the corresponding financial transactions have exploded in volume. The three major centres of international finance, London, New York and Tokyo, have received the lion's share of that great rise in volume.

Table 17.4   US merchandise trade, 1992 ($US billion)

	Exports	Imports
Trade attributed to TNCs	351.8	391.9
Total trade	440.4	536.5
TNC trade as % of total	80%	73%

Source: Bureau of Economic Analysis (1994).

CONCENTRATION OF FINANCIAL ACTIVITY IN LONDON, NEW YORK AND TOKYO

International trade, FDI, income repatriation from foreign subsidiaries, cross-border purchase of equities, bonds, options and futures, plus commercial bank lending, all require the exchange of currency. London is the unrivalled centre of currency trading or foreign exchange. Daily volume is currently over one trillion dollars, about one-fifth of annual US GDP (*Wall Street Journal*, 11 July 1994), and one-quarter of that daily volume occurs in the London foreign exchange market. Two decades ago when the international economic activities described above were a small fraction of what they are today, daily foreign exchange volume was also a small fraction of what it is today. Consequently, market intervention by concerted action of the Group of Seven monetary authorities could make a big difference in supporting a currency. That is no longer true. The combined foreign exchange markets in London, New York and Tokyo are too big to be significantly moved by government intervention, as became clear in July 1994 when an attempt to prop up the falling dollar was aborted.

Equity and debt markets are largest in London, New York and Tokyo, as shown in Table 17.5. The value of stocks listed on the New York Stock Exchange was almost $US4 trillion at the end of 1992, over $US2 trillion on the Tokyo Stock Exchange, and almost $US1 trillion on the London exchange. By comparison, the combined value of stocks listed in Frankfurt plus Paris, the fourth and fifth ranked exchanges, was two-thirds of the London total.

The London Stock Exchange is the most international of the three. More than 500 of the almost 2400 corporations listed in London are foreign. New York and Tokyo each have somewhat more than 100 foreign corporations listed out of totals around 2000 each (London Stock Exchange, 1994), but the Tokyo total has been falling and is now 92 (*Wall Street Journal*, 3 October 1994).

A great deal of international financial transactions flow through large commercial banks. Unlike the case of TNCs, where the US and the UK are among the top three, large commercial banks in Japan, France and Germany account for two-thirds of the assets of the 100 largest commercial banks in the world. The seven US banks and six UK banks in the top 100 together have assets

Table 17.5 Volume and capitalization, major stock exchanges, 1992 ($US billion)

	New York	Tokyo	London	Frankfurt	Paris	Other[a]
Value of stocks traded	1745	476	674	300	121	713
Value of bonds traded	12	117	1171	700	817	139
Total market value of stocks	3878	2321	933	321	328	1289
Total market value of bonds	2044	1278	608	993	578	1281

[a] Toronto, Zurich, Amsterdam, Milan, Austria, Hong Kong, Singapore, Taiwan, and Korea.
Source: Tokyo Stock Exchange (1994).

only about equal to the top 11 French banks (*Wall Street Journal*, 24 September 1993). Although the US and the UK banks do not dominate commercial banking, New York and London are the unrivalled centres of international commercial banking. There are more foreign banks with branches in New York, 342, than in any other city. London is second with 312, Tokyo third with 97 (Thomson Ltd, 1993). Also, as Sassen (1994) shows, international lending by banks tripled from 1981 to 1991 and the three major centres, London, New York and Tokyo, maintained their collective share of 41 per cent of that $US6 trillion market.

Twenty-two of the 25 largest securities firms in the world are either US (11), Japanese (9) or British (2) (*Wall Street Journal*, 24 September 1993). The largest securities firms are all present in London. In 1988 there were 122 foreign securities houses in London, of which the majority were American (37), Japanese (36) and Canadian (36) (King, 1990).

The above facts establish that London, New York and Tokyo are the dominant centres of international finance. A host of additional data on location of industrial headquarters, large commercial banks, insurance companies, service firms and pension funds are presented by Sassen (1991, 1994), showing that those three cities are at the pinnacle of a world financial hierarchy. What is absent is a theory to explain their dominance.

OUTLINE OF A THEORY OF INTERNATIONAL FINANCIAL DOMINANCE BY LONDON, NEW YORK AND TOKYO WITHIN THE NEOCLASSICAL ECONOMIC PARADIGM

The theoretical literature on world cities or global cities can be characterized as a political economy literature (Hymer, 1972a; Castells, 1989; Cohen, 1981; Mollenkopf and Castells, 1991; Fainstein and Harloe, 1992; Sassen, 1991, 1994). The empirical literature is in a host of disciplines: urban economics and regional science (Drennan, 1987, 1992), planning (Moss, 1988; Goldsmith and Blakely, 1992), politics (Shefter, 1993; Vogel, 1993), and geography (Hall, 1966; Pred, 1977; Daniels, 1993). The empirical literature lacks an analytical framework and therefore intellectual coherence. The political economy literature does not lack an analytical framework but the framework is foreign to mainstream economists. Consequently and unfortunately, the world city literature has been ignored by neoclassical economists.

In order to develop or outline a neoclassical theory of development of London, New York and Tokyo as the major centres of international finance, it is first necessary to relax a key assumption of the neoclassical regional economic growth paradigm. That assumption is constant returns to scale and therefore the absence of agglomeration economies in production. Constant returns to scale has a venerable history. The Cobb–Douglas production function exhibits constant returns to scale, which means that if all inputs are multiplied by some factor, then output will be multiplied by the same factor. But if space (separation) and therefore positive transportation costs and communication costs are introduced into that model, then constant returns to scale, and its corollary of infinitely divisible inputs, implies that every good and service will be produced everywhere. By admitting increasing returns to scale and external economies of scale, i.e. agglomeration economies, then concentration of production in space is efficient. Ohlin, the co-founder of modern trade theory, clearly saw that concentration of production in space is efficient and can lead to trade among regions (Ohlin, 1933). But his followers in international trade theory ignored the gains from concentration in space for two reasons: first, because their analysis is aspatial; and second, because comparative advantage as the basis for trade leads to a neat mathematical model whereas increasing returns as the basis for trade leads to a messy and complex model. In his restatement of international trade theory, Krugman (1990) has rediscovered what regional economists have known at least since Ohlin, namely the importance of increasing returns to scale as a basis for trade. One reason for a certain tension between urban and regional economics and neoclassical economic theory is that in a world with space, the central reasons for spatial concentration of economic activity, i.e. urban areas, are scale economies and agglomeration economies. But scale economies and agglomeration economies are the camel's nose in the tent, leading inexorably to models without unique equilibrium solutions, an anathema to neoclassical 'normal science'. Hence the important phenomenon of emerging global cities has been ignored by neoclassical economists. Mathematical models of general equilibrium analysis assume perfect competition, which has as two necessary conditions constant returns to scale and perfect information. Global cities cannot be encompassed in such models.

Scale economies, agglomeration economies, and urban form

Scale economies may be internal or external to the firm. External scale economies are agglomeration economies. For example, firms in the same industry which cluster together spatially may gain collective economies in purchasing inputs, such as specialized labour or materials, or in selling and transporting output. Noted above, one necessary condition for the existence of perfect competition is perfect information, i.e. all buyers and sellers in all markets have complete information. Thus a central reason for certain firms clustering together in space is assumed away. Information is not costless, and the more complex and developed the industry, the more important is information. Stigler noted the critical importance of information for reducing uncertainty for the firm (Stigler, 1961).

If scale economies and agglomeration economies matter in reality, then urban areas would be expected to show high specialization and concentration in particular traded goods and services as opposed to non-traded goods and services (retail trade, utilities, construction, etc.). And generations of urban economists, beginning with Frederick S. Hall in the first decade of this century (1902), have shown that to be the case. In a recent analysis of US metropolitan areas at the most detailed industry level, Henderson (1988) found that 80 per cent or more of national employment in a particular manufacturing industry tended to be concentrated in five or fewer metropolitan areas, while the other hundreds of metropolitan areas would have trivial numbers of jobs in that industry. This pattern was obviously not true for manufacturing activities characterized by high-weight and low-value output such as cement production, bottling plants and newspapers, which tend to be ubiquitous. Thus scale economies and agglomeration economies appear to matter in reality.

But if scale economies matter for local economic activity, then scale diseconomies probably matter too. Increases in urban size lead to diseconomies such as rising money and time cost of transporting goods and people, rising land costs and rising wages. In the same study, Henderson performed a sophisticated regression analysis which identified empirically an optimum urban size for different economic sectors. He found that resource-based manufacturing reached relative maximum concentration (i.e. share of local employment) in rather small-sized metropolitan areas. Footloose manufacturing reached relative maximum concentration in mid-sized metropolitan areas. The financial part of producer services reached maximum share in metropolitan areas of 10 million population. But most interesting, for the professional service part of the producer services sector, Henderson found no optimum size. That is, the relative share of producer services tends to rise continuously with urban size and is highest in the very largest US metropolitan area: New York (Henderson, 1988).

A defining characteristic of producer services industries is that non-routine information is a major input and output (Machlup, 1962; Porat, 1977; Pred, 1977; Drennan, 1989). With the highest concentration (employment share) of producer services in the largest urban area in the US, and in the UK too (see Buck *et al.*, 1992), one would infer that the agglomeration economies for producer services firms in the largest places are not offset by diseconomies. Further, the largest producer services firms are concentrated in the largest urban areas (Sassen, 1991, 1994; Drennan, 1992). Pred's concept of spatial bias in information flows provides insight into that high concentration of producer services in the largest urban areas.

> With increasing frequency, informational spatial biases are also affecting explicit locational decisions in the sense that place-to-place variations in the availability and accessibility – or cost – of information are deliberately considered as a factor of location for administrative headquarters, advertising agencies, banks, other financial intermediaries, law firms, ... Metropolitan locations where activities of this type are already clustered, are generally perceived to offer new or relocating sister units the advantages of, first, easily arranged short-notice group meetings and face-to-face contacts between client and customer; second, a greater choice of opportunities; and third, risk reducing 'knowledge in a hurry' about changes in the economic or technological environment.... The costs of not having a location in a large metropolitan complex favored by spatial biases in the availability and accessibility of information are ordinarily regarded as prohibitive, especially since numerous office and business-service personnel spend 20 hours or more per week exchanging information. (Pred, 1977, p. 24)

The economic value of agglomeration economies to producer services firms has been an elusive concept, but it need not be. First, the agglomeration economies for producer services firms do not appear to be ubiquitous within urban areas (Schwartz, 1992; Mills, 1988; Drennan, 1992) but rather are concentrated in the central business district (CBD) of the central city. The rent gradient, the very strong tendency for urban land values and rents to fall with increasing distance from the CBD, could be used to empirically approximate the value of agglomeration economies. Given that some large urban areas specialize in producer services, and given that producer services concentrate in the CBD, then the difference in rents paid in the CBD, peak rents, and the next highest zone is some measure of the economic rent earned by producer services firms in the CBD, i.e. the value of the site-specific agglomeration economies. This leads to a testable hypothesis; CBD premium rents and land values are highest in major centres of producer services, and over time CBD rents in major centres of producer services have risen relative to CBD rents in manufacturing cities.

None of the above explains why some urban areas developed as major centres of producer services rather than others. History and regulation provide insights. We observe profit-seeking firms, for which some major inputs and outputs are non-routine information, concentrated in the CBDs of some large urban areas and so we infer that they are minimizing costs of information inputs and/or maximizing information outputs.

Growth theory of global cities, complementarity and the unimportance of comparative advantage

Why have the producer services sectors of the advanced economies, and particularly the producer services sectors of the largest urban areas, London, New York and Tokyo, grown so much? The growth of major centres of producer services in the past two decades can be understood with reference to three economic concepts. First, as an economy becomes more complex, the production of all goods becomes more roundabout, i.e. inputs become more diverse. Second, there is Colin Clark's (1940) idea of secular economic growth whereby as per capita incomes rise over time, composition of final demand changes, favouring tertiary and quaternary sectors because of different income elasticities of demand. Third, there is Henderson's (1988) idea that, given the specialized character of different-sized urban places, a change in the composition of national and international demand can stimulate growth in certain size classes of urban places. Changing national and international demand favours producer services, a quaternary sector, that will have the effect of earlier stimulating growth in the largest urban places which are most specialized in producer services. As shown, the increasing importance of TNCs, the relative rise in world trade (stimulated by the TNCs), and the rise in FDI by TNCs all produced differentially strong growth in producer services. That differentially strong growth stimulated the economies of urban areas most specialized in producer services and most closely linked to large TNCs. Recall that the US, Japan and the UK are the three top home countries for the 100 largest, and 500 largest, TNCs. Therefore the three financial centres of those nations, London, New York and Tokyo, had strong economic growth.

Comparative advantage means that nations with *different* specializations gain from trade with each other. Krugman (1991) has argued that comparative advantage cannot explain the phenomenon of nations with the *same* specialization having most trade in that item with each other. For example, the production of sophisticated machine tools is dominated by Germany, Japan and the United States. The lion's share of world exports and imports of machine tools is among those three nations. Much of that represents trade between foreign subsidiaries and the parent. This phenomenon is relevant to Pred's (1977) empirical analysis of corporate headquarters in San Francisco. He noted that growth impulses (or contractions) in other urban areas resulted from decisions in San Francisco headquarters. The magnitude of the growth impact had no relation to distance from San Francisco but rather to the size of the subsidiary units in the affected urban areas. This strikes a critical blow to central place theory: the idea of a proximate hinterland dependent on the urban centre, with dependence decaying with distance. The same concept applies to financial services and other producer services. That is, it is wrong to view the three global cities as only competing international financial centres with separate spheres of influence. They stimulate each other through choices made regarding expansion and contraction of subsidiaries. Because the producer services sectors are so large in those three cities and so intertwined with each other through subsidiaries, they are 'unhinged' from their national system of urban places. That is, the economic fortunes of Birmingham and Manchester, for example, may be less important for London's economy than the economic fortunes of producer services firms in New York and Tokyo.

INSTITUTIONAL AND HISTORICAL FACTORS IN THE RISE OF THREE CITIES

Britain was the first industrial nation and had the largest overseas empire, so it is not surprising that London emerged as the world's major financial centre in the eighteenth and nineteenth centuries. The financial institutions of London expanded through financing and insuring the huge volume of British foreign trade and through marshalling the long-term capital for financing industrial development throughout the world. In this century two world wars, the end of the international gold standard managed by the Bank of England, the dismemberment of the empire, the displacement of sterling by the dollar as the major currency for trade and bank reserves, and the relative decline of the British economy should have transformed London into a pickled city like Venice. But that did not happen.

On the contrary, the City has held its own in recent decades as a leading financial center. London may be located geographically in the United Kingdom, but 'economically it may just as well be in international waters or in orbit'. Britain is no longer one of the world's three industrial nations, but London is unequivocally one of the three major centers of global finance. (Vogel, 1993, p. 53)

What explains the continued importance of London? One part of the explanation has been covered above, namely the number and size and international character of British TNCs, more international than their US or Japanese counterparts. Vogel (1993) notes that 45 of the 500 largest corporations in the world have their headquarters in London. The long-term capital exported over two centuries, owned and controlled by British corporations, has mostly not been expropriated or destroyed.

Just as the disappearance of the Victorian and Edwardian world did not make the overseas investments of British TNCs vanish, or change ownership, the agglomeration economies achieved in London through the concentration of financial institutions with unparalleled international experience were not dissipated. The intra-industry and cross-industry flows of complex information among professionals in London is critical for the competitive position and profitability of its major financial institutions. That includes the branches of foreign financial firms which have flocked there. If those amorphous agglomeration economies are indeed important, then they would be reflected in differentially high office rents, land prices, and returns to professional labour in London. It is well known, anecdotally, that London (and New York and Tokyo) has the highest office rents and land prices in the UK, rising and falling as they do with real estate cycles. What needs to be determined empirically is whether or not real rents and real earnings of labour in London and the other two centres of global finance are differentially higher than in other urban centres. Further, have those hypothetical premiums risen or fallen over the past few decades? Given the vast expansion of international demand for financial services described above, those hypothesized premiums probably rose through 1989, the peak of the 1980s economic boom.

Another reason for the continued importance of London as a major centre of finance is that *international* finance is far more important, measured by transactions, earnings and employment, than it was 20 years ago. This is related to Henderson's (1988) point, namely that on the eve of the explosion of international financial transactions, which was a shift in national and international composition of demand, London's specialization in international finance gave it a competitive advantage. The same is true of New York and Tokyo. And all these places exploited that competitive advantage, in part through public policy.

The history of capitalism is a history of breaking down barriers to the allocation of capital and to the liquidity of capital. The technological barriers have fallen rapidly in the second half of this century, leading to inexorable pressure on the political barriers, i.e. pressure to waive the rules. Foreign exchange controls and the pegging of currencies were major political barriers, the fall of which ushered in truly global capital markets (see also Chapter 8). Deregulation of financial markets in the UK and the US, and much more slowly in Japan, has been instrumental in enhancing the volume of international financial flows and therefore enhancing the competitive position of London, New York and Tokyo. There is a curious lack of symmetry, however. Deregulation in London and New York drew Japanese financial institutions into those cities with their access to massive amounts of capital generated by Japan's trade surpluses and that nation's unusually high savings. Political barriers in Japan to foreign financial institutions prevented a similar move on a comparable scale by London and New York financial institutions.

The political barriers or rules in some cases are not waived but circumvented and in so doing international finance is substituted for domestic finance. The huge Eurodollar market centred in London was born in the 1960s to avoid US interest rate ceilings and the requirement that banks hold reserves which do not earn interest. There was originally competition between London and Paris for the fledgling Eurodollar market, but because the French favoured regulation and the British did not, London won (Hamilton, 1986). In some cases historical shocks overwhelm regulatory structures. The first oil price shock of 1973 made the big New York and London banks recyclers of massive amounts of international short-term capital. The New York banks were not free to expand aggressively in the US because of rules against interstate banking. So the only route to growth was outside the US. The unprecedented inflation of the late 1970s ended the quiet orderly world of US savings institutions and UK building societies. Their traditional sources of cheap capital fled to earn higher returns.

Just as technology and historical events have swept away much of the financial regulatory framework which circumscribed financial transactions and kept markets insulated from foreign influence, will technology render international financial centres an anachronism? If modern financial markets can exist in computer networks or 'cyberspace', as does NASDAQ, who needs high-cost locations in real space such as London, New York or Tokyo? Apparently major financial institutions and markets do need such locations, and it is their demand which keeps the rents high.

> . . . the proximity of like-minded people, are essential to a market. Technology will not alter this. What it is doing is to make the competition over where the market is concentrated that much more intense. There is no room for an infinite number of major international exchanges. . . . What technology is also doing is to make it impossible for national regulators to turn the clock back. (Hamilton, 1986, p. 49)

IMPACT OF PRODUCER SERVICES CONCENTRATION ON THE ECONOMIES OF LONDON, NEW YORK AND TOKYO

The great expansion in international financial transactions and the concentration of those financial transactions in the three urban centres which has been documented above is manifest in the parallel great expansion of employment and earnings in the financial and related sectors, i.e. producer services in those cities. Further, the size of the producer services sector in those places renders it the premier export sector or driving sector of those urban economies. The international economy determines the fortunes of the producer services sector in those cities. And the producer services sector determines the fortunes of the urban economies of London and New York, and less so of Tokyo. They are global cities in the sense that their economic conditions are more unhinged from the economic conditions of their respective national economies than is the case for other urban areas.

Over the past two decades, the only sector which has had consistent employment growth in central London, or indeed in Greater London, has been producer services (Buck *et al.*, 1992). In 1971, Greater London had 3.9 million jobs of which 0.5 million or 13 per cent were in producer services. By 1989, Greater London total employment was down to 3.5 million jobs, of which 0.8 million or 23 per cent were in producer services. In 1971, Greater London had two manufacturing jobs to every producer services job. By 1989 the ratio was reversed with two producer services jobs for every manufacturing job. The producer services jobs are highly concentrated with 38 per cent of the 1.2 million central London jobs in producer services. Such an enormous economic restructuring in two decades has doubtless changed the mix of consumer goods and services demanded in London.

Financial services are the most concentrated part of the London producer services sector:

> The financial and producer services sector itself is rather diverse. Agglomeration economies are vitally important for those parts of the sector involved with the financial markets, international business and company headquarters, which tend to be concentrated in the City and West End. Other elements, including back offices carrying out more routine functions, and establishments serving a more local and regional market, are dispersed among a series of subsidiary centers with lower rent levels. Thus the central area accounts for only about 44% of employment in the sector, though for 53% of that in financial services, and 62% of company headquarters. (Buck *et al.*, 1992)

The tale of employment restructuring is remarkably similar for New York. In 1969, there were 3.8 million jobs in New York, about equal to the Greater London total around that time, of which 0.7 million were in producer services. By 1994, total employment in New York was down to 3.3 million, but producer services employment was up to 1.0 million. As with central London, producer services employment is highly concentrated in Manhattan. There were 1.0

million manufacturing jobs in New York in 1969, or 1.5 for every producer services job. By 1994, manufacturing employment was down to 0.3 million, so there were three producer services jobs for every manufacturing job (Drennan, 1995).

Earnings data for New York show that in dollar terms the producer services sector is a larger part of the local economy than the employment numbers indicate, and also show that Manhattan is highly specialized in producer services. Before the recession at the end of the 1980s, producer services earnings throughout the United States were 17 per cent of all earnings. In the New York region, producer services earnings were 28 per cent of all earnings in the region, and in Manhattan producer services earnings were 47 per cent of all earnings (Drennan, 1992). The producer services sector, with all of its business travellers, plus tourism in London and New York, supports the hotels, restaurants, theatre, entertainment, culture and private transportation sectors of the local economy.

The Tokyo metropolitan area had 6.0 million jobs in 1969, of which almost one-third were in manufacturing. By 1991, total employment was up to 8.8 million but manufacturing employment was down to 1.5 million or 17 per cent of all jobs. So like London and New York, the importance of the manufacturing sector has diminished in Tokyo. Producer services (defined as finance and insurance plus real estate and business services) employment in Tokyo almost doubled in that period, rising from 381000 to 741000. Tokyo is clearly specialized in producer services because 23 per cent of Japan's producer services employment is in Tokyo while 15 per cent of total national employment is in Tokyo. Tokyo is not specialized in manufacturing for it has only 11 per cent of Japan's manufacturing employment (Tokyo Metropolitan Government, 1990).

Although producer services account for only 8 per cent of Tokyo jobs compared with 38 per cent in central London and 30 per cent in New York city, that in part reflects the geographic areas covered (Table 17.6). Metropolitan Tokyo includes the entire urbanized area whereas central London and New York city include only the urban core of much larger urbanized areas. Because producer services employment tends to be concentrated in the urban core, the London and New York shares are much higher. If data were available for the urban core of Tokyo, the share of producer services jobs would doubtless be much higher.

Table 17.6   Producer services in London, New York and Tokyo

	Central London	New York City	Metropolitan Tokyo
Producer services employment (millions)	0.5	1.0	0.7
Total employment (millions)	1.2	3.3	8.8
Producer services employment as % of total employment	38%	30%	8%

THREATS TO POSITIONS OF DOMINANCE

What are the factors which could unravel the agglomeration economies of producer services firms in a global city? The first and most central would be a return to the rigid financial regulatory framework of the past. That would raise the cost of allocating capital and reduce the liquidity of capital so the real return on capital would be reduced. If a major centre of international finance reimposed the rules of the past, it would quickly become a minor centre or a former centre. The second factor relates to the home country of the largest TNCs. Because the major clients of large financial institutions are TNCs, a long-run shift in composition of the world's largest TNCs from the US, Japan and the UK to say China, India and Brazil could make financial centres in those countries contenders for status as top international financial centres. Of course they would need to have regulatory regimes compatible with such potential positions and status as hard currency countries.

Tokyo is the most recent city to emerge in the triumvirate of international centres of finance and its position is least secure. One reason for that is that the Japanese, like the French, are not as enamoured with *laissez faire* finance as are the Americans and British. In 1990 there were 125 foreign corporations, mostly TNCs, listed on the Tokyo stock exchange. In late 1994 that number was down to 92. Purchases by Japanese investors of foreign stocks tend to occur outside Japan to avoid the Japanese tax on trades and high fixed commissions. The minimum asset requirement for a foreign corporation to be listed on the Tokyo Stock Exchange is one billion dollars. So big new initial public offerings from China or elsewhere in Asia go to London or New York rather than Tokyo (*Wall Street Journal*, 3 October 1994). The *Wall Street Journal* has charged that '... Japan remains a museum of the financial services of the 1970s' (3 October 1994). Deregulation of financial markets in Japan will probably continue to lag. By dragging their feet in the waiving of rules, Tokyo is less attractive to foreign financial institutions and may indeed be less attractive even to huge Japanese financial institutions (Vogel, 1993). *Laissez faire* is not easily embraced by Japanese bureaucrats. The rise of Tokyo has been bound up with Japan as a major *source* of international capital. The collapse of the Nikkei index plus the slowness to deregulate makes Japan less attractive as a major *destination* for international capital. Tokyo is less congenial to foreigners than Hong Kong. If the Chinese government clearly demonstrates that foreign capital is safe and welcome in Hong Kong after the city passes to Chinese control, and is less hamstrung with regulation than in Japan, then Hong Kong will challenge the position of Tokyo. No European city poses a similar threat to London.

There are global and local threats to the dominance of New York. One global threat is the status of the dollar as the major currency of international trade, international capital flows and bank reserves. One disaster scenario is tied to the Republican Party's sweep of Congress in the 1994 elections. Their 'Contract with America' resurrects the discredited supply-side economic policies of cutting taxes and boosting defence spending while holding harmless middle-class entitlements. As *The Economist* noted (21 November 1994), the numbers do not add up, i.e. the deficit will zoom upward again. The Republican leadership counters that 'dynamic scoring', a method for projecting revenues and expenditures which embodies the magic of rising future revenues from present tax cuts, will prove on paper that their programme will not produce massive deficits. If they succeed in selling that Reaganesque nostrum, bond yields will soar as bond prices plummet because financial markets will, quite rationally, expect much increased US budget deficits and inflation. The dollar will fall more. The disaster would be reluctance by foreigners to continue buying US Treasury bonds at any interest rate given the massive losses foreign holders of existing US bonds would suffer from rising interest rates and the falling dollar. A flight from the dollar would permanently diminish the currency's importance in trade, in capital flows and as a reserve currency, and therefore diminish the importance of New York in international finance.

A less dramatic and more long-run threat to the dominance of New York is posed by the gradual shift in economic power from Atlantic nations to Pacific nations. Although the US is both, Los Angeles or San Francisco could replace New York as the major centre of international finance in the nation. The same cast of financial institutions massed in New York would simply diminish there and expand, and eventually shift headquarters, to one of those west coast cities. Of course with present laws, the commercial banks in New York could not shift location, but the days of those political barriers are numbered.

The local threat to the position of New York is what Hamilton (1986) has called the '. . . self-inflicted wounds of metropolitan chaos and urban decay . . . .' If the public infrastructure of airports, roads, bridges and transit systems plus the social infrastructure of education, public safety, public health and income support should deteriorate much more under chronic fiscal stress, then the critical mass of highly educated professionals so central to the competitive success of New York's producer services sector might diminish there. If the Republican Congress downloads to the states responsibility for funding major social welfare programmes and the new Republican governor of New York state downloads more of that to localities like New York city, the resulting new wound would not be self-inflicted but critical. The irony is that the star performer of US exports, producer services (contributing more to US net exports than aerospace, computers and semiconductors combined), is centred in New York city. The *laissez faire* fundamentalists ascendant in the US Congress could damage the competitive position of New York, and therefore the United States, in their zeal to unravel the welfare state.

The only major threat to the position of London as one of the three centres of international finance are a stall or reversal of European union, or a re-emergence of British xenophobia strong enough to catapult the UK out of the union. So long as the UK remains in the union and London has the blessing of the Bundesbank, then the centuries of international financial expertise concentrated in London will not shift to some other European city. London does not face the extent of capital infrastructure and social infrastructure decay that New York does. The ideological committment to *laissez faire* by the British government is rational and therefore selective. The importance of London for the UK economy is understood and defended by the national government. New York is not so fortunate because its importance for the US economy is not understood and not defended.

FURTHER READING

Carnoy, M. 1993 Multinationals in a changing world economy. In Carnoy, M., Castells, M., Cohen, S.S., Cardoso, F.H. (eds) *The new global economy in the information age.* Pennsylvania State University Press, University Park, PA: 45–96.

Castells, M. 1989 *The informational city.* Blackwell, Oxford.

Drennan, M. 1992 Gateway cities: the metropolitan sources of U.S. producer service exports. *Urban Studies* **29**(2): 217–35.

Hamilton, A. 1986 *The financial revolution.* Penguin Books, Harmondsworth.

King, A. 1990 *Global cities.* Routledge, Chapman and Hall, London and New York.

Pred, A. 1977 *City systems in advanced economies.* Halstead Press, New York.

Sassen, S. 1994 *Cities in a world economy.* Pine Forge Press, Thousand Oaks.

Shefter, M. (ed.) 1993 *Capital of the American century.* Russell Sage, New York.

CHAPTER 18

OVERVIEW AND SYNTHESIS
Peter Daniels and William Lever

On the evidence of the preceding chapters, the global economy has always been in transition. The concept of transition implies change, usually gradual and evolutionary, from one condition to another – political, economic or social factors have always ensured that equilibrium in the operation and organization of the global economy is the exception rather than the rule. Economic uncertainty on the part of firms and countries is greater than ever and adjustments to their behaviour are therefore all the more necessary, even if the costs or the benefits are elusive. The dynamics of disequilibrium have more recently been supplemented with advances in telecommunications and information technology, the growing influence of multinational organizations on the form and structure of the global economy, the flight of certain kinds of capital from high-to low-cost countries as the development gap remains as wide as ever, and the recent and rapid emergence of the newly industrialized countries. Depending on the perspective from which we interpret change, the very recent changes in the economic organization and orientation of the post-socialist economies of eastern Europe and the former Soviet Union can be seen as offering new growth opportunities or, conversely, as introducing yet more disequilibrium into the global economy.

The contributions to this volume reflect the diversity of the paradigms and interpretations of the factors driving change in the global economy and some of the spatial consequences. Indeed, Thrift (Chapter 2) provokes us to think about the fact that while nobody doubts that changes are taking place in the world economy, we remain as far as ever (perhaps even further than we have previously thought) from understanding why it has been happening. Crucially, he suggests that this is not just the product of the fuzzy intellect of academic observers but is the position in which the business community also finds itself. Without the privilege of a brief to stand back from the details of their particular research interests, most of the contributions to this volume do, in their own way, conform to the Thrift thesis. The restructuring of production such as the rise of networks of flexible specialization (Holly, Chapter 3; Cooke, Chapter 15); the uncertainty about the relative significance of global versus more local impacts of information and communications technology (Charles, Chapter 6); the emergence of what

Coffey (Chapter 4) calls the 'newer' international division of labour; the inexorable growth and expansion of multinational enterprises (Clegg, Chapter 7); and the transfer of production offshore (Howland, Chapter 16) are not only causing a major shift of selected parts of the production systems of advanced economies to the emerging economies of the developing world but also sending contradictory signals about where the process of transition is taking the global economy. Core production activities, including research and development (Hayter, Chapter 9), high value added products and services or technology-intensive activities remain anchored in the developed economies, where high-skill human resources (especially for the production of advanced services) are now one of the most important factor inputs. It is also much easier for corporations to shift production of products in the mature phase of the product life cycle or standardized processes such as data entry to lower cost locations because they no longer embody proprietary, state-of-the-art knowledge which can be replicated by competitors in a way that would confer competitive advantage. Innovation and knowledge-based product or service development which protects the competitive advantage of advanced economies and of the leading multinationals remains highly concentrated, as Hayter (Chapter 9) demonstrates for R&D (see also Drennan, Chapter 17). Differentials in the ability of countries to marshal the necessary education and training systems, to invest in the necessary technological infrastructure or to make the necessary social adjustments will help to perpetuate geographical unevenness and 'those societies that comprehensively organize themselves for learning and innovation will do better than those who do not' (Hayter, Chapter 9).

While acknowledging that the components of the global economy are interdependent, Drakakis-Smith (Chapter 11) shows how uneven dependence is an enduring feature. Both multinational enterprises operating from a developing country base (there are still relatively few, see Clegg, Chapter 7) and the countries themselves are impoverished in terms of capital equipment, skilled labour, capital or technology, for example, and remain dependent on the suppliers of these inputs to sustain their production infrastructure. However, we should not assume from this that dependence is an unambiguous concept; there are numerous interpretations of the economic characteristics of dependence (Drakakis-Smith, Chapter 11) and it is a concept that should therefore be used carefully. At all scales, from the global to the local, it needs to be clear how dependence is structured or influenced by the various elements that make up a relationship and Drakakis-Smith (Chapter 11) illustrates this with reference to examples of structural adjustment in Africa and the emergence of regional divisions of labour in Pacific Asia. One way for developing countries to reverse dependence and to achieve sustained economic growth is to raise the level of export growth of manufactures (Gwynne, Chapter 12). But many developing countries are heavily dependent on agricultural, mineral or energy exports, an easy but vulnerable (to world price fluctuations and demand swings, for example) source of overseas earnings. Gwynne (Chapter 12) gives details of the model of east Asian industrialization, based on human rather than natural resources, as a way forward for developing countries. Taiwan is a model that many countries would like to follow but unfortunately it seems likely that its success at achieving international competitiveness for its manufactured goods is exceptional; for most other developing countries with similar aspirations the Taiwan model simply demonstrates how much change they have yet to achieve to get anywhere near replicating that success.

Multinational enterprises are significant actors in shaping the process and the spatial outcomes of global economic transition (Clegg, Chapter 7; Hayter, Chapter 9; Daniels, Chapter 10; Howland, Chapter 16). The relocation of their activities is a recurring theme to which must be added in recent years the opportunities for organic growth resulting from the economic and political liberalization of markets in the post-socialist economies (Bradshaw, Chapter 13) and the more open economic environment of China. Clegg (Chapter 7) demonstrates how foreign direct investment by multinational enterprises is closely allied to the size and growth of markets. This means that the relatively recent emergence of integrated markets such as the European Union (Lever, Chapter 14) or the North American Free Trade Agreement (NAFTA) is causing multinationals to redirect much of their activity towards these large economic areas with, for example, their low internal tariffs, ease of movement of labour and increasingly harmonized transport and telecommunications infrastructure. These developments are part of an effort by the advanced economies to reassert their hegemony and that of their multinational enterprises, and the effect is to marginalize even further the peripheral economies in the Caribbean or Africa. In other words the notion of transition in the global economy does not mean widespread international dynamism; rather it implies a combination of highly dynamic economic environments side by side with increasing relative stagnation of economies that are already very weak and disadvantaged.

The formation of supranational integrated markets based on multilateral agreements reminds us that national comparative advantage is derived from government actions (national and regional) rather than the investment and location behaviour of multinationals (Lever, Chapter 14; Daniels, Chapter 10; Swyngedouw, Chapter 8; Cooke, Chapter 15). Cooke (Chapter 15) finds that the region state (such as Baden-Württemberg in Germany or Emilia-Romagna in Italy) has increasingly become involved with generating competitive advantage for its economic base via 'policy support instruments, institution building and information supply which contribute to its innovation capacity.' This complements the innovative business milieu of these regions based on dynamic inter-firm interaction, cross-cluster exchanges and informal groupings of small firms (networking) that enable them to meet the requirements of very large multi-national customer firms.

Perhaps the most extreme example of this is the restructuring of the world's financial and trade spaces (Swyngedouw, Chapter 8; Leyshon, Chapter 5) as expressed through the staggering volume (by value) of trading in currency, equities, futures and an extremely diverse range of financial derivatives that takes place 24 hours a day on a global basis but is managed from a relatively small number of countries. While to some extent these countries are capitalizing on historical advantages (Drennan, Chapter 17) their pivotal position has been sustained by government support or provision of deregulated fiscal or ownership regimes designed to retain or attract the dynamic, innovative financial institutions and professional services at the centre of the 'glocal' world (Swyngedouw, Chapter 8). While Leyshon (Chapter 5) goes further and suggests that the spread of money has brought about an 'annihilation of space' through time in a way which could be interpreted as making all economic spaces around the globe the same (since they all ultimately function on money as *the* form of communication), he submits that, firstly, even if financial space has become homogenized, levels of economic development vary greatly between these spaces and, secondly, the global economy still comprises several different financial systems. A truly integrated (seamless) global financial space is still an ambition rather than a reality. Meanwhile, there is no doubt that the coincidence between the nation-state and financial space often achieved through the regulatory intervention of governments is breaking down, making it difficult for those countries or trade blocs on the 'outside' to participate effectively in a dynamic global economic system.

The scale and timing of the circulation of money (see also Leyshon, Chapter 5) is such that much of the world economy is subordinate to a few countries and, in particular, a few global cities within those countries such as New York, Tokyo and London, where agglomeration economies and cumulative causation have combined to underpin national government objectives to create regulatory environments favourable to dynamic economic growth and restructuring. Drennan (Chapter 17) reminds us that at the present stage in the ongoing process of transition in the global economy the historical security of these global control points is no guarantee of their future dominance. Tokyo, for example, has asserted its role in the global economy because it is a major source of international capital but Japan's reluctance to open and deregulate its domestic markets to foreign service firms and manufactured goods (most recently exemplified by the threat by the US to double its tariffs on imported Japanese luxury cars in view of the persistent negative trade balance with Japan) may mean that more enlightened, but currently lower order, global financial centres such as Hong Kong or Singapore will threaten Tokyo's position. For New York the threats are both global and local. Globally, the future of the dollar as the major currency for international trade seems to be weakening and this could undermine New York's role as one of the three major international financial centres. The rise of the Pacific Rim as a nexus of global interaction and trade also means that the west coast cities of the US (Los Angeles, San Francisco, Seattle) might also displace New York, a process encouraged by the increasing pace of domestic deregulation of US banking. At the local scale the physical and social infrastructure of New York is deteriorating, making it a less than attractive place to locate and to transact international business.

Perhaps paradoxically, there is in fact less uncertainty about the future direction of change and transition in the post-socialist states but much more scope for uncertainty about the eventual outcome. Globalization has yet to figure strongly in the research agenda for this part of the world but its opportunities and pitfalls will have to be grasped much more quickly than was ever the case in the developed or even the developing economies if the outcomes of the contemporary economic reorientation of the post-socialist economies are to be constructive. The seven socialist states of the former 'Soviet bloc' have become 21 post-socialist states for which transition to some form of 'modern' market-based economy seems inevitable, but there are likely to major differences in the pace of change, ultimate outcomes and degree of integration into the wider European and global economies (Bradshaw, Chapter 13). Bradshaw demonstrates the way in which the post-socialist states in central Europe are already well on the road towards a market economy (in relative terms) and some may expect eventually to achieve full membership of the European Union. Russia in particular is more progressive than most of the other former CIS states but overall the picture is one of enormous diversity in both the practice and potential for economic change. Thus, as other contributors to this volume have shown in both historical and most recent contexts, economic transition in the post-socialist states will be accompanied by increasing polarization, disparity and spatial inequality.

Irrespective of how long the process of transition has been taking place or how rapidly it can occur in a technology- and information-rich late twentieth century, capitalism equals increased inequality from the local, through the regional, to the global scale. In terms of dependency theory (Drakakis-Smith, Chapter 11) countries will only succeed in a capitalist environment if they can get some other country dependent on them, thus enabling them to yield a profit. The consequent economic and social hardships then become part of the political agenda in the post-socialist countries just as much as they are part of that agenda of the developed and less developed market economies or major international development agencies such as the World Bank, the United Nations, the Organization for Economic Cooperation and Development or the General Agreement on Tariffs and Trade.

Thrift (Chapter 2) refers to the rigidities (corporate, nation-state, bureaucratic, fiscal) that characerized the world economy pre-Bretton Woods. It is clear from the contributions to this volume that many of these rigidities have since been unravelled, resulting in greater complexity and economic instability for nation-states, supranational markets such as the EU or newly emerging participants in the global economy such as the post-socialist states or China. The dynamics of identifying opportunities and shaping responses that ensure that localities, major MNEs or nation-states can adjust to the new imperatives of production (just-in-time, flexible specialization for example) are more volatile and condensed in time if not constrained by space. Economic development continues to be a process of restructuring and adjustment for all those affected, but whereas in the past there was time for a more gradual absorption of change, this has been replaced by a need for much more rapid response. It is therefore as important to be able to anticipate how and in what direction a locality or a region's role in the larger global economy will proceed as it is to be aware of what has happened thus far. To know or to anticipate is to be at a competitive advantage. Access to the requisite information, expertise or influence over the deployment of labour or the configuration of production by MNEs is, unfortunately, very uneven. We suggested in Chapter 1 that by the 1990s the world's economy had been truly integrated or globalized. It now seems that this is only the beginning of the story; a truly integrated global economy in which the economic and social benefits of development are more widely and evenly distributed is as far away as ever.

We opened our Introduction with an illustration of the likely geographical sources of the foods and implements that contributed to a typical breakfast for a child in the Britain or the United States of the 1950s. Let us assume that the child is now an adult in the mid-1990s. Breakfast may now be a more diverse affair but the basic geography of its component elements has probably not changed a great deal, although Danish bacon or Jamaican watermelon will be regarded as less 'exotic'. Consider, however, the work, domestic and leisure activities of this middle-aged adult in contemporary Britain. There is a good chance that he or she will be employed in a service industry or some form of white-collar work in manufacturing which will require using modern technology comprising, for example, computers designed in the US, assembled in Ireland, marketed by a British advertising agency, distributed by an Australian transport company and operated by software written in Seattle, downloaded to a distribution centre in Britain supported by user telephone 'hotlines' at yet another location. The computer will be linked to others inside and outside the workplace by telecommunications equipment manufactured by a Swedish MNE, connected by a British service supplier that is a subsidiary of a US-owned telecommunications conglomerate with headquarters in Atlanta. In order to keep telephone charges competitive or to avoid congestion, some calls between parties within the UK will be relayed via a satellite above the equator operated by a European consortium based in Paris. Our hard-working individual regularly receives and replies to queries via e-mail from key clients in Singapore, Rio de Janeiro and Birmingham and operates to sales targets fixed once a month by corporate headquarters in Frankfurt and transmitted at a fixed date and time via a secure company telecommunications network.

Most of these transactions are unseen, even unknown about in terms of the routes used to convey a message between any two points. The same is true at home, where our individual has a mortgage provided by a Middle Eastern bank which has more depositors outside its parent country than within. He or she has invested in shares traded on the Chicago Stock Exchange and in Hong Kong with instructions to the stockbroker in the City of London given by telephone and the transfer of additional funds to invest arranged through a telephone bank in Leeds which handles all domestic banking requirements by telephone 24 hours a day, 365 days a year. The same bank account is automatically debited when the once-weekly shopping trip to the local supermarket or shopping centre is paid for using a plastic card which also holds medical, insurance, blood group, driving licence and similar information that can be 'swiped' only for use by authorized users. Finally, in this generalized (and simplified) scenario, leisure time can comprise watching television programmes beamed by satellite from 10 EU countries as well as a live football game from an east coast city in the US, a grand prix from Australia or tennis from Paris. A film watched at the cinema or at home on the video recorder will probably be financed by US investors, filmed on location in Spain and Russia and in studios in London using equipment manufactured in Japan, with extras recruited locally and the leading roles performed by actors moving swiftly by air from one international location to the next and staying in hotels owned by a multinational group headquartered in the US. The film will be edited in New York and distributed from London. The daily newspaper can be typeset in one location and transmitted by landline or satellite to printing presses more conveniently located for efficient distribution to markets. In the US this helps to overcome time zone differences between the east and west coasts (effectively increasing many fold the number of potential readers); in the UK it avoids traffic delays and congestion.

This is a crude but hopefully useful illustration of the very different economic environment within which 1990s, as opposed to 1950s, households and businesses exist. Production and consumption are less constrained by space and time, yet as we have seen in this book this has not undermined the importance of place or locality and the synergy between the global and local. To assert the distinctiveness of the local as a place to invest, for the quality of labour or for the presence of networks that support production, is a natural antidote to the all-embracing process of globalization. But there can be no going back; the global economy will continue to evolve and to challenge social scientists trying to understand the causes and the consequences. The contributors to this book have hopefully added some useful insights to the economic dimensions of this process.

REFERENCES

Aganbegyan, A. 1988 *The challenge: economics of perestroika*. Hutchinson, London.

Aglietta, M. 1986 *Le fin des devises clés*. La Découverte, Paris.

Aglietta, M., Orléan, A. 1982 *La violence de la monnaie*. Presses Universitaires de France, Paris.

Agnew, J. 1987 *The United States in the world economy*. Cambridge University Press, Cambridge.

Agnew, J. 1994 The territorial trap: the geographical assumptions of international relations theory. *Review of International Political Economy* **1**: 53–80.

Aharoni, Y. 1966 *The foreign investment decision process*. Harvard University Press, Boston, MA.

Albert, M. 1993 *Capitalism against capitalism* (translated by Paul Haviland). Whurr, London.

Alexander, C. 1995 *Fin-de-siècle social theory: relativism, reduction and the problem of reason*. Verso, London.

Altvater, E. 1993 *The future of the market – an essay on the regulation of money and nature after the collapse of 'actually existing socialism'*. Verso, London.

Amin, A., Robins, K. 1990 The re-emergence of regional economies? The mythical geography of flexible accumulation. *Environment and Planning D, Society and Space* **8**: 7–34.

Amin, A. Thrift, N.J. 1994 Living in the global. In Amin, A., Thrift, N. (eds) *Globalization, institutions, and regional development in Europe*. Oxford University Press, Oxford: 1–22.

Anderson, K., Blackhurst, R. (eds) 1993 *Regional integration and the global trading system*. New York.

Andrae, G., Beckmann, B. 1985 *The wheat trap*. Zed Books, London.

Angel, D., Engstrom, J. 1995 Manufacturing systems and technological change: the US personal computer industry. *Economic Geography* **71**: 79–102.

Archer, C. 1994 *Organizing Europe: the institutions of integration* (2nd edition). Edward Arnold, London.

Armstrong, A., Glyn, A., Harrison, J. 1991 *Capitalism since 1945*. Blackwell, Oxford.

Armstrong, H.W. 1995 The role and evolution of European Community regional policy. In Jones, B., Keating, M. (eds) *The European Union and the regions*. Clarendon, Oxford: 23–62.

Armstrong, W. McGee, T.G. 1988 *Theatres of accumulation*, Methuen, London.

Asanuma, B. 1989 Manufacturer–supplier relationships in Japan and the concept of the relation-specific skill. *Journal of the Japanese and International Economies* **3**: 1–30.

Aslund, A. 1991 *Gorbachev's struggle for reform* (2nd edition). Pinter, London.

Atkinson, M.D., Coleman, W.D. 1989 *The state, business, and industrial change in Canada*. University of Toronto Press, Toronto.

Auty, R.M. 1990 *Resource-based industrialization: sowing the oil in eight developing countries*. Clarendon, Oxford.

Auty, R.M. 1991 Third World response to global processes; the mineral economies. *Professional Geographer* **43**(1): 68–76.

Auty, R.M. 1993 *Sustaining development in mineral economies: the resource curse thesis*. Routledge, London.

Auty, R.M. 1994 Industrial policy reform in six large newly industrializing countries: the resource curse thesis. *World Development* **22**(1): 11–26.

Aydalot, P. 1992 The reversal of spatial trends in French industry since 1974, in Lambory, J.L. (ed.) *New spatial dynamics and economic crisis*. Finn Publishers, Helsinki: 68–87.

Bachtler, J., Clement, K., Raines, P. 1993 European integration and foreign investment: the regional implications. In Lundqvist, L., Persson, L.O. (eds) *Visions and strategies in European integration: a north European perspective*. Springer-Verlag, Berlin: 81–106.

Balassa, B. *et al.* 1982 *Development strategies in semi-industrial economies*. John Hopkins University Press.

Balassa, B., Bauwens, L. 1987 Intra-industry specialization in a multi-country and multi-industry framework. *The Economic Journal*, December, 923–39.

Banco Central de Chile 1994 *Indicadores de comercio exterior: Diciembre, 1993*. Santiago.

Bank for International Settlements, 1992, *Recent developments in international interbank relations*. Report prepared by a Working Group established by the Central Banks of the Group of Ten Countries (Bank for International Settlements, Basle).

Bar, F., Borrus, Coriat, 1989 *Information networks and competitive advantage: issues for government policy and corporate strategy development*. BRIE, OECD and CEC, Berkeley, CA.

Barass, B. 1985 Office automation and women's work: the technological transformation of the insurance industry. *High technology, space, and society*, Castells, M. (ed.). Sage Press.

Barham, B., Clark, M., Katz, E., Schurman, R. 1992 Nontraditional agricultural exports in Latin America. *Latin American Research Review* **27**(2): 43–82.

Barnet, R.J., Cavanagh, J. 1994 *Global dreams: imperial corporations and the new world order*. Simon & Schuster, New York.

Barratt-Brown, M. 1974 *The economics of imperialism*. Penguin, Harmondsworth.

Bartlett, C., Ghoshal, S. 1989 *Managing across borders: the transnational solution*. Harvard Business School Press, Boston, MA.

Basle Committee 1994 The capital adequacy treatment of the credit risk associated with certain off-balance-sheet items. Internal Document, released 15 July 1994, Basle.

Bauman, Z. 1987 *Legislators and interpreters*. Polity Press, Cambridge.

Bauman, Z. 1995 Searching for a centre that holds. In Featherstone, M., Lash, S., Robertson, R. (eds) *Global modernities*. Sage, London: 140–154.

Beck, U. 1992 *Risk society*. Sage, London.

Becketti, S. 1993 Are derivatives too risky for banks? *Economic Review*, Federal Reserve

Bank of Kansas City, Third Quarter: 28–41.

Beers, D. 1987 Offshore offices: corporate paperwork sneaks out of the country. *Working Woman* September: 55–57.

Begg, I., Mayes, D. 1993 Regional restructuring: the case of decentralised industrial policy. Paper to Regional Science Association Annual Conference, September, Nottingham.

Bell, M. 1980 Imperialism: an introduction. In Peet, R. (ed.) *An introduction to Marxist theories of underdevelopment.* Monograph HG14, RSPACS, Australian National University, Canberra: 39–50.

Bello, W. 1992 Export-led development in Southeast Asia: a flawed model. *Trocaire Development Review* **4**: 11–27.

Bennett, R., Krebs, G. 1991 *Local economic development: public–private partnership initiation in Britain and Germany.* Belhaven, London.

Bernstein, H., Hewitt, T., Thomas, A. 1992 Capitalism and the expansion of Europe. In Allen, T., Thomas. A. (eds) *Poverty and development in the 1990s.* OUP, London: 168–184.

Beyers, W. 1992 Producer services and metropolitan growth and development. In Mills, E.S., McDonald, J.F. (eds) *Sources of metropolitan growth.* Center for Urban Policy Research, New Brunswick: 125–46.

Bhagwati, J. 1991 *The world trading system at risk.* Harvester Wheatsheaf, London.

BIS 1980 *Bank for International Settlements – 50th Annual Report.* BIS, Basle.

BIS 1984 *Bank for International Settlements – 54th Annual Report.* BIS, Basle.

BIS 1987 *Bank for International Settlements – 57th Annual Report.* BIS, Basle.

BIS 1990a *Bank for International Settlements – 60th Annual Report.* June 1990, BIS, Basle.

BIS 1990b *Survey of foreign exchange market activity.* February, Bank for International Settlements, Basle.

BIS 1991 *Bank for International Settlements – 61st Annual Report.* BIS, Basle.

BIS 1992 *Bank for International Settlements – 62nd Annual Report.* BIS, Basle.

BIS 1993a *Bank for International Settlements – 63rd Annual Report.* BIS, Basle.

BIS 1993b *Central bank survey of foreign exchange market activity in April 1992.* March, Bank for International Settlements, Basle.

BIS 1994 *Bank for International Settlements – 64th Annual Report*, 13th June 1994. BIS, Basle.

Black, I. 1989, Geography, political economy and the circulation of finance capital in early industrial England. *Journal of Historical Geography* **15**: 366–384.

Blacksell, M., Williams, A.M. 1995 The development of the European Community: its spatial dimension. In Blacksell, M. Williams, A.M. (eds) *The European challenge: geography and development in the European Community.* Oxford University Press, Oxford: 89–106.

Blau, J. 1994 Germany hopes new law will boost gene research. *Research-Technology Management* **37**(4): 3–4.

Blaut, J. 1993 *The colonizers model of the world.* Guildford Press, London.

Block, F., Somers, M.R. 1984 Beyond the economistic fallacy: the holistic science of Karl Polanyi. In Tskocpol (ed.) *Vision and method in historical sociology.* Cambridge University Press, Cambridge: 47–84.

Bluestone, B., Harrison, B. 1982 *The deindustrialization of America.* Basic Books, New York.

Blum, R.H. 1984 *Offshore haven banks, trusts, and companies.* Praeger Press, New York.

Boddy, M., Fudge, C. 1984 *Local socialism*. Macmillan, London.

Boden, D. 1994 *The business of talk*. Polity Press, Cambridge.

Boekholt, P. 1994 Methodology to identify regional clusters of firms and their needs. Paper to SPRINT-RITTS Workshop, Luxembourg.

Bonamy, J., Daniels, P.W. 1993 Firm organisation and spatial dynamics. In Daniels, P.W, Illeris, S., Bonamy, J., Philippe, J. (eds) *The geography of services*. Frank Cass, London: 69–75.

Bonetti, S., Cobham, D. 1992 Financial markets and the City of London. In Cobham, D. (ed.) *Markets and dealers: the economics of the London financial markets*. Longman, London: 1–24.

Booth, A. 1993 Progress and poverty in Southeast Asia. Paper presented to the British Pacific Rim Seminar Group, John Moores University, Liverpool.

Borrman, A., Koopmann, G. 1994 Regionalisation and regionalism in world trade. *Intereconomics* **29**, July/August: 163–71.

Boskin, M.J., Lau, L.J. 1992 Capital, technology, and economic growth. In Rosenberg, N., Landau, R., Mowery, D.C. (eds) *Technology and the wealth of nations*. Stanford University Press, Stanford: 17–56.

Bradshaw, M.J. 1996 The internationalization of the Post-Soviet States. In Bradshaw. M.J. (ed.) *Geography and transition in the Post-Soviet states*. Wiley, London: Forthcoming.

Bradshaw, M.J., Lynn, N. 1994 After the Soviet Union: the Post-Soviet republics in the world system. *The Professional Geographer* **46**(4): 439–49.

Britton, J.N.H. 1980 Industrial dependence and technological under-development: Canadian consequences of foreign direct investment. *Regional Studies* **14**: 181–99.

Britton, J.N.H., Gilmour, J.M. 1978 *The weakest link: a technological perspective on Canadian industrial underdevelopment*. Background Study 43, Science Council of Canada, Ottawa: Ministry of Supply and Services Canada.

Brookfield, H. 1975 *Interdependent development*. Methuen, London.

Brunn, S.D., Leinbach, T.R. 1991 (eds) *Collapsing space and time: geographic aspects of communication and information*. Harper Collins, London.

Bruno, M. 1994 Stabilization and reform in Eastern Europe: a preliminary evaluation. In Blanchard, O.J., Froot, K.A., Sachs, J.D. (eds) *Transition in Eastern Europe, vol. 1 Country studies*. MIT Press, London: 19–48.

Bruns, W. 1995 Harvard University Business School Press, Cambridge, MA.

Buck, N., Drennan, M., Newton, K. 1992 Dynamics of the metropolitan economy. In Fainstein, S.S., Gordon, I., Harloe, M. (eds) *Divided cities*. Blackwell, Oxford: 68–104.

Buckley, P.J., Casson, M.C. 1981 The optimal timing of a foreign direct investment. *Economic Journal* **91**: 75–87. Reprinted as Chapter 5 in Buckley, P.J., Casson, M.C. (eds) 1985 *The economic theory of the multinational enterprise*. Macmillan, London.

Buckley, P.J., Clegg, J. 1991 Introduction and statement of the issues. Chapter 1 in Buckley, P.J., Clegg, J. (eds) *Multinational enterprises in less developed countries*. Macmillan, London: 3–23.

Buckley, P.J., Ghauri, P. (eds) 1993 *The internationalization of the firm: a reader*. Academic Press, London.

Budd, L., Whimster, S. (eds) 1992 *Global finance and urban living*. Routledge, London and New York.

Bujra, J. 1992 Ethnicity and class: the case of East African 'Asians'. In Allen, T., Thomas, A. (eds) *Poverty and development in the 1990s*. OUP, London.

Bull, M. (ed.) 1995 *Apocalyse theory and the ends of the world*. Blackwell, Oxford.

Bureau of Economic Analysis, US Department of Commerce June 1994. *Survey of current business* Tables 1 and 7. US Government Printing Office, Washington DC.

Cain, P.J., Hopkins, A.G. 1993a *British imperialism: innovation and expansion 1688–1914*. Longman, London.

Cain, P.J., Hopkins, A.G. 1993b *British imperialism. Crisis and deconstruction 1914–1990*. Longman, London.

Callon, M. 1987 Society in the making: the study of technology as a tool for sociological analysis. In Bijker, W.E., Hughes, T.P., Pinch, T.J. (eds) *The social construction of technical systems*. MIT Press, Cambridge, MA: 83–103.

Campbell, M. (ed.) 1990 *Local economic policy*. Cassell, London.

Campbell, R.W. 1991 *The socialist economies in transition: a primer on semi-reformed systems*. Indiana University Press, Bloomington.

Camps, M. 1964 *Britain and the European Community, 1955–1963*. Oxford University Press, Oxford.

Cantor, R., Packer, F. 1994 The credit rating industry. *Federal Reserve Bank of New York Quarterly Review* **19** (2): 1–26.

Capellin, R., Molle, W. 1988 The coordination problem in theory and policy. In Molle, W., Cappellin, R. (eds) *Regional impact of community policies in Europe*. Avebury, Aldershot: 1–22.

Capello, R. 1994 Towards new industrial and spatial systems: the role of new technologies. *Papers in Regional Science* **73**: 189–208.

Carnoy, M. 1993 Multinationals in a changing world economy. In Carnoy, M., Castells, M., Cohen, S.S., Cardoso, F.H. (eds) *The new global economy in the information age*. Pennsylvania State University Press, University Park, PA: 45–96.

Casson, M.C. 1982 Transaction costs and the theory of multinational enterprise. Chapter 2. In Rugman, A.M. (ed.) *New theories of the multinational enterprise*. Croom Helm, London. Reprinted as Chapter 2 in Buckley, P.J., Casson, M.C. (eds) 1985 *The economic theory of the multinational enterprise*. Macmillan, London.

Casson, M.C. 1987 General theories of the multinational enterprise: a critical examination. Chapter 2. In Casson, M.C. (ed.) 1987 *The firm and the market*. Blackwell, Oxford.

Casson, M.C. (ed.) 1991 *Global research strategy and international competitiveness*. Blackwell, Oxford.

Castells, M. 1989 *The informational city*. Blackwell, Oxford.

Castells, M. 1993 The information economy and the new international division of labor. In Carnoy, M., Castells, M., Cohen, S., Cardoso, F.H. (eds) *The new global economy in the information age: reflections on our changing world*. Pennsylvania State University Press: University Park, PA.

Castells, M., Hall, P. 1994 *Technopoles of the world: the making of 21st century industrial complexes*. Routledge, London.

Cecchini, P. 1988 *The European challenge: 1992. The benefits of a single market*. Wildwood House, Aldershot.

Cerny, P.G. 1993 Money and power: the American financial system from free banking to global competition. PAIS Working Paper No. 116, Department of Politics and International Studies, University of Warwick.

Chandler, A. 1962 *Strategy and structure*. MIT Press, Cambridge, MA.

Chandler, A. 1977 *The visible hand*. Belknap Press, Cambridge, MA.

Chandler, A.D. 1990 *Scale and scope: the dynamics of industrial capitalism.* Belknap Press, Cambridge, MA.

Chandler, A., Redlich, F. 1961 Recent developments in American business administration and their conceptualisation. *Business History Review* **35**: 1–27.

Chandra, R. 1992 *Industrialization and development in the Third World.* Routledge, London.

Chapman, G. 1992 Introduction: Asia's future seen in the mid 1960s. In Chapman, G., Baker, K. (eds) *The changing geography of Asia.* Routledge, London: 1–9.

Chapman, K., Humphrys, G. (eds) 1987 *Technical change and industrial policy.* Basil Blackwell, Oxford.

Charles, D.R., Li, F. 1993 *Lean production, supply chain management and new industrial dynamics: logistics in the automobile industry.* PICT Working Paper, University of Newcastle-upon-Tyne.

Charles, D.R., Richardson, R. 1993 *The convergence of transport and communications: UK urban and regional implications.* Report to the Transport and Communications Programme, Centre for Exploitation of Science and Technology, London.

Cheshire, P.C. 1990 Explaining the recent performance of the European Community's major urban regions. *Urban Studies* **27**: 311–333.

Cheshire, P.C., Hay, D.G. 1989 *Urban problems in western Europe: an economic analysis.* Unwin Hyman, London.

Cheshire, P.C., Carbonaro, G., Hay, D.G. 1986 Problems of urban decline and growth in EEC countries: or measuring degrees of elephantness. *Urban Studies* **23**: 131–149.

Cho, G. 1990 *The Malaysian economy: spatial perspectives.* Routledge, London.

Christopherson, S. 1993 Market rules and territorial outcomes: the case of the United States. *International Journal of Urban and Regional Research* **17**: 274–288.

Clark, C. 1940 *The conditions of economic progress.* Macmillan, London.

Clark, G.L. 1981 The employment relation and the spatial division of labour: a hypothesis. *Annals of the Association of American Geographers* **71**: 412–24.

Clark, G.L. 1993a Global interdependence and regional development: business linkages and corporate governance in a world of financial risk. *Transactions of the Institute of British Geographers* **18**: 309–25.

Clark, G.L. 1993b *Pensions and corporate restructuring in American industry: the crisis of regulation.* Johns Hopkins University Press, Baltimore.

Clarke, A. 1994 Spatial linkages and subcontracting relationships among high-technology industries in the Northeast Ohio region. *Environment and Planning A* **26**: 1579–1603.

Clarke, J., Newman, J. 1993 The right to manage: a second managerial revolution? *Cultural Studies* **7**: 427–441.

Clegg, J. 1993 Investigating the determinants of service sector foreign direct investment. Chapter 5. In Cox, H., Clegg, J., Ietto-Gillies, G. (eds) *The growth of global business.* Routledge, London: 85–104.

Clegg, J. 1995 United States foreign direct investment in the European Community: the effects of market integration in perspective. In Burton, F., Yamin, M., Young, S. (eds) *The changing European environment.* Macmillan, London.

Coffey, W., Bailly, A. 1992 Producer services and systems of flexible production. *Urban Studies* **29**: 857–68.

Cohen, R. 1981 The new international division of labor, multinational corporations and the urban hierarchy. In Dear, M., Scott, A. (eds) *Urbanization and urban planning in capitalist society.* Methuen, New York.

Cohen, W.M., Mowery, D.C. 1984 Firm heterogeneity and R&D: an agenda for research. In Bozeman, B., Crow, M., Link, A. (eds) *Strategic management of industrial R&D*. D C Heath, Lexington: 107–32.

Collier, J. 1994 Regional disparities, the Single Market and European Monetary Union. In Michie, J. (ed.) *Unemployment in Europe*. Academic Press, London: 145–159.

Collins, J. 1995 *Architectures of excess. Cultural life in the information age*. Routledge, London.

Commission of the European Community 1991 *The regions in the 1990s: fourth report on the social and economic situation and development of the regions of the Community*. CEC, Brussels.

Confederation of British Industry 1995 *Winning the export race*. CBI, London.

Conzen, M.P. 1975 Capital flows and the developing urban hierarchy: state bank capital in Wisconsin, 1854–1895. *Economic Geography* **51**: 321–338.

Conzen, M.P. 1977 The maturing urban system in the United States, 1840–1910. *Annals of the Association of American Geographers* **67**: 88–108.

Cooke, P. (ed.) 1989 *Localities*. Unwin Hyman, London.

Cooke, P. 1995 Institutional reflexivity and the rise of the region state. In Benko, G., Strohmayer, U. (eds) *Space and social theory: geographic interpretations of postmodernity*. Blackwell, Oxford.

Cooke, P., Morgan, K. 1993 The network paradigm: new departures in corporate and regional development. *Society & Space* **11**: 543–564.

Cooke, P., Moulaert, F., Swyngedouw, E., Weinstein, O., Wells, P. 1992 *Towards global localisation*. University College Press, London.

Coombs, R., Jones, B. 1989 Alternative successors to Fordism. In Ernste, H., Jaeger, C. (eds) *Information society and spatial structure*. Belhaven, London: 105–116.

Corbett, J. 1987 International perspectives on finance: evidence from Japan. *Oxford Review of Economic Policy* **3**(4): 30–55.

Corbridge, S. 1993 *Debt and development*. Blackwell, Oxford.

Corbridge, S. 1994 Maximizing entropy? New geopolitical orders and the internationalization of business. In Demko, G., Wood, W. (eds) *Reordering the world: geopolitical perspectives on the twenty-first century*. Westview, Boulder, CO: 281–300.

Cox, A. (ed.) 1986 *State, finance and industry: a comparative analysis of trends in six advanced industrial economies*. Harvester Wheatsheaf, Brighton.

Cox, R. 1987 *Production, power and world order*. Columbia University Press, London and New York.

Coy, R. 1992 Cooperation networks and innovative roles for employers' and workers' organisations. Paper presented to an International Conference, Regional Development: the roles of technical service institutes and co-operation networks, Valencia, November.

Cronon, W. 1991 *Nature's metropolis – Chicago and the Great West*. W W Norton & Co, New York.

Daly, C. 1993 The discursive construction of economic space. *Economy and Society* **20**: 79–102.

Daniels, P.W. 1993 *Service industries in the world economy*. Blackwell, Oxford.

DATAR 1989 *Les villes Européenes*. Maison de la Géographie, Montpellier.

Davies, G. 1994a *A history of money: from ancient times to the present day*. University of Wales Press, Cardiff.

Davies, G. 1994b Interfacing universities and SMEs in North-Rhine Westphalia.

Proceedings of an International Conference, Cooperation & Competitiveness: Interfirm Cooperation – a Means Towards SME Competitiveness. PEDIP, Lisbon.

Davis, E.P., 1991 The development of pension funds – an international comparison. *Bank of England Quarterly Bulletin* **31**: 380–390.

Debagge, K.G. 1994 The international airline industry: globalisation, regulation and strategic alliances. *Transport Geography* **2**(3): 190–203.

De Benedictis, L., Padoan, P.C. 1995 EC enlargement to eastern Europe: community and incentives and sectoral resistances. In Lombardini, S., Padoan, P.C. (eds) *Europe between east and south*. Kluwer, Dordrecht: 9–35.

De Standaard 1994 Vrijhandelsakkoord kan wereld 15.000 miljard opbrengen. *De Standaard* 12/13 November: 17.

de Vet, J. 1993 Globalisation and local and regional competitiveness. *STI Review* **13**: 89–121.

Deyo, F. (ed.) 1987 *The political economy of the new Asian industrialism*. Cornell University Press, Ithaca, NY.

Diamond, C. 1991 *The realistic spirit. Wittgenstein, philosophy and the mind*. MIT Press, Cambridge, MA.

Dicken, P. 1986 *Global shift: industrial change in a turbulent world*. Harper and Row, London.

Dicken, P. 1988 *Global shift: industrial change in a turbulent world*. Paul Chapman, London.

Dicken, P. 1992 *Global shift: the internationalization of economic activity*. 2nd edition. Paul Chapman, London, and Guilford, New York.

Dicken, P. 1994 Global–local tensions: firms and states in the global space-economy. *Economic Geography* **70**(2): 101–28.

Dickenson, J. 1987 Early industrial patterns. In Preston, D. (ed.) *Latin American development*. Longman, Harlow.

Dixon, C. 1991 *Southeast Asia in the world economy*. Cambridge University Press, Cambridge.

Dixon, C., Drakakis-Smith, D. (eds) 1993 *Economic and social development in Pacific Asia*. Routledge, London.

Dixon, C., Drakakis-Smith, D. (forthcoming) *The Pacific Asian region: myth or reality*.

Dixon, R.J., Thirlwall, A.P. 1975 *Regional growth and unemployment in the United Kingdom*. Macmillan, London.

Dobozi, I., Pohl, G. 1995 Real output decline in transition economies – forget GDP, try power consumption. *Transition* **6**(1–2): 17–18.

Donaghu, M., Barff, R. 1990 Nike just did it: international subcontracting and flexibility in athletic footwear production. *Regional Studies* **24**: 537–52.

Dornbusch, R. 1992 The case for trade liberalization in developing countries. *Journal of Economic Perspectives* **6**(1): 69–85.

Dosi, G. 1988 The nature of the innovative process. In Dosi, G., Freeman, C., Nelson, R., Silverberg, G., Soete, L. (eds) *Technical change and economic theory*. Pinter, London: 221–38.

Dosi, G., Freeman, C., Nelson, R., Silverberg, G., Soete, L. (eds) 1988 *Technical change and economic theory*. Pinter, London.

Drache, D., Gertler, M. 1991 The world economy and the nation-state: the new international order. In Drache D., Gertler, M. (eds) *The new era of global competition – state policy and market power*. McGill-Queen's University Press, Montreal & Kingston: 3–25.

Drakakis-Smith, D. 1992 *Pacific Asia*. Routledge, London.

Drakakis-Smith, D. 1993 Is there still a third world? *Chronos* **1**: Kulturgeografiska Institutionen, Handelshögskolan vid Goteborgs Universitet.

Drakakis-Smith, D., Bowyer-Bower, T., Tevera, D. 1995 Urban poverty and urban agriculture: an overview of the linkages in Harare. *Habitat International* (in press).

Drennan, M. 1987 Local economy and local revenues. In Brecher, C., Horton, R.D. (eds) *Setting municipal priorities 1988*. NYU Press, New York: 15–44.

Drennan, M. 1989 Information intensive industries in metropolitan areas of the United States. *Environment and Planning A* **21**: 1603–1618.

Drennan, M. 1992 Gateway cities: the metropolitan sources of US producer service exports. *Urban Studies* **29**(2): 217–35.

Drennan, M. 1995 The changing industrial structure of the New York region. In Norton, R.D. (ed) *Upgrading the northeast*. JAI Press, Boston.

Drucker, P.F. 1989 Information and the future of the city. *Wall Street Journal* (4 April): A22.

Duncan, A. 1993 *An end to illusions*. Demos Paper No. 2. Demos, London.

Dunning, J.H. 1986a The investment cycle revisited. *Weltwirtschaftliches Archiv* **122**: 667–77.

Dunning, J.H. 1986b The investment development cycle and third world multinationals. In Khan, K.M. (ed.) *Multinationals of the south*. Frances Pinter, London.

Dunning, J.H. 1988 *Explaining international production*. Unwin Hyman, London.

Dunning, J.H. 1993 *Multinational enterprises and the global economy*. Addison-Wesley, Wokingham, Berks.

Dunning, J.H. 1994 The prospects for foreign direct investment in central and eastern Europe. In Buckley, P.J., Chauri, P.N. (eds) *The economics of change in east and central Europe: its impact on international business*. Academic Press, London: 373–388.

Dunning, J.H., Narula, R. 1994 *Transpacific foreign direct investment and the investment development path: the record assessed*. South Carolina Essays in International Business, No 10. March.

Dymski, G.A., Veitch, J.M. 1992 Race and the financial dynamics of urban growth: L.A. as Fay Wray. Working Paper 92-21, Department of Economics, University of California, Riverside, California, March.

Dyson, K. 1983 The cultural, ideological and structural context. In Dyson, K., Wilks, S. (eds) *A comparative study of state and industry*. Oxford University Press, Oxford: 26–66.

EBRD 1994 *Transition report*. EBRD, London.

Economist 1994 A survey of international banking (30 April): 1–42.

Edgington, D.W. 1994 Planning for technology development and information systems in Japanese cities and regions. In Shapira, P. (ed.) *Planning for cities and regions in Japan*. Liverpool University Press, Liverpool: 126–54.

Emery, F., Trist, E. 1965 The causal texture of organisational environments. *Human Relations* **18**: 21–32.

Enos, J.L., Park, W.H. 1988 *The adoption and diffusion of imported technology: the case of Korea*. Routledge, London.

Erickson, R.A. 1976 The filtering down process: industrial location in a non-metropolitan area. *Professional Geographer* **28**: 254–60.

Ericson, R.E. 1991 The classical Soviet-type economy: nature of the system and implications for reform. *Journal of Economic Perspectives* **5**(4): 11–27.

Ettlinger, N. 1991 The roots of competitive advantage in California and Japan. *Annals of the Association of American Geographers* **81**(3): 391–407.

Ettlinger, N. 1994 The localization of development in comparative perspective. *Economic Geography* **70**(2): 144–166.

Fainstein, S., Harloe, M. 1992 London and New York in the contemporary world. In Fainstein, S., Gordon, I., Harloe, M. (eds) *Divided cities*. Blackwell, Oxford: 1–28.

FAO 1993 *Agriculture: towards 2010*. Food and Agriculture Organisation, Rome, C93/24.

Fersko-Weiss, H. 1987 The return of outside data processing. *High Technology Business* **7** (December): 41–46.

Firn, J.R. 1975 External control and regional development: the case of Scotland. *Environment and Planning A* **7**: 393–414.

Florida, R., Kenney, M. 1990 High technology restructuring in the USA and Japan. *Environment and Planning A* **22**: 23–52.

Forbes, D. 1984 *The geography of underdevelopment*. Croom Helm, London.

Forester, T. 1987 *High-tech society: the story of the information technology revolution*. Blackwell, Oxford.

Forey, D., Freeman, C. (eds) 1993 *Technology and the wealth of nations*. Pinter, London.

Forgacs, O.L. 1979 The role of industry research. Paper presented at British Columbia's Future in Science and Research Executive Seminar. British Columbia Ministry of Education, Science and Technology, Delta, June 25.

Fothergill, S., Guy, N. 1990 *Retreat from the regions: corporate change and the closure of factories*. Jessica Kingsley Press, London.

Franchi, M. 1994 Developments in the districts of Emilia-Romagna. Paper to conference on Industrial Districts & Local Economic Development in Italy: Challenges & Policy Perspective, Bologna, May.

Frank, A.G. 1994 Soviet and East European socialism: a review of the international political economy on what went wrong. *Review of International Political Economy* **1**(2): 317–43.

Freeman, C. 1982 *The economics of industrial innovation*. Frances Pinter, London.

Freeman, C. 1987 *Technology policy and economic performance: lessons from Japan*. Frances Pinter, London.

Freeman, C. 1988 Japan: a new national system of innovation? In Dosi, G., Freeman, C., Nelson, R. Silverberg, G. (eds) *Technical change and economic theory*. Frances Pinter, London: 330–48.

Freeman, C., Perez, C. 1988 Structural crises of adjustment, business cycles and investment behaviour. In Dois, G., Freeman, C., Nelson, R., Silverberg, G. (eds) *Technical change and economic theory*. Frances Pinter, London: 38–66.

Fröbel, F., Heinrichs, J., Kreye, O. 1980 *The new international division of labour*. Cambridge University Press, Cambridge.

Fruin, M.W. 1992 *The Japanese enterprise system*. Clarendon Press, Oxford.

Fukuyama, F. 1992 *The end of history and the last man*. Hamish Hamilton, London.

Furness, C.C. 1958 *Research in industry: its organization and management*. Nostrand, Toronto.

Galbraith, J.K. 1967 *The new industrial state*. Hamish Hamilton, London.

Garofoli, G. 1992 *Endogenous development and southern Europe*. Avebury, Aldershot.

Gassmann, P., Hansen, I., Herzer, H., Pitz, K., Roth, S. 1993 *Innovation und soziale unternehmenskultur: fallbeispiel mettler-toledo*. I G Metall, Albstadt, Frankfurt.

GATT 1993 *International trade 1993: statistics.* General Agreement on Tariffs and Trade, Geneva.

Geddes, M., Benington, J. (eds) 1992 *Restructuring the local economy.* Longman, London.

Gelsing, L., Knop, P. 1991 Status of the network programme – the results from a questionnaire survey (mimeo, University of Aalborg, Denmark).

Gelb, A.H. 1988 *Oil windfalls: blessing or curse?* Oxford University Press, Oxford.

Geron, L. 1990 *Soviet foreign economic policy under perestroika.* RIIA/Pinter, London.

Gerschenkron, A. 1962 *Economic backwardness in historical perspective.* Harvard University Press, Cambridge.

Gertler, M.S. 1988 The limits to flexibility: comments on the post-Fordist vision of production and its geography. *Transactions of the Institute of British Geographers* **13**: 419–42.

Ghoschal, S., Bartlett, C.A. 1995 Changing the role of top management: beyond structure to process. *Harvard Business Review* **73**: 86–96.

Gibb R., Michalak, W. 1993 The European Community and Central Europe: prospects for integration. *Geography* **78**: 16–30.

Gibbon, P. 1992 The World Bank and African poverty 1973–1991. *Journal of Modern African Studies* **30**(2): 193–302.

Gibbon, P., Bangura, Y. Ofstad, A. 1992 *Authoritarianism, democracy and adjustment.* Seminar Proceedings No 26, Scandinavian Institute for Development Studies, Uppsala.

Giddens, A. 1981 *A contemporary critique of historical materialism.* Macmillan, London.

Giddens, A. 1984 *The constitution of society.* Polity, Cambridge.

Giddens, A. 1985 *The nation state and violence.* Polity, Cambridge.

Giddens, A. 1990 *The consequences of modernity.* Polity, Cambridge.

Giddens, A. 1991 *Modernity and self-identity: self and society in the late modern age.* Polity, Cambridge.

Gilbert, A. 1990 *Latin America.* Routledge, London.

Gillespie, A. 1993 Telematics and its implications for industrial and spatial organisation. *Regional Development Dialogue* **14**(2): 138–150.

Gilman, M.G. 1981 *The financing of foreign direct investment: a study of the determinants of capital flows in multinational enterprises.* Frances Pinter, London.

Glasmeier, A.K. 1986 High-tech industries and the regional division of labor. *Industrial Relations* **25**: 197–211.

Glasmeier, A., Howland, M. 1995 *From combines to computers: rural development in the information age.* State University of New York Press, Albany, New York.

Glyn, A., Hughes, A., Lipietz, A., Singh, H. 1988 The rise and fall of the golden age. Working Paper 43, World Institute for Development Economics Research, United Nations University, Helsinki.

Goldsmith, W., Blakely, E. 1992 *Separate societies.* Temple University Press, Philadelphia.

Gomes-Casseres, B. 1994 Group versus group: how alliance networks compete. *Harvard Business Review* July–August: 62–73.

Goss, T., Pascale, R., Athos, R. 1993 Reinvention roller coaster: risking the present for a powerful future. *Harvard Business Review* January–February: 1–12.

Gowa, J. 1983 *Closing the gold window.* Cornell University Press, Ithaca, NY.

Graham, M.B.W., Pruitt, B.H. 1990 *R&D for industry: a century of technical innovation.* Cambridge University Press, Cambridge.

Gregory, R.R., Stuart, R.C. 1992 *Comparative economic systems* (4th edition). Houghton Mifflin, Boston.

Gregory, R.R., Stuart, R.C. 1994 *Soviet and post-Soviet economic structure* (5th edition). Harper Collins, New York.

Gros, D., Thygesen, N. 1992 *European monetary integration: from the European monetary system towards monetary union.* Longman, London.

Grossman, G. 1963 Notes for a theory of the command economy. *Soviet Studies* **15**: 101–23.

Group of Thirty 1993 *Derivatives: practices and principles.* Global Derivatives Study Group, Washington, DC.

Grupp, H., Schnoring, T. 1992 Research and development telecommunications. *Telecommunications Policy* **16**: 46–66.

Gumbrecht, H.U., Pfeiffer, K.L. (eds) 1994 *Materialities of communication.* Stanford University Press, Stanford.

Gwynne, R.N. 1985 *Industrialisation and urbanisation in Latin America.* Croom Helm.

Gwynne, R. 1990 *New horizons: third world industrialization in an international framework.* Longman, Harlow.

Gwynne, R.N., 1992 Copper policy and the democratic transition in Chile. In Angell, A., Pollack, B. (eds) *The legacy of dictatorship: political, economic and social change in Pinochet's Chile.* Institute of Latin American Studies, University of Liverpool: 13–26.

Gwynne, R.N. 1994 *Chile 1994: report on government, economy, the business environment and industry.* Business Monitor International.

Haas, G. 1992 Testimony before the subcommittee on housing and community development and the subcommittee on consumer affairs and coinage of the U.S. House of Representatives Committee on Banking, Finance and Urban Affairs, 7 May.

Habeeb, A. 1981 Economic structure of colonial cities in India: a review of sectoral trends, 1872–1921. *Studies in Urban History.* Guru Nanak Dev University, Amritsar.

Hagstrom, P. 1992 Inside the 'wired' MNC. In Antonelli, C. (ed.) *The economics of information networks.* Elsevier.

Hall, F.S. 1902 The localization of industries. *Twelfth Census of the United States Manufacturing Part I.* US Government Printing Office, Washington: cxc–ccxiv.

Hall, P. 1966 *The world cities.* Weidenfeld and Nicolson Ltd, London.

Hall, P., Breheny, M., McQuaid, R., Hart, D. 1987 *Western sunrise: the genesis and growth of Britain's major high tech corridor.* UnwinHyman, London.

Hamilton, A. 1986 *The financial revolution.* Penguin Books, Harmondsworth.

Hamilton, C. 1992 Can the rest of Asia emulate the NIEs? In Walker, C.K., Jameson, K.P. (eds) *The political economy of development and underdevelopment.* McGraw Hill, Singapore: 112–145.

Handy, C. 1989 *The age of unreason.* Arrow, London.

Handy, C. 1991 *The empty raincoat.* Hutchinson, London.

Hansen, N. 1995 Small and medium-sized enterprises, innovative milieux, and regional development: some evidence from the US. Annual meeting, Western Regional Science Association, San Diego.

Harberger, A. 1988 Growth, industrialization and economic structure: Latin America and East Asia compared. In Hughes, H. (ed.) *Achieving industrialization in East Asia.* Cambridge University Press: 164–194.

Harrington, J.W. 1995 Empirical research on producer service growth and regional development: international comparisons. *The Professional Geographer*, **47**(1): 66–69.

Harris, N. 1986 *The end of the third world: newly industrialising countries and the decline of an ideology*. Penguin, Harmondsworth.

Harrison, B. 1994a The Italian industrial districts and the crisis of the cooperative form: part 1. *European Planning Studies* **2**: 3–22.

Harrison, B. 1994b *Lean and mean: the changing landscape of corporate power in the age of flexibility*. Basic Books, New York.

Harvey, D. 1982 *The limits to capital*. Blackwell, Oxford.

Harvey, D. 1985 *Consciousness and the urban experience*. The Johns Hopkins University Press, Baltimore.

Harvey, D. 1989 *The condition of postmodernity*. Blackwell, Oxford.

Hassink, R. 1992 Regional innovation policy: case studies from the Ruhr area, Baden-Württemberg and NE England. NGS, Utrecht.

Havinden, M., Meredith, D. 1993 *Colonialism and development*. Routledge, London.

Hayter, R. 1981 Patterns of entry and the role of foreign-controlled investments in the forest products sector of British Columbia. *Tidschrift voor Economische en Sociale Geografie* **72**: 99–113.

Hayter, R. 1982 Research and development in the Canadian forest product sector – another weak link. *Canadian Geographer* **26**: 256–63.

Hayter, R. 1985 The evolution and structure of the Canadian forest product sector: an assessment of the role of foreign ownership and control. *Fennia* **163**: 439–50.

Hayter, R. 1988 *Technology and the Canadian forest-product industries: a policy perspective*. Background Study 54, Science Council of Canada, Ottawa: Ministry of Supply and Services.

Hebbert, M. Hansen, J.C. 1990 *Unfamiliar territory: the reshaping of European geography*. Avebury, Aldershot.

Held, D. 1991 Democracy, the nation-state, and the global system. *Economy & Society* **20**: 138–172.

Helpman, E., Krugman, P. 1985 *Market structure and foreign trade: increasing returns, imperfect competition and the international economy*. MIT Press, Cambridge, MA.

Henderson, J.V. 1988 *Urban development*. Oxford University Press, Oxford.

Henderson, J. 1989 *The globalisation of high technology production*. Routledge, London.

Henderson, J., Castells, M. (eds) 1987 *Global restructuring and territorial development*. Sage, London.

Hepworth, M. 1989 *The geography of the information economy*. Belhaven, London.

Hepworth, M., Ducatel, K. 1992 *Transport in the information age*. Belhaven, London.

Hettne, B. 1990 *Development theory and the three worlds*. Longman, Harlow.

Higgins, A. 1994 Speculators hasten collapse of rouble. *The Independent* 12 October 1994: 11.

Hilferding, R. 1981 *Finance capital*. Routledge and Kegan Paul, London.

Hill, R.C. 1989 Comparing transnational production systems: the automobile industry in the USA and Japan. *International Journal of Urban and Regional Research* **13**: 462–80.

Hindle, T. 1994 *Pocket finance*. The Economist Books, London.

Hirsch, S. 1972 The United States electronics industry in international trade. In Wells, L.T. (ed.) *The product life cycle and international trade*. Harvard Business School, Boston.

Ho, S.P.S., Huenemann, R.W. 1984 *China's open door policy: the question of foreign technology and capital*. University of British Columbia Press, Vancouver.

Hodder, R. 1992 *The West Pacific Rim*. Belhaven.

Holmes, J. 1986 The organization and locational structure of production subcontracting. In Scott, A.J., Storper, M. (eds) *Production, work, territory: the geographical anatomy of industrial capitalism*. Allen and Unwin, Boston: 80–106.

Hoogvelt, A. 1987 *Multinational enterprise – an encyclopaedic dictionary of concepts and terms*. Macmillan, London.

Howells, J.R.L. 1990 The internationalization of R&D and the development of global research networks. *Regional Studies* **24**: 495–512.

Howells, J., Wood, M. 1992 *The globalisation of production and technology*. Belhaven Press, London.

Hsiao, M. 1992 The Taiwanese experience. *Development and Democracy* **2**: 17–32.

Hymer, S. 1972a The multinational corporation and the law of uneven development. In Bagwati, J. (ed.) *Economics and world order from the 1970s to the 1990s*. Macmillan, New York.

Hymer, S. 1972b The efficiency (contradictions) of multinational corporations. In Paquet, G. (ed.) *The multinational firm and the nation state*. Collier-MacMillan, Toronto: 49–65.

IBM 1993 *Annual report*. New York.

IMF, World Bank, OECD & EBRD 1991 *A study of the Soviet economy*. 3 Vols. OECD, Paris.

Ingham, G. 1994 States and markets in the production of world money. In Corbridge S., Martin, R., Thrift, N. (eds) *Money, power and space*. Blackwell, Oxford: 29–48.

Ingham, G. 1995 British capitalism: empire, merchants and decline. *Social History* (forthcoming).

Ingold, T. 1995 Man: the story so far. *Times Higher Education Supplement* June 2: 16–17.

International Monetary Fund 1977 *Balance of payments manual*. 4th edition. IMF, Washington DC.

International Monetary Fund 1992 *International financial statistics yearbook*. Vol XLV, Washington DC.

Jeelof, G. 1989 Global strategies of Philips. *European Management Journal* **7**(1): 84–91.

Jefferies, I. 1993 *Socialist economies and the transition to the market, a guide*. Routledge, London.

Jenkins, R. 1991a Learning from the gang: are there lessons for Latin America from East Asia? *Bulletin of Latin American Research* **10**(1): 37–54.

Jenkins, R. 1991b The impact of foreign investment on less developed countries: cross-section analysis versus industry studies. Chapter 6. In Buckley, P.J., Clegg, J. (eds) *Multinational enterprises in less developed countries*. Macmillan, London: 111–30.

Jessop, B. 1992 Fordism and post-Fordism: a critical reformulation. In Storper, M., Scott, A.J. (eds) *Pathways to industrialisation and regional development*. Routledge, London: 46–69.

Johansson, J.K., Yip, G.S. 1994 Exploiting globalization potential: U.S. and Japanese strategies. *Strategic Management Journal*.

Johns, A. 1994 Not tax havens, havens for transnational invisible trade enterprise. *Intereconomics* **29**, January/February: 26–32.

Johnstone, R.J. 1980 *City and society*. Penguin, Harmondsworth.

Jones, G. 1993 British multinational banking strategies over time. Chapter 3. In Cox, H., Clegg, J., Ietto-Gillies, G. (eds) *The growth of global business*. Routledge, London: 38–61.

Journal of Management Inquiry 1994 Special issue on chaos and complexity. *Journal of Management Inquiry* **3**(4).

Jowitt, K. 1992 *New world disorder. The Leninist extinction*. University of California Press, Berkeley.

Kanter, R.M. 1991 *When giants learn to dance*. Routledge, New York.

Kapstein, E.B. 1994 *Governing the global economy: international finance and the state*. Harvard University Press, Cambridge MA.

Kay, J. 1993 *Foundations of corporate success*. Oxford University Press, Oxford.

Kay, J. 1995 The foundations of national competitive advantage. *Fifth ESRC Annual Lecture*. London.

Keating, M. 1995 Europeanism and regionalism. In Jones, B., Keating, M. (eds) *The European Union and the regions*. Clarendon Press, Oxford: 1–22.

Keeble, D., Offord, J., Walker, S. 1988 *Peripheral regions in a community of twelve member states*. Commission of the European Community, Luxembourg.

Keen, P. 1988 *Competing in time: using telecommunications for competitive advantage*. Ballinger, Cambridge MA.

Kelly, T., Keeble, D. 1990 IBM: the corporate chameleon. In de Smidt, M., Wever, E. (eds) *The corporate firm in a changing world economy: case studies in the geography of enterprise*. Routledge, London: 21–54.

Kenney, M., Florida, R. 1993 *Beyond mass production: the Japanese system and its transfer to the US*. Oxford University Press, Oxford and New York.

Kern, S. 1983 *The culture of time and space, 1880–1918*. Harvard University Press, Cambridge MA.

Khambata, D. 1986 *The practice of multinational banking*. Greenwood Press, Westport CT.

Khanin, G. 1992 Economic growth in the 1980s. In Ellman, M., Kontorovich, V. (eds) *The disintegration of the Soviet economic system*. Routledge, London: 73–85.

King, A. 1990 *Global cities*. Routledge Chapman and Hall, London and New York.

Kitching, G. 1982 *Development and underdevelopment in historical perspective*. Methuen.

Knights, D., Sturdy, A. 1990 New technology and the self-disciplined worker in the insurance industry. In Varcoe, I., McNeil, M., Yearley, S. (eds) *Deciphering science and technology: the social relations of expertise*. Macmillan, Basingstoke.

Knox, P., Agnew, J. 1989 *The geography of the world economy*. Edward Arnold, London.

Knudsen, D. 1994 Flexible manufacturing. *Growth and Change* **25**: 135–49.

Kojima, K. 1978 *Direct foreign investment: a Japanese model of mutinational business operations*. Croom Helm, London.

Kojima, K. 1990 *Japanese direct investment abroad*. International Christian University, Social Science Research Institute Monograph Series 1. Mitaka, Tokyo.

Kornai, J. 1980 *Economics of shortage*. North Holland, Amsterdam.

Kredietbank 1992 De nieuwe financiële instrumenten – weldaad of kwaad? *Week-berichten* **47**(36): 1–5.

Krueger, A. 1985 The experience and lessons of Asia's super exporters. In Corbo, V., Krueger, A., Ossa, F. (eds) *Export-oriented development strategies*. Westview: 187–212.

Krugman, P. 1986 *Strategic trade policy and the new international economics*. MIT Press, Cambridge MA.

Krugman, P. 1990 *Rethinking international trade*. MIT Press, Cambridge MA.

Krugman, P. 1991 *Geography and trade*. MIT Press, Cambridge MA.

Kudo, A. 1994 I.G. Farben in Japan: the transfer of technology and managerial skills. In Jones, G. (ed.) *The making of global enterprise*. Frank Cass, London: 159–83.

Kuzela, L. 1987 New Jamaican teleport to serve US business. *Industry Week* **234** (August 10): 64–65.

Ladreit de Lacharrière, G. 1969 La nouvelle division internationale de travail. Droz, Geneva.

Lakoff, G. 1987 *Women, fire and dangerous things*. Chicago University Press, Chicago.

Lall, S. 1983 *The new multinationals*. John Wiley, Chichester and New York.

Langdale, J.V. 1989 The geography of international business telecommunications: the role of leased networks. *Annals of the Association of American Geographers* **79**: 501–22.

Lash, S., Urry, J. 1994 *Economies of signs and space*. Sage, London.

Latour, B. 1987 The enlightment without the critique: a word on Michel Seres' philosophy. In Griffiths, A.P. (ed.) *Contemporary French Philosophy*. Cambridge University Press, Cambridge: 83–97.

Latour, B. 1993 *We have never been modern*. Harvester Wheatsheaf, Brighton.

Law, J. 1994 *Organising modernity*. Blackwell, Oxford.

Law, J., Mol, A. 1995 Notes on materiality and sociality. *Sociological Review* **28**: 274–294.

Lawniczak, R. 1992 Post-CMEA integration of Soviet and East European economies – challenges and perspectives. *International Social Science Journal* **131**: 91–106.

Lecraw, D. 1991 Factors influencing foreign direct investment by transnational corporations in host developing countries: a preliminary report. Chapter 8 in Buckley, P.J., Clegg, J. (eds) *Multinational enterprises in less developed countries*. Macmillan, London: 163–80.

Lehmann, J.P. 1982 *The roots of modern Japan*. Macmillan, London.

Lever, W.F. 1993 Competition within the European urban system. *Urban Studies* **30**: 935–948.

Levitt, T. 1983 The globalization of markets. *Harvard Business Review* May–June: 92–102.

Leyshon, A. 1993 Crawling from the wreckage: speculating on the future of the European Exchange Rate Mechanism. *Environment and Planning A* **25**: 1553–1557.

Leyshon, A. 1995 Annihilating space? the speed-up of communications. In Allen, J., Hamnett, C. (eds) *A shrinking world?* Oxford University Press, Oxford: 11–54.

Leyshon, A., Thrift, N. 1992 Liberalisation and consolidation: the Single European Market and the remaking of the European Financial Capital. *Environment and Planning A* **24**: 49–81.

Leyshon, A., Thrift, N. 1993 The restructuring of the financial services industry in the 1990s: a reversal of fortune. *Journal of Rural Studies* **9**: 223–241.

Leyshon, A., Thrift, N. 1994 Access to financial services and financial infrastructure withdrawal: problems and policies. *Area* **26**: 268–275.

Leyshon, A., Thrift, N. 1995 Geographies of financial exclusion: financial abandonment in Britain and the United States. *Transactions of the Institute of British Geographers* **20**: 312–341.

Leyshon, A., Tickell, A. 1994 Money order? The discursive construction of Bretton

Woods and the making and breaking of regulatory space. *Environment and Planning A* **26**: 1861–1890.

Lin, C. 1989 *Latin America versus East Asia.* M.E. Sharpe.

Lintner, V., Mazey, S. 1991 *The European Community: economic and political aspects.* McGraw-Hill, London.

Lipietz, A. 1982 Towards global Fordism? *New Left Review* (March/April).

Lipietz, A. 1987 *Mirages and miracles: the crisis of global Fordism.* Verso, London.

Littler, C. 1985 Taylorism, Fordism and job design. In Knights, D., Willmott, H., Collinson, D. (eds) *Job redisign.* Gower, Aldershot: 1–9.

Locke, J. 1994 Home and away. *Risk* **7**(9), September.

Loh, C. 1993 The rights stuff. *Far Eastern Economic Review* July 8: 15.

London Stock Exchange 1994 *Official yearbook 1993–94.* Stockton Press, London.

Lorenz, C. 1989 The rise and fall of business fads. *Financial Times* June 24th, 24.

Lowder, S. 1986 *Inside third world cities.* Croom Helm, London.

Lubeck, P. 1992 Malaysian industrialization, ethnic divisions and the NIC model. In Appelbaum, R., Henderson, J. (eds) *States and development in the Pacific Asian Rim.* Sage, London: 177–199.

Lucas, R.E. 1988 On the mechanics of economic development. *Journal of Monetary Economics* **22**: 3–32.

Ludlum, D.A. 1986 Offshore data entry pays off. *Computerworld* **20** (June 9): 103, 112.

Lundvall, B.-A. 1988 Innovation as an interactive process: from user-producer interaction to the national system of innovation. In Dosi, G., Freeman, C., Nelson, R., Silverberg, G., Soete, L. (eds) *Technical change and economic theory.* Frances Pinter, London: 349–69.

Lutz, R.A. 1994 Implementing technical change with cross functional teams. *Research-Technology Management* **37**(2): 14–18.

MacDonald, H.I. 1992 Special interest politics and the crisis of financial institutions in the USA. *Environment and Planning C: Government and Policy* **10**: 123–146.

Machlup, F. 1962 *The production and distribution of knowledge in the United States.* Princeton University Press, Princeton NJ.

Mair, A. 1993 New growth poles? Just-in-time manufacturing and local economic development strategy. *Regional Studies* **27**: 207–222.

Malecki, E.J. 1979 Locational trends in R&D by large US corporations, 1965–1977. *Economic Geography* **55**: 309–23.

Malecki, E.J. 1980 Corporate organization of R&D and the location of technological activities. *Regional Studies* **14**: 219–34.

Malecki, E.J. 1985 Industrial location and corporate organization in high technology industries. *Economic Geography* **61**: 345–69.

Malecki, E.J. 1991 *Technology and economic development: the dynamics of local, regional and national change.* Longman, Harlow and New York.

Malecki, E.J., Bradbury, S. 1992 R&D facilities and professional labor: labor force dynamics in high technology. *Regional Studies* **26**: 123–36.

Manners, G. 1986 Multinationals and the exploitation of non-renewable resources. In Dixon, C.J., Drakakis-Smith, D., Watts, H.D. (eds) *Multinational corporations and the third world.* Croom Helm: 25–38.

Mansfield, E., Rappart, J., Romeo, J., Villani, E., Wagner, S., Husic, F. 1977 *The production and application of new industrial technology.* Norton, New York.

Mansfield, E., Teece, D., Romeo, R. 1979 Overseas research and development by US-based firms. *Economica* **46**: 187–96.

Marden, P. 1992 'Real' regulation reconsidered. *Environment and Planning A* **24**: 751–67.

Marer, P. 1991 Pitfalls in transferring market-economy experiences to the European economies in transition. In Marer, P., Zecchini, S. (eds) *The transition to a market economy, vol. 1 the broad issues.* OECD, Paris: 38–56.

Markusen, J.R. 1986 Explaining the volume of trade: an eclectic approach. *American Economic Review* December: 1002–1011.

Marrese, M., Vanous, J. 1983 *Soviet subsidisation of trade with Eastern Europe: a Soviet perspective.* University of California Press, Berkeley.

Marshall, R., Tucker, M. 1992 *Thinking for a living: work, skills and the future of the American economy.* Basic Books, New York.

Martin, R. 1994 Stateless monies, global financial integration and national economic autonomy: the end of geography? In Corbridge S, Martin, R., Thrift, N. (eds) *Money, power and space.* Blackwell, Oxford: 253–78.

Massey, D. 1984 *Spatial divisions of labour: social structure and the geography of production.* Macmillan, London.

Massey, D. 1992 Politics and space/time. *New Left Review* **196**: 65–84.

Massey, D. 1993 Power-geometry and a progressive sense of place. In Bird, J., Curtis, B., Putnam, T., Robertson, G., Tickner, L. (eds) *Mapping the future – local cultures, global change.* Routledge, London: 59–69.

Massey, D., Meegan, R. 1979 The geography of industrial reorganisation: the spatial effects of the restructuring of the electrical engineering industry under the Industrial Reorganisation Corporation. *Progress in Planning* **10**: 155–237.

Matthews, R.C.O. 1968 Why has Britain had full employment since the war? *Economic Journal* **78**: 556–69.

McCauley, R., Seth, R. 1992 Foreign bank credit to US corporations: the implications of offshore loans. *Federal Reserve Bank of New York, Quarterly Review*, Spring: 52–63.

McDonough, W.J. 1993 The global derivatives market. *Federal Reserve Bank of New York, Quarterly Review*, Autumn: 1–5.

McGee, T.G. 1967 *The Southeast Asian city.* Bell, London.

McGregor, D. 1960 *The human side of enterprise.* New York.

McLuhan, M. 1964 *Understanding media: extensions of man.* Routledge and Kegan Paul, London.

Messner, D. 1993 Shaping competitiveness in the Chilean wood-processing industry. *CEPAL Review* **49**: 117–137.

Michalak, W.Z. 1993 Foreign direct investment and joint ventures in East-Central Europe: a geographical analysis. *Environment and Planning A* **25**: 1573–91.

Michalak, W. 1994 Regional integration in eastern Europe. In Gibb R., Michalak, W. (eds) *Continental trading blocs: the growth of regionalism in the world economy.* Wiley, London: 111–32.

Mills, E. 1988 Service sector suburbanization. In Sternlieb, G., Hughes, J. (eds) *America's new market geography.* Center for Urban Policy Research, New Brunswick NJ: 243–54.

Minc, A. 1994 *The great European illusion: business in the wider community.* Blackwell, Oxford.

Molle, W.K., van Mourik, A. 1988 International movements of labour under conditions of economic integration: the case of western Europe. *Journal of Common Market Studies* **26**: 317–42.

Molle, W., Breumer, L., Boeckhout, I. 1989 The location of information intensive activities in the European Community. In Punset, E., Sweeney, G. (eds) *Information resources and corporate growth*. Pinter, London: 161–72.

Mollenkopf, J., Castells, M. 1991 Introduction. In Mollenkopf, J., Castells, M. (eds) *Dual city*. Russell Sage, New York: 3–22.

Moody's 1991 Credit implications for firms that use derivatives. *Moody's Special Comment* November, 10 pp.

Moran, M. 1991 *The politics of the financial services revolution: the USA, UK and Japan*. Macmillan, London.

Morris, J. 1989 Japanese inward investment and the 'importation' of subcontracting complexes: three case studies. *Area* **21**: 269–77.

Moss, M. 1988 Telecommunications and international financial centers. *Information and Behavior* **3**: 239–52.

Mowery, D., Rosenberg, N. 1989 *Technology and the pursuit of economic growth*. Cambridge University Press, Cambridge.

Murphy, A.B. 1992 Western investment in the East: national and international strategies. *The Professional Geographer* **44**: 249–59.

Myers, Alberga 1992 Cayman Islands. *Offshore financial centres*, Euromoney Publications, International Financial Law Review, Special Supplement, September: 14–20.

Nations Bank Annual Report 1993 Charlotte, North Carolina.

Nelson, R.R. 1988 Institutions supporting technical change in the United States. In Dosi, G., Freeman, C., Nelson, R., Silverberg, G. (eds) *Technical change and economic theory*. Frances Pinter, London: 312–29.

Nelson, R.R. 1993 *National innovation systems: a comparative analysis*. Oxford University Press, New York.

New York State Department of Labor 1994 *Employment trends*. Albany NY.

Newfarmer, R. (ed.) 1985 *Profits, progress, poverty: studies of international industries in Latin America*. Notre Dame University Press.

Nicoll, W., Salmon, T.C. 1994 *Understanding the new European Community*. Harvester Wheatsheaf, London.

Nishioka, H., Takeuchi, A. 1989 The development of high technology industry in Japan. In Breheny, M.J., McQuaid, R. (eds) *The development of high technology industries*. Croom Helm, London: 262–95.

Norris, C. 1995 Versions of apocalypse: Kant, Derrida, Foucault. In Bull, M. (ed.) *Apocalypse theory and the ends of the world*. Blackwell, Oxford: 227–249.

Nove, A. 1987 *The Soviet economic system* (3rd edition). Allen & Unwin, London.

Nove, A. 1992 *An economic history of the USSR, 1917–1991*. Penguin, Harmondsworth.

Nurske, R., Haberler, B., Stern, R.N. (eds) 1961 *Equilibrium and growth in the world economy*. Harvard University Press, Cambridge MA.

Oakey, R.P., Thwaites, A.T., Nash, P.A. 1980 The regional distribution of innovative activity in Britain. *Regional Studies* **14**: 235–53.

Oakey, R.P., Thwaites, A.T., Nash, P.A. 1982 Technological change and regional development: some evidence on regional variations in product and process innovation. *Environment and Planning A* **14**: 1073–86.

O'Brien, R. 1991 *Global financial integration: the end of geography*. Pinter, London.

OECD 1971 *R&D in OECD member countries: trends and objectives*. Organization for Economic Cooperation and Development, Paris.

OECD 1981a *The measurement of scientific and technical activities: proposed standard practice for surveys of research and experimental development* (Frascati Manual).

Organization for Economic Cooperation and Development, Paris.

OECD 1981b *Science and technology indicators: trends in science and technology in the OECD area in the 1970s.* Organization for Economic Cooperation and Development, Paris.

OECD 1986 *Science and technology indicators, no. 2: R&D invention and competitiveness.* Organization for Economic Cooperation and Development, Paris.

OECD 1990 *Towards techno-globalisation: summary paper.* Organization for Economic Cooperation and Development, Paris.

OECD 1991 *The transition to a market economy, vol. 1 the broad issues.* OECD, Paris.

OECD 1993 *National accounts 1960–1991.* Organization for Economic Cooperation and Development, Paris.

OECD 1994 *The OECD jobs study: facts, analysis, strategy.* Organization for Economic Cooperation and Development, Paris.

Office of Technology Assessment 1994 *Multinationals and the US technology base.* Office of Technology Assessment, Washington DC.

Ofori-Amoah, B. 1988a Ghana's informal aluminium pottery: another grass-roots industrial revolution? *Appropriate Technology* **14**: 17–19.

Ofori-Amoah, B. 1988b Improving existing indigenous technologies as a strategy for the appropriate technology concept in Ghana. *Industry and Development* **23**: 57–79.

Ofori-Amoah, B. 1994 Technical change strategy for economic development in Africa. In Ezeala-Harrison, F., Adjibolosoo, S.B.-S.-K. (eds) *Perspectives on economic development in Africa.* Praeger, Westport: 85–102.

Ohlin, B. 1933 revised edition 1967 *Interregional and international trade.* Harvard University Press, Cambridge MA.

Ohmae, K. 1990 *The borderless world: power and strategy in the interlinked economy.* Harper, New York.

Ohmae, K. 1993 The rise of the region state. *Foreign Affairs* **72**: 78–87.

O hUallachain, B. Matthews, R.A. 1994 Economic restructuring in primary industries: transaction costs and corporate vertical integration in the Arizona copper industry, 1980–1991. *Annals of the Association of American Geographers* **84**(3): 399–417.

Oum, T.H., Taylor, A.J., Zhang, A. 1993 Strategic airline policy in the globalising airline networks. *Transportation Journal* **32**: 14–30.

Palloix, C. 1977 The self-expansion of capital on a world scale. *Review of Radical Political Economics* **9**: 1–28.

Pallot, J. Shaw, D.J.B. 1981 *Planning in the Soviet Union.* Croom Helm, London.

Parboni, R. 1981 *The dollar and its rivals: recession, inflation and international finance.* Verso, London.

Patchell, J. 1993a Composing robot systems: Japan as a flexible manufacturing system. *Environment and Planning A* **25**: 923–44.

Patchell, J. 1993b From production systems to learning systems: lessons from Japan. *Environment and Planning A* **25**: 797–819.

Patel, P., Pavitt, K. 1991 Large firms in the production of the world's technology: an important case of non-globalisation. *Journal of International Business Studies* **22**: 1–21.

Pearce, R.D. 1990 *The internationalisation of research and development by multi-national enterprises.* Macmillan, Basingstoke.

Pearce, R.D., Singh, S. 1992 *Globalizing research and development.* MacMillan, London.

Peck, F., Townsend, A. 1984 Contrasting experience of recession and spatial restructuring: British shipbuilders, Plessey and Metal Box. *Regional Studies* **18**: 319–38.

Peet, R. (ed.) 1987 *International capitalism and industrial restructuring*. Allen and Unwin, Boston.

Pelkmans, J. 1987 The new approach to technical harmonization and standardization. *Journal of Common Market Studies* **25**: 249–69.

Pelzman, J., Schoepfle, G.K. 1988 The impact of the Caribbean Basin Economic Recovery Act on Caribbean nations' exports and development. *Economic Development and Cultural Change* **36** (July): 753–796.

Perniola, M. 1995 *Enigmas. The Egyptian movement in society and art*. Verso, London.

Perrons, D. 1992 The regions and the Single Market. In Dunford, M., Kafkalas, G. (eds) *Cities and regions in the new Europe*. Belhaven, London: 170–94.

Peters, T. 1989 *Thriving on chaos*. Pan, London.

Peters, T., Austin, N. 1985 *A passion for excellence: the leadership difference*. Fontana, London.

Pettanati, P., Camillo, G. 1994 Regional convergence in the European Community. In Hajdu, Z., Horvath, G. (eds) *European challenges and Hungarian responses in regional policy*. Centre for Regional Studies, Pécs: 37–47.

Pfeffer, T., Salancik, G.R. 1978 *The external control of organisations*. Harper and Row, New York.

Pianta, M. 1988 *New technologies across the Atlantic: US leadership or European autonomy?* Harvester Wheatsheaf, Hemel Hempstead.

Pilbeam, K. 1992 *International finance*. Macmillan, London.

Piore, M., Sabel, C. 1984 *The second industrial divide*. Basic Books, New York.

PlanEcon 1994 Economic recovery in the East. *PlanEcon Report* Nos. 49–52.

Polanyi, K. 1944 *The great transformation*. Farrarand Reinhart, New York.

Porat, M. 1977 *The information economy: definition and measurement*. U.S. Department of Commerce, Office of Telecommunications Special Publication 77-12(1), Washington DC.

Porter, M. 1990 *The competitive advantage of nations*. Macmillan, New York and London.

Prahalad, C.K., Doz, Y.L. 1987 *The multinational mission: balancing local demands and global vision*. Free Press, New York.

Pratt, D.J. 1995 Re-placing money. *Environment and Planning A* (forthcoming).

Prebisch, R. 1950 *The economic development of Latin America and its principal problems*. UNECLA.

Pred, A. 1977 *City systems in advanced economies*. Halsted Press, New York.

Preston, S.H. 1988 Urban growth in developing countries: a demographic reappraisal. In Gugler, J. (ed.) *The urbanization of the third world*. Oxford University Press, Oxford: 11–31.

Price, A., Morgan, K., Cooke, P. 1994 *The Welsh renaissance: inward investment and industrial innovation*. RIR Report No. 14 CASS-UWCC, Cardiff CF1 3EB.

Putnam, H. 1981 *Reason, truth, and history*. Cambridge University Press, Cambridge.

Pyke, F., Sengenberger, W. (eds) 1992 *Industrial districts and local economic regeneration*. International Institute for Labour Studies, Geneva.

Pyke, F., Becattini, G., Sengenberger, W. (eds) 1990 *Industrial districts and inter-firm co-operation in Italy*. International Institute for Labour Studies, Geneva.

Randzio-Plath, C. 1994 Exchange rates and the volume of trade – the case for fixed exchange rates. *Intereconomics* **29**(4): 171–75.

Reddaway, P., Lapidus, G.W., Schroeder, G.E., Winston, V., Breslauer, G. 1993 Two years after the collapse of the USSR: a panel of specialists. *Post-Soviet Affairs* **9**(4): 281–313.

Rehfeld, D. 1993 *Patterns of economic restructuring in an area of industrial decline: industrial development, change factors and regional policy in the Ruhrgebiet.* IAT, Gelsenkirchen.

Reich, R.B. 1990 *The work of nations.* Random House, New York.

Remolona, E.M. 1993 The recent growth of financial derivative markets. *Federal Reserve Bank of New York Quarterly Review* Winter 1992–93, **17**: 28–43.

Reszat, B. 1993 Twenty years of flexible exchange rates: experiences and developments. *Intereconomics* **28**(3): 107–10.

Riddell, B. 1992 Things fall apart again: structural adjustment programmes in sub-Saharan Africa. *Journal of Modern African Studies* **39**(1): 53–68.

Risk Technology Supplement, Vol. 7, August 1994.

Roberts, S. 1994 Fictitious capital, fictitious spaces: the geography of offshore financial flows. In Corbridge, S., Martin, R., Thrift, N. (eds) *Money, power and space.* Blackwell, Oxford: 91–115.

Robins, K. 1991 Prisoners of the city: whatever could a postmodern city be? *New Formations* **8**: 1–22.

Robinson, N. 1992 Financial building blocks in the context of a changing national and international environment. In Budd, L., Whimster, S. (eds) *Global finance and urban living: a study of metropolitan change.* Routledge, London: 73–95.

Robison, R. 1994 The emergence of the middle class in Southeast Asia. Paper presented at a conference on Emerging Classes and Growing Inequalities in Southeast Asia, Nordic Association for Southeast Asian Studies, Aalborg University.

Roddick, J. 1988 *The dance of the millions: Latin America and the debt crisis.* Latin American Bureau, London.

Rodrik, D. 1992 The limits of trade policy reform in developing countries. *The Journal of Economic Perspectives* **6**(1): 87–105.

Rosenberg, N. 1992 Science and technology in the twentieth century. In Dosi, G., Giannetti, R., Toninelli, P.A. (eds) *Technology and enterprise in a historical perspective.* Clarendon, Oxford: 63–96.

Rostow, W.W. 1960 *The stages of economic growth.* Cambridge University Press, Cambridge.

Roth, T. 1994 Gap widens between winner and losers. *Central European Economic Review* Spring: 5–7.

Roxborough, I. 1979 *Theories of underdevelopment.* Macmillan, London.

Rubinstein, W.D. 1991 Gentlemen, capitalism, and British industry, 1820–1914. *Past and Present* **132**: 159–164.

Sabel, C. 1994 Bootstrapping reform: rebuilding firms, the welfare state and unions. Paper presented to Confédération des Syndicats Nationaux, Montreal, March.

Sachs, G. (ed.) 1992 *The development dictionary.* Zed Books, London.

Sadler, D., Swain, A., Hudson, R. 1993 The automotive industry and Eastern Europe: new production strategies or old solutions? *Area* **25**(4): 339–49.

Sampson, A. 1995 *Company man. The rise and fall of corporate life.* Harper Collins, London.

Sandhu, K., Wheatley, P. (eds) 1989 *The management of success: the moulding of modern Singapore.* Institute of Southeast Asian Studies, Singapore.

Sassen, S. 1991 *The global city – London, New York, Tokyo.* Princeton University Press, Princeton NJ.

Sassen, S. 1994 *Cities in a world economy.* Pine Forge Press, Thousand Oaks.

Saxenian, A. 1983 The genesis of Silicon Valley. *Built Environment* **9**: 7–17.

Sayer, A., Walker, R. 1992 *The new social economy: reworking the division of labour.* Blackwell, Oxford.

Sayers, A. 1986 Industrial location on a world scale: the case of the semiconductor industry. A.J. Scott and M. Storper (eds) *In Production, work, and territory.* Allen and Unwin Press, Winchester MA.

Schatzl, L. 1995 Economic restructuring in East Germany. In Lever W.F., Bailly, A. (eds) *The spatial impact of economic change in Europe.* Avebury, Aldershot.

Schmitz, H. 1984 Industrialization strategies in less developed countries: some lessons of historical experience. *Journal of Development Studies* **21**: 1–21.

Schoenberger, E. 1988 Multinational corporations and the new international division of labour: a critical appraisal. *International Regional Science Review* **11**: 105–19.

Schoenberger, E. 1989 Thinking about flexibility: a response to Gertler. *Transactions of the Institute of British Geographers* **14**: 98–108.

Schroeder, G.E. 1993 Post-Soviet economic reforms in perspective. In Kaufman, R.F., Hardt, J.P. (eds) *The former Soviet Union in transition.* M E Sharpe, New York: 57–80.

Schroeder, G.E. 1994 Observation on economic performance in the successor states. *Post-Soviet Geography* **15**(1): 1–12.

Schwartz, A. 1992 Corporate service linkages in large metropolitan areas. *Urban Affairs Quarterly* **28**(2): 276–96.

Scott, A.J. 1983 Industrial organisation and the logic of intra-metropolitan location I: theoretical considerations. *Economic Geography* **59**: 233–50.

Scott, A.J. 1988a *New industrial spaces.* Pion, London.

Scott, A.J. 1988b *Metropolis: from the division of labor to urban form.* University of California Press, Berkeley.

Scott, A.J. 1993 *Technopolis: high-technology industry and regional development in southern California.* University of California, Berkeley.

Scott, A.J., Bergman, D. 1993 *Advanced ground transportation equipment manufacturing and local economic development: lessons for southern California.* UCLA, Los Angeles.

Scott, A.J., Storper, M. 1992 Regional development reconsidered. In Ernste, H., Meier, V. (eds) *Regional development and contemporary industrial response.* Belhaven, London.

Scott, N. 1992 The implications of the transition for foreign trade and investment. *Oxford Review of Economic Policy* **8**(1): 44–57.

Serapio, M.G., Dalton, D.H. 1993 Foreign R&D facilities in the United States. *Research-Technology Management* **36**(6): 33–39.

Serjeant, G. 1995 Second successive boom year for world trade forecast. *The Times* 3 April.

Serres, M. 1982 *Hermes. Literature, science, philosophy.* Johns Hopkins University Press, Baltimore MD.

Serres, M. 1995 *Genesis.* University of Michigan Press, Ann Arbor MI.

Shefter, M. 1993 New York's national and international influence. In Shefter, M. (ed.) *Capital of the American century.* Russell Sage, New York.

Shilling, C. 1993 *The body and social theory.* Sage Publications, London.

Silversides, C.R. 1984 Mechanized forestry: World War II to the present. *Forest Chronicle* August: 231–35.

Simmel, G. 1979 *The philosophy of money*. Routledge, London.

Sinclair, T.J. 1994 Passing judgement: credit rating processes as regulatory mechanisms of governance in the emerging world order. *Review of International Political Economy* **1**: 133–159.

Skinner, E. 1994 The Caribbean data processors. Unpublished paper, Bowling Green State University.

Smith, A. 1994 East European economies. In *Eastern Europe and the Commonwealth of Independent States* (2nd edition). Europa Publications, London: 32–42.

Solomon, E.H. (ed.) 1991 *Electronic money flows: the molding of a new financial order*. Kluwer, Boston.

Stafford, L. 1992 London's financial markets: perspectives and prospects. In Budd, L., Whimster, S. (eds) *Global finance and urban living: a study of metropolitan change*. Routledge, London: 31–51.

Stanback, T., Noyelle, T. 1982 *Cities in transition*. Allenheld, Osmun, Totow NJ.

Stewart, J.M. 1992 *The Soviet environment: problems, policies and politics*. Cambridge University Press, Cambridge.

Stigler, G. 1961 The economics of information. *Journal of Political Economy* **69**: 213–25.

Storper, M. 1994 The resurgence of regional economies, ten years later – the region as a nexus of untraded interdependencies. Paper presented in *Regions, institutions, and technology: reorganizing economic geography in Canada and the Anglo-American world*. A conference held in honour of H A Innis: September 23–25, Toronto.

Storper, M.J., Harrison, B. 1991 Flexibility, hierarchy and regional development: the changing structure of industrial production systems and their forms of governance in the 1990s. *Research Policy* **20**: 407–22.

Storper, M., Scott, A.J. 1992 *Pathways to industrialisation and regional development*. Routledge, London.

Storper, M., Walker, R. 1984 The spatial division of labor: labor and the location of industries. In Sawers, L., Tabb, W.K. (eds), *Sunbelt – snowbelt: urban development and regional restructuring*. Oxford University Press, New York.

Storper, M., Walker, R. 1989 *The capitalist imperative: territory, technology and industrial growth*. Blackwell, Oxford and New York.

Strange, R. 1993 *Japanese manufacturing investment in Europe: its impact on the UK economy*. Routledge: London.

Strange, S. 1971 *Sterling and British policy*. Oxford University Press, Oxford.

Strange, S. 1986 *Casino capitalism*. Blackwell, Oxford.

Strange, S. 1988 *States and markets: an introduction to international political economy*. Pinter, London.

Strange, S. 1994 From Bretton Woods to the casino economy. In Corbridge, S., Martin, R., Thrift, N. (eds) *Money, power and space*. Blackwell, Oxford: 49–62.

Straubhaar, T. 1988 International labour migration within a common market: some aspects of EC experience. *Journal of Common Market Studies* **27**: 55–62.

Streeck, W. 1989 Skills and the limits of neo-liberalism: the enterprise of the future as a place of learning. *Work, Employment and Society* **3**: 89–104.

Swinbanks, D. 1994 Governments urged to move ahead with Japan's proposal for 21st century global manufacturing. *Research-Technology Management* **37**(4): 2–3.

Swyngedouw, E. 1989 The heart of the place: the resurrection of locality in an age of hyperspace. *Geographisker Annaler* **71B**(1): 31–42.

Swyngedouw, E. 1992 The mammon quest. 'Glocalization', interspatial competition and the monetary order: the construction of new scales. In Dunford, M., Kafkalas, G. (eds) *Cities and regions in the new Europe.* Belhaven Press, London: 39–67.

Takeda, Y. 1993 Managing technology for the 21st century. *Research-Technology Management* **36**(6): 8–9.

Takeuchi, A. 1990 Nissan Motor Company: stages of international growth, locational profile, and subcontracting in the Tokyo region. In Smidt, M.D., Wever, E. (eds) *The corporate firm in a changing world economy.* Routledge, London: 166–182.

Taylor, M., Thrift, N. (eds) 1982 *The geography of multinationals.* Croom Helm, London.

Taylor, M.J., Thrift, N.J. 1983 Business organisation, segmentation, and location. *Regional Studies* **17**: 445–465.

Taylor, P. 1985 *Political geography.* Longman, Harlow.

Teece, D.J. 1988 Technical change and the theory of the firm. In Dosi, G., Freeman, C., Nelson, R., Silverberg, G., Soete, L. (eds) *Technical change and economic theory.* Pinter, London: 256–81.

Teitel, S. 1989 Industrialisation, primary commodities and exports of manufactures. In Islam, N. (ed.) *The balance between industry and agriculture in economic development.* Macmillan.

The Economist 1994 The banking sector. *The Economist* 18 May: supplement.

The Economist 1995 The collapse of Barings – a fallen star. *The Economist* 4 March: 19–21.

The Group of Lisbon 1994 *Grenzen aan de concurrentie.* Group of Lisbon/R Petrella. University of Brussels Press, Brussels.

The Orange County Register 1994 O.C. seeks breathing room by filing bankruptcy. 7 December: 1.

Thomas, E., Jr. 1994 NationsBank expansion plans go beyond US brokers. *Wall Street Journal* (April 26): B4.

Thompson, G.F. 1993 *The economic emergence of a new Europe? The political economy of cooperation and competition in the 1990s.* Edward Elgar, Aldershot.

Thomson Ltd 1993 *Thomson bank directory international.* Thomson Ltd, London.

Thorngren, B. 1970 How do contact systems affect regional development? *Environment and Planning A* **2**: 409–27.

Thrift, N.J. 1986 The geography of world economic disorder. In Johnston, R.J., Taylor, P.J. (eds) *A world in crisis? Geographical perspectives.* Blackwell, Oxford: 12–76.

Thrift, N.J. 1990 Transport and communication 1730–1914. In Dodgshon, R.A., Butlin, R.A. (eds) *An historical geography of England and Wales* (second edition). Academic Press, London: 453–486.

Thrift, N.J. 1991 For a new regional geography 2. *Progress in Human Geography* **15**: 456–466.

Thrift, N.J. 1994 On the social and cultural determinants of international financial centres: the case of the City of London. In Corbridge, S., Martin, R., Thrift, N. (eds) *Money, power and space.* Blackwell, Oxford: 327–355.

Thrift, N.J. 1995 A hyperactive world? In Johnston, R.J., Taylor, P.J., Watts, M. (eds) *Geographies of global change.* Blackwell, Oxford: 18–35.

Thrift, N., Leyshon, A. 1994 A phantom state? The de-traditionalization of money, the international financial system and international financial centres. *Political Geography* **13**(4): 299–327.

Thrift, N.J., Olds, K. 1996 *Progress in human geography* (forthcoming).

Thurow, L. 1992 *Head to head: the coming economic battle between Japan, Europe and America*. Time Warner, New York.

Thurston, C. 1990 US company joins with Jamaicans in data processing. *The Journal of Commerce* **383** (March 23): 4a.

Thwaites, A.T. 1978 Technological change, mobile plants and regional development. *Regional Studies* **16**: 445–61.

Tickell, A. 1995 Making a melodrama out of a crisis: interpreting the collapse of Barings Bank. Mimeographed Paper, School of Geography, University of Manchester, Manchester M13 9PL.

Tillman, D.A. 1985 *Forest products: advanced technologies and economic analyses*. Academic Press, New York.

Todaro, M. 1994 *Economic development*. Longman.

Tokyo Metropolitan Government 1990 *Tokyo industry 1989*. Tokyo Metropolitan Government, Tokyo.

Tokyo Stock Exchange 1994 *Fact book*. Tokyo Stock Exchange, Tokyo.

Triffin, R. 1961 *Gold and the dollar crisis*. Yale University Press, New Haven CT.

Ullman, E.L. 1958 Regional development and the geography of concentration. *Papers and Proceedings, Regional Science Association* **4**: 179–98.

UNDP 1993 *Human development report*. United Nations, New York.

UN ECE 1993 *Economic survey of Europe in 1992–1993*. United Nations Economic Commission for Europe, New York.

UN ECE 1994 *East–West investment news* (1). United Nations Economic Commission for Europe, New York.

United Nations 1991a *World investment report: the triad in foreign direct investment*. United Nations Centre on Transnational Corporations, New York.

United Nations 1991b *Directory of transnational corporations*. United Nations Centre on Transnational Corporations, New York.

United Nations 1992a *World investment report: transnational corporations as engines of growth*. United Nations Transnational Corporations and Management Division, New York.

United Nations 1992b *The determinants of foreign direct investment*. United Nations Centre on Transnational Corporations, New York.

United Nations Centre on Transnational Corporations (UNCTC) 1992 *World investment directory 1992: foreign direct investment, legal framework and corporate data, volume I Asia and the Pacific*. United Nations, New York.

United Nations Conference on Trade and Development (UNCTAD) 1993a *World investment report 1993: transnational corporations and integrated international production*. Programme on Transnational Corporations. United Nations, New York.

United Nations Conference on Trade and Development (UNCTAD) 1993b *Small and medium-sized transnational corporations*. Programme on Transnational Corporations. United Nations, New York.

United Nations Transnational Corporations and Management Division 1992 *World investment directory 1992: foreign direct investment, legal framework and corporate data, volume II Central and Eastern Europe*. Department of Economic and Social Development and Economic Commission for Europe. United Nations, New York.

United Nations Transnational Corporations and Management Division 1993 *World investment directory 1992: foreign direct investment, legal framework and corporate data, volume III developed countries*. Department of Economic and Social Development. United Nations, New York.

United States Census Bureau 1993 *Statistical abstract of the United States 1993*. US Government Printing Office, Washington DC.

United States Congress, Office of Technology Assessment 1987 *International competition in services*. US Government Printing Office, Washington, DC: Chapter 5.

United States Department of Commerce, Bureau of the Census 1988 *Educational attainment in the US*. March 1986–87, Series P-20, No. 428, Table 10.

United States General Accounting Office 1994 *Financial derivatives – actions needed to protect the financial system*. Report to Congressional Requesters, Washington DC.

United States Information Service 1993 *Atlantic Outlook*. No. 49, March, 5.

Urry, J. 1986 Capitalist production, scientific management and the service class. In Scott, A.J., Storper, M. (eds) *Production, work, territory: the geographical anatomy of industrial capitalism*. Allen and Unwin, Boston: 43–66.

Van der Pijl, K. 1984 *The making of an Atlantic ruling class*. Verso, London.

Van der Pijl, K. 1994 The cadre class and public multilateralism. In Sakamoto, Y. (ed.) *Global transformation: challenges to the state system*. United Nations University Press, Tokyo: 200–249.

Vaughan, R. 1976 *Post-war integration in Europe*. Edward Arnold, London.

Verbraeken, P. 1994 Spekuleren in riskante niches. *De Morgen* 16 April 1994: 34.

Vernon, R. 1966 International investment and international trade in the product life cycle. *Quarterly Journal of Economics* **80**(2): 190–207.

Vernon, R. 1970 Organization as a scale factor in the growth of firms. In Makham, J.W., Papanek, G.F. (eds) *Industrial organization and economic development*. Houghton Mifflin, Boston: 47–66.

Vernon, R. 1979 The product cycle hypothesis in a new international environment. *Oxford Bulletin of Economics and Statistics* Special Issue: The Multi-National Corporation **41**(4): 255–67.

Vienna Institute for Comparative Economic Studies 1990 *Comecon data 1989*. Macmillan, London.

Virilio, P. 1986 *Speed and politics: an essay on dromology*. Columbia University Press, New York.

Vogel, D. 1993 New York City as a national and global financial centre. In Shefter, M. (ed.) *Capital of the American century*. Russell Sage, New York.

Wade, R. 1990 *Governing the market: economic theory and the role of government in East Asian industrialization*. Princeton University Press.

Walker, R. 1988 The geographical organization of production systems. *Society and Space* **6**: 377–408.

Wall Street Journal 24 September 1993.

Wall Street Journal 1994 Corporate banking, given up for dead, is reinventing itself. 31 January 1994, page 1.

Wall Street Journal 11 July 1994.

Wall Street Journal 3 October 1994.

Walter, A. 1993 *World power and world money*. Harvester Wheatsheaf, London.

Walton, J. 1985 The third 'new' international division of labour. In Walton, J. (ed.) *Capital and labour in the urbanized world*. Sage, London: 3–14.

Warf, B. 1989 Telecommunications and the globalization of financial services. *Professional Geographer* **41**(3): 257–71.

Warren, B. 1980 *Imperialism: pioneer of capitalism*. Verso, London.

Waugh, D. 1990 *Geography: an integrated approach*. Nelson, Walton-on-Thames.

Weiss, J. 1990 *Industry in developing countries: theory, policy and evidence*. Routledge, London.

Wells, P., Rawlinson, M. 1992 New procurement regimes and the spatial distribution of suppliers: the case of Ford in Europe. *Area* **24**: 380–390.

Westlake, M. 1993 Latin lovers. *Risk* **6**(9): 51–60.

Whyte, W.H. 1957 *The organisation man*. Cape, New York.

Wiener, M.J. 1981 *English culture and the decline of the industrial spirit, 1850–1986*. Cambridge University Press, Cambridge.

Williams, A.M. 1991 *The European Community*. Blackwell, Oxford.

Williams, C. 1994 Informal networks as a means of local economic development: the case of Local Exchange Trading Systems (LETS). Paper presented to the Institute of British Geographers Annual Conference, 3–6 January, University of Northumbria at Newcastle.

Willmore, L. 1993 Export processing in Jamaica: ownership, linkages, and transfer of technology. Unpublished paper prepared for the Economic Commission for Latin America and the Caribbean.

Willmore, L. 1995 Data processing: a case study of the effect of technological change on global employment. Unpublished paper, United Nations Microeconomic Issues and Policies Unit (February).

Wilson, M. 1995 The office farther back: business services, productivity, and the offshore back office. In Horler, P. (ed.) *The Service Productivity Challenge*. Kluwer Press, Boston.

Wilson, N. 1994 Scratching the surface. *Futures and Options World* September: 22–23.

Winiecki, E., Winiecki, J. 1992 *The structural legacy of the Soviet-type economy*. The Centre for Research into Communist Economies, London.

Winiecki, J. 1991 The inevitability of a fall in output in the early stages of transition to the market: theoretical underpinnings. *Soviet Studies* **43**(4): 669–76.

Winiecki, J. 1994 East-Central Europe: a regional survey – the Czech Republic, Hungary, Poland and Slovakia in 1993. *Europe-Asia Studies* **46**(5): 709–34.

Wise, M., Gibb, R. 1993 *Single market to social Europe: the European Community in the 1990s*. Longman, Harlow.

Wittgenstein, L. 1978 *Remarks on the philosophy of mathematics*. Oxford University Press, Oxford.

Wolff, M.F. 1994 Meet your competition: data from the IRI R&D survey. *Research-Technology Management* **37**(1): 18–24.

Womack, J., Jones, D. 1994 From lean production to lean enterprise. *Harvard Business Review* March–April: 93–103.

Womack, J.P., Jones, D.T., Roos, D. 1990 *The machine that changed the world*. Rawson Associates, New York.

Wood, R. 1986 *From Marshall Plan to debt crisis*. University of California Press, Berkeley.

Woodridge, A. 1995 Big is back. A survey of multinationals. *The Economist* June 24th–30th: 1–22.

World Bank 1982 *World development report 1982*. Oxford University Press, Oxford.

World Bank 1986 *World development report 1986*. Oxford University Press, Oxford.

World Bank 1987 *World development report 1987*. Oxford University Press, Oxford.

World Bank 1992 *Russian economic reform: crossing the threshold of structural change*. The World Bank, Washington DC.

World Bank 1993 *The East Asian miracle*. Oxford University Press, Oxford.

World Bank 1994a *World development report 1994*. Oxford University Press, Oxford.

World Bank 1994b *Structural adjustment programmes in Africa*. Oxford University Press, Oxford.

Wriston, W. 1986 *Risk and other four letter words*. Harper and Row, New York.

Yamamoto, H. 1994 Complementary competition in Japan. *Research-Technology Management* **37**(2): 49–56.

Yeung, H.W.-C. 1994 Third world multinationals revisited: a research critique and future agenda. *Third World Quarterly* **15**(2): 297–317.

Yip, G.S. 1989 Global strategy . . . in a world of nations? *Sloan Management Review* **31**: 29–41.

Yip, G.S. 1992 *Total global strategy: managing for worldwide competitive advantage*. Prentice Hall, Englewood Cliffs NJ.

Young S.J., Hamill C., Wheeler, Davies, J.R. 1989 *International market entry and development: strategies and management*. Harvester Wheatsheaf, Hemel Hempstead.

Zelizer, V.A. 1989 The social meaning of money: 'special monies'. *American Journal of Sociology* **95**: 342–377.

Zelizer, V.A. 1994 *The social meaning of money: pin money, paychecks, poor relief, and other currencies*. Basic Books, New York.

Zuboff, S. 1988 *In the age of the smart machine*. Basic Books, New York.

INDEX